PERFORMING ARTS

A GUIDE TO PRACTICE AND APPRECIATION

PERFORMING ARTS

A GUIDE TO PRACTICE AND APPRECIATION

CONSULTANT EDITOR: MICHAEL BILLINGTON

NEW BURLINGTON BOOKS

A QED BOOK

This edition published 1988 by
New Burlington Books
6 Blundell Street
London N7 9BH

ISBN 1–85348–115–7

This book was designed and produced by
QED Publishing Limited
6 Blundell Street
London N7 9BH

Art Director Alastair Campbell
Production director Edward Kinsey
Editorial directors Jeremy Harwood
Editor Kathy Rooney

Assistant editors Nicola Thompson, Marion Casey

Designers Heather Jackson, Marnie Searchwell

Illustrators Elain Keenan, Edwina Keene, Abdul Aziz Khan,
John Woodcock, Martin Woodford

Editorial Tony Duncan, John Hantken, Jenny Mulherin, Peter Phillips,
Derek Prigent, George Short, Keith Walker, Neil Wenborn

Photographers John Barr, Michael Bussell, Michael Fear, Roger Pring,
Walter Rawlings, Jon Wyand

Picture research Anne Lyons, Linda Proud

Paste-up Gunner Finsdottir, Anne Lloyd

Filmset in Great Britain by Filmtype Services Limited,
Scarborough, and Abbettatype Limited, London
Colour origination in Hong Kong by Sakai Lithocolour Limited
Printed in Hong Kong by Leefung-Asco Limited

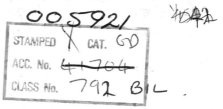
QED would like to thank the many individuals and organizations who have helped in the preparation of this book. Invaluable assistance was given by: Ballet Rambert; Colin Blakely; Borovicks; Centre Georges—Pompidou; Citizens' Theatre, Glasgow; Patience Collier; Comédie Francaise; Graham Turnbull of Decca records; William Dudley; David Edelstein and the workshop staff of the National Theatre; Festival Ballet; Greater London Council Department of Architecture and Civic Design; Trevor R. Griffiths; Norma Bishop of Hit and Run; Barbara Houseman; Institute of Choreology; David Jamieson; Sheelagh Killean; Denys Lasdun and Partners; Vivian Liff; London Symphony Orchestra; Lou the One Man Band; Gillian Lynne; George Bailey of The Magnificent Seven stunt team; Mercury Theatre Trust Ltd; John Moss; Tony Wells of Moss Empires; The National Theatre; Polish Cultural Institute; Brian Legge of Rank Strand Electric; Richard Rogers and Partners; Christine Rowlands and the wardrobe department of The Young Vic; Royal Ballet; Royal Opera House Covent Garden; Jamie Phillips of Trends Management; Victoria and Albert Theatre Museum; Mac Wilson.

CONTENTS

FOREWORD

BY SIR JOHN GIELGUD·

Most children are fond of dressing up and showing off. In past generations they were encouraged to try out their performing skills, for the benefit and criticism of their elders by reading aloud, acting, or playing some musical instrument. As they grew older they were taken to public places of entertainment for the first time, dressed up in their best clothes, to watch other people showing off. They looked forward to these occasions—first visits to the theatre, opera-house, circus or the ballet—with great excitement, and would remember and discuss what they had seen for many weeks afterwards. Nowadays, with television and radio tending to supply an endless stream of second-rate and too easily available forms of so-called entertainment, children quickly begin to accept these marvellous inventions as commonplace accompaniments to the routine of their daily lives, and the sense of 'occasion' which once served as an added spur to their concentration and delight is gone forever. All the same, thousands of people, both young and old, have become used to listening to words and music as a completely new experience, with easy and expert information con-

stantly provided for them, on subjects which formerly they could only find in books, newspapers and magazines, besides the opportunity of watching plays, operas, recitals and films of every kind, with a number of alternatives to choose from. This easy acceptance and availability of the mechanical media may have encouraged too lazy a response from audiences in their own homes, but the individual urge of those with ambitions to develop into performing artists themselves seems to be not at all diminished. Live performances in public are as popular as ever. Audiences have, on the whole, become more discriminating, better equipped to expect higher standards in what they have paid to see and hear. Bookshops are crammed with customers, and the texts of plays and musical scores are sought and studied with eager appreciation.

The art of the performer has always, until now, remained a mystery, handed down to us in criticisms and diaries, but quite impossible for us to apprehend with any certainty. Today, for the first time in history, personalities will be preserved, in every detail of physical appearance, voice and mannerisms, for future generations to assess. (We would, perhaps, prefer that they should remain as we remember them with the flattering nostalgia of our youth.) Performances before a live audience are a unique and personal experience on both sides. Modern actors have needed to learn how to perform in a variety of different media, without the sounding-board of a live audience to crystallize their sense of timing and the skill of holding a mass of restless onlookers in a silence of rapt attention. This problem, of course, is less complicated in the case of musicians, though equally important for lecturers, politicians and public speakers, when they are heard and seen, on radio or the screen, without the stimulating reaction which, in a public arena, kindles a mutual spark between performer and audience alike.

The general public is perhaps more aware than one might suppose in realizing the enormously wide development in the presentation of entertainment which has evolved in the last two decades. For there appears to be a new and increasing interest in the background of artistic endeavour in every field—master classes, talks and interviews with actors, musicians, poets, painters, and writers discussing their individual methods, opinions and experiences, for the benefit of the uninitiated.

This book should be an invaluable asset to those who are fascinated by the developments of what we call 'performance' and who wish to examine in detail the traditions as well as the new inventions which contribute to the presentation of all kinds of entertainments from the earliest time until our own.

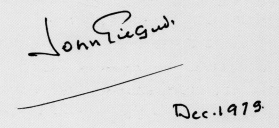

John Gielgud.

Dec. 1979.

ROOTS OF PERFORMANCE

FROM ANCIENT GREEK TO MODERN THEATRICAL PRACTICE

The primary activity which we associate with a theatre is a play or stage-play, but this is by no means the only one: opera, ballet, pantomime and musicals are the nearest in kind, but music-hall, variety, vaudeville, circuses, ice-spectaculars and military tattoos cannot be excluded. Nor can dramatic activities on a more intimate scale like puppet shows, revue, mime, recitals, monologues, cabaret or burlesque.

This loose linkage of many distinct and different kinds of spectacle has a long history. Even the word 'play' is itself still ambiguous enough to suggest a wide variety of recreational activity ranging from children's games to grand opera rather than one specific theatrical stage form.

All early concepts of theatrical production carried with them a sense of recreation, a sense of make-believe as opposed to actuality, and a sense of order within rules supplied by the individual in charge: but the range of such recreations was very wide. To the Romans it included both athletic games and stage plays, although they distinguished those recreational activities associated with the theatre from those of the amphitheatre or the circus. Some vestiges of the gladiatorial combats and the military exercises of the Roman amphitheatres survived in the tournaments of the Middle Ages, as did the sports of the circus in the athletic games and the animal baitings of Anglo-Saxon and Norman times — in the South of France bull-fights are still held in the Roman arenas at Nimes and Arles.

The revival of interest in classical antiquity that marked the Renaissance ensured the survival of these ideas. The old words 'theatre', 'amphitheatre', 'arena' and 'circus' came back into current use as places respectively appropriate for the production of stage plays, athletic and equestrian spectacles, fencing and wrestling matches, and performances by animals and their trainers.

In the past three centuries these concepts have not changed much except that they have proliferated and been sub-divided. Starting with Italian opera and French ballet and *carrousels* (equestrian ballets) in the seventeenth century, changes in taste and social conditions have introduced many variants, ranging from such costly and elaborate productions as music-hall, musicals, military tattoos and historical pageants, to such intimate production concepts as cabaret and strip-shows. Fundamentally, however, they have remained unchanged, retaining the game/play ambiguity of earlier epochs.

Right This family tree of the performing arts shows the development of 'theatre' from its primitive origins in religious ritual to its most recent manifestations. The unifying feature is that they are all presented to a live audience.

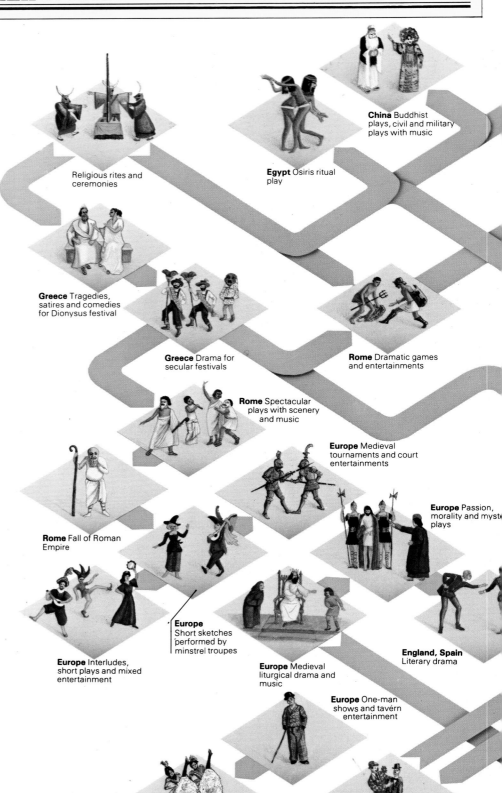

Religious rites and ceremonies

Egypt Osiris ritual play

China Buddhist plays, civil and military plays with music

Greece Tragedies, satires and comedies for Dionysus festival

Greece Drama for secular festivals

Rome Dramatic games and entertainments

Rome Spectacular plays with scenery and music

Europe Medieval tournaments and court entertainments

Europe Passion, morality and myste plays

Rome Fall of Roman Empire

Europe Short sketches performed by minstrel troupes

Europe Medieval liturgical drama and music

England, Spain Literary drama

Europe Interludes, short plays and mixed entertainment

Europe One-man shows and tavern entertainment

France Cabaret

Britain Music hall

Europe, USA Variety

Europe, USA Ma

10

India Hindu plays performed by nomadic acting troupes

Europe, USA Circus

Japan Ningyo-Shibai, marionette theatre

Europe Harlequinades

Japan Kabuki, popular theatre

Japan Shinto rituals

Japan Noh plays, classical drama

Europe Commedia dell' arte

Europe Renaissance and Neo-classical drama

Britain Pantomime

Italy, Europe Opera

Europe Farces

France, Europe Ballet

USA Burlesque and vaudeville

USA Blues

Europe, USA Modern dance

Europe, USA Melodrama

USA, Europe Musical comedy

USA, Europe Jazz

Europe Concerts

Europe, USA Modern drama

USA Musicals

USA, Europe Pop and rock music

11

The direction of theatrical productions

All of these activities required careful preparation and regulation, with a controller or director assuming responsibility for both the form and manner of their presentation. These responsibilities obviously differed widely according to the nature and sophistication of the spectacle. During the Middle Ages, for example, an elaborate tournament might involve participants from many countries and last for several weeks. This would necessarily demand far greater administrative skills and resources than the production of a folk-play in a small country village. However, both the title of 'director' and the word 'production' have become established only during the past hundred years. Yet the notions of the theatrical production (an ordered entertainment) and of direction (the ordering of the production) go as far back as performance itself.

Common to all such organized recreational activities was a sense of special occasion and the notion of witnessing an unusual happening or event – a marvel. 'Feast', 'festival', 'holyday' and 'holiday' are all words associated with this sense of special occasion. Successful entertainments called for training or rehearsal; they had to be advertised; the order of the action needed careful regulation. Last, but not least, success could lead to a demand for repeated performances and thus enable the organizers to place the entertainments on a commercial footing, partly in order to recover their outgoings and partly to reap a reward for the time, labour and skill expended.

Such entertainments also needed a guiding hand. The figure now called 'producer' or 'director' had counterparts in earlier ages. The differences that distinguish the playmasters of Greek and Roman theatres, and the *trouvère*, *Spielmeister* and pageant-master of the Middle Ages, from today's producer or director owe more to the steady increase in sophistication and accompanying complexity of spectacular entertainments than to any real change in the nature of the entertainments themselves.

In former centuries the master or leader was normally himself a practical performer of outstanding personality, skill and experience. For example, the Greek dramatist Aeschylus (c.525–456 BC) was also an actor, as was William Shakespeare (1564–1616). The French comic dramatist Molière (1622–1673) and the British dramatist Richard Brinsley Sheridan (1751–1816) were also theatre managers. Both the American Edwin Booth (1833–1893) and the British actor Sir Henry Irving (1838–1903) were also managers. Sometimes, however, responsibility was shared between two people, one of whom concentrated on the financial and organizational side of theatrical production and the other on its artistic aspects. One example of this was the management of the Rose and Fortune theatres in Elizabethan and Jaco-

Left This Roman manuscript of a play by Terence dates from the second century B.C.
Below The battle between amateur and professional actors is satirized in this early nineteenth century cartoon showing Sheridan in harlequin costume followed by John Philip Kemble (as Hamlet) and Sarah Siddons (as Lady Macbeth) driving a group of aristocratic amateurs from the stage.

bean London by Philip Henslowe (died 1616) and Edward Alleyn (1566 – 1626), or the collaborative management of the Duke of Saxe-Meiningen and Ludwig Chronegk in Germany in the mid-nineteenth century.

In general until late in the nineteenth century, the control of theatrical production was autocratic, and the style of the productions strongly flavoured by the personality and tastes of the leader of the company, normally the theatre manager. Notable British nineteenth century theatre managers included Madame Vestris (1797 – 1856) of the Olympic Theatre, Charles Kean (1811 – 1868) who managed the Princess's Theatre, and John Philip Kemble (1757 – 1823) of Drury Lane and later Covent Garden theatres.

Towards the middle of the nineteenth century, responsibility for theatrical production began to become too onerous for one person to handle successfully. Larger theatres, more machinery and a rapid improvement in the speed and comfort of travel all served to accelerate this process, spelling the end of the tight-knit stock company both in metropolitan centres and in the provinces, in America as in Europe, and to herald the advent of what was to become known as the 'star system'. The advent of the railways enabled managers to take their companies and productions on tour, instead of waiting for audiences to visit them in their own theatres; productions could even be taken abroad, sometimes with a leading actor or actress whose reputation would ensure large audiences wherever they appeared. This development in turn encouraged businessmen to enter theatre management, to acquire chains of theatres and, thus to keep a single production running for as long as the drawing-power of the actors and actresses at the head of the company would attract patrons. The economic advantages offered by star-billing and long runs both came to assume an overriding importance in theatrical production, at the expense of the quality of the plays and production.

In America Augustin Daly (1836 – 1899) followed by Daniel Frohman (1851 – 1941), and in Britain Sir Edward Moss (1852 – 1912), followed by Sir Oswald Stoll (1866 – 1942) pioneered this new style of production organization, Daly coming to the theatre from journalism, Moss from the circus. Their successors grouped themselves into syndicates which, by virtue of owning the buildings, could virtually dictate what productions the public should be allowed to see and which they should not. Syndicates were more powerful in the United States than in Britain or on the continent of Europe (where old traditions of theatrical management and production still exercised a strong conservative influence). However, they over-reached themselves in their monopolistic fervour and by 1914, found themselves challenged on three fronts: by rival syndicates; by the Little Theatre movement which was initiated by

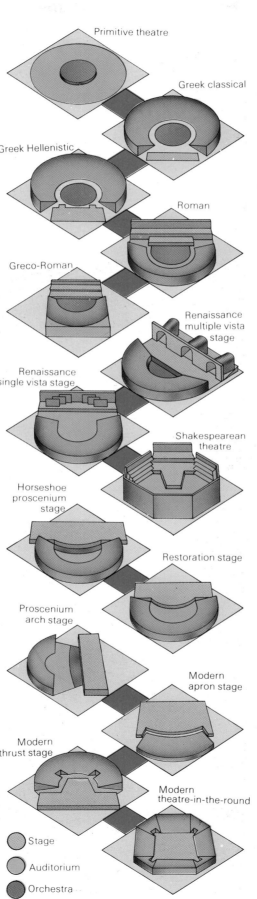

Primitive theatre
Greek classical
Greek Hellenistic
Roman
Greco-Roman
Renaissance multiple vista stage
Renaissance single vista stage
Shakespearean theatre
Horseshoe proscenium stage
Restoration stage
Proscenium arch stage
Modern apron stage
Modern thrust stage
Modern theatre-in-the-round

○ Stage
○ Auditorium
● Orchestra

Left The Western theatre in its most primitive form was simply an area surrounded by a circular arena. By Elizabethan times this had developed to include the apron stage. A most significant innovation in the mid-seventeenth century was the introduction of the proscenium arch, a feature still retained by many modern theatres. **Above** This Assyrian relief shows the enactment of a primitive folk drama.

theatre artists who were determined to free themselves from the commercial slavery which syndicates, long runs and the star system had come to represent; and by a new form of entertainment – the cinema.

Historical development

It is generally agreed that the origins of drama – and therefore of theatrical production – are to be found in the rites or ceremonies associated with religious festivals in honour of gods, spirits, ancestors or heroes. It is likely, therefore, that the first director was a priest. This relationship certainly existed in Greece and Rome, in Christian countries in Western Europe in the tenth and eleventh centuries, and in India, China and later Japan, as it still does in certain African communities today.

The priest in any relatively undeveloped society would be expected to know how best to communicate with the supernatural forces of climate and environment and their deities and thus how to organize and administer festivals in their honour. The early festivals would probably have taken the form of specially costumed dances and songs, to banish the fear of death, and give thanks for survival, especially in spring-time, and for deliverance from plague or famine. Gradually the rituals evolved; for example, as simple chanted texts for a solo voice, alternating with a response from a chorus. The priest, or festival leader, had not only to devise the festivity but also ensure that it was presented in the traditional manner. It is thought that Thespis, the legendary 'father' of drama, either inherited or established such a relationship in ancient Greece in the sixth century BC.

Greece and Rome

In 534 BC a prize was endowed for the performance of serious plays in association with the festival of the god Dionysus in Athens. From its ecstatic and orgiastic beginnings, the worship of Dionysus had become tamed, although it still retained its close association with spring and fertility. There were four annual festivals in the god's honour, all controlled by the government, which also gave special funds (including the prize) to the spring festival, known as the *City Dionysia*. By about 499 BC Aeschylus (c.525–456 BC) was contributing tragedies and satyr plays to this competition, followed later in the century by Sophocles (c.497–406 BC) and Euripides (c.484–406 BC). The texts of many of these plays have come down to us, as well as some of the theatres in which they were presented, but very little is known about how they were directed and acted. It seems likely that each of the five competing playwrights had to assemble his own company of actors, for they had to parade in Athens, under orders from the chief magistrate, to advertise the subjects of their plays. Later in the century (c.432 BC) contests were added for comic plays. The magistrate (*archon*) selected the plays and then appointed a business manager (*choregus*) who put up the money to pay for the chorus, the costumes and other production items including musicians and a leader or trainer for the chorus. The playwright directed the ensemble. Aeschylus is known to have handled every aspect of production himself and to have acted in his plays; but, as such festivals spread outwards into the Greek world, it became normal to delegate responsibility for music, costumes and so on to specialists, doubtless under pressure from the competitive element in the festivals.

After 449 BC prizes were also offered for the best acting, another competitive element which may explain the restriction on the number of actors permitted to each playwright — one at the start of the fifth century, three at the end of it — and the allocation of

The Greek theatres at Epidaurus (**left**) and Delphi (**above**) are two of the best preserved of their kind. Epidaurus held about 16,000 spectators and its acoustics were remarkably good.

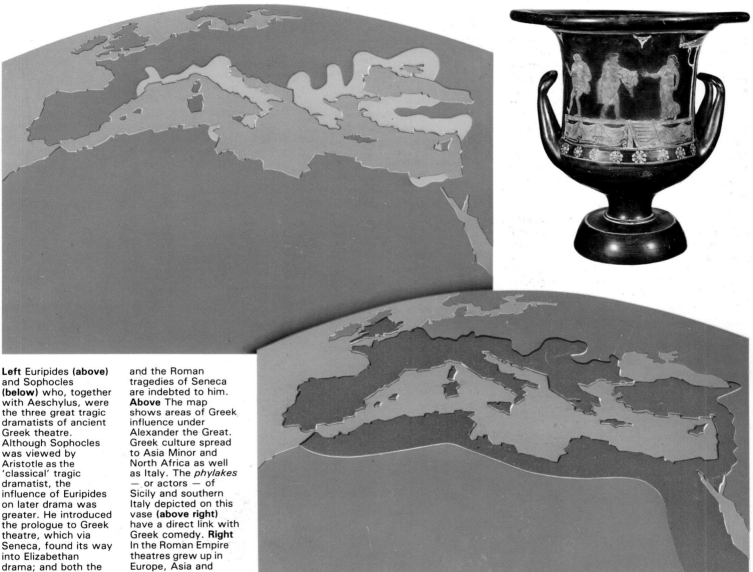

Left Euripides **(above)** and Sophocles **(below)** who, together with Aeschylus, were the three great tragic dramatists of ancient Greek theatre. Although Sophocles was viewed by Aristotle as the 'classical' tragic dramatist, the influence of Euripides on later drama was greater. He introduced the prologue to Greek theatre, which via Seneca, found its way into Elizabethan drama; and both the Greek 'New Comedy' and the Roman tragedies of Seneca are indebted to him. **Above** The map shows areas of Greek influence under Alexander the Great. Greek culture spread to Asia Minor and North Africa as well as Italy. The *phylakes* — or actors — of Sicily and southern Italy depicted on this vase **(above right)** have a direct link with Greek comedy. **Right** In the Roman Empire theatres grew up in Europe, Asia and Africa

actors to playwrights by lottery. Actors thus doubled parts using face masks. Singing and dancing remained important skills in all Athenian drama, together with clowning and acrobatics for comic and satyric actors. Much the most difficult part of the director's task was the handling of the chorus and the integration of the actors' performances with that of the chorus. However, since the plays for the following year were normally selected a month after the end of the preceding festival, the director had almost eleven months to assemble his cast and rehearse the production. The city supplied the place of performance (*theatron*).

In costume, colour was used symbolically, and some distinction in dress was made between Greeks and foreigners. Platform-soled boots (*cothurnus*) gave actors additional height. Masks were obligatory and covered the head, including face and hair.

In the fourth century BC the tendency towards specialization developed to the point where both actors and their trainers had become professionals. At the same time, dramatic performances of the kind established in Athens spread, under Alexander the Great, through Asia Minor and Palestine into North Africa and became linked with festivities celebrating his victories as well as the traditional religious festivals. This new relationship with secular festivals was accompanied by the formation of a guild of professional performers, the Artists of Dionysus, who contracted with individual cities for the production of plays at festivals.

There were also troupes of mimes, who were especially popular in Alexandria, Sicily and southern Italy. Using booth theatres, they specialized in short comic sketches, with or without a formal text, and lived a nomadic existence financed and directed by the leader of the troupe. The artists included women and were probably recruited and retained on a family basis. Known as *phylakes* in southern Italy, they provide the connection between Greek professional production and primitive Italian folk drama out of which grew the sophisticated Roman games, the *ludi*.

Dramatic games came to be associated with Roman religious festivals at the same time as regular forms of drama were developing in Greece. By the end of the third century BC there were six such festivals each year; three in April given in honour of the goddesses Flora, Ceres, and Mother Earth, one in July for Apollo, one in September and one in November, both in honour of Jupiter.

As in Greece, the management of these festivals was entrusted to the city magistrates: they contracted directly with the *domini* — leaders — of the gladiators, animal trainers, dancers and actors, for the provision of entertainments suitable for the festival and in the organization of which they proved themselves specialists. Among the most spectacular of these games were chariot-races and mock sea-battles on artificial lakes. Performances involving texts and actors were called *ludi scenici*. To begin with, the buildings housing all the games were temporary structures, but in the course of the first century BC they were replaced by permanent buildings which, under the Empire, became increasingly sumptuous and costly. Architects, too, were at pains to match the design of their buildings to the different types of entertainment offered — thus developed performance spaces such as the circus, arena and amphitheatre.

Considerable efforts were made to cater for the comfort of the audiences, including roofing and air-conditioning. Audiences, however, were not obliged to see one entertainment through from start to finish, but moved freely from one to another. In part to retain the attention of audiences, productions grew increasingly spectacular, introducing crowd scenes, processions, scenery and curtains, and machinery with which to achieve surprise scenic effects.

The *domini* in charge of the productions were professionals, but it is uncertain whether they concerned themselves as actively with artistic matters as with financial and organizational ones. Actors varied in social status from being respected citizens, such as the Roman comic actor Roscius (c.125 – 62 BC), to being no more than slaves. Although most surviving Roman plays usually require only five or six actors, the diversity of the entertainments offered, including many items now considered more appropriate to music hall or circus than to stage plays, could multiply these numbers ten times or more. With the decline of the Empire and the waning of traditional values, regular plays derived from Greek models steadily lost ground to increasingly crude and obscene entertainments, which used music and spectacle. Productions such as these provoked mounting opposition from Christian communities, which saw theatre

Above Roman circuses, like this one, were the scenes of gladiatorial contests, a form of entertainment immensely popular with the Romans.

The grotesque masks **(left, right)** worn by Roman comic actors were based on Greek models, but more realistic masks were also used in Roman drama. The mask covered the whole head and increased the volume and projection of the voice, a useful device in a large theatre.

as a direct contributor to the decadence and corruption of the Roman imperial governments which sponsored it. In their efforts to curb the theatre, the Christians were assisted first by the conversion of the Emperor in the fourth century AD and then by the barbarian invaders of the fifth and sixth centuries, who destroyed and pillaged most of the theatre buildings and finally abolished the festivals. After this, those professional performers who persevered in earning a living from mimes and pantomimes took to the roads with a small stock of costumes, masks and stage-properties, finding audiences where they could and avoiding arrest and imprisonment by travelling constantly.

Below The gigantic Colosseum in Rome is not a true theatre but was built as a sporting arena by Vespasian and Titus. Gladiatorial contests and even naval battles, with the arena filled with water, were held here up to the sixth century. The amphitheatre was 612 feet long and 515 feet wide at its widest point and seated about 87,000 people with standing room for 15,000.

Above This Roman amphitheatre at Dougga, North Africa, shows that the Roman theatre differed from the Greek in many ways. It was almost always built on level ground, not a hill slope. Stone steps led to the comparatively low stage (it was rarely more than five feet in height). There was often an imposing architectural structure behind the stage **(left)**.

Right This mosaic from Pompeii shows actors rehearsing a satyr play. This essentially Greek form of drama was a burlesque in which a hero, often taken from mythology together with a group of satyrs, is involved in some ludicrously improbable situation. The drama was characterized by boisterous action, much dancing and bawdy dialogue and gesture. Surprisingly, it was always performed along with three tragedies.

The Far East

The roots of performance in oriental countries also lie in religious observances. Records of a literary drama in India begin with Hindu plays in Sanskrit about 100 AD. Actors and actresses formed a separate caste in society, working in troupes under a leader (*Sudtrahara*) and living nomadically as in Christian Europe. There were no regular theatres, performances normally being given at major religious or civic festivals associated with temples and palaces. and on specially constructed stages (*ranja*), with a painted curtain at the back providing the only scenery. Plays included song, dance, music, mime and acrobatics and were usually stirring and melodramatic with a happy ending.

In China, drama grew out of Buddhist worship in the fifth century AD, and had become sufficiently well established by 720 AD to warrant the founding of a school of acting, called 'The Pear Garden'. The subject-matter of plays tended to be restricted to two types: civilian and military. As in Europe, women's roles were played by men. Scenery likewise was symbolic. Here too music featured prominently, the

芝居大繁昌之圖

orchestra sat on the stage itself. A special feature of Chinese drama was the painted face (*hua-lien*), in which the colours designated character symbolically.

Japanese drama began later still (c.1300 AD), and derived from Shinto religious ritual. It took four principal forms: *Nó* (serious and lyrical); *Kabuki* (popular and comic); *Kyógen* (brief farces); and *Nìngyoshibai*

(marionettes). As in Indian and Chinese drama, spectacle was provided by the costumes, facial make-up and acrobatics of the actors, not by the scenery. The actors themselves began their training as children and stayed together in companies, living like a family. The subject-matter of their plays covered history and melodramatic fiction, with music, dance, fights and clowning.

Above The Kabuki theatre, a form of popular drama, was developed in Japan in the early seventeenth century and has remained virtually unchanged to this day. The stage itself has a special device, the *hanamichi* (flower-

way), running down one side from the back of the hall to the stage, on which characters make their exits and entrances. Masks are not worn in Kabuki. Costumes can be plain or elaborate, depending on the subject matter.

The Christian Middle Ages

After the decline of the Roman Empire, such dramatic entertainment as Europe knew lay in the hands of wandering players. Their leaders alone were capable of, or interested in, the direction of theatrical production. Mingling with Northern and Western peoples, and gaining a footing as entertainers at fairs and other large gatherings, they succeeded in keeping alive a memory of Roman mimetic art.

It was not until the tenth century that new signs of dramatic activity began to appear in the West, and then, by a curious irony, it emerged in the ritual of the Christian Church. A number of Benedictine monasteries were allowed to dramatize part of the liturgies for the principal calendar festivals of thanksgiving. This started with an Easter playlet that recounted the meeting of the three Marys with the Angel at Christ's tomb, which preceded the Mass on Easter Sunday. Other plays followed: the story of Christ's Nativity was re-enacted on Christmas morning, the Visit of the Magi at the Feast of the Epiphany. So popular did these plays become that, with the approval of the Pope, rules as to their conduct were laid down by each bishop and their direction entrusted to the officiating priest.

The performers were drawn from the clergy and/or the choir. Normal vestments were used for costumes, with only slight concessions to naturalism in order to differentiate one character from another. The *Concordia Regularis* of St Ethelwold, Bishop of Winchester, written about 975 AD, clearly lays down how these liturgical dramas should be 'produced'.

Later, additional stories were added to these Biblical dramas, together with secular music and emblematic devices to identify the locality of the action and the characters. These relatively elaborate plays include the Anglo-Norman *Jeu d'Adam*, the *Antichristus* from Tegernsee in Bavaria and the *Ludus Danielis* from Beauvais in northern France.

Outside the Church, other forms of organized entertainment began to develop in the eleventh century. The most important of these was the tournament, which, from its origins as a battle school for horse and foot soldiers, emerged as a sophisticated spectacle formally enacted in an amphitheatre in the presence of ladies, with prizes and all the romantic overtones of heraldry and chivalry. The introduction of costumes and scenic emblems translated the combatants into the heroes of medieval romances, such as King Arthur and his knights.

Simple farces and short sketches developed later. These were acted in the evening at banquets accompanying these martial sports, or on such major festivals as the twelve days of the Christmas holiday. The household servants responsible for producing these pieces were known as minstrels and they gradually banded themselves into troupes of entertainers, linking up with groups of wandering players, and forming themselves into guilds. The entertainments they offered ranged from music, juggling, dancing and acrobatics to recitations of poetry, mime and short plays called interludes. Priests or schoolmasters wrote the scripts.

The growth of these small-scale secular entertainments may well have encouraged the Church to extend its own forms of drama. The year 1311 saw the establishment of the Feast of Corpus Christi, a festival that was to become associated with cycles of epic religious plays produced as part of a missionary crusade, spearheaded by mendicant friars. The Passion plays, Corpus Christi cycles, morality plays and Saint plays were imaginatively conceived on a grand scale, which involved laymen in every sphere of production from finance to acting and making costumes. A committee, jointly set up by ecclesiastical and municipal authorities, appointed the author – a cleric – and the director, who was known in England as the *pageant-master*, in Germany as the *Spielmeister* and in France as the *maître de jeu* or *régisseur*. The director secured the actors, musicians and technicians, and rehearsed the plays – in some places he also supervised transport arrangements and crowd control. He might, too, be assisted by several actor-managers, each responsible for a specific section of the production.

An important part of these duties involved the provision of a fixed stage or several transportable stages, of stage machinery to deal with ascents into heaven and descents into hell, floods, fires and the destruction of scenic buildings, and of meals for the actors and technicians during rehearsals and performance. Playing-time varied from several hours to whole days. Most plays were performed in high summer because of the paramount need for fine weather for such large-scale open air productions. Performances were well advertised. Advertising methods included elaborate costume parades in processions on the eve of the festival, in the town of performance. Plays normally began with a prayer and ended with a hymn, thus planting the entertainment firmly in its religious context. Despite the many local variations, the Church imposed a general uniformity of approach on this type of play-production throughout medieval Christendom.

The Renaissance

In Europe, from the fifteenth century onwards, two new factors became important. The first was a keen awareness of the Roman, and later of the Greek, theatre, mainly to be found in Court and academic circles; the second was a growing professionalism, which arose in the popular theatre where actors and managers looked to the financial returns from performances to acquire capital, and to free themselves from

Above The Swan Theatre London seen in this sketch (c. 1596) is the only surviving contemporary representation of the interior of the Elizabethan theatre. The circular structure is open to the sky and has three tiers of galleries for spectators. Most of the action took place on the apron stage.

dependence on a princely patron.

Thus at Court and at the universities, research and experiment tended to hold sway in dramatic productions. Elsewhere, traditional forms of drama continued to predominate unless novelty could command public support. The wars of religion that marked the sixteenth century resulted in social and political pressures which helped reinforce this process. In Catholic countries, except Spain, popular entertainments in the medieval, Gothic style swiftly lost ground before the advancing tide of classically influenced drama; in Protestant countries, except Germany, amateur interest in the theatre found itself facing ever stiffer competition from tightly organized professional companies.

The new drama based upon Greek and Roman models came to be known in Italy as *commedia erudita*. It was encouraged by princely patrons who built theatres to house the productions. The most famous of these was the *Teatro Olimpico*, designed by Andrea Palladio, in Vicenza; it opened with a performance of Sophocles's *Oedipus Rex*, in Italian, in 1585, and is still standing today.

There was a growing interest, too, in the spectacle, as well as in song and dance. In Florence, experiments with the chorus in Greek plays led to the invention of new forms of drama, from which opera emerged to dominate the stages of Italy, while ballet came to play a similar role in France at the expense of tragedy and comedy. No expense

Commedia dell'arte
The stock characters of this popular, improvised Italian comedy, which flourished from the sixteenth to the eighteenth century, can be grouped according to their functions in the plot. The non-comic characters were a pair of lovers, the *innamorati* — such as Lucia **(bottom)**. They usually did not wear masks. The series of illustrations **(left, below)** depict the masked comic characters.

The *commedia* has had a wide-ranging influence on theatre, pantomime, circus and many other performing arts.

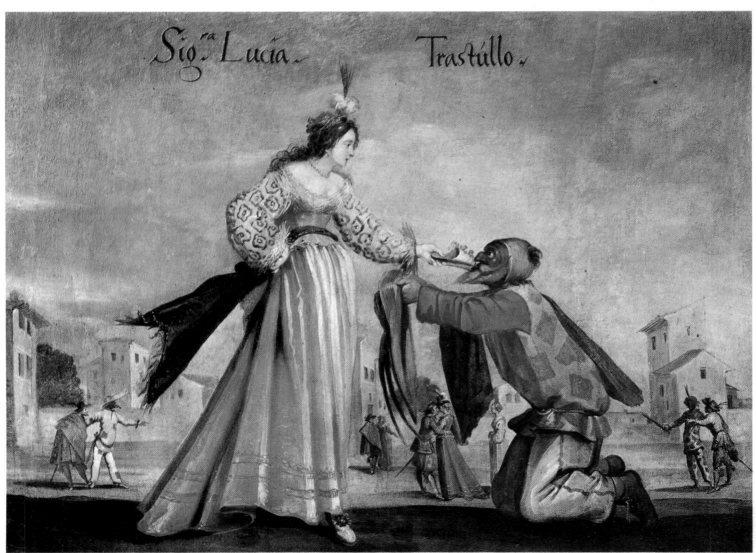

Sigᵃ Lucia.   Trastúllo.

was spared to mount these entertainments: lavish costumes and scenic spectacle came to be taken for granted, and tournaments or water-spectacles were often incorporated into the performances.

Sometimes the patrons themselves took part in the production, which came to be regarded as a co-ordination of several specialist activities. The singers, dancers, musicians, painters, horsemen and machinists were each rehearsed independently by their respective trainers and brought together into a single ensemble by the stage-manager, who today would be called the director. This way of organizing productions reflected the structure of a princely household in which the master of the music, dancing-master and so on would assume responsibility for their respective sectors. Princely patronage also encouraged visits from professional companies of touring players.

In Italy towards the end of the sixteenth century, these professional touring companies began to specialize in a form of improvised drama based on the characters and plots of Latin comedy. This gained a vitality drawn from direct observation of contemporary bourgeois and peasant life. These entertainments were known as *commedia dell'arte*, and were very much under the control of the leading actor, whose com-

pany usually travelled and was known under his name – although some companies received regular support from aristocratic patrons. During the seventeenth and eighteenth centuries, *commedia erudita* (with its extensions into opera, ballet and circus) and *commedia dell'arte* came to dominate Europe. This was accompanied by the relative eclipse of the dramatist as the dominant force in theatrical production and the rise in importance of painters and scenic engineers like Inigo Jones (1573–1652) in England, Giacomo Torrelli (1608–1678) in France and the Bibiena family in Italy, Austria and France.

In England and Spain, however, the Italian, neo-classical drama failed to become established to the same extent as in the rest of Europe. There was far stiffer opposition from the theatre itself, and less lavish support from Court and academic patrons. This atmosphere favoured the survival of medieval stage conventions and also helped playwrights and actors to flourish. Literary drama and professional standards of presentation led to the building of permanent public playhouses. This was accompanied by the emergence of the actor who was also playwright and director. The renowned Spanish dramatists Lope de Vega (1562–1635) and Calderon de la Barca (1600–1681) performed these functions, as did in England Ben Jonson (c.1572–1637), Thomas Heywood (c.1573–1641), William Shake-

speare (1564–1616) and William Davenant (1606–1668). Such men were open to all the new ideas of the time, which by their genius they were able to project to the public; they were lucky enough, too, to enjoy the protection of powerful patrons. It was an enviable position of strength and they used it to bring to the popular theatre a form of management that was at once coherent yet flexible, conservative yet progressive, which was thus able to speak simultaneously to courtier, artisan and peasant.

Their theatres also reflected this flexibility and could stage entertainments ranging from bear-baiting, cock-fighting and sword fights to secular and religious stage plays. Flexibility, too, marked the way in which the actors moved easily between public amphitheatres, provincial town halls and banquet-halls, and stages in royal palaces. With equal ease the new men of the theatre – Calderon as Master of the Revels to King Philip IV, Jonson as Poet Laureate to James I and Shakespeare as principal playwright to the King's own company of actors from 1603 to 1616 – created works that appealed to all levels of society. They revealed to popular audiences the views of their royal masters and, at the same time, the plays included characters drawn from the ordinary people that gave their masters some indication of the tastes and interests of their subjects. Censorship in both Spain and England was strict; but having once obtained a licence to

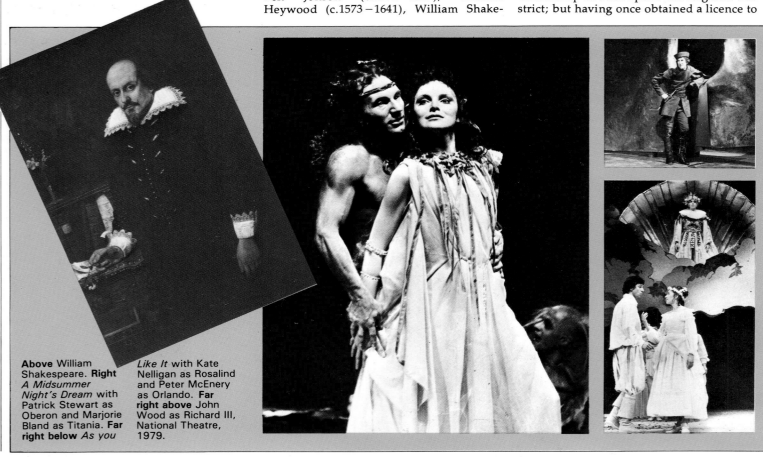

Above William Shakespeare. **Right** *A Midsummer Night's Dream* with Patrick Stewart as Oberon and Marjorie Bland as Titania. **Far right below** *As you Like It* with Kate Nelligan as Rosalind and Peter McEnery as Orlando. **Far right above** John Wood as Richard III, National Theatre, 1979.

present a play, author, leading actor and
manager were free to rehearse and direct it as
they pleased.

It was not unusual for a company to perform up to 40 different plays in the season,
which lasted from October to June. About
one third of these might be new plays, which
were rehearsed for about four weeks — as
long as it took to make the costumes. These
were luxurious and, like the settings, were
intended more as a means of identification
than as exact reproductions — although there
were some concessions to realism in foreign
or classical dress, such as turbans for Turks
or togas for Romans. Music and dance featured regularly in the productions, as did
fights and battles, but never at the expense of
dialogue and plot.

There were losses as well as gains in the
triumph of professionalism in the theatre.
One casualty was the decline of amateur
dramatic activity. In addition, before the end
of the seventeenth century, Court taste
gradually became more important in the
English and Spanish theatre, as it had
already done in the rest of Europe. In both
countries, however, the author in his dual
role of playwright and actor or manager
retained a controlling influence. In France
the emergence of Molière (1622–1673),
Racine (1639–1679) and later Voltaire
(1694–1778) in similar capacities began to
effect changes which, in association with the
commedia dell'arte, were destined to spark off

Right Shakespeare's
Henry VI Part II with
Helen Mirren as
Queen Margaret and
Peter McEnery as
Suffolk produced at
Stratford-upon-
Avon, 1977. **Below**
Alan Howard as
Henry V in the RSC's
1977 production at
Stratford-upon-
Avon.

reactions in other countries during the eighteenth century.

Later innovations

One of the principal changes to appear in the public theatres of England, France and Spain during the seventeenth century was the introduction of movable scenery. Roofed over, illuminated by candelabra and intimate in atmosphere, the new public theatres attracted middle-class audiences whose tastes and interests were to determine standards of theatrical production during the eighteenth century. Actresses took over female roles, scenery became simplified, stereotyped and romanticized. In costume and acting, extravagance gave way to some degree of naturalism, and prose replaced verse. In Italy, the dramatist Carlo Goldoni (1707–1793) attacked the *commedia dell'arte*, forcing its actors to substitute scripted parts for improvisation, to abandon their masks and to soften their attacks on the bourgeoisie. Goldoni is now best remembered for his comedies such as *Il Servitore di due Padroni* (*The Servant of Two Masters*), first performed in 1746.

Elsewhere the changed climate brought sentimental comedy and bourgeois tragedy into vogue. The sentimental moralizing of *The Conscious Lovers* by Sir Richard Steele (1672–1729) was extremely popular, while in Germany Gotthold Ephraim Lessing (1729–1781) wrote a successful bourgeois tragedy called *Miss Sara Sampson*. First performed in 1755, it was taken from the earlier English success *The London Merchant* by George Lillo (1693–1739). The constant moralizing of both types of drama, however, served to popularize a wide variety of short after-pieces — farces, pantomimes and harlequinades — heavily indebted to the *commedia dell'arte*. Managers, as a result, gave a high priority to variety in their programme planning. Playwrights, actors and stage-managers, however, continued to respect traditional methods of rehearsal and presentation, despite the successful production of plays like *The Rehearsal* by George Villiers (1628–1687), in 1671, and Sheridan's *The Critic*, in 1779, which ridiculed the theatre's own practices.

Late in the eighteenth century and early in the nineteenth century, however, a number of architectural and technical changes in theatre building and equipment had wide-ranging effects on actors, audiences and scene designers. These changes obliged managers to alter the traditional concepts of theatrical production.

To accommodate the rapid increase in the number of theatre-goers, theatres were enlarged. In London, for example, both Covent Garden and the Theatre Royal, Drury Lane were enlarged during the 1790s. New theatres were constructed in provincial cities, such as the theatre in Richmond, Yorkshire, which opened in 1788. The same

Left This scene is from *Le Bourgeois Gentilhomme* by Molière.

Above Thomas King as Puff in Sheridan's *The Critic*, first produced in 1779.

period saw the beginnings of a largely English-speaking theatre in North America. America's first theatre, the Southwark, opened in Philadelphia in 1766, followed by the Chestnut Street Theatre in 1794. In New York the John Street Theatre opened in 1767. British actor-managers seized the new opportunities offered by this new market to establish new stock companies and to tour successful productions. On the technical side, the introduction of gas lighting to theatres after 1815 made it possible to darken the auditorium. This was one main reason for another change which was fundamentally to alter both the theatre and the nature of theatrical performance. The forestage disappeared and the action retreated behind the proscenium arch. This form of stage dominated the theatre until the mid twentieth century.

These changes led to the total separation of the actor-manager's twin functions. His authority was divided between three individuals — the business manager or the producer, the director, and the star performer. The stage manager and the designer became accepted as the individuals best equipped to supervise and direct the growing complexities of the stage action into a coherent pictorial ensemble.

Still more radical change was stimulated by the redistribution of wealth that accompanied the industrial and political revolutions during the early years of the nineteenth century. Theatre-going, in both Europe and America, came to be regarded as the right of everyone, rather than the prerogative of the few. Theatres multiplied in number and further increased in size.

Alongside them, in taverns, large annexes grew up, equipped to offer music, dancing and comedy. Here, the amateur talent of coffee-houses and music rooms gave way to professionals — women as well as men. The most popular artists soon found that they could demand large fees and dictate the moment within the miscellaneous programme at which they appeared. In order to steal custom from their rivals, the more enterprising publican-managers quickly took to equipping their halls with stages, scenery and lighting, and the artists appearing in them with glittering costumes. Music-hall, variety, vaudeville, all brash but slick, offered wine, women, song and spectacle at very low cost to a wide public.

Something of the vigour and energy of all this brushed off on to all other forms of drama. The larger theatres called for larger voices and larger orchestras; the technical improvements in stage lighting and machinery allowed for greater spectacle; while the larger, more diverse audiences demanded a greater variety of specialist techniques. Failure to please the public, however, brought with it a risk of heavy losses — the history of theatrical production in both Europe and America during the nineteenth century is strewn with bankruptcies.

The stars of the music-halls, were able to command success through their personal relationship with their audience. However, leading actors, singers and dancers in straight theatre, opera and ballet found themselves losing control of their careers to theatrical business executives — house managers, tour managers, and eventually to management syndicates.

At the same time, darkened auditoria and more brightly illuminated stages forced actors to tone down their performances to correspond more naturalistically with the increasing realism of the scenery around them and to relinquish to the stage managers much of their former directorial authority within their own companies. The American actor-manager, Edwin Booth (1833–1893), wrote to a friend following his own bankruptcy in 1873 advising him to put the money wasted on realistic scenery into finding good actors and regaining control of artistic direction.

However, Booth and his fellow actor-managers learned this lesson too late. By the end of the century the tension between star performer and business and stage manager under the stress of touring and of huge financial investments had reached a point where the weakest member of the triumvirate, the actor, had to concede defeat. In this maelstrom of divided loyalties the theatre had to face an unprecedented threat to its continued existence from the advent of the cinema as a rival. In the confusion accompanying this development in the early years of the twentieth century the director arose as the dominant figure in theatrical production, and the reaction against spectacle and rhetoric began.

PLACES OF PERFORMANCE
FROM THE CLASSICAL ARENA TO MODERN THEATRE

THEATRES

Theatres have had a circular history. They started out as bowl-shaped amphitheatres and that is increasingly the form to which they are returning. There is a direct link between the Greek Theatre at Epidaurus and the Olivier auditorium at Britain's National Theatre in London, or the Festival Theatre at Stratford, Ontario. Increasingly, audiences are wrapped around a stage area instead of being placed squarely in front of it. The proscenium arch theatre, in which the actors are confined behind a picture frame, will no doubt survive; but today it is progressive to favour either the non-proscenium, open stage or the intimacy of the studio theatre which is often little more than a converted room.

The stage itself is quite simply the space on or in which the actors appear before the audience. Originally in the Greek theatre it was no more than a small plateau on the hill below the Acropolis with the audience sitting round on rudely constructed wooden benches or squatting among the rocks; it gradually became more sophisticated. The still-surviving theatre at Epidaurus has a carefully tiered space for the audience (the auditorium), a circular area where the choric action took place (the orchestra) and an area behind for the main action (the stage). It is interesting to note that Peter Hall's early productions of *Tamburlaine, Hamlet* and *Volpone* at the Olivier Theatre, which were designed by John Bury, employed the idea of a circular acting area, though with time this form has been abandoned.

Auditorium, orchestra and stage were the three separate parts of Greek theatre. The Romans modified this by making theatre

Above, right The ancient theatre at Epidaurus in Greece is the best preserved theatre of its kind. In the fourth century BC tiers were carved out of hill sides in semi-circles. Stone slabs were then placed on these tiers as seats for as many as 12,000 people. The acoustics in this theatre are still excellent. The Greek theatre influenced the construction of all subsequent theatres The gradual development is shown in colour. The auditorium is in orange and the stage pink. The blue area between them is the orchestra, which is where the Greek chorus used to sing and dance.

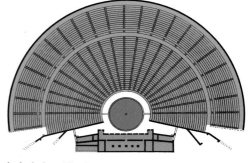

Left, below The Roman theatre differed in many respects from the Greek. Most theatres were built on a level plain, rather than on a hillside, as the Romans preferred a more enclosed setting. In addition, the stage (shown in pink) was surrounded by buildings on three sides, and the auditorium (orange) was fenced in by a large, ornately decorated wall. The stage was raised up to five feet and was sheltered by a permanent wooden roof. If necessary, a covering could be draped from tall poles on the wall, to shelter the auditorium.

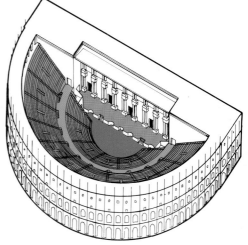

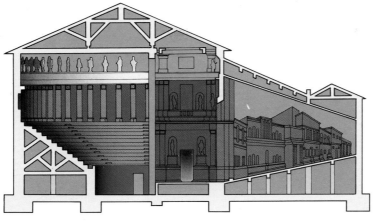

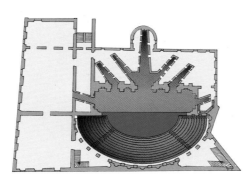

Above, left The Teatro Olimpico at Vicenza in Italy was the first permanent indoor theatre. Andrea Palladio designed it in 1580 as a reconstructed Roman theatre. It therefore retains the semi-circular orchestra (shown in blue) and auditorium (orange); but the stage (pink) has become more complicated. One large central stage entrance and four smaller ones were added by Scamozzi, who completed the theatre in 1584. Vistas of streets were painted in perspective onto back-cloths. These were then hung behind the stage entrances so that the theatre gained a new depth.

much more an indoor affair. A roof jutted out over the stage; awnings could be spread over the audience; scenery was displayed on the ornate facades against which the actors were revealed. Even a front curtain was introduced. Greek theatres were formed out of natural structures, such as hillsides, and the sea or the mountains often served as a permanent backcloth. The Romans usually performed on the plains and added the idea of decorative scenery and protective covering.

Theatre can take many forms. Throughout history there has been a constant battle between simplicity and elaboration. In the early medieval period, plays were often presented on rough carts, and later on decorated platforms or 'mansions' arranged before the audience in a straight line or semi-circle. Spectacular effects became possible. A record of a production at Valenciennes, France, in 1547 tells us that: 'From Hell, Lucifer rose, how one could not tell, on a dragon's back. Moses' staff, dry and withered, suddenly burst forth with flowers and fruit; the souls of Herod and Judas were borne into the air by devils.' Man's residual hunger for spectacle had to be satisfied.

Simplicity fought with elaboration; openness with formality. The Renaissance theatres of Italy, particularly the famous Teatro Olimpico at Vicenza built in 1584, show formality winning. The Olimpico has a semi-circular auditorium, a long narrow stage backed by a richly designed facade and in the facade itself a large central opening with four other entrance doors. By 1618, the Teatro Farnese at Parma had an elongated auditorium and a richly sculptured proscenium-arch firmly separating the actors from the audience. The straight-edged stage with the audience in front of it obviously

Right The Teatro Farnese at Parma was designed by Aleotti in 1618. It was the first proscenium arch theatre to be constructed with moving scenery, and it became the model for other stages and theatres during the next 250 years. The Farnese was badly damaged in the Second World War but it has since been fully restored. In this theatre the ancient orchestra area was turned into a large arena.

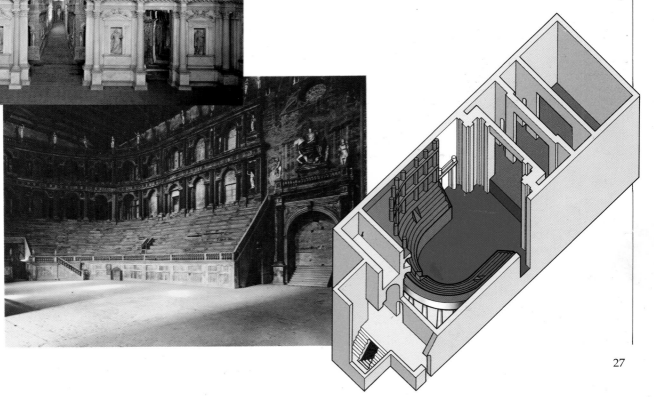

27

allows for greater use of pictorial effect.

In England, the same battle was fought between two kinds of theatre. It is possible to work out from contemporary sources roughly what the Elizabethan Globe Theatre, built in 1599 on the south bank of the Thames, must have looked like: an open platform providing scope for movement, an inner stage beyond for particular localities, an upper gallery that allowed for vertical action. The Globe, with its Shakespearean associations, has fascinated historians and theatrical practitioners alike. Even today, attempts are still being made to reproduce the Globe format: the St George's Theatre, Tufnell Park, London, is one such and in Detroit great sums are being spent on a reconstructed Globe.

In the early seventeenth century there was a shift from open-air to roofed-in theatres. The company run by Richard Burbage (1567 – 1619) played in the indoor Blackfriars Theatre in London which had been built by Burbage's actor-manager father. Shakespeare's later plays were first performed here.

As time went on scenery and spectacle became more important. However, English Restoration playhouses still had a curved projection beyond the curtain called the apron which allowed for direct contact with an audience and was similar to the Elizabethan platform.

But the seventeenth and eighteenth centuries saw increasing scenic and theatrical elaboration. Italy, especially with its passion for opera, built baroque houses like the Teatro San Carlo of Naples (1737) or La Scala Milan (1778) which allowed for rich scenery and machine effects and which turned the horseshoe auditorium into the most sophisticated of box-filled curves where spectators could both see and be seen. At Drottningholm Theatre near Stockholm, built in 1754 and still very much in use for opera, the original machinery remains intact and the view from the back of the stalls gives a perfect vision of the proportions of classical theatre.

Throughout the nineteenth century realistic illusion and scenic spectacle became more important and the proscenium arch held sway. Drury Lane, Covent Garden, the Haymarket and Her Majesty's in London, the Burgtheater in Vienna, the Comédie Française in Paris, and the National Theatre in Stockholm all enclosed the actors behind an arch. The dominance of the proscenium arch stage must be seen in conjunction with other developments. From the early nineteenth century it became possible to darken the auditorium and stage lighting became more versatile and technically complex. The extravagant scenic effects of many nineteenth century melodramas of necessity fed the idea of a demarcation line between the watchers and the watched; for example a play like *The Whip* which put a real horse race on

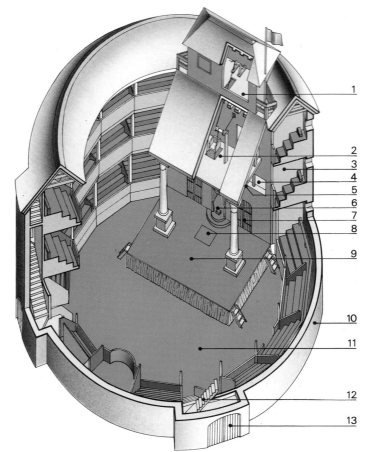

Left This scale reconstruction of the Swan Theatre shows the basic features of the Elizabethan playhouse. These were the hut *(1)*; the machinery rooms *(2)* where props were kept; the two penny rooms *(3)*; the gallery *(4)* used by both players and musicians; the heavens *(5)* on the underside of machinery rooms, which formed a canopy over the stage; the inner stage *(6)*; the stage doors *(7)*; the trap door *(8)* used, for example in graveyard scenes; the stage *(9)*; the outer walls of the theatre made of flint *(10)*; the yard or pit *(11)* where the audience could pay for standing room only; the stairs leading to the tiered galleries *(12)* where the more expensive seats were covered against the weather; the entrance to the yard *(13)*.

Right The second Theatre Royal, Drury Lane, seen here from the stage, was designed by Sir Christopher Wren and opened in 1674. It was an elaborate structure and the scale reproduction **(below)** shows the entrance doors*(1)*; pit door *(2)*; upper gallery *(3)*; gallery *(4)*; pit *(5)*; amphitheatre *(6)*; lobby *(7)*; pit passage *(8)*; vista stage *(9)*; tiring rooms *(10)*; scenic stage *(11)*; the proscenium *(12)*; side boxes *(13)*; stair to boxes *(14)*; and rooms for making costumes, stage scenery, props and so on *(15)*.

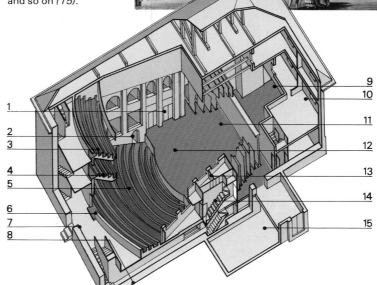

Right This print by Thomas Rowlandson shows the Theatre Royal, Drury Lane in 1809. This is not, in fact, Wren's building but a new theatre which was constructed in 1794. This, however, was destroyed by fire in 1809 soon after Rowlandson's sketch was made. The theatre was rebuilt in 1812 in very much the same style as the 1794 construction.

Left This eighteenth century theatre shows how the stage itself had developed since Elizabethan times. The principal acting area is still the forestage; it is flanked on both sides by the proscenium doors and framed by the proscenium arch, a Restoration development.

Below Extravagant scenic effects, like this real horse race on stage at Sadler's Wells, were a feature of nineteenth century drama. Sadler's Wells was also well-known as the home of aquatic drama. A gigantic tank filled with water was used for naval battles and other spectacles.

Below These simplified diagrams of the auditoria of La Scala, Milan **(top)** and the Comedie Francaise **(bottom)** in Paris show the relative size of audience space and stage.

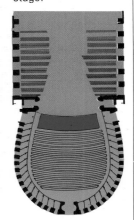

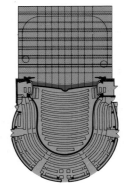

stage at Drury Lane demands both complex machinery and a certain physical distance.

However, inevitably a reaction against the comfort of illusion was to come; and it has arrived like a landslide in the current century. Theatre-in-the-round (with the audience on all sides of the actors) came into prominence in Russia in the 1930s with productions by Nikolai Okhlopkov (1900–1967) at the Realistic Theatre in Moscow. He also experimented with gangways leading into the auditorium with platforms spread throughout. In England in the 1930s, the actor and director Robert Atkins (1886–1972) produced Shakespeare plays in a boxing ring in Blackfriars, London. In America, the theatre-in-the-round movement flourished on the campus circuit starting with the Penthouse Theatre at the University of Washington in Seattle, which had an elliptical acting area and auditorium contained in a circular foyer.

Not everyone, however, thought theatre-in-the-round was the ideal solution to the flight from illusion. Others favoured the open stage, going back to the Greeks and Elizabethans, with the audience on three sides of the main acting area. The British director Tyrone Guthrie (1900–1971) was a pioneer of this method and used it decisively when for the 1948 Edinburgh Festival he produced a sixteenth-century Scottish morality play, *The Three Estates*, in the Assembly Hall of the Church of Scotland. It was a huge success and Guthrie himself wrote: 'One of the most pleasing effects of the performance was the physical relation of the audience to the stage. The audience did not look on the actors against a background of pictorial and illusionary scenery. Seated around three sides of the stage, they focused upon the actors in the brightly lit acting area, but the background was of the dimly lit rows of people similarly focused on the actors. All the time, each member of the audience was being reminded that he was not lost in an illusion but was a member of a large audience "assisting", as the French very properly express it, in a performance, a participant in a ritual.'

The Assembly Hall became a permanent part of the Festival, and Guthrie was invited to apply similar principles elsewhere: to a new festival at Stratford, Ontario, which began in a tent in 1953 and which now takes place in a superb open-stage building where an actor can stand down-stage and still command the whole house. The same principles were used, for example, in two British theatres, the Chichester Festival Theatre which opened in 1962 and which was directly inspired by Stratford's success; and the Crucible Theatre in Sheffield which can — and does — house everything from a Broadway musical like *Chicago* to a snooker championship. Everywhere, open stages now prosper: the Olivier at the National is simply the latest in a long line.

Nikolai Okhlopkov's period as director of the Moscow Realistic Theatre from 1934 to 1938 was a time of major experimentation with staging. His production of *The Iron Stream* (**below**) shows in its crowd scenes a fine sense of spatial relationships. Okhlopkov's staging was influenced by the Greek, Elizabethan and Far Eastern theatres. In 1957 he revived his production of Pogodin's *Aristocrats* which is set in a labour camp (**right**).

Right The Olivier auditorium at London's National Theatre has an open stage. Its design looks back to the Greek and Elizabethan theatres.

Below Many modern theatre complexes have a small studio theatre. London's National has its Cottesloe auditorium, and the Lincoln Center in New York has a small auditorium in the Vivian Beaumont Theater which seats 299 people. Studio theatres are used mainly for small scale and experimental productions.

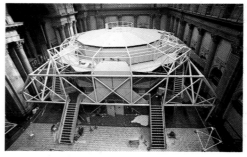

Left, above The Royal Exchange Theatre in Manchester's former Cotton Exchange is one of the most exciting theatre buildings in Britain. This theatre-in-the-round is built inside the huge exchange building; this gives the stage its unusual acoustics. Gangways lead through the auditorium and onto the stage.

Below This plan of the Penthouse Theater, Washington University, Seattle, shows the way the whole theatre is laid out, including stage, auditorium, dressing rooms, box office, foyer, props room and so on. The provision of adequate dressing rooms for the acting and stage staff is no less important than providing good seats and visibility for the audience.

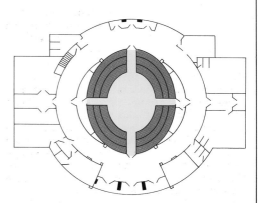

The Royal Exchange Theatre in Manchester, which is an incredibly intimate circular theatre situated within the cavernous framework of the old Mancunian Cotton Exchange has proved that theatre-in-the-round can also be made to work. When the Royal Exchange company came to the Roundhouse in London in the summer of 1979 with productions of *Gilbert Pinfold*, *The Family Reunion* and *The Lady from the Sea*, even the metropolitan audience quickly adjusted to the problems of periodically confronting an actor's back.

Today, in addition to the increasing return to first principles of Greek and Elizabethan theatre, there is also an exploration of the theatrical possibilities of small spaces. In New York, Off-Off-Broadway theatre happens in rooms, temples, attics and garages all over Manhattan. The Royal Shakespeare Company has done much of its best work in a shed in Stratford-upon-Avon called The Other Place and in a converted rehearsal room in London's Covent Garden known as The Warehouse. For years, the theatre-in-the-round in Scarborough, Yorkshire, in which most of the popular social comedies by the British playwright Alan Ayckbourn (born 1939) are first performed, was simply a room in the public library.

However, even if the open stage and the studio are the currently popular modes, all theatres have certain features in common. Apart from the stage and auditorium, there is invariably a foyer where the audience congregates. This may be plush and carpeted, like the Lincoln Centre in New York. It may itself contain pre-play musical recitals as at the Olivier in London, or it may be simply a converted butcher's shop as at the Young Vic just off London's Waterloo Road.

Again, backstage there are always dressing-rooms and a green room where the actors can mingle, though these vary with the size of the theatre. In many of London's older theatres, the dressing rooms are dreary; to visit the star of whatever is playing at the Savoy requires a descent down a precipitous flight of steps into something rather like an upholstered cellar. At the Young Vic there are simply two dressing-rooms: one each for men and women. In contrast, at the Royal Shakespeare Theatre in Stratford-upon-Avon, the dressing-rooms command a handsome view of the river with swans drifting past.

Theatres, apart from studio theatres, also share certain common features: wings (where the actors wait to make their entrances); flies (a space above the stage from which scenery may be flown in); a control panel (containing a lighting board that regulates the numerous lighting cues a play may require); a below-stage area (used for storage or for entrances through a trap door in the stage); a stage door (usually manned by a white-thatched octogenarian who remembers the legendary Mrs Patrick Campbell). Most theatres also have a capacious front-of-house area that houses all the non-

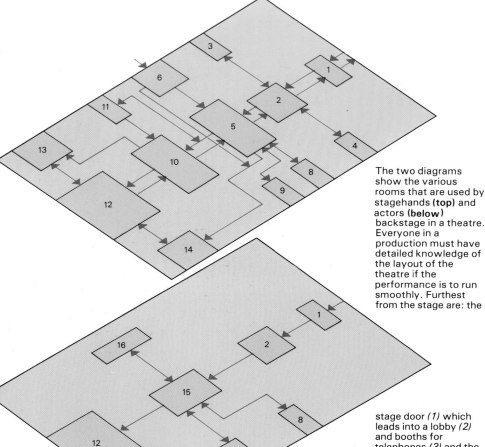

The two diagrams show the various rooms that are used by stagehands (**top**) and actors (**below**) backstage in a theatre. Everyone in a production must have detailed knowledge of the layout of the theatre if the performance is to run smoothly. Furthest from the stage are: the stage door (1) which leads into a lobby (2) and booths for telephones (3) and the doorman (4). The dressing rooms (5) are close to the costumes (7) which are kept in the wardrobe rooms (6) the showers and toilets (8) and the make-up room (9). When the actors have changed they wait for their call onstage in the green room (11) and from the stage anteroom (10) they make their entrances. The stage (12) has screened off areas where actors can wait, and dressing rooms for quick changes (14) are as near to the acting area as possible. In most theatres, a trap room (13), which has a passage leading to beneath the stage, is on the opposite side to the quick change dressing rooms. Also behind the stage are locker rooms (15), a lounge (16) and a room for first-aid (17).
Left This caricature of 'the life of an actor' is dated 1824 and satirizes the apparent backstage chaos which often reigns in the theatre before the curtain goes up on a performance.

performing people who help to keep the building ticking over: the theatre manager responsible for the bricks and mortar; the front-of-house manager who supervises the audience; the press and publicity staff; the secretaries. These days, theatres can be very complex mechanisms requiring huge operating staffs. Big enterprises like the National Theatre and the Royal Shakespeare Company in Britain employ hundreds. But at the other end of the scale there are, in every major city, fringe theatres that deliberately cut back on administration and rely on a small band of dedicated, underpaid workers.

Today, theatre is, in fact, a term that can apply to an extraordinary variety of buildings: the Sydney Opera House or the Edinburgh Traverse – which is a room off the Royal Mile; in London, the National Theatre or the dining area of the King's Head, an Islington pub; The Palace on Times Square, New York, or the Hudson Bay Theatre Guild which is a tiny arts centre in downtown Manhattan.

In the end, it is impossible to define what a theatre is or should be. Even to say that it is people at one end of a room watching people at the other end is no longer true, since street theatre has once more become a widespread phenomenon. Theatre – that is to say theatrical performance – basically consists of someone watching someone else performing. The theatre is the building in which that performance takes place – whether in Greece in the fifth century BC, or in London, Paris, New York, Rome or Berlin today.

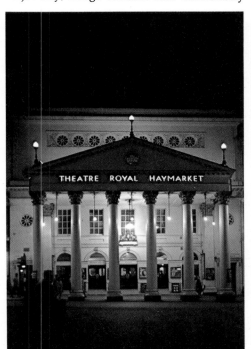

Varieties of theatre
These illustrations show the wide range of theatrical buildings. The simplest forms include the Greek theatre (**far right**), a modern travelling theatre on wheels (**above centre**), a pub room converted into a theatre (**right**) and a simple outdoor structure used for mystery plays (**right centre**). The Theatre Royal, Haymarket (**above**) and the Drottningholm in Sweden (**bottom right**) are traditional buildings. The theatre in the Manchester Royal Exchange, (**top centre**), London's National Theatre (**top right**) and the New York Met (**bottom far right**) are diverse examples of complex, modern theatres.

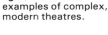

Opera Houses

During the eighteenth and nineteenth centuries opera became increasingly popular, so, in order to accommodate the larger audiences, lavish opera houses were built. These vary considerably in size. The old Metropolitan Opera House in New York was built in 1883 to seat 3,639 people. However, La Scala in Milan *(9)* and the Royal Opera House, Covent Garden, London, *(5)* seat about 2,500 La Fenice in Venice *(8),* one of the world's most elegant opera houses, was burned down during its construction. It was rebuilt and eventually opened in May 1792. The Opéra in Paris *(2)* was founded in 1669. After a series of fires and temporary sites, it moved to a new building, which also burned down and was replaced by the present building in 1875. The Bolshoi Theatre in Moscow *(1)* also suffered badly. It was first destroyed in 1805 and reconstructed to its present design in 1856.

Other opera houses were damaged during the Second World war. La Scala was repaired but the State Opera House in Vienna *(3)* was completely rebuilt, and opened in 1953.

Opera houses tend to be plagued by financial problems. For example, the Festival Theatre at Bayreuth in Germany *(7)* had many difficulties when it first opened in 1876, and the Wagner festival was inaugurated there in the same year. More recently, the Sydney Opera House *(6),* designed by a Danish architect in 1955, only opened in 1973 after many delays and difficulties. The Metropolitan moved from its old site in New York to the Lincoln Center *(4).* It is a very successful building built specifically for opera.

1△

2△

7▽

8▽

5▽

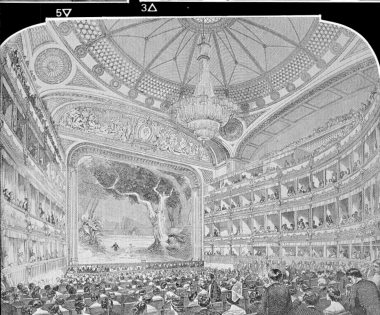

3△

9▽   6△

CONCERT HALLS

The concert hall, designed and used solely for the purpose of non-dramatic and non-religious music, is a relatively modern phenomenon. Up to the end of the eighteenth century, most sacred music, whether or not liturgical, would have been performed in a church, while secular music was usually to be heard in opera houses, theatres, taverns or private houses.

In European countries such as Italy and Germany, which were divided into a multiplicity of kingdoms and princely states, music was primarily a court entertainment, apart from chamber music which was played in the home.

In England the position was rather different. The flourishing middle classes who supported the public theatres in Elizabethan and Jacobean times, and again in the Restoration period, also provided the first audiences for musical performances outside the court or the university.

On December 30, 1672, John Banister (1630–1679), chief violinist to King Charles II, advertised in the *London Gazette* that from 'this present Monday, will be musick performed by excellent masters, beginning precisely at four of the clock in the afternoon, and every afternoon for the future' at his house by the George Tavern in Whitefriars, which was henceforth called the 'Musick-School'. Banister's concerts flourished, continuing until 1678, the year before his death. The next series of public concerts in London was given in the converted loft of a coal-house in Clerkenwell, where Thomas Britton (1651–1714), small-coal hawker by profession and self-taught amateur musician, held weekly gatherings for 36 years. A yearly subscription to his concerts cost 10 shillings, while a cup of coffee was one penny.

Other venues for London concerts in the first half of the eighteenth century included the Crown and Anchor Tavern in the Strand where the Academy of Ancient Music met for many years; the Castle Tavern in Paternoster Row which gave its name to the Castle Concerts; and Hickford's Room in James Street, Piccadilly.

During the latter part of the century, Carlisle House, Soho Square, was the setting for musical entertainments and concerts run by Mrs Cornelys who, as Teresa Pompeati, had sung in Italian opera at the King's Theatre some years before.

At first the musicians who took part in her subscription concerts were of the calibre of Johann Christian Bach (1732–1795) and Karl Frederick Abel (1723–1787), the viola da gamba player, who jointly conducted the proceedings.

J. C. Bach and Abel also played at the Hanover Square Rooms, inaugurating the hall in 1775 with a series of concerts. The Hanover Square Rooms remained one of the chief musical centres of London for nearly a century. It was here that Haydn appeared under the aegis of J. P. Salomon (1745–1815), at whose subscription concerts he introduced and conducted his so-called London or Salomon symphonies. After its original home, the elegant Argyll Rooms in Regent Street, was destroyed by fire in 1830, the Philharmonic Society held its concerts in the Hanover Square Rooms, and most of the best-known musicians in Europe, including Richard Wagner (1813–1883), conducted or played there.

Meanwhile, orchestras as well as audiences were steadily increasing in size, both in London and in the provincial cities where special halls were also beginning to be built. Though neither the Birmingham Town Hall, an edifice modelled on the Parthenon and completed in 1834, nor the Manchester Free Trade Hall, opened nine years later, was exclusively designed for musical activity, both buildings have provided a firm foundation for the musical life of the two cities.

At first the Birmingham Town Hall, with a capacity of 2,000, was chiefly used for the Triennial Musical Festival. The impressive organ, built by William Hill, was inaugurated in 1846 at the first performance of the *Elijah* by Felix Mendelssohn (1809–1847). The City Orchestra, now the City of Birmingham Symphony Orchestra, has been based in the Town Hall since its foundation in 1920.

In the same way, the Manchester Free Trade Hall became the home of the Hallé Orchestra which grew out of the old Gentlemen's Concerts' Society, originally founded

in 1770. The first public concert of Charles Hallé with the newly reconstituted orchestra took place in the Free Trade Hall on January 30, 1858. The hall was destroyed in the Second World War but reopened again in 1951.

The Liverpool Philharmonic Society, founded in 1840, which at first used the Lascelles Rooms for its concerts, had expanded sufficiently by 1849 to build its own hall. This auditorium, renowned for its particularly fine acoustics, burnt down in 1933, and the present Philharmonic Hall, which seats 1,771, was opened six years later. It too, has excellent acoustics.

The trend towards ever larger halls continued. St James's Hall, between Piccadilly and Regent Street, could hold 2,127 in its rectangular, balconied auditorium.

Left This eighteenth century picture shows a concert at the rooms of the Venice Philharmonic Society. It is interesting to note the resemblance between the concert room and domestic architecture; and the height above the audience at which the choir and orchestra sit. The performance is of a cantata, a form of music popular in cultured Italian society of the eighteenth century, which was made up of extended vocal solos with some instrumental accompaniment. Here the orchestra apparently consists exclusively of violins.

Above The Hanover Square Rooms in London were opened in 1775 and were a major concert venue until they closed in 1874. One of the most famous of British concert masters, J.P. Salomon **(right)** inaugurated a series of subscription concerts there at which Haydn appeared in 1791 and 1794, and for which he wrote his Salomon or London Symphonies.

Right St James's Hall was London's leading concert hall during the second half of the nineteenth century. It staged very popular chamber concerts called the 'Monday Pops' between 1859 and 1898 and also the 'Saturday Pops' between 1865 and 1898. The auditorium, which could hold an audience of 2,127, was balconied and rectangular in form.

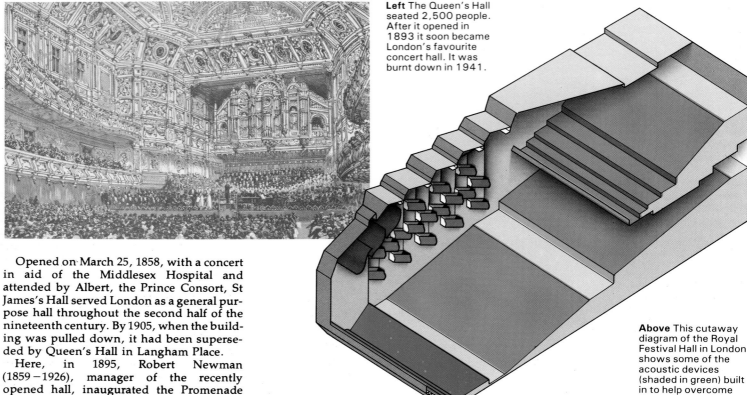

Opened on March 25, 1858, with a concert in aid of the Middlesex Hospital and attended by Albert, the Prince Consort, St James's Hall served London as a general purpose hall throughout the second half of the nineteenth century. By 1905, when the building was pulled down, it had been superseded by Queen's Hall in Langham Place.

Here, in 1895, Robert Newman (1859–1926), manager of the recently opened hall, inaugurated the Promenade Concerts which still flourish. Promenade concerts were not new to London, and the success of the Queen's Hall Proms, while chiefly due to the efforts of Sir Henry Wood (1869–1944), their conductor from their inception until his death, can also be attributed, in part, to the ambience of the hall.

With a seating capacity of 2,500, the Queen's Hall yet retained an intimacy of atmosphere lacking in smaller halls, and its destruction by fire in an air raid in May 1941, left London without a suitable all-purpose concert hall for almost a decade, until the construction of the Royal Festival Hall.

The Festival Hall was designed as part of the Festival of Britain exhibition on the South Bank of the Thames. Exactly 100 years previously, the Great Exhibition of 1851 was responsible for two of the most famous buildings used as London concert halls. The Crystal Palace, designed by Sir Joseph Paxton, originally covered a 20 acre site in Hyde Park. After the closure of the exhibition, Paxton's huge glass and iron structure was taken down and re-erected at Sydenham in southeast London. Regular musical events became a feature there in 1855 when the British musician of German origin Augustus Manns (1825–1907) introduced the Saturday afternoon concerts which continued annually, from the beginning of October to the end of April, until 1901.

The concert room was situated in the north-east corner of the central transept which itself was used for mammoth-scale performances such as the triennial Handel Festival. After a trial run in 1857, the centen-

Above This cutaway diagram of the Royal Festival Hall in London shows some of the acoustic devices (shaded in green) built in to help overcome the problems of the acoustics which are still considered very dry. The hall is good for much eighteenth century and modern music which demands a clear tonal quality. However, the Festival Hall is less suitable, for example, for symphonic music which, to some extent, depends for its effect on a long reverberation time.

Left The Queen Elizabeth Hall has more resonant acoustics than the Festival Hall and seats 1,100.

Right London's South Bank arts complex seen here as an architect's model houses the Queen Elizabeth Hall, the smaller auditorium called the Purcell Room, and the larger Festival Hall. Nearby are the National Theatre, with its three auditoriums, the National Film Theatre and the Hayward Art Gallery.

Above, right The Royal Albert Hall was opened in 1871 as an auditorium for many different types of event. It has a circular auditorium which is well suited to orchestral and choral concerts. It is London's largest hall and can accommodate over 7,000 people both sitting and promenading.

Left Snape Maltings in Suffolk, England, is perhaps one of the most unusual concert halls in the world. The original building was a malt house. The reconstruction involved remodelling the interior entirely **(above)**. The hall immediately became popular with players and audience alike because of its excellent acoustics. However, the original building was gutted by fire in 1969. It was rebuilt, reopened the following year, and the acoustics, amazingly, remained as good as ever.

ary of Handel's death was commemorated in 1859 with a festival involving nearly 3,000 performers. By 1926, the year of the final festival, the number had grown to more than 4,000 participants, while Handel's scoring was augmented by Sir Henry Wood to support the weight of the huge choral forces. Ten years later, on the night of November 30, 1936, the Crystal Palace was destroyed by a fire.

The Royal Albert Hall, built on land bought with the proceeds of the Great Exhibition, served as a memorial to the Prince Consort who had died a decade before the formal opening of the hall on March 29, 1871.

The circular auditorium, 264ft long and 231ft wide, has been used for many activities other than music since it was built. The Albert Hall, most suitable for choral and orchestral concerts involving a large number of performers, became a general concert venue after the destruction of Queen's Hall in 1941.

With the opening of the Festival Hall in 1951, the Albert Hall reverted to its role of a multi-purpose auditorium, though the Promenade concerts, inherited from Queen's Hall, were retained and have grown in scope and popularity ever since. Seating 5,604 in the stalls, the orchestra, two tiers of boxes and the balcony, the Albert Hall can also accommodate 1,500 promenaders.

The notorious echo, which for many years marred the performance of music in the hall, has been significantly reduced by sound-baffles suspended from the huge dome but the tone-quality remains extremely resonant. The Festival Hall, on the other hand, has exceptionally clear, dry acoustics which though suitable for much eighteenth or twentieth century music, are far from ideal for the romantic, nineteenth century symphonic repertory.

The Festival Hall is the prototype of many general purpose halls that have been built since. With its sharply raked stalls, grand tier and side boxes staggered like the open drawers of a display cabinet, it holds nearly 3,500 people. The adjacent Queen Elizabeth Hall with its capacity of 1,100 and the Purcell Room, which seats 370, are both much more resonant than the Festival Hall.

Perhaps the most striking concert hall to be built in Britain since the Second World War is Snape Maltings, near Aldeburgh, in which the shell of an old malt house has been adapted to its new purpose with complete success.

First opened in 1967, the Maltings can seat 820 people. The plain brick walls of the rectangular auditorium, with its handsome, raftered roof, provide acoustics perfect for orchestral music of all kinds. When the Maltings burned down in 1969 and had to be rebuilt, this acoustical miracle survived when it was opened in the following year.

In Germany and Austria many of the orchestral societies are of great venerability.

The *Dresdener Staatskapelle*, for instance, was founded in 1548. At that time musicians were usually in the pay of the local princely ruler or nobleman and concerts took place mainly in court theatres until the nineteenth century.

Some orchestras acquired both independence and a concert hall of their own earlier than that. The most famous example is the Leipzig Gewandhaus orchestra which evolved out of a society called *Das Grosse Konzert* which in 1781 started to give its concerts in the Gewandhaus, or ancient market hall of the Saxon linen merchants. Here Mendelssohn directed the orchestra from 1835 to 1843.

In Cologne, the ancient Gürzenich building, a fifteenth century banqueting hall, was first used as a concert hall in 1857. Destroyed in the Second World War, the Gürzenich was re-opened in 1955 as a modern concert hall inside a carefully restored Gothic exterior.

In Vienna the Musikverein, a neo-Renaissance building designed by Theophil Hansen, was built in 1870, since when it has been the home of the Vienna Philharmonic Orchestra. The smaller Brahms Hall is in gold and white. The hall has a reverberation time of just over two seconds giving a rich sound, appropriate to nineteenth century symphonic music.

In Holland, the Concertgebouw (literally, concert-building) Society of Amsterdam was founded in 1883, though its hall, with an imposing neo-classical facade, was not opened until five years later. Seating 2,219, the rectangular auditorium is unusually wide (30 metres) for its length. Staircases ascend from the platform to the balcony which runs around approximately two-thirds of the hall. The acoustics, with a reverberation time of two seconds, are particularly good for the music of Mahler and other late Romantic composers favoured by the Dutch conductor Willem Mengelberg (1871–1951), conductor of the Concertgebouw Orchestra from 1895 to 1941.

European concert halls dating from the inter-war years include the Stockholm Konserthuset, completed in 1926. Designed by Ivar Tengbom in the style of a Greek temple and situated in Hötorget, a square that serves the Swedish capital as a flower, fruit and vegetable market, the Konserthuset has two auditoria. The interior of the larger hall, which seats 1,500, maintains the classical effect with Greek columns.

In Moscow, the Tchaikovsky Hall, built between 1938 and 1940 has a massive front portico facing on to Gorky Street. The auditorium is in the form of an amphitheatre, with honeycombed ceiling and staircases and corridors of white marble.

Another Moscow hall used for concert purposes is the Hall of Columns in Trade Union House, an eighteenth century palace on Pushkin Street. A pillared gallery runs around the entire auditorium with enormous chandeliers hanging between each pair of white marble columns.

There is also the Great Hall of Moscow Conservatory, opened in 1866 and renamed the Tchaikovsky Conservatory in 1940. It seats more than 2,000 and every Russian musician of note over the last 100 years, including Tchaikovsky; has appeared here.

The post-war tendency has been to build all-purpose halls that can be used as conference centres or exhibition areas as well as for musical performances. The Beethoven-Halle in Bonn, perched on a splendid site overlooking the Rhine, is an example of this type. It seats 1,000 and every two years plays host to the Beethoven Festival.

Another multi-purpose building, the Finlandia Hall in Helsinki, was designed by the famous Finnish architect Alvar Aalto to attract a wide cross-section of the city's population. It was opened in 1972 and has two auditoria. The large one seats 1,750 and the smaller, 350. There is also a cinema, exhibition galleries, restaurants and conference rooms.

In Paris the huge Palais des Congrès has a seating capacity of 3,700, but although the acoustics are adequate for music, the atmosphere is bleak and cold. On a totally different scale, the new Pompidou Arts Centre includes an acoustic-research concert hall with movable walls, floor and ceiling as well as changeable surfaces, that can seat 400 people. The building also houses the laboratories and computer rooms of the Institute for Research and Co-ordination into Acoustics and Music.

In the Music Centre at Utrecht, the concert hall forms the hub of a vast complex of buildings including shops and offices as well as restaurants and galleries. The auditorium is broken up into many different-sized seating areas, on varying levels, rather in the manner of the new Berlin Philharmonic.

Above The Finlandia Hall in Helsinki has two rooms that are used for concerts. Between them these can hold an audience of 2,100. In addition to these concert rooms, the Finlandia Hall houses a cinema and several galleries

Left In 1941 the Moscow Conservatory was renamed after one of Russia's best-known composers, Tchaikovsky. In recognition of his brilliance and the appearances he made here, his portrait now hangs on a wall behind the orchestra. The large concert hall, built in 1866, seats over 2,000 people.

Below This exceptional concert hall is the result of modern technology and electronics. It was designed for the Institute for Research and Co-ordination into Acoustics and Music in the Georges Pompidou Arts Centre in Paris. The room has only enough seats for 400 people but its main features are a ceiling and walls that can be moved around during research. The flexibility of this room means that the quality of the sound and the acoustics are almost perfect.

Right The Musikverein, built in Vienna in 1870, has most impressive architecture and an ornate interior. There are over 40 high arched windows and 20 doors above the balcony around the side walls. The room is lit by 10 enormous crystal chandeliers which hang from the richly decorated ceiling. This relatively small concert hall has 1,680 seats.

But the Berlin Philharmonic Hall, unlike so many other post-war buildings of a similar nature, is intended solely for music. Designed by Hans Scharoun and completed in 1963, the asymetrical structure replaces the Berlin Philharmonic Orchestra's old home, destroyed by bombing. The octagonal auditorium is arranged in terraces that surround the orchestral platform almost completely. The triple curve of the ceiling, 70 feet above the platform, corresponds with the tent-like roof that gives the exterior of the building much of its character. Sound, rising from the centre of the hall, is dispersed by the ceiling and descends on the listener from above. Acoustics are clear and immediate.

In the United States, as in Europe, concerts were first given in opera houses or musical academies. As the individual orchestras came into existence they built permanent halls.

In New York, where the Philharmonic Society had been founded as early as 1842, Carnegie Hall was constructed with money supplied by the Scottish-born millionaire, Andrew Carnegie. The Hall was, at first, simply known as the Music Hall but was renamed in 1891. The building was inaugurated in May 1891 with a five-day music festival at which Tchaikovsky was the guest conductor. The spacious auditorium, with two tiers of boxes and two balconies, can seat 3,000 people. There is also a small chamber music hall holding 300.

The very fine acoustics, bright but sufficiently resonant, together with the comfortable, old fashioned interior have endeared Carnegie Hall to thousands of New York music lovers. When, after construction of the Lincoln Center for the Performing Arts, it was proposed to demolish the Carnegie Hall, the public outcry was loud enough to ensure a reprieve for the building.

Meanwhile, Philharmonic Hall, the first of the Lincoln Center auditoria to be completed, was opened on September 23, 1962. Designed by Max Abramovitz in the style of a Greek temple, with a peristyle of 44 columns on the north side of the plaza, the hall seats 2,836 people in three tiers.

Although special care had been taken over the acoustical properties, these proved to be unsatisfactory from the start, and the interior of the auditorium, now renamed Avery Fisher Hall, was later completely redesigned and rebuilt. The resulting quality of sound, although undoubtedly improved, is still not nearly as good as the fine natural acoustics of Carnegie Hall.

American orchestras are apt to have a more muscular tone than central European ones, and generally their concert halls reflect this tendency. Symphony Hall in Boston, which was opened on September 15, 1900, proved an ideal setting to show off the brilliance of the Boston Symphony Orchestra during the years 1924 to 1949 when Koussevitsky (1876–1951) was its musical director.

In Chicago, Orchestra Hall, dating from 1904, was funded by popular subscription. Facing Lake Michigan, the hall seats 2,500 and has housed the Chicago Symphony Orchestra, with its particularly brilliant timbre, for some 75 years.

In Cleveland, the Symphony Orchestra, founded in 1919, originally played in the Masonic Hall. But in 1931 a fine new auditorium, the Severance Hall, was donated by John L. Severance in memory of his wife.

Finally, a controversial building, used at least partly for concert-giving, should be mentioned: the Sydney Opera House. Conceived by the Danish architect Joern Utzon, who won the competition for its design in 1956, the complex was not ready for another 17 years, opening in October, 1973.

The largest of the five auditoria, with a capacity of 2,800, had originally been planned as the opera house, with stage machinery in the interlocking shells that reflect the sails in the harbour so faithfully. But for various technical reasons it proved necessary to use this auditorium as the concert hall. Acoustics are forward and bright, with a reverberation period suitable to most forms of orchestral music.

Concert halls have developed out of all recognition since the period, three centuries ago, when John Banister and Thomas Britton promoted their modest series of concerts. The size of the orchestra has increased four- or five-fold; the price of a subscription, and of a cup of coffee, has escalated enormously. What was once the part-time occupation of one man, has become a business employing hundreds of people over and above the musicians themselves.

Audiences may have grown hugely in numbers but have not changed totally in character. The young people who pack the Albert Hall arena during the Proms are not so very different from the crowds who thronged the Crystal Palace on Saturday afternoons, or from that audience at the Hanover Square Rooms which, according to Dr Burney, greeted Haydn with 'such a degree of enthusiasm as almost amounts to frenzy'.

Far left The Orchestra Hall in Chicago was designed by Daniel Burnham under the supervision of Theodore Thomas, the conductor of the Chicago Symphony Orchestra. The Hall was built in 1904 because the previous home of the CSO had very inferior acoustics. However, the unusual shape of the Orchestra Hall, with its curved stage ceiling and nearly circular rear stage wall, still causes an imbalance of sound.
Top left and **centre left** The Berlin Philharmonic Hall was designed specifically for concerts. The auditorium is arranged in tiers so that it can seat over 2,000 people. It is the largest concert hall in Berlin.
Bottom left The Carnegie Hall in New York is named after its sponsor Andrew Carnegie, the Scottish-born industrialist millionaire. The hall has very fine acoustics.
Bottom right The Avery Fisher Hall at the Lincoln Center, New York was formerly the Philharmonic Hall. Nearly 3,000 people can be seated in the body of the hall and in the three tiers constructed around the walls.

JAZZ CLUBS

Never afraid of appearing nostalgic, jazz musicians have seldom hesitated to celebrate − in the titles of blues or other compositions − those places where joys or miseries have seemed exceptionally great. Plenty of thoroughfares have been honoured in this way − Chicago's State Street, Basin Street in New Orleans, Beale Street in Memphis, Chestnut Street in Los Angeles, even, thanks to Fats Waller, London's Bond Street. It is odd, however, that no lyric extols the virtues of New York's 52nd Street.

Known in its heyday − the 1930s and 1940s − as 'Swing Street', or simply 'The Street', it was lined with clubs which between them presented an extraordinary range of jazz performers. Joe Marsala's Chicagoans, for example, with the teenaged Buddy Rich at the drums and Marsala's wife, Adèle Girard, plucing a harp, held forth at the Hickory House, a second-hand car salesroom before it was equipped with a forty-foot-long oval bar. But that was in the block between Seventh and Sixth Avenues. Most of the action took place further on, between Sixth and Fifth.

During Prohibition the Onyx Club had been a speak-easy. After the visitor had climbed to the second floor and tapped on a mottled silver door, an eye peering through a Judas hole decided whether he could be admitted. Having money mattered less than being on nodding terms with Benny Goodman, a busy studio man in those days, or Joe Sullivan or Benny Carter. For this was a musicians' hang-out, a place for leaving instruments, for chatting, drinking − and playing. For a while the resident pianist was Art Tatum.

Further along 52nd Street was The Famous Door, insufferably hot, a kind of glorified cubbyhole with musicians. Elsewhere were the two Café Society clubs, one uptown, the other downtown, run by Barney Josephson and deliberately setting out to encourage a mixed clientele of black and white. It was at the Downtown Café that Billie Holiday created something of a sensation with her anti-lynching song, 'Strange Fruit'. Over in Greenwich Village was Nick's, full of stuffed birds in glass cases, with moth-eaten moose-heads on the walls. It was very much the headquarters of those musicians − mostly from Chicago − who revolved around the wise-cracking, often inebriated guitarist, Eddie Condon.

These were all establishments where music generally came first. It had been different earlier. The Cotton Club and Connie's Inn, for example, were both located in Harlem, yet catered exclusively for whites, although all the performers happened to be black. But jazz was considered to be part of the exotica, something that added atmosphere. Nevertheless, Duke Ellington made

his name at the Cotton Club while Louis Armstrong sang 'Ain't Misbehavin' at Connie's Inn in 1929, as part of the all-black revue, *Hot Chocolates*.

Sleaziness was commonplace as well. The red-light district of New Orleans, which was closed down by the U.S. Navy in 1917, had jazz musicians working in cabarets, such as Billie Phillips' or Gyp the Blood's, where the girls would be paid 25 cents for a dance. Only the pianists − Jelly Roll Morton and Tony Jackson were two of them − played in brothels like Lulu White's baroque Mahogany Hall. Some patrons even hired a

pianist to provide appropriate music while they took their pleasure.

In Chicago, not surprisingly, many clubs were run by the mob. However, the mob were never a menace to individual musicians − 'Look kid', a club-owner reassured the 18-year-old Bud Freeman, 'None of these guys would hurt you unless they got paid for it!' According to popular anecdotes, the band would continue playing while bullets whirred between the tables. But corrupt civic authorities also meant that clubs stayed open around the clock. Musicians never earned much money in Kansas City, but at least they

Above The Cotton Club was one of the most famous of New York's jazz clubs particularly in the 1920s and 1930s. This show features Ethel Waters and Duke Ellington's orchestra around 1933.
Left The Mahogany Hall in New Orleans was a brothel at which several major jazz musicians played,

including Jelly Roll Morton and Tony Jackson.

Below Jazz also made an impact in Britain. 'Bottle clubs', clubs which managed to circumvent the licensing regulations, flourished during the 1950s. Here George Chisholm and his band are playing at The Nest in London.

Left Jazz was not just for listening to, it was also for dancing. These dancers were jitterbugging at the Savoy Ballroom in Harlem.
Below right The 'jazz loft' idea was started by Ornette Coleman in the 1960s and became very popular in the USA. At this loft session in New York in 1971 Arthur Doyle played tenor sax and Milford Graves drums.
Below left Eddie 'Cleanhead' Vinson is playing at the Berlin Jazz Club.
Bottom Ronnie Scott's is one of London's foremost jazz clubs.

could play as much as they wanted to. A sideman in Count Basie's band at the Reno Club was paid 18 dollars a week for working seven nights from 9 pm to 5 am, except Sundays, when the Breakfast Dance stretched things out until 10 am or noon.

Prohibition was responsible for the underworld becoming involved in running clubs. Bootleggers did not give up these particular interests once the law was repealed in 1933, nor did the drinking stop. 'That damn cash register ringing', moaned Charles Mingus, complaining indignantly about the working conditions in clubs of a later era, the 1950s and 1960s, places such as the Five Spot, Village Vanguard and Birdland. The last was named in honour of Charlie 'Bird' Parker, although he was eventually barred from going there.

In London during the 1930s the licensing laws were evaded by patrons bringing their own bottles. 'Bottle parties', as they were called, took place six nights a week at Soho clubs such as the Nest and the Nuthouse, where dance band musicians who liked to play jazz would drop in to jam after finishing work at their hotel or restaurant. Visiting Americans such as Coleman Hawkins, Benny Carter or Fats Waller would turn up too, playing alongside overwhelmed locals, like the trombonist George Chisholm.

The popular British image of a jazz club, however, was a product of the post-war New Orleans or 'trad' jazz revival. At first the approach was over-reverent, a matter of listening devotedly. Those purists received a rude awakening in 1948 with the arrival from Australia of Graham Bell's Dixielanders, who actually encouraged people to dance to their music. Something of that sort still goes on in rooms over or attached to many English pubs. Things are very different at Ronnie Scott's Club, designed as a place in which to hear jazz — mostly modern — and with a proprietor capable of holding his own on tenor saxophone with the best of his highly talented performers.

Jazz is played in clubs all over Europe — even behind the Iron Curtain — as well as in Tokyo and the Antipodes. Indeed, jazz is played all over the world. So far, however, the jazz loft, started by Ornette Coleman in the 1960s but taken up wholeheartedly by young black musicians in New York during the following decade, has not spread outside America. In many ways it represents a return to basics. The names given to the lofts are sometimes picturesque, such as The Ladies' Fort, sometimes functional, for example The Kitchen. Audiences tend to be small, comprising friends and initiates. Very often performers such as the tenor saxophonist David Murray or the baritone saxophonist Hamiet Blueitt will play entirely alone, without even bass and drums. This is not what they were used to on 'The Street' a third of a century ago, but at least jazz — and the jazz performer — is very much alive and kicking.

PLAYS

Play-acting began about 2,500 years ago in open-air theatres carved from the hillsides in Greece. The acoustics were good in these horse-shoe shaped excavations which were often arranged so that the afternoon sun came from behind the audience and flooded the performing area with light. There may be earlier roots, of course, but the generally agreed starting point for world drama lies in the large-scale public festivals of Dionysus, a nature-god associated with wine. Choirs would chant legends in the god's honour. Out of this grew Greek tragedy, the traditional father of which is said to be Thespis who added a prologue and a set speech spoken by a costumed actor. Thespis apparently presented his plays first at country festivals but in 535 BC he gave a performance at the Great Dionysus in Athens — first recorded evidence of a successful show brought 'into town'.

Contests were often staged in which dramatists produced four plays, the first three tragedies and the fourth a satyric drama — a less serious piece in which the chorus was played by Satyrs, the traditional companions of Dionysus. Prizes were awarded. In the plays, all the parts were taken by men or boys and a single actor often took several different parts in the same play.

Aeschylus (525 – 456 BC), Sophocles (495 – 406 BC) and Euripides (480 – 407 BC) became masters of the Greek tragic form. These writers fashioned their plays out of popular myth. Drama, in other words, began as a re-enactment of something the audience already knew. Because of this association with ancient myths, the audience knew the plot as soon as the play began. Most Greek tragedies were about events purported to have happened long before, but there is one exception, Aeschylus's *The Persians*, produced in 472 BC, only eight years after the Athenians had shattered the Persian fleet in the Battle of Salamis.

For the Greeks, drama was a form of ritual. It was also an outdoor affair, seen against the background of sea and mountainous landscape. Drama went indoors with the Romans. They staged plays both in simple wooden structures and in quite elaborate buildings. They introduced the idea of scenic display and of the front curtain.

Enduring comic characters

In Roman comedy and farce which is rather neglected today one finds the origins of much Western drama. Plautus (254 – 184 BC) wrote the *Menaechmi*, about the complications caused by the presence in the same city of long-separated twins. Out of this, Shakespeare spun *The Comedy of Errors*. In other plays, Plautus created a foolish braggart, Pyrgopolinices, who has the characteristics of an early Falstaff, and an aged miser, Euclio, who is Molière's Harpagon in embryo. Although they may not have realized it, Broadway and London audiences who revelled in the Stephen Sondheim musical *A Funny Thing Happened on the Way to the Forum* were enjoying Roman farce at second hand. In fact, the authors of the book, Burt Shevelove and Larry Gelbart, researched all 21 surviving comedies by Plautus and used all the standard Plautine characters: the conniving servants, the lascivious master, the domineering mistress, the self-centred warrior. The Romans gave the modern world not only scenic theatre and standard comic characters but also a dramatic structure which endured until the end of the nineteenth century. The Roman comic writer Terence (195 – 159 BC) and the tragedian Seneca (4 BC – AD 65) introduced the idea of the five-act drama which was to have an enormous influence on Western drama. Roman theatre even pioneered the concept of the star actor. One of them, Roscius (c.126 BC – 62 BC), had his name handed down to future generations.

Right This drawing of the stage for a mystery play at Valenciennes in 1547 shows an elaborate version of the medieval practice of designating areas of the stage to different locations. Heaven is on the left, and Hell on the right.
Left This nineteenth century painting shows that century's view of Roman comedy. The grotesque expression, stylized gesture and ornate wig of the figure on the left are particularly noteworthy.
Below Even the Romans had theatre tickets. These tokens in the shapes of animals and objects were found at Pompei.

World drama, however, did not evolve logically and coherently. What happened in Europe, at least, was that it got off to a flying start with the Greeks and the Romans and then virtually came to an end with the fall of the Roman Empire. It began to grow again from the beginning of the tenth century and, though the classics were not entirely forgotten, it was not until the Renaissance that dramatists turned to them again as a model.

Medieval drama had didactic elements. Out of its strict form came the mystery plays which demonstrated the basis of Christian faith, and miracle plays mainly derived from the lives of the saints. In the fourteenth and fifteenth centuries came the morality plays which showed how Christians should act to obtain salvation.

Yet, despite the sermonizing nature of medieval drama, comedy and tragedy could be mixed up together in a way the classical theorists would never have approved. An example comes in one play from the Wakefield Mystery Cycle. The sacred theme of Christ's birth is echoed in the story of Mak the sheep-stealer and his wife, Gill, who make off with a sheep, wrap it in swaddling clothes and hide it in Gill's cradle. It is a very funny bit of farce which also paves the way for the central scene in Bethlehem. This peculiarity anticipates the rich impurity of Shakespeare who at the high point of *Macbeth* would bring on a drunken porter or who just before Cleopatra's death would dare to bring on the resident funny-man clutching a box of asps.

Drama in the Renaissance

With the Renaissance came a break with explicitly religious subject matter. The best of Renaissance drama combined a core of medieval thought with a search for fresh means of expression. Shakespeare is the supreme example of this in the way he combines in one person three diverse forces. The classical influence contributes to his sense of form. The spirit of his own Elizabethan and Jacobean age is reflected strongly in his work. Beyond these there is the powerful tradition of the medieval theatre. The result is something wonderful and new in the history of drama.

This did not happen everywhere. In Italy, for instance, the stage was split between literary and popular theatre. Court productions obeyed the classical unities and, on the other hand, there was the *commedia dell'arte* (literally: 'the play of *the* profession') which was an improvisation around a given scenario using stock characters like Pantalone, the Venetian merchant, and Capitano, the boasting soldier. This was a kind of theatre played in squares and market places on hastily built platforms before large crowds. Obviously it was fun. But the divorce between Court theatre and popular theatre had a divisive effect on Italian drama.

Much the same thing happened in France in the sixteenth century. But in Spain the emergence of one great genius, Lope de Vega (1562–1635), helped to bring together classic and popular styles. When he died aged 73 Lope left behind him a host of plays: 470 are still extant; many more have perished. The greatest of them, such as *Fuente Ovejuna* (*The Sheep Well*), anticipate later developments in drama. The hero of this play is not one person but a crowd of village peasants enraged by the rapacity and high-handedness of a libertine Commander. 'And if life be honour, how shall we fare,' someone asks at a village council, 'since there breathes not one among us whom this savage has not offended?' The crowd storms the palace, the Commander is slain, and when the officers of justice arrive the entire population of the village decides to declare its collective responsibility.

Lope's successor, Pedro Calderon de la

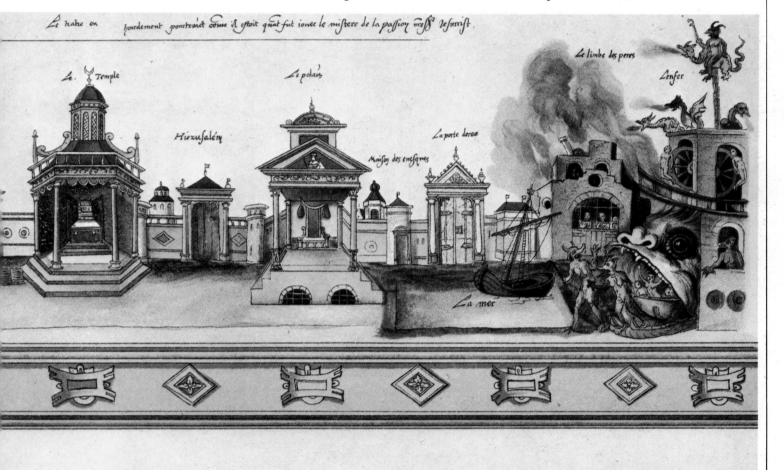

Barca (1600–1681), also wrote some 200 full-length plays of which half are still extant. They, too, cover an astonishing range – family plays, chronicles, plays on legendary and folklore subjects, on the Moorish wars, Old Testament stories as well as comedies of intrigue and honour plays which deal with the virtues of free conscience and personal sacrifice as against the cruel fixation of preserving one's reputation.

In England the Renaissance also led to a great explosion of energy in the theatre. In France and Italy, writers paid homage to classical civilization and often wrote drama according to the rule book. In England there was a spirit of scepticism which led to the classic rules being bent in accordance with the national temper. William Shakespeare (1564–1616) is the dominant example, although English drama was already flourishing when he came on to the London scene. *The Spanish Tragedy*, by Thomas Kyd

1△

4△

Right These productions of Shakespeare's *A Midsummer Night's Dream* show the wide variety of possible interpretations. Samuel Phelps played Bottom in his own 1875 production *(1)*; while Madame Vestris played Oberon in her 1840 production *(10)*. Harley Granville Barker's controversial and innovatory production at the Savoy *(2)* opened in 1914. Peter Brook's 1970 Stratford production, one of the most startling recent productions, met with almost universal critical acclaim *(8)*. The other productions took place in 1905, directed by Oscar Asche *(3)*; in 1906, directed by Frank Benson *(6)*; in 1937 at the Old Vic with Vivien Leigh as Titania *(9)*; at Stratford in 1954 *(7)*; At Stratford also in 1962 directed by Peter Hall *(5)*, and in 1977, directed by John Barton *(4)*.
Left This 1499 woodcut shows a view of a classical theatre.
Left below This is a contemporary illustration of Shakespeare's *Titus Andronicus*.

2△

3△

8▽   6△

9▽

10▽

(c.1557 – c.1595), a bloodthirsty revenge drama, was London's first great commercial hit in the late 1580s. Christopher Marlowe (1564 – 1593) had written such works as *Tamburlaine the Great*. Robert Greene (1560 – 1592) in works like *Friar Bacon and Friar Bungay* had shown that one play could bring together clownery and romantic seriousness.

Shakespeare remains the towering figure of English drama. It has become evident, though, in recent years that the plays once accepted as his masterpieces (*Hamlet, King Lear, Othello* and *Macbeth*) no longer seem the dramatic Everests they once did. In fact, both Shakespeare's early and late plays have come in for a good deal of re-assessment. For example, *Love's Labours Lost*, conventionally regarded as a flawed piece of prentice work, today seems like a masterly blend of verbal satire and true feeling. Likewise, when the three *Henry VI* plays were revived in their entirety by Terry Hands for the Royal Shakespeare Company in 1977 people were struck by their comprehensive portrait of English society and by the pathos of the image of the solitary king. Much the same is true of the late romances. Ben Jonson thought *Pericles* a 'mouldy tale'. Bernard Shaw described *Cymbeline* as 'for the most part stagey trash of the lowest melodramatic order' while Dr Johnson talked of its descent into 'unresisting imbecility'. *The Winter's Tale* has often been regarded as a study in sexual jealousy much inferior to *Othello*. Today, however, it is easier to appreciate the plays at their true worth. Parallels have been drawn between Shakespeare's romances and Beethoven's late quartets and the last poems of Yeats. There is in them a hunger for reconciliation between the generations and belief in the regenerative power of love that suggest Shakespeare was consciously moving towards such ideas at the end of his creative life.

The more one studies Shakespeare, the more one becomes aware that he drew heavily on his predecessors and contemporaries while managing to create something which was uniquely and individually his own. One also becomes aware of the way he bent rules of drama so that comedy intruded upon tragedy (as with the gravedigger in *Hamlet*), tragedy upon comedy (witness the fearsome final exits of Malvolio in *Twelfth Night* and Shylock in *The Merchant of Venice*). The grandiose and the commonplace existed side by side. If the history of drama is one of collapsing and blurring categories, then Shakespeare is instrumental in that process.

Alongside and shortly after Shakespeare there are many other dramatists of prodigious talent. One can mention Ben Jonson (1577 – 1637), Thomas Middleton (1580 – 1627), John Webster (c.1580 – 1625) and John Ford (1586 – 1639).

This vigorous movement gradually declined into spectacle and sensationalism, but from the 1580s to the 1630s English drama produced a body of work still without parallel, work which gives a total picture of a society, which rejoices in the poetic use of language and which is filled with flamboyant character and incident.

Giants of France

England and Spain dominated drama during the Renaissance. In the latter half of the seventeenth century the focus moves to France, which produced two dominant figures of genius, Jean Racine (1639–1699) and Molière, which was the pen-name of Jean Baptiste Poquelin (1622–1673). The French revival was helped by several things. One was a desire for classical precision and control after the heady excitement of the Renaissance. Another factor was an awareness of the poverty of French theatre in the sixteenth century, and conscious desire to create a national literature centred on Paris. Racine wrote a number of very different plays on a single theme — the destructiveness of passion. He also created a sense of fatality through language — every speech in a Racine play is an act that wounds or moves others or that involves the character more deeply in his fate.

Molière, though he was a provoker of laughter, has a certain similarity to Racine. His characters, pursued by inner demons, have an obsessive quality that marks them out as blood brothers and sisters to the great tragedian's creations. Like all great comic writers, Molière also touches on the darker side of life. *Le Misanthrope*, his greatest play and one in which many of the finest modern actors from Jean-Louis Barrault (born 1910) to Alec McCowan (born 1929) have made a great impression, deals with a profound and universal human dilemma — whether or not to accept the standards of the society into which one is born. The hero is enthralled by the frivolously delicious Celimène but is appalled by the prattling, gossipy world in which she moves. Out of this tension comes superb drama. Though technically a comedy, *Tartuffe* has tragedy lurking within it. Orgon, a Parisian bourgeois, is ready to sacrifice his family for a religious ideal embodied by Tartuffe, a sensual parasite. Hypocrisy and sincere piety are thus mocked with equal force and effect.

At this time, England was busy with Restoration Comedy, a classic example of elitist drama. Records indicate that the courtiers regarded the playhouses as their own domain. The theatres became like clubs attached to Whitehall in which assignations were made and quarrels sparked off. Out of this atmosphere came a surprisingly durable comedy of manners — *The Country Wife* by William Wycherley (1640–1716), *The Way of the World* by William Congreve (1670–1729), and *She Would if She Could* by Sir George Etherege (1635–1691) with its young gallants in quest of amorous adventure. This

Right, below French theatre in the seventeenth century was dominated by three figures — the comic dramatist Molière and the tragedians Racine and Corneille. The portrait of French and Italian actors and comedians **(right)** shows Molière as well as some of the traditional *commedia dell' arte* characters such as Harlequin in the centre foreground. Molière's plays ridicule social pretentiousness, contemporary weaknesses and general failings such as avarice, and favour reason and moderation. The tragedies of Racine, on the other hand, show characters as the victims of destructive passions and in the grip of an external fate. The plots of Racine's plays focus almost exclusively on the hero or heroine. The richness of the language and imagery is conveyed in alexandrines, the twelve-stress iambic line in which all French classical tragedies were written. Racine looked mainly to classical Greece and Rome for his plots, for example, *Andromaque* (1667), *Phèdre* (1677) and *Britannicus* (1669).

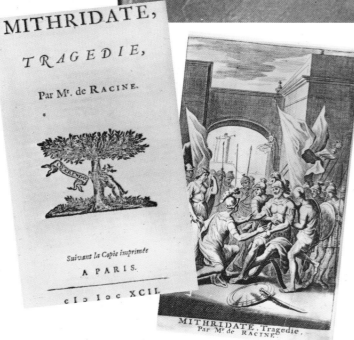

MITHRIDATE, TRAGEDIE, Par Mr. de RACINE.

Suivant la Copie imprimée A PARIS.

cIɔ Iɔc XCII.

MITHRIDATE, Tragedie, Par Mr de RACINE.

Right Sheridan's fine comedy of manners, *School for Scandal*, was first performed in 1777 and published in 1783 **(far right)**. Sheridan came from a theatrical family and became manager of Drury Lane Theatre in 1777, taking over from David Garrick. Sheridan's work ridicules sentimentality and deceit through wit and perceptive observation. His earlier comedy, *The Rivals* (1775), is also still produced. The great British actress, Edith Evans, played a memorable Mrs Malaprop **(right)**.

was aristocratic drama *par excellence*, yet because of its style, its wit and its satire it is still capable of revival.

The eighteenth century

The eighteenth century produced surprisingly little in the way of great drama. It was, in England an age of great actors and actresses such as David Garrick (1717–1779), Peg Woffington (c.1714–1760), Sarah Siddons (1755–1831) and her brother John Philip Kemble (1757–1823). On continental Europe it was an era for the establishment of great playhouses: the Burgtheater in Vienna, the New National Theatre in Stockholm, the Royal Theatre in Copenhagen and Berlin. Some important plays were written within the bourgeois comic tradition, especially in Italy where Carlo Goldoni (1707–1792) wrote spritely farces such as *Il Servatore di due Padroni* (*The Servant of Two Masters*) and *Trilogia della villeggiatura* (*Trilogy on Holidays in the Country*) which showed the newly-leisured class falling in and out of love in the course of a long summer. Social bitterness also surfaced in a revolutionary work like *The Marriage of Figaro* by the French dramatist Beaumarchais (1732–1799) in which the hero-servant seems a figure of honest virtue when set against the proud and worthless aristocrats. Despite these occasional heights, the eighteenth century saw the philosophic decline into the sentimental and the plays themselves were often less important than the playhouses and the players.

In Germany the work of several dramatists put that country on the dramatic map of Europe. Gotthold Ephraim Lessing (1729–1781) was one of the most important literary figures of the Enlightenment in Germany. His major plays included *Minna von Barnhelm*, first performed in 1767, and his bourgeois tragedy *Emilia Galotti* (1772). One of Lessing's early plays, *Miss Sara Sampson* (1755) was a version of the first ever English bourgeois tragedy *The London Merchant* (1731) by George Lillo (1693–1739). The literary giant, Johann Wolfgang von Goethe (1749–1832) was director of the court theatre at Weimar from 1791 to 1817, although many of his major plays such as *Götz von Berlichingen* (*Ironhand*) and *Egmont* were first performed much earlier. Goethe collaborated closely with Friedrich von Schiller (1759–1805) in devising a theory of drama. Schiller's first play *Die Räuber* (*The Robbers*), premiered when he was only 22, and the later tragic work *Don Carlos* are perhaps his best known works today.

It was in the following century that the theatre, after a period of romanticism, extravagance and fantasy, began to put down the realistic roots which are still familiar to audiences today.

Realism and Naturalism

In France, Emile Augier (1820–1889) in the middle of the century wrote works such as *Le*

Gendre de M. Poirier (*The Son-in-Law of M. Poirier*) which dealt faithfully with the conflict between a proud but magnanimous aristocrat and a hardworking yet vulgar bourgeois. In Germany, Friedrich Hebbel (1813–1863) wrote plays like *Judith* and *Agnes Bernauer* in which historical figures were given a modern motivation and tone of voice. By the mid nineteenth century the notion that a tragic hero had to be a noble character who falls from a great height had given way to the idea of bourgeois tragedy which had seen its beginnings in the previous century.

Realism and naturalism had many sources. One was the weakening of religious and moral concepts which led writers to the conviction that all they could do was observe life. Another was the growth of stage lighting (gas was first used around 1820, electric light later in the century) which made it possible to produce realistic effects. Yet another was the development of theatrical equipment. In 1881 Steele MacKaye displayed to wondering American audiences a double elevator stage by means of which entire sets, with their actors ready placed, could be raised or lowered into position.

The greatest exponent of the naturalistic theatre was the Norwegian Henrik Ibsen (1828–1906). Others, like André Antoine with the Théâtre Libre in Paris in 1887 and Otto Brahm with the Freie Bühne in Berlin in 1889, specialized in presenting naturalistic plays. But it was Ibsen's work which showed the power of naturalism – paradoxically partly because it was never purely and simply naturalistic. As the critic Eric Bentley once pointed out: 'Inside the skins of these prim-looking women and beefy-looking men lurk the trolls and devils of *Peer Gynt*, that is to say, the trolls and devils of Norse folk tale, the trolls and devils of Ibsen's inner consciousness.' His work can be divided

Right Chekhov is perhaps Russia's greatest and most influential dramatist. His plays portray complex relationships between varied groups of people. The creation of atmosphere is extremely important. The first production of *The Seagull* in 1896 was not a success, it was revived successfully by Stanislavsky at the Moscow Arts Theatre in 1898. The programme is shown **right**. Chekhov's plays have remained in the world repertory since then. For example Britain's National Theatre produced *The Cherry Orchard* in 1978 **(far right)**.

into the early poetic dramas (such as *Brand* and *Peer Gynt*), the middle period naturalistic plays (like *Pillars of Society, Ghosts* and *A Doll's House*) and the later more symbolic plays (beginning with *The Master Builder* and ending with *When We Dead Awaken*).

The great Russian dramatist, Anton Chekhov (1860–1904) also shows that naturalism and realism are not just so simple. From *The Seagull* onwards, his plays seem like a slice of life, but they are much more. As Bentley says: 'Cuts in Chekhov — as in Shakespeare — are like vandalism in an art gallery. It is as if you cut every tenth bar out of a Beethoven trio . . . Chekhov gives the illusion of a slice of life by being not less but more skilful in construction than the playwrights of the boulevards.' Chekhov's plays also burst with a sense of wasted potential. When the hero of *Uncle Vanya* says that he might have been a Dostoyevsky or a Schopenhauer, he may be talking nonsense,

but it is a heroic nonsense filled with a sense of the possibilities of life. That sense of the might-have-been gives his plays their richness — that, plus the combination of minute attention to realistic detail with a musical sense of form.

Since Ibsen and Chekhov the theatre has explored many different forms. In the early twentieth century Expressionism, especially in Germany, made a great impact on theatrical form and convention. In the mid twentieth century there was talk of a poetic revival — led by W. B. Yeats (1865–1939) in Ireland by T. S. Eliot (1888–1965) and Christopher Fry (born 1907) in Britain.

However, one characteristic of drama in the twentieth century seems to be the tenacity of realism and its variety. The writers whose works dominate the century are all, in different ways, apostles of realism rather than merchants of fantasy and shock.

The twentieth century

All such writers had their own particular ways of handling realism. George Bernard Shaw (1856–1950) would try on whatever cap suited him at the time, sometimes the jester's tricorne, sometimes the sober cap of argument. His initial influence, however, rested upon his ability to present social problems on the stage (professional prostitution in *Mrs Warren's Profession*, slum landlordism in *Widowers' Houses*) and even when he was concerned to provoke laughter it was nearly always a purposeful fun that he was after. In 1919 he wrote *Heartbreak House* which represents an image of a country morally adrift, ideologically bankrupt and floating along in a haze of pleasurable talk. Shaw has undeniably been a powerful influence.

Just as the word 'Shavian' has entered the language, so has the adjective 'Brechtian'. Loosely applied, Brechtian means 'political, epic, visually simple and even stark'. It derives from the great German dramatist Bertolt Brecht (1898–1956). He has made us re-think our notions of what the theatre is; yet the root of his art still seems to be a realistic concern with human behaviour.

It has been said of Brecht that he did not believe in an inner reality, a higher reality or a deeper reality but simply in reality. This is why he presented on the stage the things of this world in all their solidity and with all the appreciation of their corporeality which is found in a painter like Brueghel. In Brecht not only is a stage a stage but a lamp is also a lamp.

The visits of the Berliner Ensemble to London in 1956 and 1965 and their performances of Brecht's plays had a profound influence on British theatre. Shortly after their first visit an English designer talked of the 'unlimited possibilities for the destruction of scenery'. The effect can still be seen in the bare-stage productions of groups such as the Royal Shakespeare Company.

As well as having theories about the

Top *Ghosts* is one of Ibsen's major plays. Here Beatrix Lehmann plays Mrs Alving.
Middle Bertolt Brecht and Kurt Weill collaborated on *The Threepenny Opera*, first produced in Berlin in 1928. Based on John Gay's eighteenth century play *The Beggar's Opera*, Brecht's version has remained consistently successful. This picture shows the 1956 production at London's Royal Court Theatre.
Bottom Shaw's work has been both popular and influential. London's National Theatre produced *The Philanderer* in 1978.

theatre Brecht, of course, was a great play-wright. His plays, such as *The Threepenny Opera* (with music by Kurt Weill), *Mother Courage, The Caucasian Chalk Circle, Galileo* and *Arturo Ui* are constantly in production.

Brecht's plays have promoted the notion that the spectator should become detached from the action and consider the play's ideas and arguments, steadfastly refusing to succumb to the blandishments of illusion. Brecht used the term 'alienation effect' to describe what he wanted in terms of theatre. Instead of the actor immersing himself or herself totally in the character's emotions, he or she stands slightly apart from the role and 'presents' it so that the audience does not lose itself in compassion. Conceived originally as a counter to the rhetorical style of German acting, it is a method which several prominent British actors have long instinctively adopted. Actors like Olivier, Donald Sinden, Leonard Rossiter and John Wood have for years been giving performances which appeal to the audience's judgment as much as to its sympathy.

If Brecht towers over the modern theatre, many other playwrights from different countries have also made this a rich century. The United States has produced a prize-winning heavyweight in Eugene O'Neill (1888–1953). The son of a romantic actor, he flirted in his early work with Germanic Expressionism before settling down to the lengthy, confessional masterpieces by which he is still remembered, in particular *The Iceman Cometh* and *Long Day's Journey Into Night*. Set in a cavernous bar, the former play presents a set of alcoholic derelicts whose only alternative to despair lies in pipe-dreams. They tolerate one another as long as each tolerates the others' illusions. Through the four-hour length of the play, one is gripped by O'Neill's autobiographical intensity and also the sardonic humour which undermines it. In *Long Day's Journey* the audience sees a crucial day in O'Neill's late youth covered with a thin gauze of fiction. A family is torn between official Irish-Catholic morality and the sordid facts of drink and dope (the father is addicted to booze, the mother to morphine). As well as being personal in tone and content, the play has universality in its portrayal of a family tearing itself apart. No-one who saw the British National Theatre production, in which Laurence Olivier played the father and Constance Cummings the mother, is ever likely to forget it.

On another side of American drama, the comedies of George Kaufman (1889–1961) and Moss Hart (1904–1961) are gradually being rediscovered. *The Man who Came to Dinner* and *Once in a Lifetime* are deservedly being revived. The postwar American theatre has produced fine plays by Tennessee Williams, Arthur Miller, Edward Albee, Neil Simon (born 1927) and Stephen Sondheim. The forte of Williams (born 1914) is a complete compassion for people wrestling with their own sexual natures. In *A Streetcar Named Desire* he shows decorous nymphomania and in *Cat on a Hot Tin Roof* a suppressed homosexuality. A factor often ignored about Williams is that he is also one of the funniest playwrights that America has produced. One of his latest plays, *Crève Coeur* (1978), is a balefully comic study of four very lonely women all striving to confront their solitude with a battered dignity.

The ordinary hero
Arthur Miller (born 1915) has not shown the same theatrical stamina as Williams. Yet *Death of a Salesman* written in 1949 remains one of the classic postwar tragedies. It proves that the modern theatre can still produce tragic drama.

Left *Long Day's Journey Into Night,* a scene from which is shown here, is Eugene O'Neill's masterpiece. O'Neill was America's first great dramatist, but it was Tennessee Williams who dominated American drama in the period immediately following World War II. The scene (**above right**) is from the celebrated 1947 production of his *A Streetcar Named Desire* with Marlon Brando, Jessica Tandy and Kim Hunter. George Kaufman (known as the 'Great Collaborator') with Moss Hart wrote the brilliant caricature of Hollywood life, *Once in a Lifetime* in 1930. Another notable work was *The Man Who Came to Dinner* (**right**), a play about the critic, Alexander Woollcott written in 1939. This recent New York production features James Whitmore and Bill Macy.

Edward Albee (born 1928) in *Who's Afraid of Virginia Woolf* has also written a study of marital rancour which is both exhilaratingly comic and mordantly savage, showing that the old categories of comedy and tragedy have in this century fruitfully come together. American drama, which languished somewhat in the 1960s when the trend was towards groupwork by ephemeral ensembles, has undergone a renaissance in the 1970s with the emergence of such promising playwrights as David Rabe, Thomas Babe, David Mamet and Martin Sherman.

In the last 25 years there has been a marked flowering of drama in Britain. Since *Look Back in Anger* by John Osborne (born 1929) made its debut at the Royal Court Theatre in 1956, new plays have poured out in abundance. Perhaps this is partly because Britain's search for a new identity following the end of the Empire has led to an especially prolonged period of self-examination. Osborne, David Hare, Howard Brenton, Peter Nichols, Alan Bennett and many others have constantly taken the moral temperature of the nation. The founding of the Royal Court as a writer's theatre in 1955, the creation of a National Theatre Company in 1962 and the steady expansion of the Royal Shakespeare Company throughout the 1960s have inspired new writing (as has the bustling fringe theatre). All this has compensated for the fact that Britain came late to the idea of institutional theatre.

Harold Pinter (born 1930) has in many ways revolutionized drama by assuming that an author knows no more about his characters than the audience. Tom Stoppard (born 1937), in plays like *Jumpers* and *Travesties*, has sent language out on a drunken spree. David Hare, in *Plenty*, took the most ironic look at the collapse of postwar ideals yet seen on the British stage. Trevor Griffiths (born 1935), in *Comedians*, combined the

Below This scene is from Neil Simon's semi-autobiographical play, *Chapter Two* (based partly on the author's second marriage). The actors in this New York production are (**left** to **right**) Anita Gillette, Ann Wedgeworth, Cliff Gorman and Judd Hirsch. Simon's witty domestic comedies have been very successful on Broadway.

class conflict with a bracing study of a night-school course for apprentice laughter-makers.

Many of these dramatists show clearly the influence of Brecht, many of them are also indebted to the work of Samuel Beckett (born 1906). The individual talent of this Irish dramatist who lives and works in France has had a tremendous impact on theatre – the first night of *Waiting for Godot* in London in 1955 was a theatrical landmark in the revival of British theatre.

These developments, along with an upsurge of new writing in Australia and Canada recently, as well as the emergence of drama in the Third World, have strengthened theatre world-wide. The Nigerian dramatist Wole Soyinka (born 1934), for example, has done much to develop theatre in Nigeria as well as making an impact in Britain and the USA.

Drama has been written off many times during this century. First the cinema was going to kill it, then television. But the hunger for live theatre experience seems to grow all the time.

The making of a play

To have a play accepted, a writer or writer's agent sends it to a theatrical producer. Once accepted, the search begins for a director willing to stage it. The director is the author's first critic, suggesting cuts, offering ideas for re-writes and trying to tighten and sharpen the text. In modern theatre, writer-director partnerships such as that of Peter Hall and Harold Pinter have grown up.

The role of directors is constantly changing. Once, 'blocking' was more extensively and rigidly used – the director would turn up on the first morning of rehearsal with every move by the performers plotted or worked out in a book. Today the trend is more towards letting the performers help shape the final product. Directors are more inclined to describe to the performers the general layout of a scene and leave it to them to move, sit or stand as the impulse takes them. Jonathan Miller (born 1934) once said that, when he was directing *The Merchant of Venice* at the National Theatre, he had a general idea of how the court room scene should look with figures seated round a table, but how the performers actually reached their positions was left to them.

Three other figures have a major influence on the production – the scenic designer, the lighting designer and the costume designer. In the nineteenth century, independent actor-managers, stock companies and travelling troupes ordered ready-made sets from firms which manufactured replicas of woodlands, mountains, castles and so on, churning them out in bulk. Some firms printed catalogues of completed background settings. In the United States right up into the 1920s a ground plan was handed to a scenic shop which made up the setting. A common

Above The first production of John Osborne's *Look Back in Anger* at London's Royal Court Theatre in 1956 established Osborne as one of the 'angry young men' of the British theatre. The production starred Kenneth Haigh as Jimmy Porter and Mary Ure as his wife Alison. One of the most important London theatres, The Royal Court has also launched the careers of many British playwrights such as Harold Pinter and Edward Bond.

Left The first London production of Beckett's *Waiting for Godot* also had a huge impact. It was produced in 1955 at the Arts Theatre, directed by Peter Hall.

Above right
Programmes for some significant recent British productions include (from **left** to **right**) the première of Osborne's *Look back in Anger* in 1955 Tom Stoppard's *Travesties* at the Aldwych, Pinter's *No Man's Land* at the National Theatre with Ralph Richardson and John Gielgud (**top row**); and (**bottom row**) Beckett's *Waiting for Godot, Comedians* by Trevor Griffiths and David Hare's *Plenty*.

Right This diagram illustrates the steps in producing a play. The time-scale will vary according to what type of play and company is involved.

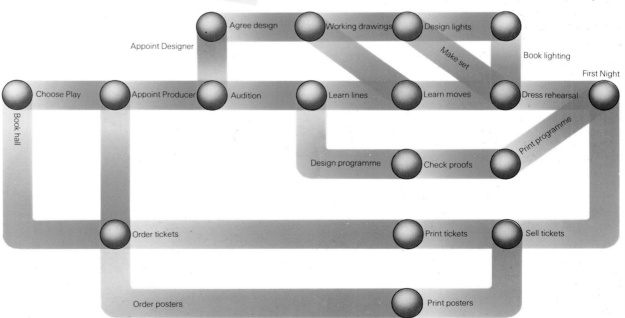

Book hall · Choose Play · Appoint Producer · Audition · Learn lines · Learn moves · Dress rehearsal · First Night

Appoint Designer · Agree design · Working drawings · Design lights · Make set · Book lighting

Design programme · Check proofs · Print programme

Order tickets · Print tickets · Sell tickets

Order posters · Print posters

Costume design
Designing the costumes is a very important element in the production of a show. The designer first consults with the director and set designer to gain an impression of the whole production. The costumes are worked up from sketches, often with swatches of material attached. The costumes shown here **(left)** are for a production of Shakespeare's *Pericles*. The designer also writes comments and clarification on the sketch to help convey the idea of the costume to the director and designer as well as to the person making up the costume. It is also important that the costumes enhance the individuality of the character as well as fitting in to the overall concept of the play. That concept — as well as financial considerations — may affect the costume designer's approach.

After the costume designs have been completed the process of making up the garments begins. The material has to be chosen with care **(above)**. For work under stage lights, texture is important. The costumes are then cut out **(above right)**, sewn **(above far right)**, and fitted **(right)**. The designer and wardrobe supervisor work in close consultation **(far right)**. A large company would have both costume designer and wardrobe supervisor.

Scene design
Scene designers now use models to work out their designs. Previously scene painters worked only from sketches provided by the designer. These designs (**right**) are for the 1980 Glyndebourne Festival Opera production of Mozart's *Seraglio*. The designer draws first a rough sketch (**above**), and works up a scale drawing (**above centre**). The model is then constructed (**above right**). Any scenery to be dropped from the flies has to be checked on an exact scale plan of the stage (**right**). The finished model (**far right**) will be reconstructed in full size for the production.

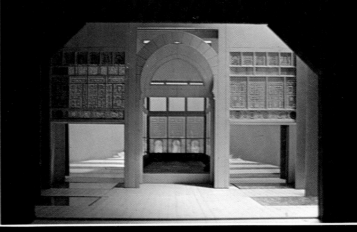

Props and scenery
As with scenery and costumes, props vary tremendously depending on the production. Larger theatres often have props and scenery building departments. London's National Theatre has a complex of workshops which serve its three auditoria. The woodwork shop (**below left**) is here making scenery for the National's production of *Thee and Me*. Scenery is painted in the paint shop (**below centre**). Here the Olivier Theatre's production of

Amadeus is being worked on. Props are made in the prop shop (**left**). The metal workshop (**above**) has responsibility, for example, for the arms and armour used in the theatres.

Far left This stage setting for a tragedy was devised by the Renaissance architect, Sebastiano Serlio in 1545. Serlio designed his sets for a royal banqueting-hall and was one of the first to use perspective in his designs. The 'houses', arranged on both sides of the street, recede at right angles from the front of the stage. They were two-sided and fore-shortened.
Left This stark set design is by Ralph Koltai for Ibsen's *Brand* at the National Theatre, 1978.

Right, below Various types of stage design used by modern designers are illustrated here. The arena and theatre-in-the-round *(1)* is the simplest of settings. The thrust or open setting *(2)* is a rostrum backed by a curtain or cut-out screen. The screen setting *(3)* is an extension of open setting. Curtain sets *(4)* are common in schools and church halls. Wing and cloth sets *(5)* are often used in pantomime and revue. The box set *(6)* is for a realistic interior setting. When two or more interiors are needed the box-within-a-box *(7)* is used. The cyclorama set *(8)* is suitable when there is a minimum of stage furniture. Composite sets *(9)* are used when there are several locations in the play. Permanent sets *(10)*, which have a structural framework, are used for plays with long runs.

1

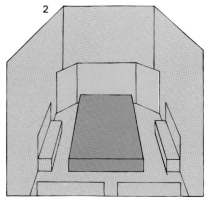

2

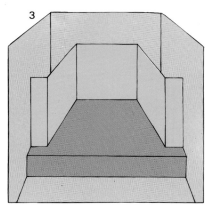

3

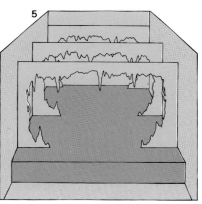

4

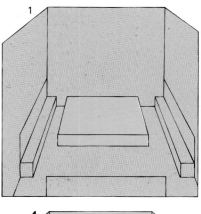

5

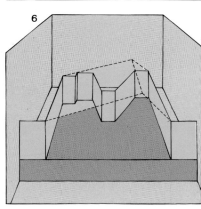

6

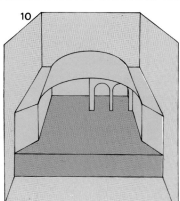

7

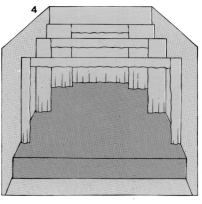

8

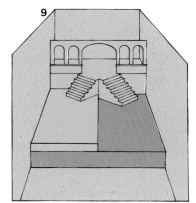

9

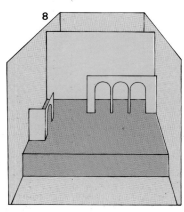

10

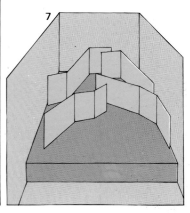

Stage lighting
When theatres moved indoors around 1600, they were illuminated using candles and oil lamps. These remained the standard forms of theatre lighting until the nineteenth century, when gas lights were introduced. Gas allowed greater control of the quality of light and made it possible to vary the levels of light on stage. It only became standard practice to darken the auditorium in the latter half of the nineteenth century. Before then the auditorium was lit in the same way as the stage. Footlights were used before gas light was introduced. The term 'float' which is occasionally still used to describe footlights, refers to the wick floating in the old oil lamps. Theatres needed many lights — in 1810 Covent Garden used 270 candles and 300 oil lamps just to light the stage and scenery. Since the introduction of electricity in the late nineteenth century, lighting has become more and more sophisticated.

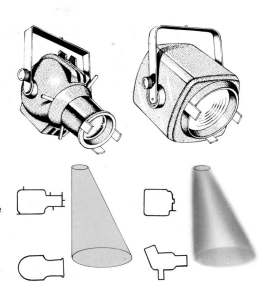
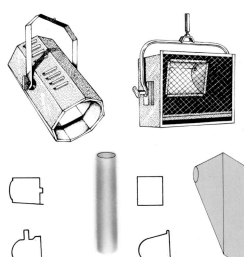

Above Stage lighting designers use four basic types of light. These are (from **left** to **right**) profile spot, fresnel spot, beam light, and floodlight. The profile spot gives a hard beam. Types of filters called gobos can be inserted to give, for example, a leaf effect. The fresnel gives a softer, narrower beam and its size is varied using the 'barn doors', a type of shutter, in front of the lamp. The beam light can be either hard or soft focus. On hard focus its beam is very intense. The light is very white and the beam light is often used for back lighting and pop concerts. The flood is used to provide large areas of light, for example on to a cyclorama. The type of lamp is indicated on the lighting plan using standard symbols. The British symbols are shown in the diagram above the American ones.

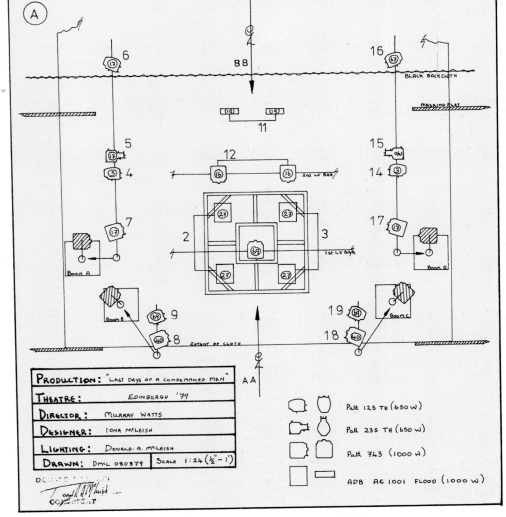

	Patt 123 TH (650 W)
	Patt 235 TH (650 W)
	Patt 743 (1000 W)
	ADB AC 1001 FLOOD (1000 W)

PRODUCTION: "LAST DAYS OF A CONDEMNED MAN"
THEATRE: EDINBURGH '79
DIRECTOR: MURRAY WATTS
DESIGNER: IONA McLEISH
LIGHTING: DONALD A. McLEISH
DRAWN: DMcL 080879   SCALE 1:24 (½" = 1')

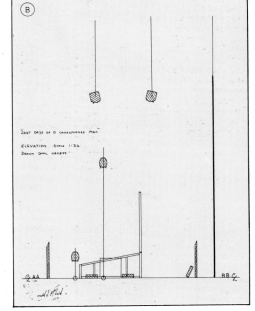

Above The lighting plan is the scale drawing of the set which shows the position of all the lights. The plan is drawn up after detailed consultation between the lighting designer and the director. The diagram shows the position of the lights, their type and the angle at which they hang. The lighting and its intensity is controlled from a board which has a given number of circuits marked. The circuit numbers are marked on the diagram with large numerals. Levels of the lights are established and marked on the lighting plot with which the lighting operator follows the play. The side elevation (**above right**) shows the vertical relationships of the scenery, lights and curtains.

Below The lighting plan on the previous page is realized. The set for *Last Days of a Condemned Man* at the 1979 Edinburgh Festival was to give the impression of a cell. A dentist's chair was used to give some movement to the sitting figure. Under the solid metal framework, a cage-like effect was created using a type of metal mesh which would reflect the light in different directions.

Above The strong colours and clear lines made this production very effective visually. As the production had to tour, it was vital for the set and lighting to be fairly simple. There is no standard lighting rig for drama as there is, to some extent, for opera and ballet. The lighting design evolves in discussions between the director, and the set and lighting designers. Lighting design has increased in importance and sophistication in the last 30 years.

Stage make-up
Make-up is used for most stage actors. The reasons for using make-up are varied. Make-up is needed to counteract the effect of the stage lighting which seems to flatten out an actor's features. Make-up is also used to change an actor's appearance — for example to make a young actor look older, or an older actor look younger. Early in the nineteenth century many of the principles of make-up were laid down; these became the accepted approach to stage make-up for over a century. Indeed, some actors still follow these precepts, for example, to use a hare's foot for finally powdering the made-up face. Greasepaint is the traditional form of make-up. It comes in stick form and a wide range of colours which can be easily blended. Compressed and liquid forms of make-up, applied with a damp sponge, are more popular today. Make-up can also use, for example, liquid latex to create wrinkles, or mortician's wax to improve or disfigure the shape of the actor's feature. Wigs are another important part of make-up; they can profoundly alter the shape and appearance of an actor's head. It is important that the make-up complements the character being played by the actor. In earlier times, actors would always have done their own make-up. Now a large company may have a department of make-up artists and wig-makers.

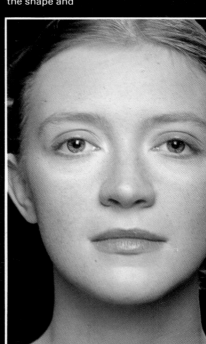

The model's face (**above**) is shown without make-up. Stage make-up need not be heavy; it should help the audience see the actor's features clearly.

In the make-up (**above, left, top right**) the person has been made to look her own age. This simple corrective make-up emphasizes the eyes and mouth slightly. In the older make-up (**above right, right**) lines have been accentuated or added and the eyes and mouth left very pale. If the actor's neck or ears will show they must also be made up.

One of the main reasons for having make-up is that the bright stage lighting tends to take colour out of the actor's face. In smaller studio theatres today, however, it is possible for actors to wear little or no make-up, because the distance between the actor and audience is very small.

These pictures show Maggie Smith with make-ups designed for different roles. In Molnar's *The Guardsman* (left) she plays an actress. For the dual role of Rosalind/Ganymede in Shakespeare's *As You Like It,* she has a younger make-up designed to complement the eighteenth century style of the production. For the role of Hippolyta in *A Midsummer Night's Dream,* (right) Maggie Smith was made up to look like Queen Elizabeth I.

Right Colin Blakeley played the role of Captain Shotover in the National Theatre's production of Shaw's *Heartbreak House.* The bald wig and false nose are ready to be put on **(top left)** and are applied **(top centre)**. No foundation was applied, the actor started to draw in lines and age spots to create the wrinkles **(top right)**. The beard is then applied in layers **(bottom left, centre)**, then the wig is put on. The end result is a remarkable testimony to what make-up can achieve **(bottom right)**.

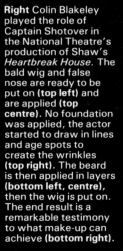

method of scenic make-up was the 'flat', a wooden frame pushed horizontally onto the stage with the background scene painted on it. Scenic designers, then, were rather like interior decorators called in to furnish a play.

In postwar years this gave way to a style known as 'skeletal' in which a graceful simple framework, with a minimum of adornment, was used to give suggestions of mood. There are exceptions, but a designer has become much more occupied in trying to capture the mood of a play through props and furniture. A classic example is the designer Ralph Koltai (born 1924) who often works through a single image or a sustained metaphor, such as the huge radar scanner he employed for Rolf Hochhuth's *Soldiers* or the cinder-track stage he created for the English National Opera's version of *The Ring*.

As scenic designers gradually destroy scenery, so lighting designs have become increasingly elaborate. Torches, pine knots, open wick lamps and tallow candles were once used to light plays. In the seventeenth century, oil lamps and candles began to be set in a row along the front edge of the stage but hidden from the audience – they were the footlights. When gaslighting was introduced in the nineteenth century, lights could be more easily darkened for effect. Intensity was improved by shining a sharp point of oxyhydrogen flame against a cylindrical block of lime – limelight. Mirror reflectors were added and the intense limelight was used to follow individual performers about the stage. Limelight could also be used to suggest effects such as sunlight, moonlight, or cloud movements. Nowadays, lighting designers such as David Hersey (born 1939) in England or Jules Fisher (born 1937) in America have become stars in their own right, using sophisticated electronic equipment controlled by central switchboards. Pools of light are located in set areas of the stage and can be called for individually or mixed by the director. Modern lighting can use an extremely wide range of transparent coloured sheets of plastic fitted in front of lighting units for colours. In earlier times these 'gels' used to be made of gelatine. Different coloured lights can be shined on performers' faces and on the background. Effects such as rippling water or dancing flames can be produced by revolving slides. Costumes or background can be painted in different materials to show up against certain lights or fade against others. A recent example of what can be done was the production of a Sherlock Holmes drama, *The Crucifer of Blood*, in which at one point two ships were required to come alongside each other in the Thames estuary. The effect of night, of slight river-mist, of water, was entirely created in the London version by David Hersey's atmospheric lighting.

Another essential component of a play is the casting, and here a lot depends on circumstances. In the commercial theatre, production is often centred on a 'bankable' star with the smaller parts being filled in afterwards. In a company like the British National Theatre or the Royal Shakespeare Company, parts are generally cast from the talent which is available. Great importance is attached in such subsidized theatre to the casting director whose job it is to know about rising talent and to advise on the casting of specialized roles.

The process of getting a play onto the stage varies, but it is now accepted in the professional theatre that there should be a minimum rehearsal time of four weeks but, ideally, one of six weeks. Rehearsals vary. Some directors like to have run-throughs of the whole play from the second week so that the performers get the rhythm of the piece; others like to work in fragments and put the pieces together at the end.

Responsibility for costume is usually shared between the director, the designer and the specialist costume designer (if a company is big enough to afford one). Large companies like the National and the Royal Shakespeare Company have their own wardrobe departments where costumes are cut and measured according to the shape of the actor and the demands of the director. In a smaller organization, costumes may be hired from a costumier's who usually can cover every period of history. In a rep company the actor may be required to supply his or her own costume for contemporary work.

When it comes to running a show, technically, this is the job of the stage manager. He is in charge of everything which happens back-stage from the rise to the fall of the curtain. The stage manager also often becomes the director's representative after the initial performances and is responsible for company discipline, post-performance notes, payment of artists' salaries, understudy rehearsals and overseeing the work of the technicians. To the assistant stage managers fall the tasks of calling the actors on time, moving scenery, sitting with the prompt copy, helping with swift costume changes and keeping the production flowing.

Great modern performers

To the public, it is still the actor or actress who is one of the chief magnets in the business of theatregoing. The most dominant performer of the twentieth century is Laurence Olivier (born 1907). Regarded with suspicion for many years as something of a matinée-idol, a wayward verse-speaker and a play-picker of dubious taste, he came into his own in September 1944 when he first played Richard III for the Old Vic Company at the New Theatre. A critic noted that Olivier brought out the intellectual ability of his Richard – if outwardly Richard was a limping panther, there was no lameness in his mind as portrayed by Olivier.

The same quality of intellect also distinguished the Macbeth that Olivier played at Stratford-on-Avon in 1955. Starting low-keyed, he painted a picture of Macbeth as a man rather than a monster and wrung all hearts with his swooping emphasis on the phrase 'troops of friends' when Macbeth describes the things he must not seek to have. His performance as the third-rate music-hall artist Archie Rice in John Osborne's *The Entertainer* in April 1957 was also a wonderful anthology of all-round Olivier: the faint androgynous touch, the savage irony and the ability to hit the emotion without rant or sentimentality.

Olivier's contemporary, John Gielgud (born 1904), was a famous Hamlet and Richard II in the Old Vic seasons of 1929 and 1930, went on through more classical parts and latterly has scored notable successes in modern plays. Ralph Richardson (born 1902) is a superb embodiment of robust eccentricity who, in famous seasons with the Old Vic Company from 1944–5, was an outstanding Peer Gynt, Falstaff and Uncle Vanya. Another noteworthy British actor, Paul Scofield (born 1922) has a magnificent voice that can turn from autumn-softness to the icy blast of winter in a second. Only a few of America's host of talented stars can be mentioned here. John Barrymore (1882–1942) electrified the New York and London stages with his Hamlet in the 1920s. In the postwar Broadway world, one performance above all others is constantly used as both a yardstick and as a demonstration of the wastefulness of a system that allows so much talent to escape to Hollywood. This is Marlon Brando's (born 1924) performance as Stanley Kowalski in the original 1947 production of *A Streetcar Named Desire*. No list of American players can omit the veteran Helen Hayes (born 1900) who scored her greatest triumph in the American production of Laurence Housman's *Victoria Regina* in 1935; Laurette Taylor (1884–1946) with her performance in Tennessee Williams's *The Glass Menagerie* in 1944: Jason Robards (born 1920) who has become the foremost living interpreter of Eugene O'Neill; and Jack Lemmon (born 1925) who returned to Broadway in triumph in 1978 as the gag-peddling, life-evading hero of a play called *Tribute*.

The story of French acting is very much dominated by great actresses such as Elisa Rachel (1820–1858) and Sarah Bernhardt (1845–1923), and in more recent times Madeleine Renaud (born 1903) and Maria Casarès (born 1922). In Germany there is a long line of great actors such as Alexander Moissi (1880–1935), Werner Krauss (1884–1959), and Gustaf Grundgens (1899–1963). Today the tradition is carried on by such performers as Martin Held (born 1908) who played Osborne's Archie Rice as a sweaty, crude cabaret M.C.

People may pay tribute to the virtues of ensemble teamwork and company discipline, but the spine-tingling, magnetism of a star can still hold the public enthralled.

Great performers **Right** (from **left** to **right**) These illustrations show Mrs Patrick Campbell as Eliza Doolittle; Laurence Olivier as Henry V; and Henry Irving. **Below** (from **left** to **right**) Shown here are the inimitable Sarah Bernhardt; the American actor-manager, Edwin Booth; the great Shakespearean actress, Ellen Terry; and John Gielgud as Hamlet in his 1934 interpretation. **Bottom** This engraving (**left**) shows the great eighteenth century actor, David Garrick. John Barrymore (**right**) made his British debut as Hamlet in 1925.

OPERA

FROM THE CAMERATA TO STAGING AND PRODUCTION TODAY

Opera, probably the most complex of all the traditional performing arts, was actually the fruit of a fortunate mistake. It stemmed from the studies of a group of late sixteenth century Florentine humanists known as the Camerata, who met in the house of a nobleman to discuss aesthetic issues and ideas.

The group — mainly poets and musicians — were particularly interested in the tremendous importance attached to music in antiquity and they concluded that this was due to the dramatic uses to which it had once been put. As they discovered through ancient writings, music had been allied to language to reinforce its meaning, resulting in what, to the Camerata, was the peak of expressive art, namely Greek tragedy.

Where the members of the Camerata were mistaken was their belief that Greek tragedy was sung throughout. As it is now known that, only the choruses were sung (or chanted), though music was probably used

to accentuate dramatic climaxes. However faulty the Camerata's scholarship was, their creative instincts were sound. In attempting to emulate Greek tragedy they paradoxically achieved something of startling originality. It was a mode of dramatic presentation which the Camerata and their immediate successors called 'dramma per musica' —

drama through music — or 'favola in musica' — fable in music. It was this which eventually became known as opera.

Opera composers

Opera was the culmination — albeit accidental — of a long-felt desire to simplify and humanize music. The earlier part of the sixteenth century was still dominated musically by polyphony, the densely written ceremonial music developed for Church rituals which, though vocal, was not verbal. Yet, as the Camerata saw, music could hardly mirror human behaviour unless the words were understandable. Thus the Florentines threw themselves behind the movement for reform. The result was a new, monodic style of music, that is music with a single vocal line, which could reflect the meaning of the words and which, apart from a few instrumental chords or flourishes, was essentially self-sufficient.

Left Wolfgang Amadeus Mozart poured his most intense music into operas such as *The Marriage of Figaro* and *Don Giovanni*.

Left Guiseppe Verdi is recognized as one of the world's greatest opera composers. His combination of passionate melody with gripping, if sometimes complex, plots brought opera closer to the people and away from stylized entertainments like the intermezzo (**above**). **Below** This scene is from one of Verdi's greatest operas, *La Traviata*. Verdi originally intended this to be played in contemporary dress.

Sadly, the music of the world's first opera, *Dafne*, completed in 1597 by the Italian Jacopo Peri (1561–1633) and performed in the presence of Giovanni de Medici and other Florentine nobles, is lost. But the second opera, *Euridice*, also by Peri, survives complete. Given in Florence in 1600 to celebrate the wedding of Henry IV of France and Maria de Medici, *Euridice* is historically important; but musically it is inferior.

Yet so significant were the aesthetic implications of opera and so tantalizing its expressive possibilities, that no Italian composer could fail to be tempted by the new art form. Within seven years of Peri's *Dafne* a work showing unmistakable signs of genius had been presented, first at a private academy and then at the court of Mantua. This was *Orfeo*, by the Italian composer, Claudio Monteverdi (1567–1643).

Like its predecessors, this 'favola in musica', in which for the first time the rich possibilities of opera — musical, dramatic and formal — were foreshadowed, was written for private performances before exclusively aristocratic and courtly audiences. Opera did not remain so limited in appeal for long. In 1637 the first public opera house was opened in Venice. By the end of the century, 10 had been built there (of which eight were still flourishing) and more than 350 different works had been presented.

Until the age of Mozart, public and private opera had a great deal in common. Works commissioned by the courts tended to be frigidly ceremonial in tone, scenically lavish and slow-moving. Almost invariably they made use of a familiar tale from mythology or ancient history that could serve as an allegory in praise of the virtues of the sponsoring ruler. Operas written for public theatres depicted the same kind of subject. For example, Monteverdi's first opera for a public theatre was *Il Ritorno d'Ulisse in Patria* (*The Return of Ulysses to his Homeland*), first performed in 1641; the only true opera by the English composer Henry Purcell (1659–1695), completed in 1690, was *Dido and Aeneas*, another legendary epic; one of the most decisive successes of the German George Frideric Handel (1685–1759) at the King's Theatre, London, was *Giulio Cesare* (*Julius Caesar*, 1724); another German, Christoph Willibald Gluck (1714–1787) had his greatest triumph in Vienna with *Orfeo ed Euridice* (1762).

Gluck in particular, first in *Orfeo* and a few years later in *Alceste* (1767), helped to make opera once again the fully expressive medium it had originally been in the minds of the Camerata and in the music of Monteverdi. For despite the genius of Purcell and Handel the period between Monteverdi's last opera *L'Incoronazione di Poppea* (*The Coronation of Poppaea*), first performed in 1642, and Gluck's *Orfeo* was in many ways

Left Richard Wagner revolutionized opera with his concept of continuous music drama. His most ambitious composition was the four-opera cycle *The Ring of the Nibelungs*, based on Norse and German myth, and charting the decline and fall of the gods. **Far left** This scene from the second opera *The Valkyrie* shows Amalie Materna playing Brünnhilde.

Right Giacomo Puccini was the leading Italian opera composer of his day. This series of illustrations comes from one of his best-known operas, *Madame Butterfly* (**below**). The singer shown here, Rosina Storchio, created the title role at La Scala, Milan, in 1904.

one of severe artistic decline. Psychological truth was sacrificed to the virtuosity of star singers, particularly sopranos and *castrati* – neutered boys who developed into technical prodigies, combining female vocal flexibility with male strength and possessing what all agreed was an affectingly spiritual timbre.

It was not that brilliant sopranos or *castrati* were in themselves bad – Gluck, after all, wrote the role of Orfeo for a *castrato* – but that the vanity of some of these stars and the delight the public took in their vocal skills led even serious composers like the Italian Allessandro Scarlatti (1660–1725) to ignore expressiveness in favour of showmanship.

With the advent of the extraordinarily comprehensive genius of the Austrian Wolfgang Amadeus Mozart (1756–1791), opera extended its reach to reflect not only human feelings but subjects which featured ordinary people as opposed to kings or gods.

In opera, Mozart is the poet of social behaviour. In his comedies *Così fan tutte (All Women Behave Alike)*, first performed in 1790, and *Le Nozze di Figaro (The Marriage of Figaro)*, first performed in 1786, he shows the confusions and misunderstandings of daily life and the harmony, both personal and social, in which they can be resolved. *Don Giovanni* (1787), the story of a rake dragged

down to hell, shows the sinister underside of human absurdity, while *Die Zauberflöte (The Magic Flute)*, first performed in 1791, a mixture of fairytale, vaudeville comedy and ethical allegory, depicts its solemn foundation.

With *Die Zauberflöte* and the earlier *Singspiel* (opera with spoken dialogue), *Die Entführung aus dem Serail (The Abduction from the Seraglio)*, which had its first performance in 1782, Mozart helped to break the spell of formal Italian opera which had dominated the whole of Europe, except France, since the beginning of the eighteenth century. The yearning for a native form of art, which in the nineteenth century was to make opera indi-

genous, particularly in Germany, Austria, Russia, Hungary and what is today Czechoslovakia, was intensified by the break-up of the old aristocratic order under the impact of the French Revolution and the Napoleonic Wars.

Social and psychological upheaval brought to opera new subjects, new audiences and new techniques, including a highly sophisticated and emotive use of the orchestra. *Der Freischütz (The Freeshooter)*, by the German composer Carl Maria von Weber (1786–1826) is the story of the triumph of innocence over the diabolic. First performed in 1821, it sought to stir in audiences alternating feelings of reverence and fear. By blending in the age-old beliefs of the German peasantry and by revealing the relationship of character to landscape, Weber changed the course of opera.

The great contribution of the Italian Gioacchino Rossini (1792–1868) was to bring Mediterranean brio and vivacity to the whole of Europe – and indeed even farther afield, for in 1828 his *Barbiere di Siviglia (Barber of Seville)*, which had been premiered in 1816, became the first Italian opera to be heard in the United States. Yet even Rossini was prone to northern introspection, and the heroine – Mathilde – of his last opera, *Guil-*

Left, below Dame Nellie Melba was one of the greatest sopranos of her day. **Right** Joan Sutherland, regarded by many as Melba's natural successor, sings the title role in Donizetti's *Maria Stuarda*.

laume Tell (*William Tell*), first performed in 1829, sings mournfully of sombre forests and storm-shrouded hills.

With another Italian, Vincenzo Bellini (1801–1835), melancholy became the dominating strain. The vulnerable, sweetly carolling heroines of his *La Sonnambula* (*The Sleepwalker*, 1831), *Norma* (1831) and *I Puritani* (*The Puritans*, 1835) went straight to the heart of nineteenth century audiences – now dominated by the bourgeoisie – as did the jilted, demented heroine of *Lucia di Lammermoor* (1835) by Bellini's fellow countryman Gaetano Donizetti (1797–1848). He took his plot from the novel *The Bride of Lammermoor* by Sir Walter Scott (1771–1832).

A new, native vigour entered opera with Giuseppe Verdi (1813–1901). By ancestry an Italian peasant, by instinct a patriot, by nature a pragmatist and by birth a genius, he was not a theoretician but a practical man of the theatre for whom success was an acknowledgement that he had satisfied a felt need. Opera to Verdi meant the dramatic expression of primal states of feeling. All his characters, from the raw, exciting hero of *Ernani* (1844) to the deeply satisfying, fastidiously conceived hero of *Otello* (1887), exemplify emotions rather than merely feel them. By his third opera, *Nabucco* (1842), in the chorus

of lamentation sung by the Hebrews exiled from their homeland, he found that he could touch not merely an audience but an entire people, yearning as it was for political unification.

In the operas of his mid-career, *Rigoletto* (1851), *Il Trovatore* (*The Troubadour*, 1853) and *La Traviata* (*The Woman Gone Astray*, 1853), Verdi's irrepressible flood of melody creates character and action with incomparable vividness. The later *Don Carlos* (1867) and *Aida* (1871) express his compassion for the individual, helpless before the claims of society. *Falstaff* (1893), his farewell to the stage, is at once knockabout farce and a benediction on behalf of all his fellow creatures.

Verdi, the celebrant of the here and now, makes a striking contrast to his German contemporary, Richard Wagner (1813–1883), who called himself 'an outlaw for life' and whose aim as an artist was not so much to reach the opera-going public as to regenerate the world. Luckily he was also a great composer. Whereas Verdi accepted operatic conditions as he found them Wagner, inspired by Beethoven, sought to transform everything that stood between him and his vision of the ideal – namely, to give vastly greater importance to the orchestra than ever before,

to create a new, more heroic breed of singer, to convert grand opera into what he termed true music-drama and to change the theatre into a temple of art. While Verdi sought to provoke the enthusiasm of his audience, Wagner demanded its unquestioning devotion. In the process he created a powerful cult and eventually, in Bayreuth, a festival devoted to the fitting presentation of his masterworks.

Wagner's recognition of the importance of words led him to become his own librettist. He sought his subjects in northern history, folk narratives, myths and the workings of his own psyche. From such diverse elements he fashioned a vast, four-part epic saga, *Der Ring des Nibelungen* (*The Ring of the Nibelungs*, 1869–76), about the creation, betrayal and regeneration of the universe.

In *Tristan und Isolde* (1865) he offered a uniquely ardent depiction of sexual love and, at the same time, showed that its fulfilment could only come about by transcending the physical world and merging with the universal will. In his sole comedy, *Die Meistersinger von Nürnberg* (*The Mastersingers of Nuremberg*, 1868), his subject is the renewal of society through art. In his final work, *Parsifal* (1882), Wagner ritualizes the eternal conflict between flesh and spirit.

A natural reaction to the overwhelming insistence of Wagner's claims coalesced around the clarity, wit and grace of *Carmen* (1875), by the Frenchman Georges Bizet (1838–1875). However, Wagner's genius – like Verdi's – proved indestructible. Both had successors. Wagner was followed by another immensely popular German, Richard Strauss (1864–1949), whose early fascination with abnormal psychology was demonstrated in his works *Salome* (1905) and *Elektra* (1909). It later gave way to a faith in the traditional values of civilization when he wrote *Der Rosenkavalier* (*The Knightly Rose-Bearer*, 1911). Verdi's heir was the no-less-popular Italian Giacomo Puccini (1858–1924), who in opera after opera – *La Bohème* (*Bohemian Life*, 1896), *Tosca* (1900), *Madame Butterfly* (1904) – touched the public by the melodic coupling of love and its loss.

Modern operas

Puccini and Strauss proved to be the last universally accepted composers of opera. That is not to say that estimable and even popular composers have entirely disappeared in recent times. Two at least have proved lastingly successful: Gian-Carlo Menotti (born 1911) and Benjamin Britten (1913–1976). Menotti, born in Italy but for most of his artistic life identified with the United States, has written at least three operas that have enjoyed constant revival – *The Medium* (1946), *The Consul* (1950) and *Amahl and the Night Visitors* (1951), the last specially written for television.

Britten was the first Englishman since Purcell to write an artistically successful opera – *Peter Grimes* (1945), which soon became an international hit. He followed it with a series of works which have laid the foundations for what, only 40 years ago, seemed inconceivable: a school of native British opera.

However, Menotti has earned neither the respect of musicians nor the esteem of connoisseurs and his works are rarely seen in the world's major opera houses. While, to judge by the reception of his operas in the United States, Britten, outside his own country, has won both respect and esteem but, with the single exception of *Peter Grimes*, not affection. Although *Albert Herring* (1947), *The Turn of the Screw* (1954) and the *Church Parables* (1964–8) will doubtless continue to be performed by small groups all over the English-speaking world, to most opera-goers outside the United Kingdom Britten remains a peripheral figure. So, apart from Puccini and Strauss, do the other distinguished composers of the twentieth century.

Many remarkable operas have been produced since 1900; for example *Pelléas et Mélisande* (1902), by the Frenchman Claude Debussy (1862–1918); *Jenůfa* (1904), by the Czech Leoš Janáček (1854–1928); *Bluebeard's Castle* (1918) by the Hungarian Béla Bartók (1881–1945); *Wozzeck* (1925) and *Lulu* (1979), by the Austrian Alban Berg (1885–1935); *The*

These scenes from the Chinese opera show Hangchow Opera's *The Fallen-from-the-skies Embroidered Shoe* (left) and two scenes from the Peking Opera's *The Monkey King* (below). China has an operatic tradition dating back many hundreds of years, starting at the imperial court where opera originated in the fourteenth century AD. Various regional styles emerged; Peking opera, for instance, is a nineteenth century development, with the fiddle as the main accompanying instrument.

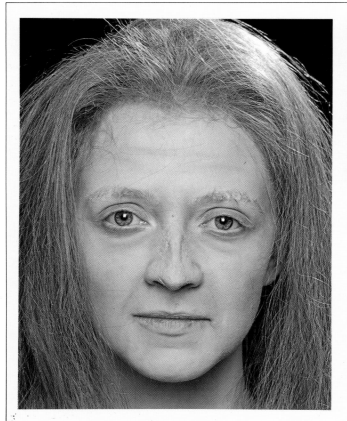

Opera make-up
Make-up for opera is traditionally more stylized than that for drama. The approach to opera make-up is also in influenced by the shape of opera singers' faces which tend to be broad at the temples because of the muscle development caused by singing. The make-up (left, above) would be suitable for a character such as one of the witches in Verdi's *Macbeth*.

Mother of Us All (1947), by the American Virgil Thomson; *The Rake's Progress* (1951), by Russia's Igor Stravinsky (1882–1971); *Moses und Aron*, by the Austrian–born composer, Arnold Schoenberg (1874–1951); and *The Midsummer Marriage* (1955) by the English composer Michael Tippett (born 1905). Most of these are performed fairly regularly, but few have established themselves as yet with the opera-going public.

Season after season in many of the principal centres of Europe and the Americas a handful of new operas are presented.

Right This caricature shows a dandy fainting with delight in his box at the opera house. **Below** In this 1907 view, the opera audience is socializing between the acts. Until relatively recent times, opera was the preserve of the wealthy, fashionable and socially prominent.

Though these are often warmly received, few, if any, are likely to join the standard operatic repertory. This is because most contemporary operas seem to lack theatrical conviction, clarity of aim, creative personality and melody.

Opera audiences

Experimentation in other theatrical forms is often welcomed by the public, but opera audiences tend to shy away from works with non-narrative structures. They also do not seem to like those in which theory supersedes theatrical effectiveness, or those in which the voice is used not as a revelation of human personality but as just another musical instrument, particularly an unconventional one.

Caution, however, has proved perfectly compatible with enthusiasm. Since the end of the Second World War the audience for opera has soared. All across the United States – in Houston, Minneapolis, Seattle, Baltimore, San Diego, Washington DC – there are new opera companies. New York, which until 1944 had only a single major company, now has two, as well as a dozen or so minor ones. Covent Garden, which in 1938 managed no more than nine weeks of opera, presently offers it for ten months a year. In recent years Sadler's Wells Opera has been transformed into the English National Opera and has been joined by Welsh National Opera, Scottish Opera and English National Opera North.

Opera singers

Inseparable from the appeal of opera as a genre is the excitement and emotion with which audiences continue to respond to trained human voices of exceptional quality. The mutation from polyphony to monody after the sixteenth century inevitably led to the emergence of the individual vocal personality. In rendering vivid the meaning of the text singers were expected to make their own musical contribution by improvising ornaments on whatever words they consi-

71

dered of particular dramatic significance.

In the eighteenth and early nineteenth centuries singers were required to demonstrate all kinds of technical marvels. According to the accounts of the time the results were often transfixingly beautiful. Once, in Rome, the *castrato* Pacchierotti (1740–1821) is said to have sung so ravishingly that the performance broke down because the entire orchestra and its conductor were in tears.

However, audiences needed to identify with the characters of opera, not simply marvel at the virtuosity of the singers. Eventually the old order passed, largely under the influence of Rossini who, despite (or perhaps because of) the fact that he married a soprano, sought to curb the musical independence of his interpreters.

Nearly all the celebrated singers of his age – for example Maria Malibran (1808–1836) and Wilhelmine Schröder-Devrient (1804–1860) among the sopranos, and Adolphe Nourrit (1802–1839), Gilbert-Louis Duprez (1806–1896) and Joseph Tichatschek (1807–1886) among the tenors – were noted less for their vocal perfection than for their fire and commitment. At 16 years of age Richard Wagner, seeing Schröder-Devrient, herself only aged 24, for the first time in Leipzig in 1829, was so carried away by what he called her 'Satanic ardour' that he resolved to dedicate the rest of his life to the highest

artistic ideals. He said years later: 'She had no voice, but when we heard her we thought of neither voice nor singing, so moving was her dramatic appeal.'

Among the great singers of the nineteenth century the Swedish soprano Jenny Lind (1820–1887) still stirs the imagination. She caused a sensation in 1847 when she appeared in London for the first time and won the admiration of, among others, Queen Victoria on account of her demureness of manner and purity of voice. Prudish about appearing in the theatre she retired from opera at the age of 28 and because of the brevity of her operatic career quickly became a legend.

So did Adelina Patti (1843–1919), but for exactly the opposite reason. She first sang at a concert in New York in 1850 when she was seven and bade her adoring public a final farewell in 1914 when she was 71. In between, she saw opera pass from the age of Rossini, Bellini and Donizetti to that of Verdi, Bizet and Wagner. She made her theatrical debut in 1859 as Lucia di Lammermoor. She enchanted Verdi by her singing of his operas, including *Aida*, and she even took

on, though with less success, the fiery role of Bizet's Carmen. Late in her career, in the concert hall, she sang Wagner superbly.

Great vocalist as she indisputably was, she did not pretend to be an actress. A clause in all her contracts absolved her from attendance at rehearsals, so that often she did not meet her fellow artists until the actual performance. This mattered less than it might have done since she usually addressed her arias not to her stage companions but straight to the auditorium – after having marched right down to the footlights to get as close to her public as possible. Patti's lack of involvement in the drama of a stage performance provoked the scorn of her contemporary, the American soprano Clara Louise Kellog (1842–1916). Nevertheless the beauty of Patti's voice and her instinct for expressive phrasing provided the public, like Verdi, with more than sufficient reward.

Much the same is true of Patti's successor as queen of Covent Garden (and a great favourite in New York), Nellie Melba (1859–1931), the first of many great Australian stars. Again, though no actress, she possessed a voice of such luminescent

Right These great singers range from the age of *bel canto* to the present day. Of the figures portrayed here, Guiditta Pasta was as legendary in her time as Maria Callas is to present-day opera lovers.

Jenny Lind

Adelina Patti

Guiditta Pasta

Galli Marie

Wilhelmine Schröder-Devrient

Mary Garden

beauty which enchanted audiences for nearly 40 years. Her retirement from the stage in 1926, when she was 65, signified the passing of an epoch.

In Melba's salad days, during the 1890s and the years up to the First World War, opera was at its most resplendent. The 'golden age' of opera was also the golden age of untaxed private fortunes. The self-confidence of the new American millionaires and, in England, of a hereditary aristocracy at the height of its splendour found in 'grand opera' its most satisfying symbol. Blazing with diamonds, loud with the rustling of silks, the Golden Horseshoe at the New York

Maria Callas

Rosa Ponselle

Enrico Caruso

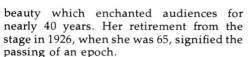

Kirsten Flagstad

Feodor Chaliapin

Metropolitan and the Grand Tier at Covent Garden represented everything that money, power and taste could bring into existence.

A decade later, when Enrico Caruso (1873–1921) had become the most idolized tenor of his time, the operatic scene had begun to change. A stronger brand of drama, a more overt emotionalism, entered the scene with composers such as Puccini and fellow Italians Pietro Mascagni (1863–1945), who wrote *Cavalleria Rusticana* (*Rustic Chivalry*, 1890), and Ruggiero Leoncavallo (1858–1919), composer of *Pagliacci* (*The Clowns*, 1892). The gramophone, to which Caruso gave respectability and which in turn gave him unprecedented fame, spread the influence of opera wider than ever before.

Like so many of the greatest operatic singers Caruso seems not to have been a very good actor except perhaps in comedy, although, unlike some others, he was a dedicated stage performer. Yet in the theatre, as on the phonograph, he touched the emotions in a way none of his rivals could approach.

Caruso's career demonstrates that while all

great singing rests on a foundation of first-rate technique, no singing that fails to go directly to the heart will ever be considered great by the opera audience. Caruso also shows that the basis of operatic acting is musicianship, an instinct for shaping sound and text so that the listener feels he is not so much being sung at as spoken to – and spoken to, moreover, personally. One fundamental quality of great singing is individuality. Good singers are sometimes interchangeable. Great singers never are.

Other artists in Caruso's time had similar gifts – for example, the Russian bass Feodor Chaliapine (1873–1938) and the American soprano Rosa Ponselle (born 1897). So, later, did the Norwegian soprano Kirsten Flagstad (1895–1962) and, closer to the present, the Greek-American soprano Maria Callas (1923–1977). They were all very different.

As the tragic protagonist of *Boris Godunov*, by the Russian composer Modeste Mussorgsky (1839–81), Chaliapine was gigantic in personality – the sort of awesome character who leaves a feeling of amazement as well

as pity in his wake. In roles such as Bellini's Norma, or Leonora in Verdi's *La Forza del Destino* (*The Force of Destiny*, 1862), Ponselle achieved an unforgettable balance between the warring elements of her artistic personality – earthiness and aristocratic fineness – so that her characterizations were both moving and sublime. The heroic Flagstad sang Wagner's later heroines like a force of nature. Through the boundless, calm radiance of her voice in full cry one understood as never before the full reach of Wagner's imagination.

In the 1950s Maria Callas, in her incomparably vibrant portrayals of Norma, Tosca, Lucia and Violetta in *Traviata*, made intelligence – the ability to comprehend motives, causes, consequences, to seize upon the essentials of any dramatic situation – into an emotional faculty. For her, analysis and feeling were one. She knew more exactly than any of her contemporaries why these characters suffered as they did, and simultaneously she absorbed that suffering into her entire stage being.

However there is evidence today to suggest that the noble art of singing is in a state of serious decline. Though there are more outstanding women than men, certain female roles, like Aida and her rival, Amneris, are becoming increasingly difficult to cast satisfactorily.

Operatic conductors

For a long time the domination of opera by star singers was virtually unchallenged except by strong-willed composers such as Verdi and Wagner, and then only in their

1△

2▽   3▽   4▽

These designs are by the British artist David Hockney for Stravinsky's *The Rake's Progress* (above) and Mozart's *The Magic Flute* (right), both for the Glyndebourne Festival Opera. In both these productions, Hockney has tried to capture the particular flavour of the story being told by both words and music. In the Stravinsky opera, the composer and librettist deliberately set out to create a modern morality play and this formalized approach is perfectly captured in Stravinsky's neo-classical music. Hockney therefore follows the same approach, with black and white as the predominant colours. The whole tone of the designs is closely linked to the work of the eighteenth century satirists. The examples shown here are the London home of the tragic hero, Tom Rakewell *(1)*, Mother Goose's brothel *(2)*, where 'the progress of the Rake begins', the auction scene *(3)* and the churchyard scene *(4)*. Here, Tom's companion and mentor, Nick Shadow, finally reveals himself as the Devil. The two play cards for Tom's soul, but, though Tom wins, the enraged Nick condemns him to insanity and Bedlam. Mozart's elaborate fantasy, however, demanded a totally different treatment from the designer. Here, Hockney has been inspired by the magical nature of the story — and the music — to create a similarly fantastical world in his designs. The opera tells the story of the quest by Tamino, the hero, and Pamina, the heroine, for truth and purity, the dominating theme being the

5△

8△

6▽

7▽

9▽

search for light. Thus, the Queen of Night *(5)*, who represents the power of evil, superstition and ignorance, is portrayed in shadow against a background of stars — her natural domain. Guided through the ordeals of fire *(7)* and water *(6)* by their love and the power of the magic flute, the couple finally achieve enlightenment at the high altar of the temple of Isis and Osiris *(8 9)* Hockney's designs have aroused controversy in the operatic world, but no one can dispute the care with which they are executed. In this, he was fortunate to be working in the conditions of a festival opera house, for the designer's task is never an easy one. It obviously involves a close liaison at all stages with the producer or stage director and very elaborate planning. Work generally begins with a close study of the libretto, backed up with records and tapes, of the opera concerned. Sometimes further study may be required. The designer then produces sketches of the scenes concerned for discussion; it is these views — with whatever modifications are necessary — that are eventually transferred to a three-dimensional model. Here, there needs to be close liaison with the technical staff of the opera house, who will have to fit the designer's demands to the resources of the stage. Lighting also must be planned, particularly where special effects are required and sets and costumes made and constructed. The whole task can take as much as a year.

own works. Then at the end of the nineteenth century a new phenomenon began to make itself felt in the opera houses of the world: the star conductor.

In 1897 the Austrian composer Gustav Mahler (1860–1911), having shown his worth as a conductor in Prague, Budapest, Hamburg and elsewhere, became artistic director of the Vienna Court Opera and inaugurated the most brilliant period in that city's operatic history. Though the company's singers were outstanding the leading star and chief guarantor of musical excitement was Mahler himself. When he resigned in 1907 standards in Vienna quickly reverted to their former, far less distinguished level.

From 1908 to 1910 Mahler conducted at New York's Metropolitan Opera House, where he shared the chief honours in the orchestra pit with the Italian Arturo Toscanini (1867–1957). Like Mahler, Toscanini was prodigiously gifted and a charismatic performer. Both were thoroughgoing autocrats. Both felt that in the opera house they carried the major responsibility for the primacy of musical matters and the realization of the composer's original intentions.

Toscanini, appointed principal conductor of La Scala, Milan, in 1898, resigned four years later because of a disagreement over his refusal to allow one of the theatre's most popular tenors, Giovanni Zenatello (1876–1949), an encore in Verdi's opera *Ballo in Maschera* (*A Masked Ball*). Toscanini returned to La Scala from 1906 to 1908 and again from 1921 to 1929, at which point he resigned rather than begin performances with the Fascist national anthem.

Italy subsequently produced several fine conductors, especially Tullio Serafin (1878–1968), Vittorio Gui (1885–1975), Victor de Sabata (1892–1967) and Guido Cantelli (1920–1956), though none ever exercised the authority that had formerly belonged to Toscanini, possibly because he had established once and for all the importance of the conductor in the creation of a first-rate operatic performance.

For similar reasons Mahler had no successor as musical 'dictator' of the Vienna Court Opera for nearly half a century, though the company, which became the Vienna State

Opera after 1918, enjoyed the services of many distinguished conductors, among them Bruno Walter (1876–1962) and Karl Böhm (born 1894). In Herbert von Karajan (born 1908), artistic director from 1956 to 1964, Mahler's view of the conductor's supremacy found a temporarily triumphant champion.

In Germany the most notable operatic conductors of the twentieth century were Wilhelm Furtwängler (1886–1954), Erich Kleiber (1890–1956) and Otto Klemperer (1885–1973). In Britain in the days before the Second World War the dominant figure was Sir Thomas Beecham (1879–1961), who combined great musical talent with a gift for

administration and who had that other essential, the financial backing to carry out his plans.

Among the many changes visible in opera since 1945 none is more far-reaching than the unwillingness of important conductors to devote the bulk of their careers to a single institution, though both La Scala and Covent Garden are fortunate in being able to rely on the dedication of their gifted music directors and chief conductors, Claudio Abbado (born 1933) and Colin Davis (born 1927) respectively. For its part, the Metropolitan has the highly talented James Levine (born 1943) who, in 1973 at the age of only 30, became the Metropolitan Opera's chief conductor and

Opera tends to use elaborate sets and costumes which are usually made in the opera house itself. Most opera houses have large staffs for wardrobe, props and sets. These costumes **(left)** are being made for the New York Met production of *Carmen*, as are the sets **(below). Left** Eric Crozier, the producer, is working with the model set for *Peter Grimes*.

Right Staging an opera is a complex process which often takes five years from inception to first night. This type of production schedule, the 'stagione' method, is used for a small repertoire. Each

3 months
Outline lighting plot ready. Extras engaged.

3-5 years
Opera decided on by management. Director, leading singers and conductor engaged.

2-3 years
Director chooses designer.

1½ years
Budget decided on.

6 months-1 year
Design agreed. Technical matters put in hand. Smaller parts cast from company. Principals begin to rehearse.

6 months
Sets and costumes started. Chorus begins to learn music.

production receives intense rehearsal followed by a short series of performances. For any revival, the production would be rehearsed almost as much as an entirely new show.

three years later its music director. In the minds of many opera lovers, he is the company's chief artistic asset.

Stage directors

Possibly because of the reluctance of most conductors to seize dictatorial power during the past half century, another figure has recently tended to gain ascendency in opera: the stage director. Unknown until the twentieth century and ubiquitous only since the 1920s, the director is nowadays responsible for all the theatrical aspects of a performance, usually decides on the designer, often chooses the choreographer and is sometimes even consulted about casting.

Max Reinhardt (1873–1943), the Austrian who helped to stage Richard Strauss's *Der Rosenkavalier* in Dresden in 1911, was one of the first directors of note to work in opera. The German Carl Ebert (born 1887), who rose to prominence in Germany in the 1920s and subsequently transferred to Glyndebourne in the mid-1930s, brought great prestige to the role of operatic director. But only since the Second World War has the star director come fully into his own.

Some have achieved notoriety by countermanding the clear intentions of composer and librettist in search of what might be called the opera's sub-text. Beginning in 1951 Wieland Wagner (1917–1966) at Bayreuth dispensed with certain features that had hitherto been taken by most people as unavoidable aspects of his grandfather's operas, especially realistic scenic details such as armour, helmets and animals.

In the 1976 *Ring* at Bayreuth the Frenchman Patrice Chéreau, dispensed, in addition, with consistency and solemnity and provoked a riot in the audience. In 1979 another Frenchman, Jean-Pierre Ponnelle (born 1932), did the same at the Metropolitan Opera with Wagner's *Der Fliegende Holländer* (*The Flying Dutchman*, 1843). He reconceived the opera as the dream of one of the minor characters. Realistic directors such as Franco Zeffirelli (born 1923) are at a disadvantage today because the cost of detailed, representational scenery has become prohibitive.

Financing opera

Despite its growing popularity, opera today is feeling the threat of financial insecurity. Government money keeps most opera houses open. Even in the United States, where subsidies are looked on with suspicion, there is often support from local government agencies. New York's two major opera houses, the Met and the City Opera, receive substantial sums each year from the New York State Council on the Arts.

Every season costs become more and more staggering. Of all the forms of serious theatre opera has the largest number of components, each requiring the services of highly skilled professionals.

A performance of *Aida*, for example, calls for a first-class soprano (Aida), mezzo-soprano (Amneris, Aida's rival), tenor (Rhadames, Aida's lover), baritone (Aida's father) and bass (High Priest); a secondary tenor (Messenger), soprano (Priestess), and bass (Amneris's father). It also calls for a chorus of about 80 mixed voices, a large crowd to fill out the pageantry scenes, a ballet troupe to provide temple dances, entertainment for Amneris and celebratory sequences, a substantial symphonic orchestra and a conductor capable of holding everything together and infusing the whole production with spirit.

Settings for *Aida* include seven scenes depicting Egypt in the time of the Pharaohs, palace interiors, the Temple of Vulcan, Amneris's boudoir, a royal parade ground, the banks of the Nile by moonlight and a two-tier scene showing the Temple of Vulcan above and a burial crypt below. There must be costumes for everyone from the King down to the meanest onlooker.

All of this is merely for the visible part of the production. In addition there is a repetiteur who prompts the singers and must be a trained musician, a huge backstage work crew for lighting, scene-shifting and other technical operations, administrative staff and maintenance workers, seamstresses, tailors, wig stylists, make-up artists, dressers, carpenters, electricians, barmen, secretaries and stage-door keepers.

A major opera house such as Covent Garden, the Met or La Scala employs more than 1,000 people, not including supers. It is little wonder that in modern times certain heads of opera houses should have developed megalomaniacal tendencies. Sir Rudolf Bing (born 1902), general manager of the Met from 1950 to 1972, once said that every decision in connection with the company down to the casting of the smallest part was his responsibility alone. Today in his place at the Met there is an executive director, a music director and a director of production.

Planning a production

No two companies are run in exactly the same way but of necessity they must go about certain aspects of their work in similar fashion. Leading singers, the supply of which seems to be constantly dwindling, now have to be signed up as much as three years in advance. No well-run company would dream of scheduling an opera such as Puccini's *Turandot* (1926), for example, unless it could count on the services of a soprano capable of meeting most of the composer's nearly superhuman vocal demands.

Another element that must be settled well in advance is the designer, who is usually chosen after consultation with the director since if they are not of like mind the director will find it impossible to realize his intentions. In a period of dizzily rising costs it is fatal to encourage a designer whose imagination can only express itself in terms of lavishness. Although the fees of star singers are climbing faster than anything else, no opera house with the highest standards can do without a certain number of top performers. Therefore managements now tend to economize on scenery, preferring sets that are light, spare and capable of being used with projections.

Today, budgets are scrutinized as never before, since serious overspending will threaten the house's future, especially in the United States, where subsidies form only a small part of the company's income. Once a budget for a new production has been agreed the director must keep within its bounds. He can leave nothing to last-minute chance. All the sets and costumes should be finished six months before the première and the lighting plot ready three months in advance.

The singers — almost invariably contracted to be on hand from the first rehearsal of a new production to the final performance — usually rehearse for three weeks. At the start they work on their stage movements to piano accompaniment. Eventually they progress to orchestral accompaniment — an expensive way to rehearse but vital for top-quality results.

By the time of the dress rehearsal, some two to five days before the first night, all is more or less ready. In fact, dress rehearsals are usually open to the public, though probably by special invitation only. At that point no major changes can be entertained. The only thing a director can do is give notes to his cast and backstage crew about details to be corrected at the premiere.

The most remarkable thing about all these logistic complexities is that from them, season after season, come so many memorable artistic results.

5-6 weeks	1 month	3 weeks	1½ weeks	5 days	3-5 days	2-3 days	First night
Rehearsals for cast to piano accompaniment. Technical rehearsals (sets and lighting) on Sundays.	Set completed (but can still be altered)	Orchestral rehearsals begin in separate room.	Stage rehearsals to piano accompaniment	Stage movements to orchestral accompaniment	Sitzprobe (cast sing to orchestra accompaniment but do not act) Costumes finished. Piano and dress rehearsals.	General rehearsal	of new production

CONCERTS

FROM SALOMON AND HAYDN TO THE MODERN CONCERT

Concerts have become so much a part of artistic life around the civilized world that it is hard to realize that, in their present form, they are a comparatively modern phenomenon, indicative of the switch from more people listening to music than actually performing it. This change has taken place over the past 100 years and particularly over the past 50.

During this era there has been an enormous increase in the actual amount of musical activity, not only in concerts but also in the field of recorded music. Vast numbers of people with little or no knowledge of music and no ability to play, attend concerts, enjoy them and even criticize them. In earlier times the time now spent at concerts would have been spent performing music at home.

The history of concerts

A concert can be defined as the performance of musical works before an audience, who are admitted, in most cases, on payment. In Britain the practice began in London during the seventeenth century under the aegis of the musician John Banister (1630 – 1679). It was considerably expanded during the eighteenth century by the formation of various organizations with the express purpose of presenting musical programmes, among which the Salomon concerts at the end of that century are the most famous by virtue of the association of Josef Haydn (1732 – 1809) with them. Salomon had quarrelled with the organizers of the professional concerts and had struck out independently with his own subscription series given at the Hanover Square Rooms, where he produced symphonies by Haydn and Wolfgang Amadeus Mozart (1756 – 1791) in the 1780s.

Then in 1790 and 1795, he engaged Haydn himself to appear at his concerts and this proved an unprecedented success. It was at Salomon's instigation that the composer wrote *The Creation* although this was first performed in Vienna.

In Vienna, as in many other European centres, the beginnings of concert life arose from the activity in court chapels (hence the term *Kapellmeister*) and through private patronage. The emperor was one of the main patrons of music in the Austrian capital and also in Innsbruck and Prague for some 300 years. From the end of the eighteenth century there were also concerts in the public gardens and meadow by the Danube, similar to the London events at Ranelagh and Marylebone Gardens.

At first these appear to have been informal affairs, possibly in the open; later concert rooms were built. Works by many well-known composers, including Mozart and Ludwig van Beethoven (1770 – 1827), were given there. The Vienna Philharmonic, most notable of Austrian orchestras, began its history in 1842 under the baton of the composer K. O. E. Nicolai (1810 – 1849), a professional

Above Concerts have varied considerably through the ages. A consort of six musicians **(top)** play at the wedding feast of Sir Henry Unton. They accompany a masque, being performed by players in costume. In this eighteenth century painting **(middle)** a family group of amateur musicians gather around the piano to make music.

The Chicago Symphony Orchestra **(bottom)** are playing in a concert conducted by Hungarian-born Georg Solti, its musical director since 1969. **Right** This picture shows an ornate eighteenth century concert hall. The magnificent baroque architecture and domed ceiling would, however have distorted the sound of the music.

orchestra at last taking over the role until then assigned to amateur musicians. From that time it gradually grew in importance and has numbered among its musical directors most of the famous Austrian and German conductors.

Developments in the German states went along similar lines to those in Austria. Berlin was the most important centre. In the eighteenth century, Frederick the Great, that most musical of monarchs, had his own private orchestra.

Out of the various nineteenth century amateur orchestras giving occasional concerts, developed the Berlin Philharmonic in 1882, and the Court Orchestra which played for the opera but also gave concerts. So that, as in other European centres, concert giving, as we recognize it today, really began to become prominent about that time.

Well into the nineteenth century, listening to music in Italy meant going to a cathedral or church and hearing choirs and sacred music, or going to the opera, although there were also private court orchestras giving chamber concerts to the aristocracy in the seventeenth and eighteenth centuries. The Academy of St Cecilia, previously concerned with ecclesiastical music, established itself as a concert organization towards the end of the nineteenth century. The Philharmonic Academy of Rome, founded in 1821, did not begin to give concerts in any real sense until much later in the century.

Predictably, France, and Paris in particular, has had a longer history of music making for the public. The famous *Concerts Spirituels* were started in 1725. They were interrupted by the French Revolution but revived in 1805.

There were several such groups giving concerts in the same period. The *Société des Concerts du Conservatoire*, begun in 1828, have continued to the present day as has the *Société Philharmonique*, begun by Hector Berlioz (1803–1869) in the 1850–51 season. But the more modern kind of concert started, as in the rest of Europe, about 1880 in Paris under the aegis of the violinists and conductors Edouard Colonne (1838–1910) and Charles Lamoureux (1834–1899).

In London, the Philharmonic Society began to give concerts in 1813 at the Argyll Rooms near Oxford Circus. Gradually more and more venues became available or were purpose-built for giving concerts, the most important being St James's Hall, Piccadilly, built in 1858 for smaller events, and the Royal Albert Hall in 1871 which satisfied Victorian taste for the grandiose. It was closely followed by the popular Queen's Hall in 1893. The London Symphony Orchestra, the first major orchestra in the capital, was founded in 1904.

Thus, taking these four centres as reasonable examples of what was happening throughout Europe, we gain a picture of small but differing beginnings developing

into a relatively uniform series of well-established and well-attended orchestral, chamber and choral concerts. By the end of the nineteenth century these were being presented by fully-employed professional musicians.

Naturally, the improvement in communications was an aid to that uniformity and a work like a symphony by Johannes Brahms (1833–1897) could be given its première in one centre and be heard in others before many months were out. Such works which were being written from Beethoven's time onwards virtually required the kind of good-sized concert hall that was the *sine qua non* of concert-giving from about 1880; and the audiences were there to fill the larger halls. The concert as we know it today was thus now well established.

The United States soon caught the habit of concert promotion. The earliest known public 'concert of musik on sundry instruments' in North America took place at Boston on December 30, 1731, in Mr Pelham's Great Room. The various societies that sprang up during the next century were more or less dependent on 'imported' music, most of it from the German-speaking countries, and many of the musicians, as has been the case almost until today, have come from that part of Europe.

In 1881, the American philanthropist Henry Lee Higginson (1834–1919) formed the Boston Symphony Orchestra which was to 'play the best music in the best way and give concerts to all who could pay a small price', an aspiration, except with regard to price, that has been fulfilled until this day.

In New York, amateur orchestras came into existence in the late eighteenth century. The English traditions of the early inhabitants were soon nourished by German musicians. Choral societies and therefore choral works tended to predominate in the early days. Serious professional activity began with the formation in 1842 of the New York Philharmonic Society. It gradually increased in importance and size, boasting among its orchestra's conductors many of the greatest names. Philadelphia, at the start, rivalled New York in musical activity. After some flagging of interest in the middle of the nineteenth century there was a renewed interest in concerts about 1895 followed by the formation of the Philadelphia Orchestra in 1900. Chicago had, in fact, beaten Philadelphia to having its own orchestra by the formation of the Chicago Symphony Orchestra in 1891. So, as in Europe, or perhaps following in its shadow, America had established its own tradition of major

Above Although La Scala, Milan, is best-known as one of the most important operatic centres in the world, concerts are also regularly held here.

Above left This Promenade Concert at Queen's Hall took place in 1895. These concerts, at which part of the audience stand or walk around, were started by Henry Wood. **Above** Colin Davis conducts the First Night of the Proms, 1977.

concerts by the turn of the century.

In many people's minds, concert-going may not seem to have altered much since that time. It may have expanded vastly. In Tokyo, Adelaide and Los Angeles, one will find musical activity no less vigorous than that available in the older centres already mentioned and discussed.

The number of people who go to concerts has risen correspondingly with the increase in education. At the same time, with the enormous improvement in post-war transport facilities, it is possible for the same artist to appear in one city one evening and another the next. In this way, standards, and they are high, are much the same all over the world. Repertory is similar; orchestras fairly uniform.

Yet, if we look more closely, much has changed during the eight decades of the twentieth century. If we take repertory first, it may be true to say that concert promoters are not falling over themselves to perform new music, but they are programming a much more diverse list of works than was the case even 20 years ago. Above all, interest has gradually increased in Gustav Mahler (1860–1911) whose nine symphonies and *Das Lied von der Erde* are now as much staple fare as the orchestral pieces of Brahms, whose own contemporary, Anton Bruckner (1824–1896), has found a regular place in the hearts of many conductors, orchestras and audiences.

The French repertory of Berlioz, Claude Débussy (1862–1918), Maurice Ravel (1875–1937) is much performed. Among more recent composers, Dmitri Shostakovich (1906–1975), Igor Stravinsky (1882–1971), Benjamin Britten (1913–1976), and Béla Bartók (1881–1945) find a good deal of favour. In each centre there may be a particular bias towards one or other of these groups of composers.

Today there is certainly a greater distinction between the styles preferred by different orchestras and, perhaps, by different publics. Whereas in the earlier years of concert giving the German tradition was in the ascendant, orchestras now cultivate their own flavour.

There is the homogeneity of the Berlin Philharmonic, under its inspiring conductor Herbert von Karajan (born 1908), the svelte string character of the Vienna Philharmonic, the mercurial brilliance of the London Symphony, the big mellow sonority of the Chicago Symphony, the crisp solemnity of the Amsterdam Concertgebouw which is another orchestra with a long tradition of consistently fine performances.

The differences between the sound to be heard from any of these orchestras make their visits to the concert halls of other countries the special occasions they have become. In no field is it more true that variety is the spice of life.

Below right This diagram shows the standard seating plan for a modern orchestra. The different families of instruments — strings, woodwind, brass and percussion — are grouped together. The strings include the first and second violins, who perform different 'parts', the violas and the cellos and double basses. The woodwind instruments consist of flutes, including here a piccolo, oboes, clarinets and bassoons. The brass instruments include horns, trumpets, trombones and tuba. The percussion section contains, in this example a harpsichord, glockenspiel, tubular bells, xylophone, timpani, bass drum and cymbals. A harp is also included among the stringed instruments in this example. The large symphony orchestra such as this one dates from the nineteenth century. Composers do vary both the kind and numbers of instruments used. The percussion section particularly can be very varied in the modern orchestra and often includes the triangle, gong, tambourine and castanets. The piano, although strictly speaking a stringed instrument, is sometimes included in this section when it is used for its 'percussive' rather than melodic effect. The seating arrangement of the orchestra does, of course, affect the sound of the music and many composers and conductors will alter the typical layout of the orchestra in order to achieve a particular musical effect.

Organization and work of the modern orchestra

The London Symphony Orchestra, like many international orchestras is self-governing, with many of its directors also players. They are thus responsible for liaising with sponsors, agents, promotors and conductors, as well as overseeing the general administrative business including arranging rehearsals, concerts, recordings and tours. The personnel included on the tour consisted of 98 players and, among others, 2 stage managers, 3 conductors, 1 soloist, 3 administrators, 1 librarian (to look after the music), 1 personnel manager and several wives. Touring forms a large part of the orchestra's activities and any one tour requires formidable organization. The LSO's East European Tour in 1977 involved the performance of 19 concerts in 25 days.

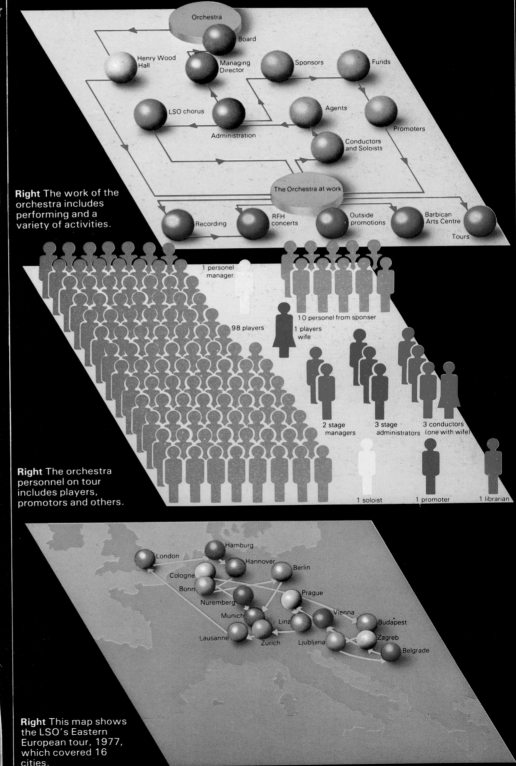

Right The work of the orchestra includes performing and a variety of activities.

Right The orchestra personnel on tour includes players, promotors and others.

Right This map shows the LSO's Eastern European tour, 1977, which covered 16 cities.

Orchestras and audiences

Audiences also differ greatly, as any peripatetic musician will acknowledge. Nowhere is attention more concentrated than in Japan where the growing interest in music-making of all kinds has brought forward a well-informed and attentive public.

In the United States, spontaneous enthusiasm is often the order of the day. Those whom the Americans take to their hearts remain there and are féted accordingly.

The British tend to be thoughtful, also, perhaps, more knowledgeable in their responses. Most artists say that a warm response from a British audience is a sign that they have fulfilled themselves. Austrians are even more discriminating but perhaps less generous. The Dutch love to jump to their feet in standing ovations. The French are not averse to the 'boo'; neither are the Germans, although this happens more often in the opera house.

Every concert hall has its own acoustics and induces different reactions. The homes of the Philadelphia and Boston are so congenial in this respect that they no doubt account for the welcoming response. The dry acoustics in London's Festival Hall demand an extra effort from the performers to promote real enthusiasm. The warm acoustics of Hollywood Bowl promote an extremely enthusiastic response in the audience.

Of course, the layout of the orchestra will affect the sound. Before the Second World War it was quite customary for conductors to place the second violins on the right, opposite the firsts. It is now usual for the seconds to sit on the same side but behind the firsts, to assist ensemble if not acoustical balance.

Some conductors now place the cellos on their right but others favour the violas in that position. Double basses will usually be behind them on the right although on occasion they will be at the back centre, perhaps behind the woodwind who almost invariably take a middle place in front of the conductor's eyes. The brass will be aligned on the right next to the basses; the percussion on the left.

Leopold Stokowski (1882–1977) was the greatest individualist in the placing of his orchestra. He was not beyond having his strings, basses excepted, placed in serried ranks on his left, the woodwind on his right and the whole brass amassed in the centre; and there were many other permutations. The results were usually arresting.

Conductors adopt different procedures in both conducting and 'acting'. Karajan stands almost motionless, directs his players with his eyes and uses very few gestures. The British conductor Sir Adrian Boult (born 1889) was accustomed to give almost all his directions with simple gestures of his right hand. The American Leonard Bernstein (born 1918) is renowned for lifting himself off the podium in an excess of zeal and emotion. The French composer and conductor

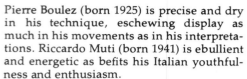

Pierre Boulez (born 1925) is precise and dry in his technique, eschewing display as much in his movements as in his interpretations. Riccardo Muti (born 1941) is ebullient and energetic as befits his Italian youthfulness and enthusiasm.

It is the individuality and eccentricities of the conductor which can galvanize an orchestra into exceptional action and give particular character and inflection to a reading. It also adds the unpredictability of the 'live' occasion of a concert that no studio-made record can achieve, however perfect in term of notes that performance may be.

Similarly, the corporate effort of listening – or, in some cases, attention wandering – is something almost tangible at a concert, catching and holding a mood unerringly. A soloist as well as a conductor can achieve it. Korean violinist Kyung-Wha Chung (born 1948) of the younger generation, the British pianist Sir Clifford Curzon (born 1907) of the older, are among those who by the personal magnetism of their playing can grasp an audience and convince it that their way is the only way to interpret the music in hand.

However, many modern concert-goers tend to regard the small as being beautiful. Chamber-music concerts have, of course, always been considered by a significant section of the musical public as the most pure and satisfying form of the art and, if anything, that opinion has been bolstered in recent times by the increasing number of quartets playing to devoted audiences.

In the last 20 years there has also been a revival of interest in medieval and preclassical music. Instruments such as the rebec, crumhorn and cornett have been rescued from the obscurity of the museum and given a fresh life in concert.

At the other end of the time scale, today's composers have written for small groups of modern instruments, or in some cases the same player has been required to play a number of instruments in the same work.

An element of economic necessity may have been a factor in the development of these groups and their repertory, but there is no doubt that they now form a vital part of concert life in several Western capitals. Their programmes also have a degree of informal-

Left Chamber music groups, such as those illustrated here, always perform in a room or small concert hall as distinct from a theatre, church or large concert hall. Such music, played by a small group of musicians, with all of them soloists on equal terms, had its origins in the private entertainments sponsored by the nobility in eighteenth century Europe.

Below The best conductors and soloists control not only the orchestra but also the audience. Georg Solti **(below** and **below right)**, is always in command of the performance. Benjamin Britten **(centre)** whose style was much less flamboyant, had immense rapport with the audience, as does Bernard Haitink **(bottom left)**. The Korean violinist, Kyung-Wha Chung **(bottom right)** also has a magnetic hold over the audience.

Above Pierre Boulez, French composer and conductor, rehearses the BBC Symphony Orchestra for a concert in London's Royal Festival Hall in November, 1972.

ity missing from the concerts of large orchestras and therefore often a greater degree of audience participation.

Another extension of concert activity, one particularly noticeable in the United States, is the college concert. Indeed, throughout campuses in North America, large music faculties encourage enthusiastic performance and the degree of experimentation is considerable.

Although the tendency in the 1970s has, perhaps, been away from the extremes of the avant-garde encountered in the 1960s when instruments and ear were often assaulted to the limits of their tolerances, there is still no lack of searching for new sonorities and new instrumental combinations.

Another important part of concert life is the solo recital. Of course, J. S. Bach (1685 – 1750) on the organ and Mozart on the clavichord were distinguished exponents of their instruments. However, the virtuoso recital, as such, was probably the product of the Romantic Movement which threw up such geniuses of execution as Nicolo Paganini (1782 – 1840) and Franz Liszt (1811 – 1886), both composers as well, who won prestige and financial reward for their prodigious deeds on violin and piano.

Since those heady days of the nineteenth century, there has never been a shortage of brilliant players to thrill audiences, but in these more sober days, there is a greater concentration on music for its own sake.

The pianist tackling a complete cycle of Beethoven sonatas in the concert hall is now perhaps a more common phenomenon than a virtuoso running through a glib programme of showpieces. Yet the exercise of personal magnetism, that indefinable factor which distinguishes a great artist from a good one, still counts for much, and indeed, is still that which brings in the paying audience.

It is perhaps not very profitable to speculate on what the future may bring, but it is still an absorbing occupation. Some people feel strongly that recorded music and the increasing difficulty in getting about city centres, may make the concert obsolete, but at the moment that is a distant prospect. There are others who think that for financial reasons the large-scale event will give way increasingly to the small-scale one. There is certainly evidence that orchestras rely more and more on what is termed the 'museum repertory', works written fifty or more years ago.

As is the case in opera, few works written in the last half-century have found their way into the repertory; two major exceptions are the very popular Britten's *War Requiem* and Shostakovich's Fifteenth Symphony.

However, concerts remain at the centre of musical activity. At their best they remain unique experiences of collective enjoyment and, as such, an essential part of our cultural heritage.

BALLET AND DANCE

FROM DAUBERVAL TO NUREYEV AND MODERN DANCE FORMS

BALLET

In 1789, the year of the French Revolution, a company of dancers gave a première at Bordeaux. They danced the ballet still known as *La Fille Mal Gardée* before an audience from this old town of shippers and wine merchants, and this can be seen as the birth of ballet as we know it today. *La Fille Mal Gardée* still remains in the repertoires of the world's ballet companies in a form that the historic audience would probably recognize.

The art of mime, music and dance as a form of entertainment had been conceived much earlier but it took more than 200 years to develop. That production at Bordeaux told a story in dance and mime without words and was directed by the French dancer and choreographer Jean Dauberval (1742–1806), devoted pupil of the great French dance innovator, Jean-Georges Noverre (1727–1810). In 1760, Noverre made the first ever statement of the principles of ballet.

Noverre passionately outlined these principles in his now famous *Lettres sur la Danse et le Ballet*. He called for an end to meaningless gestures that played no part in telling the story, and to the often elaborate masks the dancers wore to show anger, happiness or love. Ballet, said Noverre, was like a beautiful language – but you had to put the letters in the right order to make words and sentences or it was pointless. The principal dancers of the Paris Opéra were unimpressed. Noverre left Paris and toured the capitals of Europe teaching choreography for almost 20 years before he returned to put his ideas into practice.

Early development

With Dauberval's Bordeaux production, ballet emerged as an art form in its own right. However, ballet had been earlier given enthusiastic royal patronage by Louis XIV. He loved dancing and frequently took part in the dance presentations at Versailles. In 1661 he created the Royal Academy of Dance. But it was a part of the Paris Opéra and ballet remained merged with the singing, and the elaborate sets of the seventeenth and early eighteenth century theatre.

At the Drury Lane Theatre in London in 1717, John Weaver (1673–1760) staged *The Loves of Mars and Venus* – a story told entirely in mime and dance. But it seems to have been a one-off novelty. It certainly did not lead to a British ballet tradition – Britain had to wait more than 200 years for that which eventually came mainly through the efforts of two remarkable women, Dame Ninette de Valois (born 1898) and Dame Marie Rambert (born 1888).

Not all Noverre's principles, so admired today, were evident in the first great classic ballets, created in France – *La Fille Mal Gardée*, *La Sylphide* (1832), *Giselle* (1841), *Coppélia* (1870) and *Sylvia* (1876). The principles were also ignored by the great French

Top Jean-Georges Noverre was the father of modern ballet.
Above left Ninette de Valois was the founder of the Royal Ballet.

Above right Marie Rambert is one of the greatest of modern ballet teachers.

choreographer Marius Petipa (1818–1910), who worked in Russia for half a century. He created a huge number of works for the Imperial Russian Ballet in St Petersburg, with the help of his Russian assistant Lev Ivanov (1834–1901). These ballets include the famous classics by Tchaikovsky *The Sleeping Beauty*, *Swan Lake* and *The Nutcracker*, and also works like *Don Quixote*, *La Bayadère* and *Raymonda*, with less distinguished but very tuneful musical scores.

Giselle and *La Sylphide* were romantic pieces, peopled with spirits and ghosts – the *corps de ballet* of ladies in white. This is still regarded by many as an essential part of classical ballet. These ballets tend to end tragically with broken love, madness and death. Petipa's ballets were much more cheerful, ending with wedding celebrations and *divertissements* or displays of dancing virtuosity in different styles. His ballets did include the white *corps de ballet*, but he always added ballet-style versions of folk-dances from Russia, Hungary, Spain or Arabia.

All these old ballets had one thing in common – a central ballerina role. The ballerina and the female *corps de ballet* did most of the dancing, though there were speciality and national dances for the men. The poetic

princes who fell in love with the heroines rarely had much dancing to do. Their function was to look noble and to support and lift the ballerina. Modern productions of these ballets invariably insert dances for the principal men, an innovation developed and exploited by the Russian emigrant, Rudolf Nureyev (born 1938).

An earthier, folksier type of ballet, inhabited by real people rather than fairies and spirits, was created in Denmark by another French choreographer, August Bournonville (1805–1879), who came from a family of dancers. His career bears similiarities to that of Petipa. Bournonville was the founder-choreographer of the Royal Danish Ballet while Petipa founded Russian ballet. But Denmark did not have a Diaghilev or a revolution and Danish ballet remained largely unknown abroad until the middle of the twentieth century, when foreign critics discovered it and Danish dancers began to tour the world. Bournonville's version of *La Sylphide* is the version generally performed nowadays and extracts from his *Napoli* are familiar to ballet audiences all over the world.

The stories of the classical ballets cannot be taken too seriously and the music, tuneful and danceable though it is, rarely has any real connection with the period and place in which the action is allegedly taking place. The first twentieth century revolution in ballet tried to change all this. Mikhail Fokine (1880–1942), who created ballets for the legendary Russian dancers Anna Pavlova (1881–1931) and Vaslav Nijinsky (1888–1950), reformulated Noverre's principles.

Ballet, he argued, should not be a series of dances built around a ballerina, but should flow as a story with a perfect blend of dance, music and decor – with all four ingredients designed to be of equal importance. Fokine did not always succeed in this aim, but ballets like *Les Sylphides* (often confused with *La Sylphide* but actually a short abstract work), *Petrouchka*, *The Firebird* and *Spectre de la Rose* became the second generation of ballet classics. *The Swan*, often known as *The Dying Swan*, was Pavlova's signature dance and is probably the best remembered and most performed dance solo in the world.

Diaghilev and his followers

It was a former Russian law student who launched this revolution in ballet on to the receptive audiences of the twentieth century. Sergey Diaghilev (1872–1929) abandoned his law books for the stimulating company of young artists, writers and musicians. He became an impresario. In 1909 he took ballet back to Paris, its birthplace, and remained in the West to create a new taste for ballet and to spread it to wider audiences than ever before. Every major movement of modern ballet can be traced to the wealth of talent stemming from Diaghilev.

One of his star dancers, Serge Lifar (born

Below Anna Pavlova is probably the most celebrated of all ballerinas.
Right Nijinsky's Golden Slave in *Schéhérazade* around 1911, a role created for him, with choreography by Fokine and music by Rimsky-Korsakov, caused a sensation at the time.

Below This print shows Maria Taglioni as La Sylphide, her greatest role and one created especially for her. The ballet, first performed at the Paris Opéra in 1832, marked the beginning of Romantic ballet.
Bottom Rudolf Nureyev dances *The Sleeping Beauty*.

Left Sergei Diaghilev, who presented his celebrated Ballets Russes in Paris for the first time in 1909, was the greatest of ballet impresarios. His genius lay in gathering around him the most talented dancers, composers, painters and choreographers of his day, all of whom produced works of remarkable distinction for Diaghilev's company. Among the famous composers and artists who worked with him were Picasso, Stravinsky, Cocteau and Satie.

1909) gave new life to the moribund Paris Opéra. Another, Ninette de Valois, created Sadler's Wells Ballet which later became Britain's Royal Ballet. It was Diaghilev who launched Nijinsky on the Western world. Marie Rambert, who helped Nijinsky to stage his *Rite of Spring*, formed Britain's very first ballet company which was named after her and now specializes in modern dance.

Two of Diaghilev's youngest dancers, Alicia Markova (born 1910) and Anton Dolin (born 1904) became the first stars of British ballet. The great Russian's last choreographer, George Balanchine (born 1904), founded the New York City Ballet, one of the world's finest classical companies.

There was a popular explosion of ballet enthusiasm from this brilliant spring. Pavlova, with her own company, was a powerful ambassador. She toured the world, inspiring countless young girls to want to dance. Then she turned dancers into teachers so that there was someone to do the teaching.

One, Edouard Borovansky (1902–1959) launched the first regular company in Australia. Another of the thousands inspired by Pavlova was Sir Frederick Ashton (born 1904). He became director of the Royal Ballet and is recognized as Britain's greatest choreographer and one of the greatest of all time.

Today de Valois' Royal Ballet and Balanchine's New York City Ballet have given birth to new companies in their turn. Dancers and choreographers trained in London have directed and performed with companies all over the Commonwealth, in Turkey and in Iran. Sir Robert Helpmann (born 1909) who, like Ashton, was brought to ballet by Pavlova, became the first regular partner of Dame Margot Fonteyn (born 1919) and an

exciting dramatic choreographer before returning to his native Australia to become co-director of the Australian Ballet, founded by former Sadler's Wells ballerina Peggy van Praagh (born 1910). Another Sadler's Wells ballerina, Celia Franca (born 1921), founded the National Ballet of Canada and was succeeded by Alexander Grant (born 1925), for many years one of the Royal Ballet's brightest stars. Antony Tudor (born 1909), a choreographer first discovered and encouraged by Rambert but then not sufficiently employed in Britain, emigrated to the United States where he not only made outstanding ballets but also became for many years a guiding figure of American Ballet Theatre, another of the world's leading companies which was founded in New York in 1939.

The most influential of all the Royal Ballet's foreign ambassadors was John Cranko (1927–1973), the South African choreographer who started his career at Sadler's Wells in London and then put Stuttgart in West Germany back on the ballet map for the first time since Noverre by creating a company there which rapidly became acknowledged as one of the finest in the world. He made a whole repertory of highly successful new ballets, including a full-length version of Pushkin's *Eugene Onegin*, new versions of Stravinsky's *Card Game* and Prokofiev's *Romeo and Juliet*, and drastically revised versions of *Swan Lake* and *The Nutcracker*. He also developed a talented ensemble of dancers of many nationalities, headed by the Brazilian ballerina Marcia Haydée (born 1939), the American Richard Cragun (born 1944) and the Danish Egon Madsen (born 1942) all three of whom became international stars. Cranko's premature death in 1973, at the age of 45, was a tragedy.

His contemporary, the Scottish choreographer Kenneth MacMillan (born 1929), followed in his footsteps by going to West Berlin, which already had a fairly successful ballet, as director. He created new versions of *Swan Lake* and *The Sleeping Beauty*, and several important short ballets, including *Anastasia*, which he developed into a three-act work when he succeeded Ashton as director of the Royal Ballet in 1970. Unfortunately, his creativity seemed to fade with administrative responsibilities and his reign with the Royal Ballet proved controversial. Many dancers left the company and the repertoire was criticized for lack of interest.

Balanchine's influence has naturally been mainly in the United States, where virtually every city and university now has a ballet school, and where a number of regional companies regularly perform his own ballets, as well as other ballets in his distinctive, abstract, neo-classical style. Balanchine's ballets are also extensively staged all over the world and one of his former ballerinas, Patricia Neary (born 1942), became director of the ballet company in Geneva, Switzerland. Suzanne Farrell (born 1945), one of his most

distinguished ballerinas, in 1970 joined the determinedly modernistic 'Ballet of the 20th Century' company in Brussels, Belgium. This company was founded in 1960 by the French dancer and choreographer Maurice Béjart (born 1927). Farrell stimulated Béjart's choreography into a more classical style.

Balanchine's New York City Ballet has also provided a home for Jerome Robbins (born 1918), an American choreographer of Russian ancestry, whose work ranges from the dazzling show-business dances of *West Side Story* and *Fiddler on the Roof* to the romantic classicism of *Dances at a Gathering* and the comic virtuosity of *The Four Seasons*. A great choreographer in his own right, he has sometimes been underestimated because of his commercial theatre work and because of working in the shadow of Balanchine.

Another important American choreographer, John Neumeier (born 1942), emerged via the Royal Ballet School in London and John Cranko's company in Stuttgart to become the director of companies in West Germany, first in Frankfurt and then in Hamburg. Like Cranko, he has now produced an enormous body of varied ballets, many with involved intellectual ideas and themes, but also some which are purely abstract. He seems set to take Cranko's place as the leading choreographer-director in Germany, but is, curiously, unrecognized in his native United States.

All these choreographers have participated in the second revolution in twentieth century ballet – the reaction against Fokine's principles and, incidentally, against most of his ballets. This reaction has taken several forms – the revival of interest in full-length nineteenth century classics, the revival of forgotten works, the revision of well-known ones, the creation of new works in the same style and the creation of short abstract ballets, interpretations of music and movement which use no decor or drama.

Balanchine has created a vast repertory of these ballets, using composers such as Bach, Webern, Sousa, Johann Strauss, Gershwin and Hershy Kay. He has influenced not only a new generation of choreographers, but also created a new breed of dancer, capable of prodigious speed, musicality and virtuosity, but not greatly concerned with emotion or interpretation.

The third revolution is the new crossbreeding between classical ballet and more experimental forms of dance. In recent years Nureyev has appeared with the companies run by American dancer, teacher, choreographer and director Martha Graham (born 1894) and another American choreographer and dancer Paul Taylor (born 1930). Graham has collaborated with Balanchine, while modern American choreographers like Taylor, Merce Cunningham (born 1919) and Twyla Tharp (born 1942) have staged works for the Royal Danish Ballet, the Paris Opéra and American Ballet Theatre. One of the

Above Anton Dolin and Alicia Markova dance for the Festival Ballet, a company they set up in 1949 after a successful world tour together.

Above Robert Helpmann is seen here as Don Quixote. **Left** This photograph of Ashton, Fonteyn and Nureyev was taken in 1962.

Right Margot Fonteyn is seen here with George Balanchine after the revival at Covent Garden of his *Ballet Imperial* in 1950. **Below** Antony Tudor rehearses his ballet *Shadowplay*, created for and produced by the Royal Ballet in 1967. Anthony Dowell and Merle Park danced the leading roles.

Above John Cranko, seen here rehearsing the ballet, *Card Game,* was responsible for building up the Stuttgart Ballet into one of the world's leading companies.

greatest personal successes of the Russian emigrant dancer Mikhail Baryshnikov (born 1948) was in Tharp's jazzy, cabaret-like *Push Comes to Shove* in 1976. There is also a whole new breed of choreographers working in a combination of classical and modern styles. In Britain both Norman Morrice (born 1931) and Peter Darrell (born 1929), who founded Scottish Theatre Ballet, later Scottish Ballet, in 1969, have made both classical and modern works, while in the United States Twyla Tharp has moved from the extremes of the avant-garde to the choreography for the movie of *Hair*.

Glen Tetley (born 1926), an American choreographer, made his name with experimental works for the Netherlands Dance Theatre and Ballet Rambert. Tetley went on to succeed Cranko, for a brief period, as director of the Stuttgart Ballet and to create numerous works using classical technique for the world's major companies. He uses music as an atmospheric background rather than an exact accompaniment to the dance.

In the Netherlands, classical and modern techniques have been combined by the modern Dutch choreographers Rudi van Dantzig (born 1933), Hans van Manen (born 1932) and Toer van Schayk (born 1936).

The modern style abandons point work and the five positions to make the dancer walk on flat feet, lie on the ground and do a lot of seemingly gymnastic work. Music becomes simply a background atmosphere, as in a movie soundtrack. Often long sections are choreographed with no music at all — the silence punctuated only by the heavy breathing and foot-tapping of the dancers. This modern approach to ballet is intended to recognize that dancing and movement are the most important elements in ballet. Alongside the brilliant, stirringly musical beauty of classical ballet, some critics find it unattractive and not easy to watch.

The techniques

More people watch ballet today than ever before, even if many of this mass audience do not even pretend to understand what it is all about. They like the music, they like the physical excitement of the dance and its aesthetic beauty, they respond to its emotional force and sheer sex appeal. Knowing the good from the bad is easy, almost instinctive, but it is not easy to distinguish the good from the merely indifferent. Nor is it easy to define ballet in today's liberal marriage of classical ballet and contemporary dance.

Pure ballet is based on a very precise technique, which has to be learned from childhood and which can be mastered only by hard work and constant practice. The essentials are the ability to jump, to do complicated beaten steps with the legs and feet, which have to be turned out sideways from the hips, to move gracefully and musically, and — in the case of women — to dance on the points of the toes. This technique is based on five positions of the legs and feet, coupled with appropriate arm positions. Ballet can be defined in its simplest terms as dancing which is based on these positions, using that technique.

Many ballets today use bare feet instead of toe shoes for the ladies, require 'turned in' instead of 'turned out' feet, do not call for any 'elevation' or jumping, and are performed in silence or to electronic and other sound-tracks. Dancers are left to count the time to themselves rather than to follow music. It is now sometimes impossible to tell where ballet ends and mime, acrobatics, social dancing or just vaguely expressive movement begin. Ballet dancers are now even called upon to speak or sing and to do naturalistic acting instead of just conveying meaning and emotion through dance and conventional mime.

Dancers start training around the age of 10, and must do rigorous daily classes for the rest of their working lives. Their careers can be suddenly terminated by injury or illness. At best, they normally end in early middle age, just when other people are beginning to reap the fruits of success. They then face the problems of readjustment to teaching, production work, retirement or totally new careers. However, some like Massine and Helpmann, are able to continue dancing and acting careers into old age, while Fonteyn, the exception to most rules, was still dancing in her late fifties.

Brevity is one reason for the long-standing prejudice against dancing as a career for men. The other prejudice – that dancing is a feminine activity – is evaporating. Both Nureyev and Baryshnikov have done much to dispel this idea. Today we live in an age where the traditional distinctions between male and female roles are becoming less marked, while in Russia dancing has long been regarded as a manly activity.

Planning a ballet

Since the days of Dauberval and Noverre all ballet has hinged on the choreographer, and all choreographers are different. When planning a ballet, should one begin with the music, the scenario or the dance steps? Should one find all three and then meet the dancers? It has been done in every possible order.

Some choreographers, and these include the two most important contemporary figures – Ashton and Balanchine – like to choose the music and to arrive at the studio with only an outline of the ballet, leaving the precise steps to be worked out through a process of trial and error. The dancers often make suggestions and inspire the choreographer; some roles are tailor-made for particular dancers. Equally the choreographer may discover new aspects of a dancer's talent. Nowadays ballets are usually put down in written notation during the rehearsal

Far left This costume design for the Sun King is based on one worn by Louis XIV in 1653. The dancer is Anton Dolin. **Left** Leon Bakst revolutionized

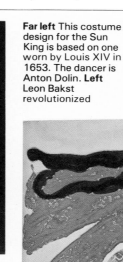

costume design by using opulent colour as in this costume for *Schéhérazade* **Below** This print shows Bakst's design for Diaghilev's *Narcisse, 1911.*

Above George Balanchine rehearses His *Union Jack,* a ballet commissioned to celebrate the US Bicentennial in 1976.
Left This costume design for a Russian peasant by Natalia Goncharova was for Diaghilev's *Le Coq d'Or,* first presented in 1914 and choreographed by Fokine.

stage, but notation in its present form is a recent invention, and not all of the world's leading choreographers know or use it. Once committed to notation, a ballet can be reproduced fairly easily, though the choreographer may well alter it, to suit himself or herself or to accommodate new dancers. Dame Ninette de Valois has likened notation to a musical score, and changes made in production to those made by the conductor of an orchestra.

Although Ashton and Balanchine usually get their first inspiration from a piece of music, they also sometimes start with a scenario. Balanchine decided to choreograph *Entente Cordiale*, consisting of three ballets, *Stars and Stripes*, *Union Jack* and *Tricolore*, and then looked around for suitable music, while Ashton took a long time finding satisfactory music for his *Marguerite and Armand* (a version of *La Dame Aux Camélias*) and *A Month in the Country*, based on Turgenev's

play. Similarly, Cranko had to have music arranged for his *Onegin* and *The Taming of the Shrew*, as did MacMillan for *Anastasia*, *Manon* and *Mayerling*.

In most of these cases, the choreographers commissioned new scores based on existing music. Ideally, they should be able to order completely new music, as Petipa used to order from Tchaikovsky. Few present-day composers would be willing to work in that way. The cost of a commissioned score could be prohibitive, and there is the added risk that the music, once composed, may not be suitable. Auber's specially written score for *Tricolore* was generally regarded as a disaster and the length of Benjamin Britten's delightful music for *The Prince of the Pagodas* is one reason for its neglect. British composers like Peter Maxwell Davies and Thea Musgrave have recently written ballet scores, but these have not as yet had a wide appeal. The most popular twentieth century full-length ballet

scores are those written by Prokofiev for *Romeo and Juliet* and *Cinderella*.

The choreographer is also generally responsible for choosing a designer. In Diaghilev's day, artists like Picasso and Bakst worked for the ballet, just as Stravinsky and Satie wrote musical scores. Leading artists seldom work for ballet today, though a number of talented designers have specialized in it, notably Rouben Ter-Arutunian and Santo Loquasto in the United States, Peter Farmer, Nicholas Georgiadis, Henry Bardon and David Walker in Britain. New York City Ballet rarely uses decors, and when it does its choice is much less distinguished than its music and choreography. The Australian artist Sidney Nolan did the decor for Helpmann's *The Display* and the celebrated British painter David Hockney is designing *Parade*, originally designed by Picasso, for the Metropolitan Opera in New York in 1981. But these are rare exceptions.

Right This stage design by Bilibine was for the 1929 production of *Tsar Saltan* by Rimsky-Korsakov. **Below** This delicate stage setting for *The Nutcracker* is by Alexandre Benois, the Russian painter and designer who greatly influenced Diaghilev.

Below This semi-Impressionistic stage setting was by Bakst for *Daphnis et Chloé*, the ballet with music by Ravel first performed by the Ballets Russes in Paris in 1912. Fokine was the choreographer.

Ballet make-up
The make-up used by ballet dancers tends to be very stylized. The most expressive areas of a dancer's face are the eyes and mouth, and the make-up emphasizes them heavily. Another reason for this style of make-up is that dancers are often lit by a follow spot, a strong, harsh light which tends to diminish the features.

All choreographers have at one time been dancers, though not necessarily good ones. Particularly in the days before effective notation, it was essential for choreographers to demonstrate steps personally to their dancers; it remains to be seen if a new breed of choreographers will arise, working entirely on paper. Some dancers turn to choreography as an escape from thwarted careers, injuries or fatigue; others are determined to be choreographers from an early age. It is certainly a more enduring career.

Great modern performers

The influence of Nureyev on world ballet has been incalculable. He is the first male dancer to become an international household name since Nijinsky, and has given more performances in more places than any dancer since Pavlova. Nureyev has raised the status of the male dancer and challenged other male dancers to achieve new technical feats. He has also been responsible for the revival of interest in nineteenth century classics like *Don Quixote*, *Raymonda* and *La Bayadère*, and for expanding the male dancer's roles in the classics. His performances with Margot Fonteyn set new standards for the interpretation of the old classic repertoire and reached an enormous new public through film and television. He has encouraged avant-garde choreographers to create works and has appeared with modern dance companies in an effort to bridge the gap between the two styles. Although his original fame in the West came partly from his dramatic dash to freedom when, in 1961, he defected in Paris from the Kirov Ballet of Leningrad, his subsequent success has been due to his unique combination of technical virtuosity, interpretative artistry and sexual charisma.

Baryshnikov, who defected from the Kirov in Toronto 13 years later, is a much more restrained personality, with an almost schoolboyish charm and innocence which is very different from Nureyev's animal magnetism. He is a definitive classical stylist, achieving technical feats which are possibly unprecedented. He is also a sincere actor and an engaging comedian. Like Nureyev, he is now reaching an enormous new public through television and the cinema.

The outstanding Western ballerina of the mid-twentieth century is Dame Margot Fonteyn, who followed years of loyalty to Sadler's Wells and then the Royal Ballet with an amazing international career, starting with Nureyev and continuing, incredibly, into late middle age with a succession of younger partners. Partnership with Nureyev provided an incalculable stimulus, at a time when she might otherwise have retired. Fonteyn's gentle artistry, her perfect physique and her endless versatility made her an unforgettable ballerina, despite the fact that she never excelled in sensational technical stunts. Neither, for that matter, did most of the world's great ballerinas, including Pavlova and the Soviet Union's Galina Ulanova (born 1910).

No-one has succeeded Fonteyn as the world's undisputed prima ballerina. There are, however, an ever-increasing number of gifted dancers.

Ballet companies

Technical standards are particularly high in the United States, in the Soviet Union and in Eastern Europe. There are more schools and ballet companies in Eastern Europe and in the United States than ever before. Even the smaller companies often astonish by the virtuosity of their dancers.

It is not uncommon to find three good ballet companies playing simultaneously in New York. The State Theatre in the Lincoln Center is the permanent home of New York City Ballet, and also plays host to visiting companies in the summer. Similarly, the Metropolitan Opera next door is the home of American Ballet Theatre and also lends its stage to foreign companies. The City Center on 55th St, the first home of New York City Ballet, is now a permanent dance theatre for smaller companies like Joffrey, Eliot Field, Alvin Ailey and Paul Taylor, as well as visitors from abroad. The beautiful Brooklyn Academy of Music also plays host to many companies of this kind, and is the regular New York home of the admirable Pennsylvania Ballet. In addition, commercial Broadway theatres like the Hellinger, the Minskoff and the Uris frequently have ballet seasons, especially when Nureyev is around to ensure box-office success.

In Britain, the Royal Ballet seems firmly entrenched at the Royal Opera House, Covent Garden, though there is periodic talk of it having a theatre of its own, not shared with the opera. The company's smaller sec-

Above These ballet positions are (**left to right**) *Arabesque (1) Arabesque penché (2), Attitude croisée (3), Attitude allongée (4)* and two positions of the *fouetté en tournant (5, 6)*. **Right** Gestures can indicate emotions or people.

Me

You

Love

Left, below Dance notation records movement through symbols on paper. Many modern ballet companies use Benesh Choreology. The basic signs for hands and feet are: in front of the body; | — level with the body; • behind the body. For flexed elbows and knees the signs are; + in front of the body; + level with the body; and X behind the body.

Of his bones are cor-   al made

These   are   pearls   that   were

his eyes nothing   of   him   that   doth   fade.

tion, which develops new dancers and choreographers, is now based at Sadler's Wells, where the Royal Ballet was born. England's other major company, the London Festival Ballet, has no regular theatre of its own yet, though it appears regularly on the makeshift stage of the Festival Hall and on the spacious one of the London Coliseum.

The Festival Ballet has always engaged exciting guest stars from all over the world, and has achieved great popularity over the years with works like Jack Carter's dramatic *Witch Boy*, Harald Lander's showpiece *Etudes* and Barry Moreland's satirical ragtime *Prodigal Son*. Originally led by Markova and Dolin, it went on to develop a number of new British stars, including John Gilpin (born 1930) one of the best British male dancers of all time. It also gave dancing experience at an early stage of their careers to Flemming Flindt (born 1936), who became a star of the

Above This scene is from Robert Helpmann's ballet *The Display*. **Right** Natalia Markarova dances in *Les Sylphides*. **Below** Lesley Collier performs in *Elite Syncopations*.

Paris Opera, director of the Royal Danish Ballet and the choreographer of several popular ballets; André Prokovsky (born 1939) and his Russian-born ballerina wife Galina Samsova (born 1937), who later formed their own company, the New London Ballet, and staged new ballets all over the world; and Peter Schaufuss (born 1949), a Danish dancer who went to New York City Ballet, the

National Ballet of Canada and had a distinguished international career.

Peter Darrell's Scottish Ballet, which emerged from a smaller and more experimental group called Western Theatre Ballet, is rapidly becoming a major classical company based in Scotland and the north of England. It has intelligent and dramatic versions of most of the classics, including the Danish *La Sylphide* and *Napoli* and shares with the Royal Danish Ballet and the Stuttgart Ballet an infectious vitality which makes their peformances a pleasure.

In general, the audience for the modern groups is still separate from that for classical ballet. Modern dancing has a strong following among art and drama aficionados. In England, Robin Howard's London Contemporary Dance Theatre, based on Martha Graham's techniques and directed by ex-Graham dancer Robert Cohan (born 1925), and the Ballet Rambert, with its similar policy, have both found enthusiastic audiences at Sadler's Wells, at the Round House, and at university theatres and colleges on tour. Classical ballet still has a much wider appeal, and can regularly fill much larger theatres.

The future of theatrical dance, classical as well as modern, seems bright, despite economic crises and constant warnings that ballet is out of date. Video cassettes and large-screen projection television are likely to bring dance to an even wider public, and may provide the much needed injection of money to finance new productions and experiments in the theatre.

OTHER DANCE FORMS

Modern dancing was born in the great revolution of art that swept the Western world in the closing years of the nineteenth century. On every front the standards and principles of traditional art were being challenged; probably, this process was most advanced in Europe.

New and revolutionary sounds created by composers such as Claude Debussy were being heard in the concert halls; abstracted visions, liberated from the constrictions of line, were being painted on canvas by the disciples of the Impressionists.

Dancing was to be liberated, too. For 150 years it had been dominated by the principles set out by the great French choreographer, Jean-Georges Noverre. There was no form of concert dance other than classical

Above Loie Fuller choreographed her dances not only for the body but also for the yards of diaphanous silk which she swirled about her. **Right** Maud Allan's most successful role was in *Vision of Salome*.

ballet. Special dances had been incorporated into many stage musical productions, but they had played only a supportive role in the shows. There had been no overall pattern, no cohesive style.

The early days

In the United States there was not even a ballet tradition. There were few ballet schools, but no ballet companies. American audiences received their dance entertainment only from touring European companies.

It was from the fertile, untapped sources of the USA that the revolution in dance sprang. It was not a conscious revolution, but an inspired one. Loie Fuller, Isadora Duncan, Maud Allan and Ruth St. Denis did not deliberately set out to lay a foundation for the theatre movement that was to become modern dance. They wanted only to express themselves and to explore the possibilities for expressive dancing. They each had their

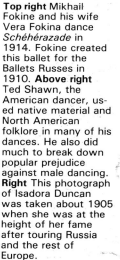

Top right Mikhail Fokine and his wife Vera Fokina dance *Schéhérazade* in 1914. Fokine created this ballet for the Ballets Russes in 1910. **Above right** Ted Shawn, the American dancer, used native material and North American folklore in many of his dances. He also did much to break down popular prejudice against male dancing. **Right** This photograph of Isadora Duncan was taken about 1905 when she was at the height of her fame after touring Russia and the rest of Europe.

Above left Ruth St Denis was one of the greatest influences on modern dance. She created a number of 'Eastern' ballets

Above These dancers are members of the Denishawn Company which was set up by Ruth St Denis and Ted Shawn.

Above Martha Graham (**left**) is shown here with her former teacher, Ruth St Denis. **Right** This scene is from one of Martha Graham's most recent ballets. **Below** Martha Graham with her company perform *Acrobats of God* (1960).

own, separate and totally divorced ideas of how dancing should develop.

Fuller (1862 – 1928) sought to create mood and nature impressions; Duncan was mesmerized by the ideals of classical Greece and the possibilities for flowing movement that seemed to be embodied in Greek sculpture; Allen was fascinated by the exotic moods of the Middle East; St. Denis wanted to interpret the mystery of the Orient.

Although the idea of modern dance sprang from the United States, it found no immediate sympathy in conservative America. Fuller and Duncan danced to unappreciative and dwindling audiences. There was no ballet tradition against which to judge their exciting innovations. It was not until they danced in Europe, where ballet was part of culture and there was a ready reception for new ideas, that they were acclaimed.

Fuller made the first break-through, causing a sensation at the *Folies Bergère*, the large boisterous music hall, that presented vigorous shows of dancing, beautiful women and popular variety. Paris, always a ferment of ideas, quickly recognized the exciting originality of Fuller's dancing. She made her debut there in a 45-minute programme, billowing in filmy fabrics, striking naturalistic poses that were a total defiance of the rigid patterns of classical ballet. She made an appeal that crossed the barriers between the noisy crowds of the music hall and the lofty intellectuals of the theatre. At the end of her career, Fuller was presenting to enthusiastic audiences whole evenings of her work, using shadow screens, phosphorescent costumes, imaginative lighting effects and draperies that became like living flames, the shapes of flowers or the wings of insects.

Fuller established her own company and it

Above The German dancer Mary Wigman is shown here in *Call of the Dead,* a ballet in memory of the dead of World War I.

Duncan founded a school outside Berlin in 1905 to spread the principles of her belief. She despised the rigidity of ballet and even urged her pupils not to go to a ballet performance lest they might become contaminated by its influence.

She had sought 'to dance a divine expression of the human spirit through body movement'. And she pleaded with her pupils: 'Listen to the music with your soul ... you will feel an inner self awakening.' But her lessons, like her dancing were purely inspirational. She died, tragically, in 1927, accidentally strangled by a scarf entangled in the back wheel of a car in which she was travelling, and it was left to others less spectacular to consolidate the revolution she and Fuller had begun.

Maud Allan (1883–1956), like Duncan, had her great successes in London. She carried modern dancing a stage beyond mere innovation to outright shock. Her most striking creation was the dance *Salomé*, heavy with menace, in which she walked on stage with the head of John the Baptist. Audiences were horrified and attracted by the sensual presentation of the work. It incarnated all the mystery and eroticism of the Middle East, and while they gasped, the fans demanded more.

The divergent courses of this new wave of dancing were all drawn together and given popular and permanent appeal in the United States by Ruth St. Denis (1877–1968) and the shrewd businessman she married, Edwin Meyers Shawn.

St. Denis, too, had her first real success in Europe. Germany was so excited by her art that impresarios offered to build a dance theatre to her specifications if she would stay there as permanent director. It was a stunning offer, but she declined and went back to the less certain American stage. She had initial success on the circuits with her programme including *Cobra, Nuatch, Rhada, Insence* and *The Yogi,* all of which showed dramatic eastern influence. But the American audiences wanted male and female teams rather than solo female dancers.

St. Denis was fortunate that among all the praise and attention that had been heaped upon her there was no more persistent admirer than Ted Shawn. He followed her to New York, became her pupil, and in a short time, her husband, too. They formed a dance team. Ted opened the act with a second female and they performed a popular dance of the day as an introduction to Ruth's solos.

While touring the West Coast they offered a prize for the best name that characterized the group. It hardly needed a competition, but the winning entry was – Denishawn. Thus was born the most successful touring dance company in America. The name became an enterprise that dominated the teaching and presentation of modern dancing for 20 years.

Denishawn had what the other innovators and the other dance teams did not have – both an inspirational figure and an organizer. Miss Ruth, as St. Denis became known to future generations performed and choreographed. Ted, known to the pupils as Papa, taught, founded schools, licensed teachers as Denishawn instructors, made the business arrangements and partnered his brilliant wife. Much of the future of modern dance development was invested in the company.

Eventually, Martha Graham, Doris Humphrey and Charles Weidman would all go to the Denishawn School in Los Angeles for instruction, tour with the Denishawn company, and carry on the message of modern dance into another era.

During the 1920s, Denishawn made an 18-month tour of the Far East. It was a triumph, and the company returned with a newly acquired repertoire of dance which fuelled a long and successful transcontinental tour. That tour finally established modern dance as a field of the performing arts that could stand proudly alone.

Shawn never missed the need to entertain the public as well as to carry over the messianic message of his wife's art about the expressive possibilities of dance. Vaudeville audiences had to understand. The costumes were sumptuous, and Shawn was always ready for a hint of scandal to keep up advance bookings. On one tour he had Miss Ruth say in an interview that the most satisfying dancing was that done while wearing the fewest clothes. Local police were on hand at the next theatre all set to arrest any offending dancers. The show opened with a danced version of *The Lord's Prayer*. The police left in silence; the crowd flocked to the box office.

The second generation
Thirty years after its dramatic birth, modern dance was an accepted art form and had already spawned a second generation of stars. They gave meaning and direction to the feeling and inspiration that had moved its creators. Modern dance began to develop themes of mythology, investigate the relationships between man and woman, and make statements on social issues.

Within just a few years, Martha Graham, Doris Humphrey and Charles Weidman all left Denishawn to found their own companies and launch modern dance on the second stage of its development.

In 1926, the year of her first independent concert, Graham (born 1894) set up her own company and studio. It was a modest beginning. She started with just herself and three young women. She built her technique on the contraction and release of energy and a natural breathing rhythm. The tenor of the dances had changed from the impressionist pieces that were pure Denishawn to driving, percussive works, beautifully and powerfully shaped, but without the delicate prettiness of earlier dances. Outstanding among

was in this fertile school that Duncan (1878–1927) perhaps the most dramatic of the dancing revolutionaries, first freed her imagination on the live stage. It was not an association that was to last long. Duncan's undisciplined talent was not to be constricted even by the loose bounds of a school like Fuller's. Duncan made her first impact in London, where she met and was greatly influenced by Edward Gordon Craig (1872–1966), a son of Ellen Terry and a theatre critic. Craig was a revolutionary himself, creating dramatic new scenic designs. He was among the crowds who rapturously greeted Duncan when her dancing took the London stage by storm in 1899.

Duncan's inspirational force was exceptional. She had a deep and fresh response to music and danced at concert level to Gluck, Chopin and Beethoven with a great imagination and popular success. Aesthetic running, skipping and gesture formed the basis of her naturalistic style. Not even her unconventional life-style – Craig fathered two of her children – in an age much less permissive than today did anything to dampen the public ardour for this very talented young lady.

this new repertoire was *Primitive Mysteries*, hinting strongly at the initiation rites of a primitive society.

There was a reaction, too, to the sumptuous costuming of the Denishawn productions. Graham confined her small company in long, simple, straight-fitting dresses. She called it later, with a smile, her 'long woollens' period. The starkness of the costuming and the identical look of the members of the group gave the whole performance a serious, sombre attitude. A mask of white make-up on the face contrasted with dark lips and eyebrows.

Martha Graham was a voracious reader with a deep interest in myth and philosophy and she allowed her dances to reflect these interests. In the 1930s she concerned herself with America and the folk and feeling of the States. *American Document*, *American Lyric* and *Letter To The World* were among the memorable productions that thrilled the devotees of the new art, who flocked as ever to a Graham show. In the 1940s she produced the masterly *Appalachian Spring*. It was virtually a dancing documentary, based on a homesteading couple settling in the wilderness and the help they receive from an older pioneer woman and a preacher. The commissioned score won a Pulitzer Prize for the composer Aaron Copland.

There was other work which continued to show Graham's deep interest in human development. *Frontier* celebrated the Western saga of a pioneering generation and added to her growing repertoire of the folklore of the United States in dance. By the 1950s, Graham had turned away from the New World to explore the old, choreographing Greek and Hebrew legends, such as the

story of Oedipus in *Night Story* and of the royal family of Atreus in *Clytemnestra*, both portrayed from a woman's point of view. She gave similar treatment to the biblical *Judith* and the story of Eden in *Embattled Garden*. Martha Graham continued to explore myth and legend right until the 1970s, and the sumptuous *Part Real-Part Dream* revealed her still considerable powers.

Doris Humphrey (1895–1958) and Charles Weidman (1901–1975) formed a team in the late 1920s that was the other great influence to come from the Denishawn modern dance school. They were unusual in that, like Denishawn, they were a team. It worked superbly because they complimented each other splendidly. She was a formal, logical choreographer with a sense of social involvement and a feeling for clear, structural development. Weidman was a wizard of spontaneous gesture and witty movement. He created dance from a truly improvisational instinct. They were able to balance both elements in a varied and exciting programme of dancing.

There was a growing awareness of modern dance in the popular theatre in the 1930s. Producers turned more and more to the choreography of Humphrey and Weidman. In 1932, the Shubert organisation's successful *Americana* included seven dances by

Humphrey and Weidman. Among them were Humphrey's examination of natural phenomena in *Water Study*, a dance still startlingly vivid today: her portrayal of a religious group in *The Shakers* and Weidman's cameo impression of the prize fighting world in *Ringside*.

There was a heroic look to the dancers trained by Humphrey and Weidman. They demonstrated the energy of movement derived from the 'fall and recovery of balance' technique articulated by Humphrey. Everyday gesture was taken and stretched to the uttermost in terms of energy. Humphrey's great monument to her concern with a humane social order was her triology *New Dance*, parts of which were choreographed by Weidman.

His special contribution lay in the realm of mimetric gesture, which he called kinetic pantomime to distinguish it from acting pantomime. He began with simple gesture and allowed it to develop its own trajectory. Logical order was abandoned, but there was always an imaginative twist or a witty ending. The major statement of his dynamic approach to choreography came in *Opus 51*, and the very name reflects his approach. He created the work without a title, then asked Humphrey for suggestions. 'How many dances have you done?' she asked. 'About

Right The American dancer and choreographer, Trisha Brown is shown here in the Judson Dance Theatre's *A String* (1966). **Below** This scene is from Balanchine's *Prodigal Son*.

50', he replied. 'Then,' she said, crisply and logically, 'call it Opus 51.'

Arthritis forced Humphrey to retire from active performing in 1945, but she carried on to choreograph and work as artistic advisor to the company formed by José Limon (1908–1972) one of the finest dancers to emerge from the Humphrey-Weidman school. Weidman formed his own concert group and continued to work separately until his death in 1975.

There were three other major contributors to the development of modern dance in the 1920s and 1930s. Hanya Holm, Helen Tamiris and Lester Horton each established schools of choreography that helped to shape

Above Members of the London Contemporary Dance Theatre perform *Nympheas.* The company was founded in 1969 by Robin Howard with Robert Cohan as director. The dancers are almost all trained in the modern dance technique of Martha Graham and many of her works have been performed by the company. **Below** Two works by the American choreographer, Alwin Nikolais, *Imago* and **(insert)** *Tensile Involvement* are shown here. Props, light, sound and colour are used with the dancers to produce a concept of total theatre.

Above, right, below From 1966 the Ballet Rambert began producing contemporary ballets. Glen Tetley became one of its leading choreographers and scenes from his works *The Tempest* **(right, bottom)** and *Pierrot Lunaire* **(below)** are shown here. *The Night of the Waning Moon* by Christopher Bruce is seen (**above** .

the progress of their art. Holm (born 1898) used space almost as a living thing, and Tamiris (1905–1966) was the first modern dancer to tap the rich source of black, spiritual music. She created new and beautiful work.

Horton (1906–1953) was the only major figure of the second generation of modern dancers who developed in isolation from the Denishawn tradition. He sprang from the creative ferment of New York, and later established a home in Los Angeles, where he set up a dance theatre that attracted a dedicated group of dancers and choreographers.

It was a small house given over exclusively to dance, and the permanent group was able to develop a wonderful sense of continuity and teamwork on stage. Horton used a fine talent to create pieces of striking originality from his deep interest in the American Indian ritual. He was obsessed by the themes of beauty and savagery, offsetting a calm, imposing deployment of the torso with eccentric movements of the limbs for dramatic effect. Based in the film capital of the States, Horton was naturally drawn into movie-making, but his first love remained the dance stage. He took his company to New York in the 1950s, and they won immediate acclaim.

He was fascinated, too, by the story of Salomé and John the Baptist, seeing in their sensual and destructive relationship the savagery and beauty that so attracted him. Between 1934 and 1950 he created six widely differing versions of the story. For the last one, he also designed the set, the costumes and wrote the sound score. He died in 1953 and his company dispersed, several forming their own groups. Among them were Alvin Ailey (born 1931), and Carmen DeLavallade (born 1931).

The European connection

Despite the resounding successes in London and Paris of Isadora Duncan and Loie Fuller, neither England nor France produced a coherent movement of modern dance during its critical development stage in the 1920s and 1930s. The whole European movement was centred in Germany – and this was to have tragic results when it was stifled in the late 1930s by the censorship of a hostile Nazi government.

Duncan and Fuller both went back to the United States after their European triumphs, leaving the stages of London and Paris to traditional ballet. When Duncan was lured back to Europe, she went to Germany.

The German school of modern dance began with Emile Jaques Dalcroze (1865–1950), who founded a school at Hellerau in 1911 and created a series of movement patterns to instruct his students in the understanding of rhythm. At the same time, Rudolf von Laban (1879–1958) founded a school in Munich, one of the homes of the expressionist art movement, and began

Folk dance
Folk dancing is as old as history itself and has always been linked with forms of social or religious ritual and used simply as a form of recreation. **Left** These ancient Egyptian dancers are depicted on a fresco from Thebes dated 1400 BC. **Right** This whirling dervishes' dance is connected with forms of Islamic religious ritual.

Left Polish folkdancers dance the Polonaise, Poland's national dance which evolved from peasant dances and court ceremonies in the late 1500s. Many great composers, notably Chopin, have written music for this slow stately dance.

Left The Morris dance is the best-known British folk dance. **Below** The Spanish flamenco was originally performed by gypsies. **Below left** Paraguayan folk dance draws heavily on native music.

Above Korean dance is frequently associated with religious ritual or theatrical drama. **Below** The Hawaiian hula dance is the best known of the Polynesian dances.

teaching his own theories of dance. It was a combination of these separate schools of thought that created the expressionist dance movement in Europe. The dancers had little interest in traditional ballet and even abandoned music at times in favour of purely percussive accompaniment.

In the 1920s, Mary Wigman (1886–1973) emerged as a major figure of European modern dance. She studied with both Dalcroze and Laban. From Dalcroze she developed flowing ideas of rhythm: from Laban she got the stimulation of his brilliance as a theorist. Wigman was drawn to the murky loftiness of primal fears and beliefs. Her presentations were stark ritual, unrelieved by the severe, dark costuming she favoured, and the basic musical accompaniment.

The other major figure in European dancing in this period was Kurt Jooss (born 1901). He, too, studied with Laban, but his approach was significantly different to that of Wigman. He attempted a synthesis of traditional ballet with the new expressive principles. He was attracted to social commentary and injustice and he created a dramatic style, backed by period stage settings, that has remained unique. During the Nazi repression, Jooss settled in Britain. He returned to his native country after the Second World War, but by that time the vitality of the movement had ebbed, and no choreographer of modern dance of any stature has emerged since from Germany.

Wigman stayed in Germany during the Nazi period, but she was barred from public performance, and the roots she had attempted to set down withered.

Fortunately, Wigman had visited the United States and, through her pupil, Hanya Holm, she was able to join the European connection to the mainstream of modern dance in the United States. Wigman opened a school of dance in New York in 1931, with the encouragement of impresario Sol Hurok (1888–1974), who had presented her company in the States. Wigman did not want to stay on, but she persuaded Holm to remain in the States and spread there the German concepts of dance. Holm later opened a summer school at the University of Colorado that further expanded her influence.

From 1934 onwards, Holm spent part of each summer at the newly formed Bennington College Summer School of Dance, which became the central focus of modern dance in America. Holm was more interested in dynamic flow and open space than in particular steps, and in 1937 at the Bennington Summer Festival she presented her masterly *Trend*. It surveyed a society falling apart, then reforming on a new and sounder basis. It was an heroic theme and remains one of Holm's most respected works.

The development of thought and choreography at Bennington was crucial to the progress of modern dance in the United States. Each autumn students returned to their colleges and universities carrying the message of modern dance, and setting up new courses where revolutionary steps and ideas spread. From these courses came the nucleus of the immense modern dance audience that exists now in the States, more than 30 years after Bennington closed in the early days of the Second World War.

The new wave

In the 1940s, large numbers of commercial theatre producers began to clamour for the major figures of modern dance to work with other performers in the musical theatre and the dramatic stage. Actors began to take regular classes in movement which opened up a new form of dramatic art for them other than the voice. The musical stage benefited greatly from this infusion of choreographic genius that freshened its somewhat thinly drawn formulas for movement. For a while, Holm, Tamiris and Weidman all abandoned the concert stage to concentrate on the commercial stage. Their students followed them into this fresh ground that opened up many more opportunities for modern dance than the constrictions of the concert hall, and gave room for many more young modern dancers to develop.

By the decade of the 1950s, dozens of new choreographers had set up on their own. Erick Hawkins, Merce Cunningham, Anna Sokolow and Paul Taylor had all worked with Martha Graham, but had left to follow their own paths in the design of dance.

Far and away the most radical of these was Cunningham (born 1919). He took the simple, but revolutionary, step of abandoning linear narrative structure in favour of a collage-like dance. The elements did not follow each other in a strict, logical order, but existed as a freely arranged jumble. Cunningham broke another tradition of modern dance – he moved the most important and dramatic moments of his work away from the centre of the stage, often filling this part with the preliminaries to a high spot that was performed almost in a corner. He opened up the proscenium stage so that it became a field of action. It was as bold as the abstract painting of its day, in which expressionists like Jackson Pollock allowed their paint to drip at will over the canvas.

Anna Sokolow (born 1915) developed a strongly committed social conscience in her dances. She maintained the vocabulary of movement that Graham had developed, but used it to explore contemporary themes like loneliness and alienation, themes that bordered at times on madness. Erick Hawkins embarked on a diametrically opposed course when he left Graham. He purged psychological and social consideration from his new dances, turning to natural phenomena in the sense of nature contemplation as understood by Zen philosophy. The stress lines, so important in Graham's dramatically orientated approach were eliminated in favour of smooth, long-phrased, gentle movements.

Paul Taylor (born 1930) measured out a middle ground for himself, directly between conventional drama and the abstract, non-linear approach. He brought a wholesome, athletic attack to everyday movements and even added touches of humour. His pieces were sometimes slightly mysterious, at other times bawdily direct. To both he added a powerful vigour that could come only from the energy of real people, no matter how dream-like the setting of his dance was.

An equally glittering team of dancers and choreographers emerged from the Humphrey-Weidman school of modern dance – José Limon, Anna Halprin, Sybil Shearer, Lucas Hoving, Katharine Litz.

Shearer and Litz drew most heavily on the kinetic pantomime approach of Weidman, in which the rationality of mind took second place to the logic of muscular development. Both created humorous pieces that were studiously vague, comprehensible only for those who stood apart from the usual process of cause and effect development. Halprin (born 1920) was more fundamental, developing dances that almost reflected an architectural idea of form following function. Movement in her dances became necessary to accomplish a given task, such as climbing, fitting so many steps into a given time, or something as simple as dressing or undressing. There were no steps as such, only solutions to given tasks.

Limon (1908–1972) remained loyal to Humphrey. He created dances concerned with human values and developed along a logical progression. He added his own brooding weight to his concern for man's place in the social order and in the conflict of interests this brought.

Experiment in the Sixties

Modern dance continued its restless search for new and original expression in the 1960s. Its mainspring in that decade seemed to be a drive for bigger and broader stages and an urge to present modern dance in totally fresh environments. The older generation of dancers who had fought to escape in the 1930s from the confines of college gymnasiums and into the theatre, doubtless looked wryly on this rush to dance elsewhere.

Some dancers went back to the spaciousness of the gymnasium; others picked even broader canvases – open fields, rooftops, in the streets, in museum galleries, even the naves of sympathetic churches.

One of these, the Judson Memorial Church in New York, provided one of the most hospitable centres for the experimental young choreographers of the 1960s, watched over by the Rev. Al Carmines. In an exciting period of development, The Judson Dance Theatre presented works by James Waring, Yvonne Rainer, Steve Paxton, Phoebe Neville, James Cunningham, Meredith Monk, Twyla Tharp, David Gordon,

Elizabeth Keen, Rudy Perez, Trisha Brown, Lucinda Childs, and Remy Charlip. Each had a distinct approach, using light, props, sound, films, movement and athleticism with lively originality.

The whole movement, freshened by its unconventionality, marched back into the theatre in the 1970s with expanded ideas of presentation in which the light, sound and films they had toyed with in the open, now played an artistic part of the dance as a whole.

In less than a century since Duncan and Fuller took their first, imaginative steps, modern dance has travelled an enormous distance to become accepted as a performing art of immense vitality. A succession of brilliant artists have released dance on a path of freedom and expression that will continue to be explored.

Where tradition lives

While modern dance and its dedicated followers explore new frontiers, many of the most popular dancers of present western society are in fact reliving old traditions. Even the go-go dancers and hip-swingers who accompany pop shows are re-awakening the past rather than experimenting with the future. They represent part of a great modern movement back towards the 'primitive', or at least to what is seen as the primitive. The popular dances – such as rock 'n roll or contemporary reggae or disco dancing – of the latter part of the twentieth century has come, via the American blacks, from the rhythmic movement commonly associated with people of African origin.

Ballroom dancing, rather than the pop or rock styles, is more truly representative of a 'progressive' or direct development in western popular dancing, although pop, with its fusion of cultures, is far more vigorous. Ballroom dancing is a descendant of ancient European dance forms, and throughout this centuries-old development there is one clear tendency: a style will, at first, be danced by everyone; then the fashion will change, and the public moves on while the out-dated style becomes a performing art.

Maypole dancing, Morris dancing, the Flamenco dancing and 'gipsy' styles used by cabaret artists in continental Europe, the sword dances of the north of England and Scotland, and Russian and Greek dancing are all examples of once popular dance movements in which ordinary people took part. They are styles kept alive and perfected by experts. Folk dancing and ballroom dancing, with their limited number of participants, are following the same trend, and already ballroom dance competitions between experts are attracting large audiences – even as the styles attract fewer actual participants.

Many popular dances appear to have begun as a circle of people singing and moving around a religious symbol. The sym-

bolism and ritual gradually disappear, leaving the circle dancing purely for pleasure. Processes such as these probably led to the development of old group dances like the Medieval carole, a dance in which the circle formation broke up into a processional line, and the branles of the late Middle Ages and Renaissance. Another stage in the development came when a couple would step forward from the line or ring and dance alone, with their friends watching perhaps a public expression of late medieval courtly love.

In sixteenth century Europe an energetic dance called the galliard became extremely popular, though it was practically a solo dance for a man, with a woman partner playing a low key role with few movements. The

Top These ballroom dancers dance in formation. **Above** Bebop dancers perform in a London club in 1949.

man jumped and hopped athletically in what became such an exhibitionist dance that it finally died out, being associated with vulgar showing off. Another flamboyant dance was the volta in which the girl was lifted by her partner, and often showed her knees as a result, shocking the watchers.

These cases, in which a popular dance was often 'taken over' by a couple or individual who had become expert, so that a mass participating activity turns into a performing art, have been repeated in modern times. Exhibitionist dancing by a few experts often marked the ballroom dances of the 1930s and 1940s, and these frequently took the form of competitions, in which skill was appraised by judges, or marathons, when the winning

couple were – quite literally – the last ones to drop to the floor, sometimes after days of non-stop dancing.

It was during the craze for ballroom dancing in America and Europe that the couple emerged who were to dominate the popular dance form – Fred Astaire (born 1899) and Ginger Rogers (born 1911). Although they danced mainly on the cinema screen in the 1930s, their style, the way their dancing enacted the conflicts between men and women, romance and sex, came to represent the height of this type of performance.

The romantic dancing of a couple can be easily understood, for the symbolism and fantasy represented are as much alive today as they ever were. But for many other types of performance-dancing it is different. They have survived partly because their meanings are so difficult. They are 'weird' and 'quaint'. Morris dancing is a typical example of this – a group of men in flower decorated hats, kicking their heels which are hung with small bells. The style is centuries old, once a common dance, now a curiosity performed by experts. The origins of 'the Morris' are believed to be pagan rituals enacted in springtime to symbolize fertility and to produce a communal feeling of well-being. The bells, attached to the ankles, are thought to have been rung originally to frighten away evil spirits, to purify the ground where the dancing was taking place.

While the Morris dance belonged to springtime and growth, the ancient sword dances were usually performed in midwinter, and they are believed to have their roots in rituals representing death and resurrection. These would be meaningful topics to ancient pagan tribes living in northern Europe and Scandinavia at the time of year when days become particularly short and the sun seems to have deserted the world.

One dance which has parted totally with its origins is the maypole dance. The maypole, a tall pole decorated with flowers and ribbons, stood on many English village greens in Elizabethan times, and was a fertility and virility symbol. People danced around it. The dance is now mainly performed by children, holding coloured ribbons attached to the top of the maypole which wind patterns around the pole as the children dance their circles. In some Devonshire market towns, the 'May fair' tradition is still strong. A young girl is elected 'May queen' and takes her seat at the foot of the pole while the other children dance around her. It is a more innocent dance now, distant from its roots; it provides a colourful springtime performance in these old English country towns, and makes a refreshing change from professional entertainment.

So from the movements of Isadora Duncan to the gyrations of today's dancers in discos, dance remains an expression of joy in movement and the human body – a joy which the audience shares with the dancers.

MIME

FROM THE COMMEDIA DELL'ARTE TO MARCEL MARCEAU

Mime is one of the oldest forms of theatrical expression. It had already been developed into an art form in the classic days of Greek theatre. Like so much of the Greek culture, it was adopted by the Romans, who added their own skills and imagination to the medium. The Roman mime artist, Esopus, had such a brilliant vocabulary of gestures that Cicero, unrivalled as the greatest orator of his age, challenged Esopus to a contest. The object was to show which of them could most eloquently convey a given idea to an audience using their respective skills. It is not recorded whether or not Esopus met the challenge – but it can be said with certainty that no one would have been in any doubt about what he had to say.

The Romans liked their mime to be a bawdy brand of entertainment, but it was none the less skilful and its techniques were imitated in all corners of the empire. Mime suffered a serious setback with the rise of Christianity. The Church frowned on the lewd excesses of Roman entertainment.

Until the Renaissance, mime was kept alive only by wandering bands of minstrels, jugglers and acrobats. The boisterous antics of these strolling players who travelled with their acts from town to town were popular with the people. This very popularity made them suspect in the eyes of the Church and local ordinances were passed to restrain them. The players were banned from speaking on stage, and this hostility gave an enormous impetus to the development of the mime's gestural vocabulary.

The large and extravagant spectacles of Roman theatre had vanished, but in the market places of Europe mime flourished. In Greek theatre the gestural language had been just one part of theatre, combined with dancing, music and drama. As Europe approached the Renaissance, mime had become a distinct and independent art form. The Church played another part in the development of mime. Miracle and mystery plays were created to carry the message of faith and truth to the people of Europe. Mime – a medium that the people of the marketplace understood well – became an integral part of the religious plays of the early Middle Ages.

In the sixteenth century the *commedia dell'arte* made its appearance in the city states of northern Italy. Here was the comedy, the music, the dancing and the drama of the market place all rolled into one coherent entertainment. To the *commedia dell'arte* can be traced directly such diverse entertainments of the modern theatre as ballet and the variety show. Stock characters grew up with the *commedia dell'arte* – Harlequin, Pantaloon, Pierrot, Columbine and the Clown. They were all instantly recognized by the audience. They all leaned heavily on the long-developed art of mime and were in part, though considerably modified, based on the classic Roman mime figures. The two

most popular were Harlequin and Columbine. He represented Eros or Cupid, and was full of daring, wit and guile, seemingly able to overcome all opposition to his quest to capture the heart and hand of the beautiful Columbine, whose character was based ultimately on Psyche, the nymph. To these characters were added Pierrot, who was a likeable old man and the butt of the inevitable jokes. Pierrot exemplified the childlike simplicity of a rustic and the Clown was a raucous prankster.

The essential power and attraction of these characters, developed forcefully over centuries and they still occur in popular and classical entertainment today. The traditional Christmas pantomime – even when staged on ice – still keeps room for these stock characters to appear in their freely-adopted fairy tales. Contemporary choreog-

Above Charlie Chaplin took the art of mime from the theatre into the cinema. He worked in pantomime, went to the USA in 1910 with a pantomime troupe and was asked to join the Keystone film company.
Right Marcel Marceau is perhaps the most influential contemporary mime artist. His one-man show featuring the character 'Bip', the archetypal little man trying to deal with the vagaries of everyday

life, has been performed internationally. Marceau typifies the versatility of the pure mime performer.
Right One of the most original modern mime troupes is the Swiss group *Mummenschanz* **(bottom right)**. They use a variety of masks lighting and props as well as dance and movement. In the East, many dance forms have much in common with Western mime traditions **(bottom left)**.

raphers, such as George Balanchine, Eliot Field and Glen Tetley have all taken these *commedia dell'arte* characters and made ballets around them. Every circus clown, of all those innumerable varieties, has his origins in the energetic, painted character who pressed on, grinning and tumbling through every performance of the *commedia dell'arte*.

The muteness of the mime has enabled him to cross national barriers and install himself in countries with widely-varied national characteristics in a way that no speaking characters have been able to do. The gestural language of Harlequin addresses a broader audience than any dramatic declamation. In this, mime shares some of the character of dance which is also a language without national frontiers. Where it differs is in its sense of time and the use of natural gesture. Time in dance is measured in the expandable and repeatable metre that is the basis of music. Mime lives in the dramatic, naturalistic span that characterizes human action.

In the sixteenth and seventeenth centuries, the *commedia dell'arte* spread to France and the rest of Europe, taking its message of mime with it. Two great schools of Western mime grew from this – the Italian tradition, which emphasizes bodily gesture, vigour and boisterousness; and the French tradition which concentrates more on facial expression. The importance of facial expression has made exponents of that school favour smaller, more intimate theatres, seating no more than 1,000 people. In a larger setting they fear that their subtleties would be lost and the logic of the presentation considerably lessened. Mimes of the French school depend on the swift play of expression across the features to make emotional declarations, while the Italian school makes primary use of the expressiveness of the whole body.

As mime spread throughout Europe it moved close to the emerging art of classical ballet. As the narrative ballet (*ballet d'action*) succeeded the court ballet (*ballet du cour*) with its singing and declamation, there was a great need to express the dramatic action of a story without words. Mime had already developed a great vocabulary of dramatic gesture and it was quickly adopted by the major innovating choreographers such as Jean-Georges Noverre, Gasparo Angiolini (1731–1803) and Franz Hilverding (1710–1768). The full evening ballets which they created had purely danced interludes, but the story was advanced and clarified by mime recitation.

The language of mime
A dozen mimes will produce at least a dozen definitions of what mime really is. Probably the only thing they will agree on is that it is a dramatic presentation that lies somewhere between dance and drama. But there is no doubt about the language of mime. They all understand that.

The hand of a man circling in front of his face clearly indicates that he has been struck by someone's beauty and the person he points to identifies the one who has caused this emotional reaction. Rapidly rolling the hands over one another above the head indicates an invitation to dance, and pointing to the ring finger on the left hand is a pledge of

Below France has produced many great mimes. Jean-Louis Barrault gave one of his most famous performances in the film *Les Enfants du Paradis* in which he played the first great French mime, Gaspard Deburau, who created the character of Pierrot in the seventeenth century.

marriage to the person addressed. Making a patting motion with one hand over the heart shows love, while extending the hands downwards with the wrists crossed is an indication of the person being tied up or under an evil spell.

The vocabulary of such gesture was exceptionally broad in the eighteenth century, but it has tended to diminish in this century. Ballet now concentrates on the expressiveness of the whole body in more musical terms rather than on conventional mime gestures which are closer to natural acting. Even so, there are gestures such as the invitation to marriage that would take an enormous amount of dancing to convey, and even then it might be ambiguous.

The language of mime can be taken so literally that it is perfectly possible to express clearly ordinary parts of verbal speech. Pro-

nouns such as 'I', 'we', 'you', and 'he', are easily conveyed. Verbs are the most dynamic part of the mime vocabulary.

These are the action words that give life and richness to the whole art. Many nouns, like fan or beggar have been turned into verbs because by doing something, by making some action, the mime can express much more obviously what he means. A person trying to mime the shape of a fan could make his point much less clear than a person who simply performs a fanning motion in front of the body. There can be no doubt about what that means. In the same way, extending the hand palm upwards in a gesture of supplication, will tell anyone that the person is a mendicant in a way that no amount of pitiful, facial expression could.

Adverbs such as 'quickly' and 'lively' become their verbal equivalents easily..

'How could I?' or 'What a mistake!' is simply a gesture of bouncing the heel of the hand against the forehead. Slapping the side of the face with one hand unmistakeably means dismay. These are gestures that are commonly used in normal communication and are so obvious one wonders: Were they adopted by mime, or did mime create them?

The great mimes

Large scale theatrical productions flourished on the stages of Europe and the United States in the nineteenth century. Many made use of mime. One of the greatest mimes was the Frenchman Jean-Baptiste Gaspard Deburau (1796 – 1846) who re-interpreted the character of Pierrot. His costume became a large baggy overblouse with floppy, long sleeves; he wore a tiny skull cap and a line of large, puffy buttons down the front of the blouse.

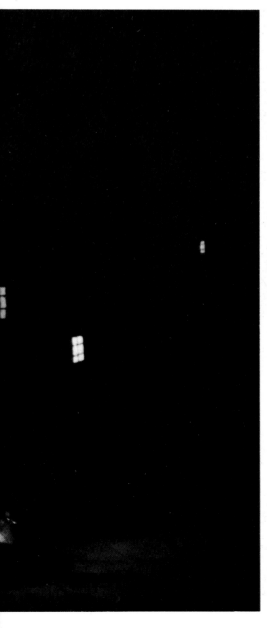

The costume was entirely white and the facial make-up was white too. Deburau dominated the art of mime from the tiny *Théâtre des Funambukes* in Paris. A beautiful photographic study of him in the part was made by the pioneer cameraman, Nadar.

In London, Joseph 'Joey' Grimaldi (1778 – 1837) dominated the stage as the clown in pantomime. He was of English-Italian parentage and first appeared on the stage of Sadler's Wells at the age of three. He played a monkey at the end of a chain held by his father. From such an unpromising beginning he went on to capture the public imagination as no other clown has ever done in Britain. After his death, Charles Dickens, who was a long-standing theatre-lover, edited his memoirs as a tribute to the great artist. His popularity is expressed in an anecdote of the day. A patient, it was said, complained to his doctor that he was suffering from deep depression. The remedy, replied the doctor, was to go to the theatre and see the great clown Grimaldi. The patient replied sadly, 'I am Grimaldi'.

No comparable figure followed Deburau and Grimaldi on to the stages of Europe for years, and by the turn of this century mime had dwindled in popularity. It was not until the 1930s that the work of the French actor Etienne Decroux (born 1898) revived mime as an art form on the stage. He believed that the art had been moved out of its most expressive boundaries by a flow of too much dance-like movement. Decroux emphasized the dramatic moment. He formed a small company that presented productions which were simply wordless plays. He dropped the broad, humourous approach of *commedia dell'arte* in favour of more precise and expressive body movement.

The invention of the silent film gave to the world another famous mime, perhaps the most famous of all – Charlie Chaplin (1889 – 1977). He caught the joy, pathos and the spirit of the *commedia dell'arte* as no other entertainer has done in this century. He was earthy, tender, boisterous, loving, and at times violent, but there was no doubting his message and most of it was given in pure mime. He was not above giving an elegant pretender a kick in the pants or tripping a pursuer with his cane. If he smelled something amiss he was likely to inspect the sole of his shoe for something foul he might have stepped into. The addition of sound to the world of films gave a new dimension to the medium, but it lost something in the vanishing tradition of Charlie Chaplin and it is no surprise that his films are as popular now as they were when they were made. Nothing has taken their place.

The vigour of Decroux and his school has, however, lived on among his pupils, the most brilliant of whom is the renowned French mime Marcel Marceau (born 1923). After leaving Decroux he worked for a short time with the Renaud-Barrault company

before forming his own small company and the memorable character of Bip. There is still some influence from the drama in Marceau's art, but it is essentially concerned with exploring the human predicament in the condition of one character. Bip is the little man trying to get on with the mounting difficulties of daily life. His are not the grand tragedies, but mere domestic irritants – the stuck window, the endless wall, the obstinate chair, the door which will not open. His weapon is ingenuity and he uses it like a rapier, with subtlety and delicacy. Bip is not the extent of Marceau's remarkable talent. His depiction of an afternoon in the park, when he brings a whole range of personalities to the stage is unforgettable. The characters demonstrate their own personalities first directly, then indirectly through the imagined encounter with the other characters, all of whom are Marceau. Through it all not a word is spoken.

Marceau has said that mime 'can come closest to identification with both human and inanimate objects'. This is something almost beyond the range of a dramatic actor or a trained dancer. The mime can openly pretend to portray a character. The actor must transform himself into it.

Like the strolling players of the medieval market place, most mime actors and performers today still live a travelling life. One major exception is the Pantomime Theatre of the Tivoli Gardens in Copenhagen, one of the world's most remarkable mime companies. Its origins are in the year 1800, when the Italian mime, Pasquale Casorti introduced the mime play, *Harlequin the Statue* to Denmark. The Tivoli Gardens opened in 1843 and a mime troupe was booked for the theatre there. The company has been at the Tivoli Gardens ever since. Each summer in the tiny theatre, the players stage traditional plays based on the old characters of the Italian *commedia dell'arte*. One of them is still *Harlequin the Statue*. The Danes love tradition, and the customs and stage practices of a long-dead age are preserved in the gardens of this northern city. Here is the closest living stage production to those noisy, laughing presentations which burst on to the Italian scene in the Renaissance.

Two very different mime companies were created in the 1950s – the companies of the Czech dancer and mime Ladislav Fialka, the Fialka Mime Group, and Henryk Tomaszewski's Polish Mime Theatre. The founders of both companies were trained ballet dancers who came to see mime as a more expressive medium. Both had wide experience of modern dance and it was from a combination of ballet, modern dance and drama that they developed their art.

Fialka (born 1931) formed his company around himself as the leading performer and he has devoted his energy to exploring serious themes, either in full-length story presentations or short sketches. He chooses

Mime is one of the oldest forms of theatrical art. Its classic simplicity has held audiences enthralled from the time of the ancient Greeks onwards. Many mimes liken their art to that of painting; Wayne Prichett, the artist who modelled for these studies, defines the art of mime as painting on a blank canvas, without the need for costume, props or scenery. Body shape and expression alone tell the story. Mime comes from within. The shape of the spine can form the basis of a character, to which can be added expression in the face, hands and other parts of the body.' All the great mime artists — from the celebrated Roman mime, Esophus, to the artists of the *commedia dell' arte,* the nineteenth century British clown, Grimaldi, Chaplin and Marceau — have followed these principles. Though the muteness of mime transcends barriers of language and nationality, two distinct European schools have evolved. One tradition — the Italian — emphasizes physical gesture, as part of its legacy from the *commedia dell' arte;* the French, on the other hand, is more subtle, concentrating on facial expression. The style is best seen in small, intimate surroundings.

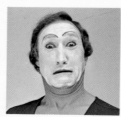

The neck is the essential creator of these different expressions.

All the characters here are formed by varying spinal position.

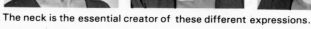

Hoy!

Quiet, please.

Tastes interesting.

Delicious.

The three stages of lifting a heavy suitcase.

small theatres and uses the full range of
modern theatrical expertise, including
music, special lighting and sound effects —
but the essence is pure mime.

Tomaszewski (born 1919) shares Fialka's
background, but his world of mime is a different one. He likes big theatres, and wit and
whimsy dominate his productions. There is
a fierce, almost sensual physicality about his
company. There is not a trace of white-faced,
romantic mime. The players are all real people, usually pretty and handsome as well as
being talented mimes. His productions are
all set within a dramatic scenario, but underlying them is a very real sense of dance and
rhythm. Tomaszewski is credited both as a
director and choreographer.

The sensibility is different, yet there is
much about the basics that is similar in both
men and their art. Both use all the stage
effects of the twentieth century and each sees
mime as a serious dramatic form capable of
great expression and philosophical depth.
There are, of course, larger and smaller roles
to be played, but the emphasis is on ensemble playing and not on solo performers. In
this sense, each man shares the vision of
Decroux that mime is a bodily expressive
form which relies on reshaping the whole
body rather than just making gestural
adjustments, and that the group is all important, not the individual.

These new companies and a spread of
annual festivals have led to a steady growth
in the popularity of mime in recent years. It
has grown from being a small, specialized
taste to reach such a broad spectrum that
the unique, Swiss three-member company,
Mummenschanz played continuously on
Broadway for several years. The company
chose the intimate Bijou Theatre, and in it
became the longest-playing mime attraction
in the United States.

The style of the company is distinctly different from any other. The body is used as an
acrobatic instrument of expression and the
face is completely masked. Watching them,
the spectator is highly conscious of movement, though it is not the graceful movement
that is normally associated with dancing. It is
athletic and eccentric with an insect quick-
ness that makes it almost eerie, despite its
humour.

The variety of masks used to hide the face
is immense, perhaps the most unusual being
made of soft clay, which the players sculpt
into expressions or designs that serve as a
sort of sculptural mime dialogue.

In a way *Mummenschanz* are returning to
the acrobatic arts of the medieval tumblers,
whose tricks were an integral part of mime
until the age of the romantic school. Props,
lights and sound are all used, but it is the
gesture of the body that speaks. It is twentieth century mime using all the trappings of
the twentieth century, but speaking in a language that has crossed the barriers of time
and nations.

The Polish mime theatre founded by Tomaszewski (far left) uses the wealth of modern theatrical effects in its productions, to produce visually exciting shows (right top). Many of the shows are based on Japanese legends (above, left) but the group also bases its work on drama.

MUSICALS

FROM MUSICAL COMEDY TO TODAY'S MUSIC AND DANCE SHOW

Musical comedy has impudently borrowed from every form of popular entertainment that could help its extravagant development. Music, dance, humour, the eccentricities of the circus, sequences of ballet, long, aria-like stretches of non-operatic song are all essential ingredients, held together by the carefully prepared plot of the straight play. Alone, these disjointed elements would not even have the coherence of the music hall, from which musical comedy largely sprang. Blended into a unified whole in which not only the dialogue, but the songs, jokes and even the dances, carry the story along, these divergent parts become a delightful art form.

Musical comedy — the musical — is thus a soufflée of the whole world of entertainment. In its most sophisticated form in the 1930s, 1940s and 1950s, staged with dazzling lighting and technical feats, it became a major performing art as well as an exciting entertainment with vast popular appeal.

The origins of musical comedy

Musical comedy is largely an American form of entertainment. In Britain, popular entertainment crystallized in the latter half of the last century into the music hall, with its expressly British traditions. Nowhere in the world did the smoke and beery jollity of the tavern and the berating banter of the cheeky chairman combine so brilliantly to create a popular entertainment so characteristic of the people who watched it — and sang and laughed with it. In Paris, the song and dance traditions of the *café chantants* had grown into the flamboyant extravaganzas built around *Les Girls*. These were glittering shows with elaborate costumes, vigorous music and sensual dance routines.

In America, early variety owed much to its European traditions. But it met, and was greatly influenced by, a uniquely American entertainment — the minstrel singer of the Southern states. In the last decade of the nineteenth century, this deep-rooted storytelling and singing tradition of the south combined with the great impresarios of Broadway to make the musical comedy — a popular entertainment form that was most brilliantly exploited in later years by the cinema. The musical comedy, more than any other form of popular variety, lent itself to the fabulous and inventive genius of Hollywood.

It is a remarkable fact, however, that the birth of the art form dates from a fire in 14th Street, New York. It was there that the New York Academy of Music burned down in the late summer of 1866 and left the two theatre producers Jarret and Palmer with a potential disaster on their hands. They had booked a travelling ballet company to appear there in a season of *La Biche au Bois*, and the company had already left Paris for the States. The autumn theatre season was about to start and the fire on 14th Street had left Jarret and Palmer with no theatre in which to put the ballet. In desperation they turned to William Wheatley, the proprietor of Niblo's Garden Theatre, for help.

Wheatley was uncertain at first. He had already planned to stage a new melodrama, *The Black Crook*. This was an improbable play about an alchemist making a pact with the devil to deliver one soul each year to Hell, and so extending his life by the same amount of time. It did not make much of an impact, and even by the standards of the time was considered preposterous and old-fashioned.

Wheatley was finally persuaded to buy up the ballet dancers' contracts and the scenery that had survived the fire. It was probably a bargain and Wheatley may have been driven to it by the dismal prospects for *The Black Crook*. Whatever the reason, Wheatley had bought himself a slice of theatrical history.

Incongruously — or perhaps to minimize his possible losses and commitments —

Right This poster for the D'Oyly Carte Opera Company advertises *The Yeoman of the Guard* the two act operetta by Gilbert and Sullivan, first performed at the Savoy Theatre, London in 1888.
Below This costume design for the Mikado was for the operetta's first production at the Savoy Theatre in 1885. *The Mikado, or The Town of Titipu,* is perhaps the best-known and loved of all the Gilbert and Sullivan operettas.

Right The fashionable poet, Bunthorne, with lily in hand is one of the main characters in Gilbert and Sullivan's *Patience,* which satirized the then popular aesthetic movement led by Oscar Wilde and Dante Gabriel Rossetti.

Below This sketch of Mr Grossmith as Ko-Ko dates from *The Mikado's* first production at the Savoy in 1885. Ko-Ko was the famous Lord High Executioner of Titipu whose ward and fiancée was the delectable Yum-Yum who eventually marries the Mikado's son, Nanki-Poo

PATIENCE

D'OYLY CARTE OPERA COMPANY

Wheatley combined the dreadful melodrama with the beautiful young women of the ballet. It was impossible simply to merge the sentimental ballet with the devilish comedy, so a friendly jumble of tunes was adapted and arranged by a local composer, Guiseppe Operti. The lovely young ladies were sent on stage in striking, leg-hugging tights, their own lavish scenery and some homely little songs for their outlandish date with the Devil.

The work — it did not fall into any previously understood category of entertainment — opened on September 16, 1866 at 7.45 pm. The final curtain did not drop until 1.15 the following morning — by which time, Wheatley can have been in no doubt that he had a triumph on his hands that would more than pay off his investment. Nothing that had gone on stage anywhere before resembled this musical production of *The Black Crook*, and this was the first musical comedy in theatre history. Soon everyone was singing the show's hit songs — 'The March of the Amazons' and 'You Naughty, Naughty Men'. *The Black Crook* was surely a remarkable theatrical beginning.

Developments in Europe

It was not just its American origins which made the musical comedy so essentially American. The social attitudes of strait-laced Europe played an unwitting part, too. In the free, frontier environment of the New World, entertainment was allowed an untrammelled development. This was not the case in Victorian Britain.

Charles Morton, the Father of Music Hall, had been presenting variety artists since 1829. By the mid-nineteenth century this form of raucous jollity had become the working man's favourite entertainment. By 1850

Above C.B. Cochran, shown here vetting costumes for *Wake up and Dream,* was a leading British producer. One of the many triumphs of his long association with Noël Coward after 1925 was *Bitter Sweet* (1929)

Below Sylvia Kingsley was one of the leading Zieglfeld girls. The American theatrical producer produced the first of 24 annual revues in 1907. His productions were renowned for their choruses of beautiful girls.

its rowdiness had caused frowns in Whitehall. Parliament decided to distinguish between what was permissible in the halls and on other stages in the world of entertainment. Theatrical entertainment was divided by government decree into the 'legitimate' theatre and the 'musical'. Music halls were restricted to singing and dancing and were forbidden to have continuous spoken dialogue — this was the exclusive right of the legitimate theatre. If this rule had been obeyed, it would have effectively banned all comedy sketches, which were the great favourites of the day. In fact, most music hall managers simply ignored the regulation, put on their sketches and paid the fine, philosophically counting the cost among their overheads.

But if Victorian moral attitudes failed to stifle the crudities of the comics, they certainly put an effective brake on any movement towards the musical comedy which was soon to arrive so surprisingly in America. Continuous dialogue, even including the songs, was an essential part of this new and exciting entertainment. The restrictions of Parliament did not even legally allow continuous spoken dialogue.

In 1860, the French government followed suit. Music hall had been adopted in France so completely, that it was even called *le music-hall*. Now artists were banned from appearing in sketches there, too, while the décor had to be one set piece fixed to the floor. The prudish elements of nineteenth century European society were obviously determined that *le music-hall* should become as dreary as possible.

It took some ingenuity to get over the problem, but the designers of the music hall sets were not to be foiled. They created revolving louvers that were indeed attached to the stage, but, when revolved, created a sumptuous variety of backing for the artists.

Governments were clearly fighting a losing battle against the lusty energy of the halls. The simple solo performer of the *café chantants* and the English pub had grown into variety bills with sometimes 20 or even more individual turns. These ranged from acrobats to magic, bellringers to boxers, bicyclists to comics, singers to strong men. The crowds were volatile and the performers had to capture their attention at once — or be bodily hauled off by stagehands waiting in the wings. Some managements even used a long shepherd's staff to hook the unfortunates off stage by the neck.

The influence of Dixie

Not only did the USA have no such restrictions; it also had a unique feature — the minstrel tradition of the South. As early as 1829, Thomas T. Rice, known as Daddy Rice, blacked his face with a burnt cork and sang on stage a negro song, 'Jim Crow'. This was the start of the minstrel tradition and imitators, such as Billy Whitlock, Dan

Emmett, Dick Pelham and Frank Brower, organized themselves as the Virginia Minstrels. They are generally credited with being the first group of minstrel showmen. They wrote and performed their own material; and it was Emmett, born in Ohio, who sat down in New York one day and wrote 'Dixieland' — the song that as 'Dixie' became the Confederate anthem.

The popularity of minstrel shows was enormous. The companies mixed songs and jokes with speciality acts, parody and satire. As a form of entertainment it did not grow into musical comedy proper, but it created a style. It was left to the Devil of *The Black Crook* and the ballet dancers to turn it into a recognisable fashion.

There was another legacy of the minstrel shows that was to play a vital role in the future of the musical comedy. This was the work of George M. Cohan (1878–1942), the son of a famous blackface singer and comedian. The paternal influence was never lost on the young George. He followed his father's footsteps into show business and for twenty years at the start of the twentieth century dominated the development of the musical comedy.

Cohan, Ziegfeld and revue

Surprisingly, there was no great rush to follow Wheatley in his success with *The Black Crook*. Burlesque was its only real and immediate successor. Legs, legs, more legs and beautiful girls — that seemed to be the first message that America's impresarios took from the success of this devilish improvisation. Showmen wandered into a cul-de-sac where crudity substituted for talent. It required a man of vision to extricate it and George M. Cohan exactly fitted the bill. Cohan was a man of prodigious talent and he pulled together most of the elements which contributed to the emergence of a unified musical comedy from the scattered turns of vaudeville.

Cohan started in vaudeville. Finding himself trapped by the repetitious nature of the work, he left the stage to become a producer. Cohan wrote his own plays, composed his own music, penned the lyrics to the songs he had composed, choreographed and danced the steps he had created, in addition to directing and producing his own shows. It was a staggering one-man display of talent. The plots of these very basic musicals were simple, direct and uncomplicated. They were carried by the brashness and energy of their creator who was unashamedly sentimental and patriotic. He caught the mood of the time, those suspended days of isolation and change in the first two decades of the century when America looked back to a nostalgic past while marching unwillingly into the future. He caught the nation at a moment when flag-waving was a national passion.

Cohan's songs were rousing or tender by turn and he had no sympathy for sophisticated themes or subtle touches. But he hit a national chord and he took musical comedy an important step forward towards its ultimate format. There was still one thing missing — spectacle. This arrived in 1905 in a sea of extravagance and theatrical excess, when the impresario Florenz Ziegfeld (1867–1932) launched his *Follies*.

The New York Hippodrome was opened in 1905. Its huge auditorium could seat 5,000 and the stage was big enough to handle elephants if necessary. Charles Dillingham and the three Schubert Brothers all produced their extravaganzas there, but it was Ziegfeld who was the most adept at combining beautiful women in lavish but revealing costumes with comedy sketches, songs and large-scale production numbers. He had a genius for balancing the elements of his productions so that they maintained a steady impetus; although towards the end of his career the public began to weary of the costume parades. They lacked the relative sophistication of the newer, more intimate reviews, such as John Murray Anderson's (1886–1954) *Village Follies* and George White's (1890–1968) *Scandals*.

These new reviews had many of the same elements as the extravaganza, but they were presented on a smaller scale and usually had an 'art spot' which presented a serious form of dance drama. Stars such as Fred and Adele Astaire, Eddie Cantor, Josephine Baker, Fanny Brice and Helen Morgan all appeared in them in the 1920s and 1930s. British performers, such as Beatrice Lillie, Gertrude Lawrence, Jack Buchanan and Noël Coward, who were to have such an influence on musicals, also emerged in these reviews successfully both in London and on Broadway.

From operetta to musicals

Yet another important influence on the development of the musical was the classic nineteenth century operetta. In France, the scintillating works of Jacques Offenbach (1819–1880), with their tuneful music and frequently satirical plots, won world-wide renown. So, too, did the works of the British partnership, Sir William Schwenk Gilbert (1836–1911) and Sir Arthur Sullivan (1842–1900). Gilbert's witty plots combined with Sullivan's music to create the celebrated 'Savoy Operas'. Tunes from these were sung in drawing rooms and whistled in the streets from London to New York and Sydney. They were the smash hits of their day.

Operetta was still a powerful attraction at the turn of the century, but it was soon to decline in popularity, although Sigmund Romberg (1887–1951) could still stage his wildly successful *Desert Song* in 1926 and *The New Moon* in 1928. Both were produced with the collaboration of a rising young lyricist — Oscar Hammerstein II (1859–1960).

Now all the ingredients of the musical comedy had been tested and tried in the live theatre. It only needed to be brought together and given a more sophisticated dramatic presentation. Songs were at last to be made an integral part of the action. They were to advance the story and not just serve as a pretty interlude. This whole process was accelerated by a succession of brilliant young lyricists.

The pioneer of this next step was Jerome Kern (1885–1945), with a series of small-scale productions at the Princess Theatre. In 1915, he collaborated with the writer Guy Bolton on *Nobody Home* and *Very Good, Eddie*. They added the novelist P. G. Wodehouse (1881–1978) to their team for their greatest successes, *Oh Boy!* in 1917 and *Oh Lady, Lady* in 1918. These were compact musical comedies based on ordinary, everyday events and they played to audiences of fewer than 300 as opposed to the gigantic crowds that filled the Hippodrome. They offered a moderating influence to the *Follies*, where all was mammoth spectacle.

The puzzled public seemed to applaud all the diversities of the musical comedy for a while, but it soon became evident that the sheer sight of beautiful women paraded as mere walking models was not enough to hold the public's attention. Audiences became increasingly attracted to the sophistication of the smaller productions.

The musical comes of age

By the early 1920s the musical comedy had truly arrived — a brilliant combination of spectacle and talent. Cohan, Kern, Irving Berlin (born 1888), George Gershwin (1898–1937) and his brother Ira (born 1896), Vincent Youmans (1898–1946) Richard Rodgers (1902–1979), and Cole Porter (1893–1964) wrote songs and shows for the stage and later the screen that still live as a monument to their age. Perhaps no other era has produced such a lasting collection of fabulous songs.

The early musicals had a set format, they were divided into two acts. A romantic couple, often from differing social strata were usually separated in Act 1, only to be happily re-united in Act 2. Each act had an opening and closing big number that filled the stage, all the principals of the show had at least one big song, and the lovers a duet. There was a comic character and unmistakable elements of the review. But the whole show hinged on a situation and the plot was carried forward by word and song.

It caught the public fancy like a wave and swept it along for decades. It was sumptuous, but not over-extravagant like the *Follies*, and it was sophisticated without being cramped like the reviews. It enchanted an entire era.

In 1927, Kern and Hammerstein produced *Show Boat*. It was a milestone in the development of the musical. Kern had always been urged by Wodehouse to 'bring on the girls' — Wodehouse even used that for

2-3 years	6 months	5 months	4 months
Writer			
Composer			
Lyricist			
Producer			

Choreographer
Musical director
Set designer — Begin mental work
Costume designer

Star performer

the title to the memoirs of his life in show business — now Kern brought on true life characters, too. There were no cardboard emotions rattling about emptily, but a real, moving plot, adapted from Edna Ferber's novel. Hammerstein wrote the lyrics for 'Make Believe', 'Old Man River' and 'Can't Help Lovin' That Man'. Kern created his most memorable score. The show ran for two years, then went on tour. Hollywood has since produced three separate musicals from it, drawn irresistibly by its magic.

The dramatic impact of *Show Boat* opened possibilities that were snapped up by other producers. In 1931, Gershwin and George S. Kaufman (1889–1961) presented *Of Thee I Sing*, the first musical to venture into politics for its plot. It dealt satirically with such cultural and political institutions as the Presidential campaign, marriage and the Supreme Court. The show won a Pulitzer Prize for drama and confirmed the arrival of the musical as a vehicle for a serious story. Richard Rodgers and Lorenz Hart (1895–1943) had collaborated for years before they took the next step and introduced a scoundrel hero in *Pal Joey*. Joey was a cynical but somehow attractive opportunist who always managed to land on his feet. The show included some of Rodger's finest music, 'If They Asked Me I Could Write A Book' and 'Bewitched, Bothered and Bewildered'. It was coolly received and did not become a hit until it was revived fourteen years later.

Disagreements broke up this gifted team — but happily they led to another when Rodgers began his masterly collaboration with Hammerstein. Shows which were to become classics flooded the stages of the next two decades. In 1943, Rodgers and Hammerstein produced their first show together, *Oklahoma!* It introduced Agnes de Mille's dream-sequence ballet to the Broadway stage, and this, too, became an almost indispensible part of successive musicals.

Season after season composers and lyricists fed on the success of the musical and, nurtured on its new seriousness, produced one classic after another. When Jerome Kern died his producers turned to Berlin and asked him to create what was to have been Kern's last musical. Berlin responded with *Annie Get Your Gun*, probably his greatest work and certainly containing a selection of his most memorable songs. These include 'They Say It's Wonderful', 'Doin' What Comes Naturally', 'The Girl That I Marry', 'Anything You Can Do', and 'There's No Business Like Show Business'.

Alan J. Lerner (born 1918) and Frederick Loewe (born 1904) produced *Brigadoon* and

Above This photograph shows a scene from *Evita*, the highly acclaimed musical based on the life of Eva Peron, by Tim Rice and Andrew Lloyd-Webber. The show opened in London in 1978 with Elaine Paige in the title role. The New York production opened on Broadway in 1979.

Above right This scene is from a 1947 production of *Oklahoma!* with music by Richard Rodgers and book and lyrics by Oscar Hammerstein II. First produced in 1941, it is one of the most popular of modern musicals and was made into a highly successful film.

Right *A Chorus Line* was first performed in New York in 1975. The music by Marvin Hamlisch and lyrics by Edward Kleban were based on a book by James Kirkwood and Nicholas Dante about an audition for eight chorus dancers. Its theme and structure marked a breakthrough in the stage musical and the show was very successful in both the USA and Britain.

3 months	2 months	7 weeks	6 weeks	1 month	**First night**

Casting begins
Extend the score

Dance arranger
Creative pianist
Extra technical staff
Deputy stage manager
Assistant stage manager
Stage director
Company manager

Singers start rehearsals
Dancers start rehearsals
Actors start rehearsals
Musicians start rehearsals

My Fair Lady; Richard Adler (born 1921) and Jerry Ross (1926–1955) created *The Pajama Game* and *Damn Yankees*; Frank Loesser (1910–1969) made *Guys and Dolls*; Leonard Bernstein (born 1918) and Stephen Sondheim (born 1930) *West Side Story*; and Cole Porter presented *Kiss Me Kate*. Rodgers and Hammerstein followed *Oklahoma!* with *Carousel*, *South Pacific*, *The King and I*, and *The Sound of Music*. The whole list is a part of Broadway history.

The variety was dazzling and the dramatic themes ranged from love on a factory floor to spy adventure in the South Sea islands. It was love among real people and real events. The music and dancing were from a fantasy, the people recognizable and the situations ordinary. The rich young couples and the fashionable settings of the early musicals had vanished. In *West Side Story*, the lovers met on a tenement fire escape, as musical comedy broadened its scope to take in the here and now. Fantasy, however, still survived in the enchanted village of *Brigadoon* and the far-off kingdom of Siam in the *King and I*. But the king and the villagers were human. The musical had reached into politics, war, social conditions, poverty, crime, and gambling and into its own golden age in the history of entertainment. Its success still lives on in many different forms. These range to-day from the intimacy of Sondheim's *Side by Side* to the memorable spectacle of *Jesus Christ Superstar* and *Evita* by Tim Rice and Andrew Lloyd-Webber.

Behind the scenes
Greater technical demands are made on the capacity of the theatre by the musical than by any other type of performing art except perhaps opera. Each production has to be planned like a military campaign, and there is as much talent, energy and administrative organization put into making the great classics by the back-stage staff as by the men and

women whose names went up in lights.

An enormous staff has to be gathered for a musical, even before a single performer has read a line, studied a score or set a dancing foot tapping on the rehearsal stage. The producer has to collect around him a composer, lyricist, director, choreographer, stage manager, technical manager, musical director, set designer and costume designer. When the rehearsal stage is reached, he has to add to the team a company manager, a stage crew manager, set construction supervisor, wardrobe mistress, lighting and special effects technician, properties manager — who has to keep track of every book, vase, table, lamp or ornament required in each and every scene — a business manager, publicity manager, box office manager and promotion director.

Most of these people need assistants.

Technical experts and backstage crews all add their touches of magic to the finished product. Lighting and effects are designed to transform scenes rapidly as are revolving stages, sliding tracks, or scenery 'flown' from joists above the stage, that is sets which can be gently lowered into position or quickly whisked upwards out of sight. Projectors, X-rays, footlights, coloured spotlights which can follow the action or turn night into day, or outdoors into indoors are among the pure lighting effects.

The musical theatre in the golden age of the musical, during the 1940s and 1950s, could create almost any atmosphere it wanted. Every element had to be worked out in advance and bound in detail into a large

book that became the bible of the show. The title page gave the name of the production, with the names of the composer and lyricist and the story credit. Inside was a complete list script, numbered with each scene and act and the list of cast.

A composite ground plan was drawn giving exact measurements for the stage. The hanging plot numbered each pipe above the stage and identified it as bearing lights or props. All the electrical equipment was listed with its function, the position where it was located and where the switchboard and dimmers were placed. It had to show each piece of property, where it had to be placed, and when and how it had to be moved, and it had to catalogue every costume. When that had all been done, then, and only then, could

the show go on. Although much of this is needed for any theatrical production, the combination of music and effects makes the musical particularly complicated.

Dance and the musical

Dancing of some sort or another has played its part in every phase of musical comedy. Individual or acrobatic numbers featured in the early spectaculars. In 1901 in London came a new innovation − the precision troupe. John Tiller picked, trained and presented his first team in that year. All the girls were between 5ft and 5ft 2in tall and they kicked their long legs in a mixture of healthy athleticism and precise timing. There arose a great demand for them on both sides of the Atlantic and they figured in stage musicals

and the great Hollywood films until well into the 1930s.

It was then that jazz gave a new impetus to dancing in the musical. The faster rhythm opened up the chance for spectacular tap routines from Fred Astaire (born 1899), which led later to complex dance duets with Ginger Rogers (born 1911). Tap routines soon developed, with exciting variations from figures such as the American choreographer and director Busby Berkeley (1895−1976). At first dances tended to be special 'production' numbers which were not fully integrated into the plot. Gradually, however, the relationship between the two became closer.

Dancing became further integrated into the plot in 1936, when Richard Rodgers and

Lorenz Hart (1895−1943) created *On Your Toes*, the first true dance-musical, which told the story of the backstage intrigues of a ballet company. The ballet director and choreographer, George Balanchine (born 1904) choreographed the show, and it included a complete ballet, 'Slaughter On Tenth Avenue'. Ray Bolger (born 1904) danced the lead with Tamara Geva (born 1907), who was a trained Russian ballet dancer. The show brought Rodgers and Hart back to Broadway after five years dedicated to Hollywood, and it launched Balanchine on a career spanning 16 Broadway shows before he returned to pure ballet.

The dancing experiment in musicals began a tradition that has grown in strength. In the 1960s and 1970s, the director-choreographer increasingly began to predominate in the world of the musical. Jerome Robbins (born 1918) forcefully turned dancing into an important part of the plot of *West Side Story*. His influence was even greater in *Fiddler On The Roof*.

Like Robbins, Bob Fosse (born 1927) choreographed musicals in the 1950s in the traditional manner. With *Chicago*, he made the reality of a murder trial merge into the musical comedy routine, making life imitate the stage rather than the other way around. In *Dancin'* he went the full distance and made the dance routines themselves the plot.

The trend has not halted, but rather urged onwards by the great burst of popular music in the late 1950s and 1960s. Michael Bennet (born 1943), an ex-dancer himself, built *A Chorus Line*, another musical hit, around the very process of selecting dancers for a show. *Grease* successfully carried the message of modern pop in an exciting display of exuberant dancing from the Broadway stage to the cinema screen.

There will always be revivals of the great classics from musical comedy's golden age and the old movies will never be lost. For all its incongruity, that inauspicious precursor of the musical comedy, *The Black Crook*, has even had its share of revivals. They are probably merited if for no more reason than the milestone it marked on the path of popular entertainment. One version was choreographed by no less a figure than Agnes de Mille for a Christopher Morley production in 1929 in New Jersey.

Perhaps the musical is stepping into the world of dance. Maybe it is not even too fanciful to imagine *The Black Crook* revived one day with Wheatley's devilish plot totally buried in the routine of a troupe of ballet dancers. It would be one of musical comedy's best jokes.

The chorus line was an essential ingredient of the musical. Glittering costumes and coordinated high kicks were also expected. In the USA, the Ziegfeld girls were popular with audiences. This picture shows their British equivalent, the Tiller girls in 1930.

VARIETY AND MUSIC HALL

FROM THE EARLY HALLS AND BURLESQUE TO THE DEATH OF VARIETY

A royal favour granted by King Charles II indirectly gave birth to the great British variety tradition. In 1663, two years before the plague and three years before the great fire destroyed half of London, he signed a decree sweeping aside the earnest Puritanism of Cromwell and opening the playhouses of England for the first time since the Commonwealth. However, royal patents were granted only to two theatres, Drury Lane and Covent Garden and, by special dispensation, to the Haymarket Theatre during the summer months when the companies of both the other theatres followed the royal court to Bath. The other English theatres could open, too, but they were expressly forbidden to produce *'wholly spoken* theatrical activity for gain.'

The impresarios of the seventeenth century were quick to find the loophole in the law. In order to present a play and make a profit they had to surround it with elements from the circus, the fairground or the world of music. In this way, they were able to maintain that the admission fee was for the song and dance part of the show. The 'wholly spoken theatrical activity', the drama which it surrounded, was merely an extra, thrown in for free.

There was nothing new in the components of such a show. They had been entertaining the town and country folk of Britain for centuries. But this was the first time they had all been presented on the same bill and the first time they had been brought together in a theatre. They were very successful. It was only a short time before the managers of the theatres expressly excluded from the royal favour, discovered that their audiences were happy to forego the plays altogether.

Before long the elements of this form of entertainment had spread to the coffee houses, taverns, glee clubs and supper rooms, all of them competing to pull in the customers. It even went back into the open air, where so many of its traditions lay in the historic art of the medieval strolling players.

Below Girls of the Folies Bergère, like these, although often more scantily clad, were one of the main attractions of this famous music hall in Paris. Built on the site of a livery stable in 1869 the hall, from the start, specialized in spectacular revues. Folies' immense promenade, where people could loiter between the variety acts, was an additional attraction and the house soon became a rendezvous for fashionable young men-about-town. Its fame spread; and both French and foreign visitors flocked to its doors. Its revues were often immensely beautiful spectacles and always featured captivating, semi-naked girls. Other acts included acrobats, singers, dancers and clowns. Many of the greatest names of French entertainment have appeared on its bills.

More than 200 pleasure gardens opened up in and around London between the middle of the eighteenth century and the latter part of the nineteenth. There, circus acts, concerts, ballets and sporting contests vied with the sideshows lining the flower-bordered lawns. Often there were firework displays, set-piece simulations of battles or the eruption of Vesuvius. Vauxhall Gardens on the south bank of the Thames was the most famous of these resorts, the Cremorne, opened across the river near the Chelsea Hospital in the 1830s the most stylish.

There were no bills of variety, the attractions were a succession of what today would be called supporting artists, who performed in separate booths or on separate pitches while the audience moved from one to the other.

In 1793 Charles Dibdin (1745–1814), an English circus promoter built a tiny playhouse in the centre of London. It was called the Sans Souci and it was designed specifically to show off Dibdin's talents as a songwriter, satirist, singer and showman.

The final step to music hall proper came in 1820. A publican, William Rhodes, took over a Strand tavern called the Coal Hole. There, and in slightly seedier quarters at the Cyder Cellars in Maiden Lane, he devised the role of a chairman or president, who introduced the performers and heckled and was heckled

by the rowdier customers. The shows were a collection of singers, sketches, conjuring acts and tableaux posed by the beefy ladies so much admired at the time.

Dibdin's one-man show and Rhodes's chairman led directly to the music hall tradition and the stand-up comic who has been its mainstay. It was from this old-time music hall, that the modern variety programme has evolved.

Publicans all over Britain soon adopted Rhodes's formula, eager to pull in the extra business it brought; but it was left to a more ambitious enterprise to install a properly equipped stage and to separate the eaters and drinkers from the performers. The first place to be described on its playbills as a music hall was the 1,000 seat Winchester Theatre which opened in 1840 just south of the Thames in Blackfriars Road — and, by an odd coincidence, on the very site of Charles Dibdin's Royal Circus which had been burned down in 1803.

The Winchester was a huge success. But if we are to put a name to the first true music hall, then it belongs not to the Winchester, but to the New Canterbury, which opened its doors 14 years later. Food, drink, and entertainment were still provided under the same roof, but, for the first time, the audience had to pay a charge at the entrance which was specifically for the performance.

The New Canterbury was the brainchild of Charles Morton (1819–1904), a slum child who had risen from being a barman to innkeeper and then to impresario by the time he was 29. His New Canterbury took six years to build. Contemporary engravings show that it was a lofty and elegant showplace, richly decorated and with marble topped tables beneath a high stage. Graceful staircases curved upwards from the wide entrance to loggias and stage boxes surrounding the main hall.

The New Canterbury even coined a new word for the great show which launched its opening in 1854. The scintillating list of entertainers was described as a 'Bill of Varieties'. It was a huge success, and there were plenty of imitators. Morton's approach seems to have been devised simultaneously by the Alhambra in Leicester Square. It opened just weeks after the New Canterbury with an elaborately designed Moorish dome and turrets — and the same formula that Morton used.

In 1861, Morton built the Oxford, which was later to become the Oxford Street Corner House. Then, he transformed the derelict Old Mogul Theatre in Cambridge Circus into the Palace, the most stylish of all the metropolitan music halls.

The New Canterbury seated 1,500. The Palace and the London Hippodrome were larger. The Coliseum in St. Martin's Lane would seat 2,200. Such florid and grandiose palaces were in direct contrast to the intimate, classic music halls like the Oxford, the

Below Covent Garden Theatre has had many forms. This version was opened in 1857.

Left This firework display is taking place at Crystal Palace in 1869, a popular recreational centre in the second half of the nineteenth century. Sir Joseph Paxton's glass and iron structure built for the Great Exhibition was re-erected there in 1854. Firework displays were among the regular entertainments which attracted the crowds.

Below A meeting of the Union Club, whose alleged aim was the union of England and Ireland. James Gillray, in this caricature of 1801, satirizes the debauchery of such gatherings.

Left This picture shows The Royal Victoria Coffee Palace and Music Hall in 1881. Although a conventional music-hall from 1871, the theatre was reopened as a temperance music-hall in 1880 and became a popular family resort.

Grecian, the Olympic or Collins's in Islington, the Edgware Road Metropolitan, the City Varieties in Leeds and Glasgow's Britannia. The smaller halls relied on local people for their audiences: the red-plush and gilt palaces catered mainly for a transient, once-only clientele. They gave rise to two quite separate types of performance.

The grander, outsize halls, with their enormous chandeliers, swagged panelling, cupids and vast promenades where lovers met, went in for productions as extravagant as their settings. Beneath the glittering dome of the Coliseum scenes from opera and drama alternated with trapeze acts and oriental dancers. Below the stage in the Hippodrome there were stables for the horses which turned machinery operating fantastic fountains and cascades. These featured in the aqua shows for which the theatre was famous. Production costs and wages for the top artists were huge. Each bill ran for a short season to attract a large number of customers, many of them from out of town.

The tiny halls, on the other hand, could make a profit in a week, and they often changed their bills weekly. They therefore included a great deal of highly topical material in songs and patter. This up-to-the-minute approach, the banter of the chairman and his cheeky exchanges with the audience, created the distinctive and intimate atmosphere of the British music hall. It has never been fully recaptured anywhere else.

Nothing remains static — least of all in

Left This cider cellar 1849 offers drink and entertainment. Music-hall began in taverns like this.
Right The Alhambra in Leicester Square was, for a short time, a circus and then, as a music hall, owed its early success to Léotard, a trapeze artist and wire-walker who drew large crowds.

show business. The links between the halls and the taverns gradually loosened. The rows of tables vanished to make room for more seating and more customers. The floors became raked and the stage, originally uncurtained, gained a proscenium arch. The audience and performers were separated for the first time. But the chivvying chairman with his pompous punning and alliteratively allusive announcements remained. There was still a bar at the back of the auditorium and through its open windows the drinkers could see and hear the show. It was still music hall.

By the late 1860s the halls had become so popular all over the country that they had practically eclipsed the theatre. However, costs were escalating and so were the fees of the topline acts. Big city centre houses like the Empire in Liverpool, the London Pavilion, the Alhambra and the Empire, Leicester Square, veered more towards the longer-running revue type of show. In a music hall bill the artists appear only once (and they would often appear in four theatres in a night); in a revue a smaller number of performers appear in a number of sketches, songs or scenes all on the same programme. The different types of show demanded different types of performer. The former favoured the blazing talent which was concentrated in a 10-minute act such as Vesta Tilley's. The revue style suited a performer such as the Australian comedienne Cicely Courtneidge (born 1893) whose talent — and act — spread over some two hours. Once the chairman and the open bar had gone, it was the blazing talents condensed into a single short performance which formed the backbone of what became known as variety.

Variety in Paris

Popular entertainment had followed a path in Paris roughly parallel to that in Britain. Singers and recitalists were hired by many of the cafés and bars — indoors and outdoors — to draw in the customers and entertain them while they ate and drank. The performances at these *cafés chantants*, as they were known, were, however, greatly inhibited by an article in the Code Napoleon, the legal constitution of France.

This banned the use of costumes, scenery, or props except in straight plays or operas. It was a law that hit even the *opéras bouffes* by Jacques Offenbach (1819–1880). These were allowed only three characters because of their 'frivolous' nature; and the producers of the café entertainments were forbidden to print posters or advertise their programmes in the street.

All this changed in 1867. Judges ruled that it was illogical that a tragedienne from the *Comédie Française* should be permitted to play, in costume, a character from Molière's *Amphitryon* on one stage, but be prohibited from playing an excerpt in the same way on another stage just around the corner.

Now, comedians, illusionists, tumblers and even skaters were added to the singers and dancers on show. The *café chantant* became the *café concert*. Later the programmes moved from the pavement cafés to smaller theatres on the fringe of the *grands boulevards* such as the Altazar, the Eldorado or *Les Ambassadeurs*, which were known by the English name, 'music hall'. The name was also adopted by the sumptuous revue spectaculars which followed soon afterwards.

The *Folies Bergères* opened in 1869, modelled unashamedly on the London Alhambra, tables and all. According to a contemporary description, it was 'a theatre which is not a theatre, a promenade where you may remain seated, a spectacle that you are not obliged to watch, with two thousand men, all smoking, drinking and joking, and seven or eight hundred women all laughing, drinking and offering themselves as happily as you could wish'. It was a great success.

Below Signor Grimondi's performing dogs. Variety acts from Paris were immensely popular in England in the early nineteenth century.

Right Charles Dibdin, one of the fathers of the music hall, also wrote naval songs such as 'Tom Bowling'.

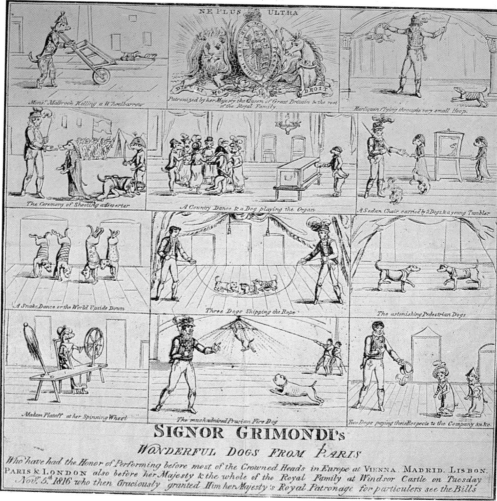

SIGNOR GRIMONDI's WONDERFUL DOGS FROM PARIS

Who have had the Honor of Performing before most of the Crowned Heads in Europe at Vienna, Madrid, Lisbon, Paris & London also before her Majesty & the whole of the Royal Family at Windsor Castle on Tuesday Nov. 5th 1816 who then Graciously granted Him her Majesty's Royal Patronage for particulars see the Bills

122 ~~Commences weekly~~ ~~Twice nightly~~ **Engagements for MONDAY,** the 1st day of May 1899 **122**

ARTISTE	Business.	Salary.	Agent	Position on Bill.	Remarks.
Salonne Family ✓	Gymnasts	IE 5%	Self.	Middle	Good
Farris & Farnley ✓	Comedians	A IE	Reel	Duet	not worth money
Geo Watson. ✓	character & speln		Duet		Good
Flo Varley ✓	Burlesque & songs	C	Reel		Fair
Arthur Glens ✓	descriptive	P 5%			Fair
~~Charles Chard~~	Comedian				brought forward to Mar 13.
~~Annie Casey~~		N 5%			cancelled.
Lottie Lennot	Comedienne	IM	G. Foster	Bottom	Very Good
Cross & Taylor	Comedians	T 5%	Self		Good
Bros Redmond ✓	Specialty	O	G. Fortune		Mod
Chas Coburn	Comedian	PE 5%		Top	poor

There were tables, too, at the *Moulin Rouge* when it opened 20 years later. The exotic showgirls, provided the main attraction. Indeed, the accessible ladies in the audience were a bigger attraction than the performers in the early days of French music hall — whether they were flinging up their petticoats in the dance that became the can-can, waiting for clients in the *Moulin Rouge* garden, or soliciting along the promenades of the *Folies* or the *Olympia*.

In summer, when the stuffy, gas-lit theatres closed, the artistes immortalized by Toulouse-Lautrec would move to pavilions in the gardens beneath the trees of the

Above This sheet lists the artists engaged at City Varieties in Leeds for 1st May, 1899. The theatre manager has included his own comments on the performers and listed their salaries in code. Interestingly, Charles Coburn, who later became a major music hall star, earned the comment 'poor'.

Champs Elysées. It had by then become fashionable for the *Belle Epoque* socialites who had earlier skated at the *Palais de Glace* and dined at Maxim's, to go to watch Jane Avril or Yvette Guilbert.

When the grander theatres began to stage lavish revues, it was often the costumes, the decor and the originality of the sets which drew the crowds as much as the performers whose names were in lights outside. Many of the starring ladies differed little from the girls in the *Moulin Rouge*. They had been booked more for their appearance than their talent. Their activities were the subject of the gossip columns rather than the critical reviews. These courtesans, delightfully called by the French *les grandes horizontales*, used the stage as a shop window for their undoubted charms.

Mimi Pinson, Blanche d'Antigny, Liane de Lancy, Manon Loti, Tica la Rousse — the names echo the frothing champagne of a fantasy world. Some did have talent. Cléo de Merode, who became mistress of King Leopold II of Belgium was a good dancer. So was La Belle Otéro, who boasted a diamond breastplate and 12-string pearl choker. She performed, according to the French writer

Colette (1873 – 1954), 'for her own enjoyment; she cared little for ours.' The most fascinating, perhaps, was Liane de Pougy, an intimate of Oscar Wilde and Aubrey Beardsley. She made her money from men and spent it on women. She ended her life as Princess Ghika, with a fabulous collection of jewellery, including emerald rings for each of her toes which she wore only in bed.

Variety stars

It was in Paris, too, that the great age of international stars was born. The year was 1900. Paris had become the pleasure capital of the world and it hosted the Universal

Left In Edwardian music hall two stock characters were Tired Tim and Weary Willie who specialized in corny jokes.
Right This Gaiety

Theatre programme dates from 1880. The theatre was famous for its burlesques and for the Gaiety girls, renowned for their looks.

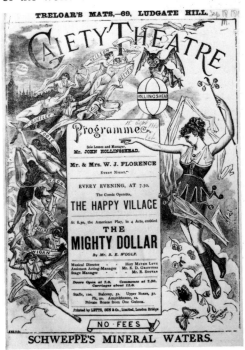

TRELOAR'S MATS.—69, LUDGATE HILL.

GAIETY THEATRE

Programme

Sole Lessee and Manager,
Mr. JOHN HOLLINGSHEAD.

Mr. & Mrs. W. J. FLORENCE
Every Night.

EVERY EVENING, AT 7.30.
The Comic Operetta,
THE HAPPY VILLAGE

At 8.30, the American Play, in 4 Acts, entitled
THE MIGHTY DOLLAR
By Mr. B. E. WOOLF.

Musical Director ... Herr MEYER LUTZ
Assistant Acting-Manager ... Mr. E. D. GRIFFITHS
Stage Manager ... Mr. R. SOUTAR

Doors Open at 7.0. Commence at 7.30.
Carriages about 11.0.

Stalls, 10s. Balcony, 5s. Upper Boxes, 5s.
Pit, 2s. Amphitheatre, 1s.
Private Boxes from One Guinea.

Printed by LUTTE, SON & Co., Limited, London Bridge.

NO FEES

SCHWEPPE'S MINERAL WATERS.

George Robey

Florrie Forde

Vesta Victoria

Polaire

Marie Lloyd

Anna Held

Little Tich'

Vesta Tilley

Exposition, one of the earliest of the great world fairs.

Speciality acts from Russia and central Europe, where the circus tradition had always been strong, featured in the fun palaces on either side of the Seine. Whirlwind tumblers from North Africa competed with jugglers and illusionists from Italy. Satirists from the cabarets of Berlin and show stoppers from Britain and the United States, sang, danced and made the people laugh.

To contend with this vast foreign influx, Paris created its own world stars — such as the singer and actress Yvette Guilbert and the folksinger Aristide Bruant, who sang about the people of the slums, the dancer and singer Mistinguett (1873–1956), and the young Maurice Chevalier (1888–1972).

Variety in the USA
Across the Atlantic there was another fertile breeding ground of talent. The stars in the United States had learned their trade in a hard school. Since the early days of the West it was traditional to provide entertainment as an extra to the booze in the beer halls. This entertainment took many and varied forms.

Above These are some of the great stars of the music-hall. Most of the famous performers had their own material and their own stage character which was immediately recognized by the audience. George Robey, with black eyebrows, was known as the 'Prime Minister of Mirth'.

Marie Lloyd, one of the best-known of all music-hall stars, epitomized Cockney London. Little Tich was renowned for his elongated boots and his diminutive size.

There were honky-tonk singers and dancers in the frontier towns and freaks in the New York museum shows. There was a touring tradition of the minstrel show and innumerable travelling specialities. One of these was called the medicine show — at which the performance merely gathered a crowd, a non-paying audience; the pay-off came with the quack who had to try and sell his medicine to the gullible public.

These touring shows were often performed non-stop, and the stars must have had some talent, or the crowds would not have watched. Artists who drew the crowds to the museum shows, which displayed

freaks and other unfortunates to a ghoulish public, sometimes had to do as many as 17 performances in a day.

After the civil war, paid-for, indoor entertainment was channelled into two main streams — vaudeville and burlesque. The distinction was quite clear in the beginning. As one wit put it, a child could take his parents to a vaudeville show; burlesque was strictly for the men.

It had not always been so. Burlesque began, as its name implies, as a stage convention full of parodies and take-offs of classical pieces. But in 1866, the producers of a melodrama called *The Black Crook* met up with a troupe of 80 girls from a *corps de ballet* who were simply stranded in town. They were drafted in to stand about agreeably on stage for no better reason than they just happened to be around at the time. It was the first time in American show business that female bodies had been exhibited on stage simply because they were good to look at. The girls wore opaque white tights which revealed parts of their legs. Puritan America was scandalized. Newspapers fulminated against this new immorality. Tights plays became synonymous with sin. *The Black Crook* became a smash hit. It can also be seen as an early musical.

The burlesque chorus developed into the American leg show. Classical parodies were dropped, leaving only coarse comedy, a minimum of spectacle and crude sexual provocation to pull in the customers from the red light districts in which most burlesque theatres were built. In 1881 Tony Pastor (1837–1908), an ex-circus performer opened the first theatre offering a variety bill clean enough for a mixed audience to attend. The hall was on New York's 14th Street. It was followed in Boston by the first playhouse owned by the impresario Benjamin F. Keith (1846–1914), who with his partner, E. F. Albee (1857–1930), was to control vaudeville's most famous touring circuit.

The Keith-Albee United Booking Office was later to comprise so many theatres, from coast to coast of the USA, that an act given a route by the organization was often assured of 80 weeks continuous work. A favourite show business anecdote sums up the size of the operation. A musician and a singer met while playing a UBO theatre in Philadelphia in 1878. The week ended, and one said to the other: 'See you around'. They toured ahead of or behind each other for 33 years and did not meet up again on the same bill until 1911!

Men like Pastor and Keith, Albee and P. T. Barnum (1810–1891) worked hard to make vaudeville family entertainment. The theatre historian Douglas Gilbert described vaudeville as 'the theatre of the people, its brassy assurance a dig in the nation's ribs . . . the trend of its humour [was] the march of those times'. If burlesque became an alliance of striptease and smut, and revue combined spectacle and exotism, then variety and vaudeville could be described as personality spiced with professionalism.

Creating a show

The very name captures its flavour – a variety show is all about variety. It matters little whether the singers come on before the dancers, or the dancers before the magicians, or the magicians before the acrobats. It matters that they have talent and timing – perhaps timing most of all.

A good variety show must be well-rehearsed. The tumblers actually bounce on to the stage the moment the orchestra plays the cue chord. The stage should never be left empty except to achieve some intentional, dramatic effect.

Nowhere is timing more important than in the compère or the stand-up comic who will introduce the acts, warm up the audience and keep the whole show together. This takes skill, feeling and lots of co-operation with the musicians. The slick and clever show led by a comedian who never misses a trick or his cue will often seem even better than the quality of the performers, and a moderate bill can be made to look good if the wise-cracker in the middle holds it all together in style.

Some producers dispense with the compère – the walk-on chairman who is the living successor to the inventive William Rhodes – and get each act to introduce the

Below This painting shows a Paris music-hall in 1897 with enthusiastic spectators crowding into the gallery. Most of the theatres were, like this one, ornate and splendid, with draped curtains, much gilt and red plush. Smoking and drinking were allowed as the audience watched the acts.

Right This sketch by Toulouse-Lautrec shows four dancers performing the can-can at the Moulin Rouge. This famous dance-hall, featured a cabaret show, in which the can-can made its first appearance in 1893.

next one. It is asking a lot of a sensitive soprano or a breathless acrobat to keep up the pace of a show. But it can work — with a cast full of stars.

For all the changes from the early days of Charles Dibdin and William Rhodes, for all the closures of those empty echoing halls which once rang with laughter, variety as it survives today — a mere facet of television — still uses a link man in most of its shows. If the compère gets the timing right, the show will get off the ground.

The great names

Long before 1900 and the arrival in Paris of the international star system, one name had already left a mark on the history of variety — Joseph 'Joey' Grimaldi (1778–1837). He was the son of a Drury Lane ballet master and he first trod the stage when only three years old. By the time he was in his twenties, Grimaldi had revolutionized the concept of English pantomime, which had grown out of the *commedia dell'arte*, the traditional Italian dance and mime entertainment, that had reached England via France in the reign of James I.

Grimaldi's genius was to bring together the talents of all speciality acts in a single performer. He switched the spotlight in Harlequinade away from Harlequin himself and on to the clown. By incorporating the fairy

Below This dance at the Moulin Rouge was painted by Toulouse-Lautrec in 1890, a year after the hall, situated in the Boulevard de Clichy, was opened. **Right** Lautrec's portrait of the singer Yvette Guilbert taking a curtain call shows her distinctive features and characteristic black gloves.

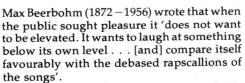

Above This Folies programme of 1900 features 14 acts. The main items are two ballets (one in 3 acts) but other acts include a trapeze artist, a juggler, an Australian dancer and the leading comic artist in Paris.

Right This revue, featuring Yvonne Ménard at the Folies in 1958 shows how spectacular and elaborate these shows were.

tale and nursery rhyme into *Mother Goose* and other pantomimes which he wrote, Grimaldi laid the foundation for the classic nineteenth century Christmas show.

The real innovation of Grimaldi's art was that he was the first performer to build a reputation solely on his ability to make people laugh. He developed the clown's exchanges with Pantaloon into something approaching the modern cross-talk act, and he introduced more and more topical allusions into his patter.

Grimaldi's impact was not restricted to variety, he was also extremely influential in pantomime and circus.

The advent of the New Canterbury boosted the star system. Morton's opening bill of varieties was topped by Sam Cowell (1820-1864), a Cockney singer. His most famous song, 'Villikins and his Dinah', was not, however, original. It had been introduced at the Grecian saloon 10 years earlier by the British singer, Frederick Robson (1821–1864), a master of the abrupt change from comedy to pathos. He had been described by the great British actor and manager Henry Irving (1839–1905) as 'great enough to know that he could only be great for three minutes'.

George Leybourne and the Great Vance in Britain, Paulus, Baldy and Felix Mayol in France entertained working class audiences by representing the fast-living playboy of the Victorian age and his conquests in an imagined paradise of the well-to-do. This dream world of gay dogs and no responsibility were crystallized in Leybourne's *Champagne Charlie*, introduced at the New Canterbury in 1867.

These characters, based on reckless extravagance, were, however, the exception rather than the rule. More typical of Victorian variety was the comic artist with a self-deflating ability, who could extract wonderment and surprise out of the obvious. The British drama critic and essayist

Max Beerbohm (1872 – 1956) wrote that when the public sought pleasure it 'does not want to be elevated. It wants to laugh at something below its own level . . . [and] compare itself favourably with the debased rapscallions of the songs'.

Some great artists have truly captured this aspect of the variety star's persona, none more so than the American comedian Jack Benny (1894 – 1974), with his carefully cultivated reputation as the meanest man in the world, Arthur Haynes, the British comedian, creator of that insolent tramp-on-the-make, and the French star Dranem, whose apparent stupidity defied belief.

The performers of the early music halls kept their material topical. The audience could identify with the social background from which it sprang. They presented a world of rent collectors, bailiffs, mothers-in-law, virago wives and husbands who drank all their wages. These were the dragons attacked — and not always vanquished by the seedy St Georges of the halls. Their songs, made famous by such stars as Albert Chevalier (1861 – 1923), Gus Elen (1862 – 1940) and Henry Champion (1866 – 1944), echoed also the conviction that of the downtrodden that all those in positions of authority are either knaves or fools.

The diminutive British singer and comedian Dan Leno (1860 – 1904) shifted the centre of gravity from the song to the monologue, while retaining as his subject the sordidness of the lower middle class, seen from within.

It was Leno, too, in pantomime partnership with the huge, stentorian-voiced Herbert Campbell (1844 – 1904), who created the prototype for such classic double acts as Hickey and Nelson, Collins and Hart, Sid Field and Jerry Desmonde, and, more recently, Morecambe and Wise.

An even smaller man than Leno was the first variety artist to make a big reputation outside his own country. The British comic Harry Relph (1868 – 1928), only 4ft 6in tall and immortalized as Little Tich, was the first truly world-wide variety star. He was a show-stopper in Paris, Berlin, Rome, London and Manchester until his death. He shared the same Leno sense that he was facing powers beyond his frail capacity and he used juggling, acrobatics, verbal pyrotechnics and eccentric dancing to create a gallery of energetic and maddening characters, full of furious indignation.

The great variety stars also share with the audience a sense of danger and the fear it inspires, and the knowledge of the impossibility of winning against a malevolent fate. The audience knows that the tottering pile of plates will end in smithereens, they know that the missing ace will not be found. In the same way we marvel at the effrontery of Arthur Haynes, wishing that we dared to emulate it, even as we convince ourselves that it is doomed to be squashed.

Such rare talents as those of the variety star do not blossom in a season. They are the results of years of hard work on particular images, routines and characters. The critic, John Barber has pinpointed the difference between the comedian and the comic actor — the latter always impersonates other people; the comic, on the other hand, is always the same. The comic will build up a public persona by devising the character pragmatically in front of many audiences, keeping and developing those aspects that proved amusing, jettisoning the rest. It has been noted that actors talk of playing and comedians of working.

Until about 1960, when there were still variety circuits operating in Britain, theatre stages would be open from 10 o'clock each morning until lunchtime. The whole com-

Left The delicate sophistication and visual impact of Korean dance owes much to opera, theatre and also to religious ritual. The *keesaengs*, cultured courtesans like the geishas of Japan, perfected the art of stylized dance, often performed as part of a poetic drama or semi-religious play.

Below Dougie Squires' Second Generation are a modern song and dance team. They have appeared in many variety shows and have toured extensively throughout the world. They owe much of their success and popularity to television appearances, as do many other modern performers.

Right Jimmy 'Schnozzle' Durante, the well-loved American comedian, began his career as a song, dance and jokes man in the beer halls of Coney Island, where entertaining a boozy and noisy audience was no easy task. He appeared in his first Broadway musical in 1929.

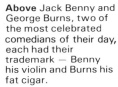

Above Jack Benny and George Burns, two of the most celebrated comedians of their day, each had their trademark — Benny his violin and Burns his fat cigar.

Below Bob Hope has been a major figure in American entertainment for over 40 years. He worked in vaudeville before films.

Below This troupe of provincial Chinese acrobats toured the whole of China with their remarkable show. The group included jugglers, gymnasts and balance performers, many of the players members of the same family.

The encouragement of small, specialized troupes like this is part of government policy in China and is aimed at preserving the varied traditional forms of entertainment which still exist in some remote rural provinces.

Right Lena Horne, the sultry black American singer and actress, began her career as a dancer in Harlem's Cotton Club. Her great success came in the 1940s when she appeared in nightclubs, musicals, Hollywood films and concerts. Records and tours have established her fame world-wide.

pany would be there trying out new bits of business, rehearsing, practising last night's turns which did not quite work. Hands, especially the hands of the specialists, had to be kept in practice and developing new tricks was just as important.

There is a great deal more to a variety star than the ability to string together a series of gags. Jimmy 'Schnozzle' Durante (born 1893) worked for years in Coney Island beer halls, bawling out songs and wisecracks to boozy customers before he got any work at all on the stage. Variety stars who subsequently had great success in the cinema like the Americans W. C. Fields (1879–1946), Fanny Brice (1891–1951) and Al Jolson (1886–1950) started in burlesque. The immortal British comedian Sid Field (1904–1950) played the provinces for 20 years before London managers would look at him.

Max Beerbohm said that we all somehow feel above these fallible geniuses. His theory, however, works less well with women. Few could feel superior to the explosive confidence of the 'red hot momma' Sophie Tucker (1884–1966) or the breezy exuberance of Two Ton Tessie O'Shea (born 1917). No-one could forget the innuendo of songs like 'Every Little Movement' as sung by the popular British artiste Marie Lloyd (1870–1922) or the brassy assurance of Eva Tanguay as she bawled out the lyrics of 'Go As Far As You Like' and 'It's All Been Done Before (But Not The Way I Do It)', on a Keith circuit where even the words slob and damn were banned.

Death of variety

Now there is almost no more live variety. The traditional circuits have gone. The Americans place the date of its death as 1932, when the UBO showplace, the New York Palace, was forced to close as a twice-nightly house. Variety struggled on in Europe until after 1945. Variety seasons are still produced, notably at the London Palladium and the Olympia in Paris. But the bills are topped by recording stars and the old artist-audience rapport has gone.

There were reasons for its death: films, radio and television lured away talent; greed played its part. There was also a disastrous failure to supply modern comforts for the paying public. Why should anyone leave a fireside chair, battle with the weather, public transport or parking problems, when they could find all the same entertainment – or better – by the flick of a switch in their own home. Television is one place where variety still flourishes today.

CABARET

FROM THE PARIS MOULIN ROUGE TO LAS VEGAS SPECTACULARS

Of all the terms used in the performing arts, cabaret is perhaps the most ill-defined. In its original French sense, it means a definite type of satirical and often political, entertainment, intensely intimate in style and frequently using material which is surreptitious or hard to handle with decency.

When it took root in other parts of the Continent, notably Germany, it preserved this meaning. However, in Britain and the United States, it usually refers to any live, light entertainment, generally presented late in the evening before an audience seated at tables and with food and drink to hand.

The early days

In one way, cabaret has always been with us because the tavern or wine cellar — the original meaning of cabaret — has often provided entertainment of a sort. In France and elsewhere it was of an informal type: the rollicking drinking song in which the customers were themselves part of the proceedings or the itinerant musician or juggler who did his turn and passed the hat around.

In France, however, café entertainment developed in a distinctive fashion in the mid-nineteenth century. In this period of unrest the café served not only as a meeting and refreshment place but almost as a living underground newspaper as the singers or *chansonniers* commented on the events of the day and gave vent to the public's grievances in between singing their age-old songs of love. Just as music hall and vaudeville grew in England and the United States from the p^ublic houses and saloons, so France developed the *café-concert*, a more staged version of the songs and skits which had characterized café life during the preceding years. Later the *café-concert* itself produced a French counterpart to the music hall. However, cabaret was a more self-conscious and deliberately intellectual and artistic offshoot.

Its genesis stems from the 'Hydropathes', a society of writers and poets who performed their works for each other at weekly meetings. Gradually the emphasis changed from the purely literary to topical satire. A permanent home was secured in 1881 for the 'Hydropathes' by the French painter Rodolphe Salis (1852–1897), whose own literary career was eclipsed by his pretensions as an artistic entrepreneur. The chosen location was Montmartre, which at that time was still a semi-rural village on the outskirts of Paris but which had nevertheless gained a raffish reputation. The name he selected for his enterprise was the *Chat Noir*.

Salis saw the *Chat Noir* as a way of life, launching a magazine of the same name and taking it into eccentric political realms. Its mixture of new work and improvisation soon attracted the smarter sections of Paris.

One of the most notable features was *Théâtre d'Ombres*, a shadow theatre which pre-dated the cinema in its screen effects. It was run by Henri Rivière (1864–1951).

Using puppets, lights, shadowgraphy and paintings, its presentations varied from the mystical to the salacious. Salis himself presided over his pioneer cabaret as *conferencier*, a combined host, narrator and comedian, and a term still in use in Europe today.

Before long, the success of the *Chat Noir* had transformed Montmatre into the cabaret district of Paris, and when it closed in 1897, it was surrounded by imitators, the most famous of which was *Le Mirliton*, which had actually taken over the original premises of the *Chat Noir* several years earlier.

The guiding spirit of *Le Mirliton* was Aristide Bruant (1862–1932), a folk singer and anarchist, immortalized in Toulouse-Lautrec's posters. Unlike Salis and his friends, with their artiness and elitist avant-gardism, Bruant was a man of the

Above This picture by Toulouse-Lautrec shows Jane Avril dancing. She was one of the most popular of the Moulin-Rouge dancers 'a wild Botticelli-like creature perverse but intelligent whose madness for dancing induced her to join this strange company'. **Right** This Lautrec painting shows La Goulue (the glutton) in a semi-oriental dance in the midst of a harem. Looking on in the foreground are Oscar Wilde, Jane Avril, Lautrec and the critic Fénéon.

people who had worked on the railway and had begun singing at the smaller *café-concerts*. Coming to Paris from the country as a lad, he had been swept up by the colour and camaraderie of the people on the streets and became their personal troubadour.

The first really great *chansonnier*, Bruant likewise attracted society to *Le Mirliton*, even though his speciality lay in insulting the guests, a tradition which continues strongly in cabaret, and his songs, in which he accompanied himself on the guitar, can be recognized now, not only as the foundation of the cabaret *chanson* tradition, but as an influence on the urban folk song of the twentieth century.

His songs were later given a wider circulation by Yvette Guilbert (1867–1944), herself the product of the *café-concerts*, and whose emotional style of acting in song can still be detected in the work of cabaret artists.

Cabaret in Paris retained its distinctive character well into the 1920s, chiefly because it was the natural gathering ground for avantgarde painters, musicians and poets. *Le Lapin Agile* was better known for its clientele, including the poet Guillaume Apollinaire (1880–1918) and the artist Maurice Utrillo (1883–1955), than its entertainment. *Le Boeuf sur le Toit* was the great Paris monument to the jazz age. But by the end of the decade the city had succumbed to the American influence, the artists returned to the cafés, and cabaret became no place for the wild, aesthetic experimentations of the Dadaists or *Les Six*.

By the 1920s, in fact, the real centre of cabaret in the style of Salis and Bruant had

Above This photograph shows the interior of *Le Chat Noir,* the celebrated cabaret in Montmartre which was established by the painter Rodolphe Salis. He stands, with pipe in hand, to the right of this photograph. The cabaret itself presented songs and skits as well as poetry readings and puppet shows. It soon attracted the fashionable intelligensia of Paris, and Montmartre was rapidly transformed into the cabaret district of Paris. *Le Chat Noir* closed in 1897 but by that time it was already surrounded by a number of imitators.

Right A typical Parisian cabaret-restaurant at the turn of the century is depicted in this painting.

shifted to Berlin, and in a way which has given that city a lasting reputation for unbridled and permissive behaviour. Cabaret took strong root in Germany at the turn of the century when Albert Langen (1869–1909) returned to Munich after a stay in Paris and transplanted something of the spirit of Montmartre, primarily through his launching of the satirical weekly *Simplicissimus*. It might be true to say that from the outset German cabaret allied itself strongly with the theatre, whereas in France it was wedded more to the arts in general. The German dramatist Frank Wedekind (1864–1918), though best known as the author of the plays *Lulu* and *Spring Awakening*, was one of the greatest exponents of cabaret, his harsh satire continually brought him into conflict with the authorities. This spirit of rebellion and even revolution was characteristic of the greatest years of German cabaret and differed from the Viennese version of the genre which was gentler and more whimsical.

Germany after the First World War probably saw the full flowering of true cabaret. Increasingly repressive government, rampant inflation, the rise of socialism and a general feeling of hopelessness combined to produce a bitter crop of writers and performers, for instance Erich Mühsam, one of the first victims of the Nazis, Kurt Tucholsky, Walter Mehring, Erich Kästner, and, of course, the major twentieth century dramatist and poet Bertolt Brecht (1898–1956).

Brecht, who emerged from the Munich cabarets, in which he sang his own songs in a distinctive voice, actually opened his own cabaret, *Die Rote Zibebe* (*The Red Grape*) as far back as 1922. In its brief life, it featured a remarkable collection of talent. There was Klabund, a fine poet of the oppressed, Joachim Ringelnatz, the dancer Valeska Gert, Karl Valentin, the comedian whose abilities inspired many writers to create sketches and characterizations especially for him, and Brecht himself.

authorized club. The complexities and quaintness of British drinking regulations have greatly shaped non-theatrical entertainment and have led to the creation of thousands of clubs throughout the country — such as the so-called working man's clubs — many of which present, either regularly or occasionally, what the British have come to regard as cabaret.

In both Britain and America the growth of cabaret was almost simultaneous with the arrival of, first ragtime, and then jazz. In its early years jazz was primarily an entertainment music and most of its performers had more in common with vaudeville than is possibly realized. It hit Europe almost immediately after the First World War, the blows being struck by dozens of American musicians, black and white, who settled for varying lengths of time in practically every European capital.

In London it rapidly caught on with the society set and found its way into the smartest hotels and an ever-increasing number of night clubs. The bands themselves were the entertainment, but in their train came other artists from the United States, who were often influenced by jazz.

When cabaret was featured, however, it was looked upon more as an interlude in the dancing rather than as an art form in its own right. Some more sophisticated variety artists found that they could adapt neatly to the style demanded, but few restricted themselves to the medium, for the bigger money was to be made in the theatres.

Indeed, as is the case today, cabaret was often regarded as an extra source of income for those already working in the West End theatre. For a time the British showman C. B. Cochran (1872–1951) put his young ladies into fairly elaborate floorshows at the Trocadero, and many stars of musical comedy, for example Jessie Matthews (born 1907), also featured in late shows. Shortly after the Second World War London had a taste of the Paris-type spectacular, with the opening of the London Casino but this venture was short-lived.

With the advent of the Second World War London's night-life scene changed dramatically. The name bands — Ambrose, Harry Roy, Lew Stone, Roy Fox and others — which had been the bedrock of prosperity in this branch of the business, were broken up or at least severely reduced in size, and late-night entertainment was largely provided through a proliferation of 'bottle parties', a law-bending device which depended on the customers bringing their own drinks or guaranteeing ownership of bottles already kept on the premises.

Al Burnett (1904–1974), an East End comedian who had been one of the bottle party kings, was one of the spearheads of a London cabaret revival after the war. He first opened the Stork Room and then the Pigalle, a much larger night spot to which he brought a

Nearly everything Brecht wrote or produced showed a cabaret influence. It might even be claimed that his celebrated 'alienation' technique, the deliberate breaking down of theatrical illusion, was inspired by *Kabarett*, which of necessity made audience and performers one.

In the late 1920s and early 1930s Berlin was arguably the greatest cabaret centre in entertainment history. Not only did the satirical cabarets thrive but there were dozens of *Amüsierkabaretten* — which literally means amusement cabaret — which had no intellectual ideals and presented spectacles for every taste, often of the most perverse type.

It is interesting to reflect on the reasons why cabaret, along the lines envisaged by Salis and Bruant, and taken up so avidly in Germany, failed to flourish in other artistic capitals like London and New York. The main one must be that both Britain and the U.S.A. have a free press and strong, democratic parliamentary traditions which make

it unnecessary for opponents of the regime to go underground. Satirical writing has been encouraged in daily papers and weekly reviews for more than a century, and in the twentieth century the theatre, radio and, latterly, television have generally been allowed to make fairly savage fun at the expense of public figures.

What is known as cabaret in Great Britain and America is much more in the nature of popular entertainment, British — or until recent years specifically London — cabaret, has a good deal more in common with music hall, American vaudeville and jazz with faint over-tones of Parisian so-called permissiveness. The artistic set of the type that haunted Paris cabarets preferred country houses and Bloomsbury and Soho pubs to Paris-style cafés.

The British licensing laws also militated against cabaret in the Continental style by insisting that anyone who wanted to stay out late at night should be a member of an

Above The Talk of the Town was opened as a theatre-restaurant in 1958 in one of London's largest theatres. Customers are not only able to dine and dance but the entertainment also includes a spectacular evening floor-show like the one illustrated here **(top)** and possibly a revue **(right)** in which a star performer may act. The late evening spot is the focal point of the entertainment when a famous cabaret or variety artist does a show. Notable performers here have been Judy Garland, Liza Minnelli, Frankie Vaughan and Matt Monroe.

Far left Danny La Rue is Britain's most famous female impersonator. He began his career in variety and then moved on to theatre. His blend of sophisticated humour with a traditional music hall style is devoid of 'camp' and is perhaps uniquely British. **Left** The American singer, Jack Jones reached the height of his popularity in the late 1960s but is still a regular night-club performer **Below left** Shirley Bassey, who rose to fame in the 1950s, has remained one of the most popular of all British female vocalists. **Below** Sammy Davis Jr. is one of the most versatile and durable of American entertainers.

number of leading American artists, including Sammy Davis Jr. (born 1925) and Peggy Lee (born 1920).

The postwar years

In the 1940s there was also the re-opening of the *Café de Paris*, scene of a bomb tragedy in 1941, which placed an emphasis on quality cabaret. It lasted only until the mid-1950s but represented a level of London cabaret which has never been repeated. The versatile Nöel Coward (1899–1973), and the incomparable Marlene Dietrich (born 1901) and many other British, American and Continental stars appeared there.

The opening of the Talk of the Town in 1958, a conversion of one of London's largest theatres, the Hippodrome, was a landmark in the popularization of cabaret and its format has, to a greater or lesser extent, been copied by venues all over Britain. Though it initially operated roughly along the lines of the pre-war London Casino, it revised its policy in 1960 to incorporate a spectacular 9.30 p.m. floorshow and a late-evening star spot, even though the star names today are not quite as lustrous as in the 1960s.

The difficulty of finding artists who can fill large cabaret rooms has become acute during the last few years and has led to either the

Right Bette Midler has been described as 'the first cabaret star of the Beatle Generation'. Her fame came when she played in cabaret shows to the homosexual clientele of a Turkish baths, in New York in 1970, singing in a camp but brassy style.

closing of many of the clubs which sprang up during the 1960s or to drastic revisions of policy. Nevertheless, even though most of the clubs are non-membership, thanks to a gradual relaxation of the licensing regulations, they still represent a major proportion of light entertainment outlets in Britain.

From time to time, attempts have been made to get closer to the spirit of cabaret as laid down in Paris a century ago. Easily the most notable was the brief era of the Establishment, opened in the early 1960s by the British comedian and satirist Peter Cook (born 1937) and others on the crest of the 'satire boom' which had started with the theatre revue *Beyond the Fringe* and continued with the founding of the magazine *Private Eye* and the memorable British television programme *That Was the Week that Was*.

The Establishment prospered in its essential form for only two or three years, staging a series of intimate revues with such British artists as John Bird (born 1936) and Eleanor Bron (born 1934), bringing in some shows from the United States and interspersing these with individual performers, the most outstanding of them was the American Lenny Bruce (1925–1966), a comedian whose black — and often obscene — humour has been a major influence on cabaret and theatre since his death.

More to the London taste was Danny La Rue (born 1927), whose club had remarkable success for eight years. La Rue, a female impersonator who began his career in variety, created a unique blend of risqué sophistication and traditional music hall, a style that has stood him in good stead in his subsequent theatrical career.

As the 1970s draw to a close there are further indications that the basic cabaret idea is not dead in London, though its more minority appeal has veered strongly towards a 'gay' influence, largely absent in the work of Danny La Rue.

As in Britain, most of the function of cabaret in the United States has been abrogated by the theatre, particularly by what is called in Britain the 'Fringe' and in New York, 'Off-' or 'Off-Off-Broadway'. Cabaret in America has, in fact, seldom adopted the European approach and has virtually never gone in for satire, save for occasional revues in Greenwich Village cafés.

On the other hand, the United States continues to produce extraordinarily vibrant and inventive performers, who create their own environment in a cabaret sense. There is Bette Midler (born 1947) who rose to prominence as resident entertainer in a gay Turkish baths in New York City. New York in particular, has a multiplicity of bars, cafés

and restaurants which might, at any time, take on the character of a cabaret, if the artists and audiences are in tune with each other.

Ever since the turn of the century, nearly all of America's leading entertainers have begun their careers in these bar-room circumstances. In fact, the lines between cabaret and other forms of entertainment are more blurred there than in other countries and there is a long tradition of night-life almost throughout the nation.

The prohibition era gave a boost, and certainly publicity, to late-night entertainment, often in a strong alliance with jazz. Sophie Tucker (1884–1966), for example, for many years renowned as a night-club artist, began as a jazz singer, and the majority of jazz or jazz-influenced performers such as Lena Horne (born 1917) and Billie Holiday (1915–1959), spent many years working within a cabaret structure. Comedians have also thrived in this milieu, whether single acts like Milton Berle (born 1908) and, more recently, Woody Allen (born 1935) or duos such as Dean Martin (born 1917) and Jerry Lewis (born 1926).

The spectacular production show, until the arrival of Las Vegas as an entertainment centre, has never played a major part in American night life, though there have been exceptions, including the Diamond Horshoe, the Copacabana, the Latin Quarter and the Cotton Club, all in New York City but now all closed. The Cotton Club in Harlem, with its ambitious all-black revues and phenomenal music by such band-leaders as Duke Ellington, represented the pinnacle of a period in which negro entertainment began to make a widespread impact on white audiences.

Cabaret or, more strictly speaking, the theatre-restaurant, has reached the height of its development with the rise of Las Vegas, a small desert town in Nevada until the early 1950s. Backed by the vast amount of money brought in by legalized gambling, entertainment of the most star-studded and spectacular type has firmly established itself. Here the intimate cabaret has given way to the mammoth show which more properly belongs in a theatre.

It is clear that in its 100 year history cabaret

Above This scene from the film *Cabaret* re-enacts a typical revue from German cabaret in the 1920s and 1930s. The film was based on Christopher Isherwood's autobiographical works about his life in the permissive, decadent Berlin of the 1930s, when all forms of cabaret, from the seedy to the most sophisticated, were flourishing.

has undergone a considerable transformation. Its birthplace, Paris, now has little that Salis and Bruant would recognize as a cabaret, but then in the Lido it has probably the most spectacular late-night showplace in the world. In Germany there is still a reminder of the days of Brecht – an irreverent satirical tradition. In other countries, if cabaret truly ever existed at all, it has been absorbed into show business and theatre.

Yet cabaret is a form of remarkable resilience, more accutely sensitive than other branches of the arts and entertainment to changes in public taste and national moods. This is because the unique artist-audience relationship still remains, even in the huge show places of Las Vegas.

MAGIC
TRICKS AND ILLUSION FROM ANCIENT EGYPT TO THE MODERN DAY

Of all the performing arts, magic is the one which crosses both borders and cultures most easily. Tribesmen to whom many art forms might be meaningless, to whom the beautiful music of one culture might be an irritating noise, would instantly recognize and warm to the magician. The language of tricks, of human dexterity and illusion, of 'sleight of hand' as it was called in the eighteenth century, is universal.

The beginnings
Magic seems to have developed as an art form spontaneously in various parts of the world, rather than having been passed from one race to another. While the Chinese and Asian Indians were impressing travellers with their tricks in the Middle Ages it seems that the American Indians were also amazing each other with 'superhuman' feats. For, as early as the sixteenth century, Spanish conquerors encountered and recorded Indian conjuring tricks in America, and there are many later records of Indian magicians bewildering white audiences in the wilds of the American West.

The link between magic and religion is very strong. Performers have had to be careful in the past, lest their work be mistaken for that of the Devil. In the case of the American Indians, it was the medicine man, the 'priest' equivalent, who was expected to perform magic arts. In Africa, too, the witch doctor was someone who could impress his audience in this way.

Some of the earliest records of magic are found in the Bible. The Old Testament tells how Moses and Aaron went to the Egyptian Pharaoh and how Aaron cast down his rod before the ruler and it turned into a serpent. Pharaoh then called his magicians who each cast down their rods and they also became serpents, but Aaron outdid Pharaoh's men — his rod swallowed up theirs.

Other early references to magic include an account extant on papyrus of how a magician was summoned to perform before the Egyptian court about 5,000 years ago. There is also a magician shown at work on a Chinese scroll painting made about 2,000 years ago.

In the ancient Middle East and Mediterranean world, there are records of tricks being used to fool people into thinking they were being addressed by the gods. One king, Cyrus the Great, executed some priests who had built a secret passageway to transport sacrificial goods and animals from an altar to their living quarters. Later an early Christian bishop of Alexandria is recorded as having shown friends a hollow statue in which a pagan priest had once stood and spoken through the lips. There is plenty more evidence that priests in ancient times used all kinds of tricks to convince their audiences of the wonders of the gods.

The Middle Ages
By the Middle Ages the practice of magic was

Above Pasha, a genuine Indian mystic, here performs what seems to be a very dangerous trick. He has raised a lady into the air and then balanced her on the pointed ends of three swords. To complete the act, he gradually removes two of the swords. The lady remains in a horizontal position, resting on just one sword under her neck.

Left This Parisian conjuror and entertainer called Philippe, has just produced a glass bowl of goldfish in water from a large cloth. All magic is the art of illusion. Magicians therefore choose their costumes and props carefully so that there is plenty to distract the audience while a trick is performed.

widespread on the continent of Europe where it was closely linked with witchcraft. Those suspected of witchcraft were often condemned and executed, yet magicians continued to produce illusions and ghosts to frighten and fascinate the populace. In the late Middle Ages, records describe the many feats of Chinese and other Asian conjurers, and these include the first mentions of the famous Indian rope trick. In the ensuing centuries down to modern times, stories have continued to be told of the rope trick in which a rope or chain was hurled into the air, became rigid and was climbed by a performer. Yet many magicians now believe this trick is a legend, that it can never be performed as described. It has been done on stage where it is possible to have part of the rope, out of sight, behind drapes, but modern magicians are sceptical as to whether it has ever been performed in the open air.

Impressive evidence appeared in the fourteenth century of an early type of entertainment now known as illusionary magic. A Chinese conjuror had been engaged by a Khan at his summer palace in central Asia, and in the course of his tricks succeeded in making his youthful assistant vanish. To cap the proceedings he then vanished himself, disappearing under the eyes of the Khan and his entourage. The performers did not reappear immediately on that occasion, but returned later to win fame and high fees for their work.

The seventeenth and eighteenth centuries

Apart from the ancient works that chronicled weird happenings, it was not until the 1630s that the first book on conjuring was printed. This was *Hocus Pocus: The Anatomy of Legerdemain*. It was extensively illustrated. Hocus was a court magician in the reign of King James I and his name has become part of the English language.

One of history's greatest magicians, Giovanni Giuseppe Pinetti (1750–1800), who conjured in Europe's leading theatres, was born in Orbitello, Tuscany. He began as a scientist, teaching in Rome and performing such amazing demonstrations of physics that he started to earn a reputation as an entertainer. He soon turned to conjuring, billed as 'Joseph Pinetti, Roman Professor of Mathematics'. He wore fashionable clothes, silk stockings, silver-buckled shoes, brocaded coat and powdered wig, and his

Right Harry Houdini is perhaps the world's most famous illusionist and escapologist. Born in 1874, he began his career in the circus ring. He was a gifted trapeze artist and horse-rider but in his early years he took most pride in his skilful card manipulation. However, it was not long before he turned to escapology. He performed one of his greatest illusions, 'Metamorphosis', first with his younger brother, Theo, and then with his wife, Bess. With the help of a spectator, Houdini's hands were tied behind his back and he was then placed inside a bag which was in turn put in a large wooden box. This box was padlocked and secured with thick ropes. Houdini's assistant then disappeared behind a screen which had been drawn around the box. Within three seconds, the transformation had taken place. Houdini drew back the screen, untied the rope binding his hands and then opened the wooden chest. Inside, tied exactly as Houdini had been, the assistant was revealed. The two appeared to have swapped places. Houdini discovered that his act was more exciting if he had to release himself from a pair of handcuffs before escaping out of anything else. He therefore spent most of his free time studying every type manacle he could find. He could open any pair of handcuffs, either with a duplicate key, which he concealed on himself, or by picking the lock with a piece of bent wire. As he became more proficient in his escapes, Houdini became more daring. In one of his tricks, he managed to get out of a water tank. He had been bound by chains and ropes and then lowered headfirst into the tank. Although it seemed impossible that anyone should escape from such a predicament, it was not too difficult for the great Houdini.

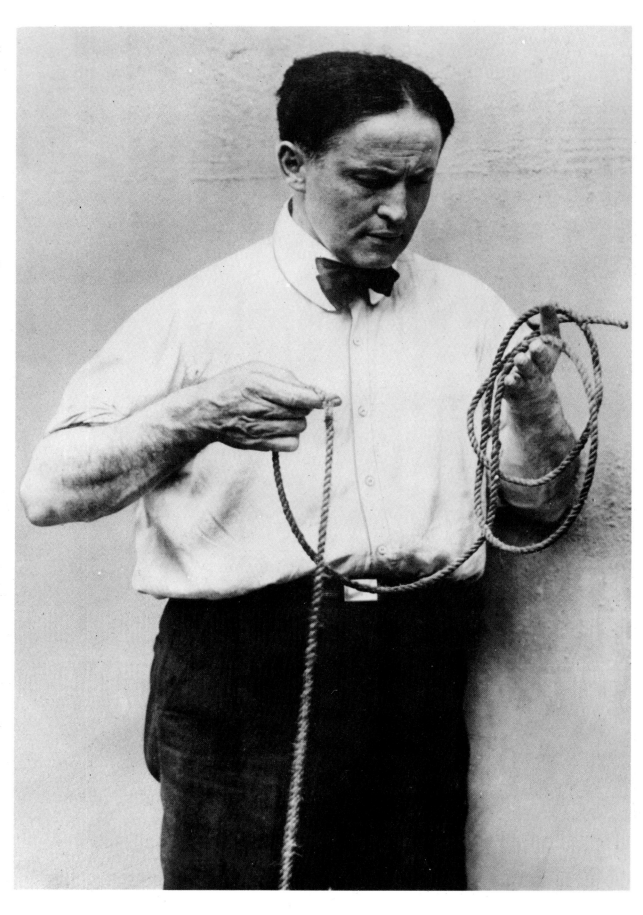

stage was often adorned with silk curtains, gilded tables and crystal chandeliers. He used a golden head that danced and struck the sides of a crystal goblet to answer questions. A 'philosophical bouquet', covered with a glass dome, produced oranges when a mysterious fluid was added.

While magicians played before kings and aristocrats in Europe in the eighteenth century, the future American President, George Washington, noted in his diary on September 19, 1769, that in Alexandria, Virginia, he 'went to see slight of hand performed'.

Magic had enjoyed no favours in early British settlements in North America. In the seventeenth century, conjurors, actors and other 'idle persons' were liable to be whipped. But in the following century the magician's art gained ground. Jacob Meyer, born in Philadelphia, Pennsylvania, in 1734, took the name 'Philadelphia' and moved to Europe to do his work, billing his magic

Above To run a sword through a person's body is an impressive trick. The hollow tube (B) is placed around the victim with the openings at his front and back. The sword (A) is extremely flexible and thin. When it is run through the tube and projects at the other side, it appears to have passed straight through the man's body.

Right This engraving shows a small audience watching an illusion that was called 'The Living Half of a Woman'. The lady appears to have no legs but in reality she is standing behind some large mirrors.
Below left and right Another popular illusion is 'The Vanishing Lady'. This has to be performed in front of a screen. The lady is hidden from the audience by a wooden box. She is then pulled out of this on a wheeled stretcher by an assistant behind the screen.

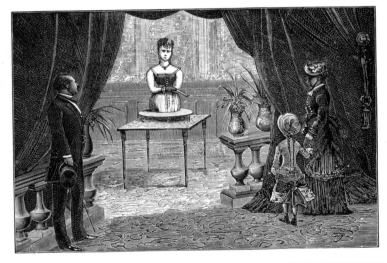

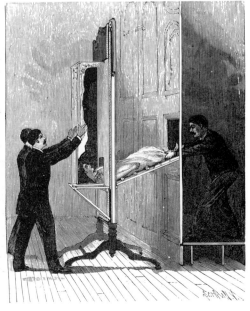

shows with lavish advertisements. Meanwhile, many prominent magicians from Europe went on tours of America. One, Antonio Blitz, who combined humour with magic — finishing his shows by rushing to and fro to correct dangerous wobbles in his display of spinning dinner plates — set sail with his family from Liverpool in August 1835 and became one of America's foremost entertainers. He once produced a bottle of whisky from the hat of a state governor who was a temperance advocate.

The American West, meanwhile, was producing evidence of magic tricks by Indians such as escapist feats by medicine men who loosed themselves from ropes and nets, and performed such tricks as making tents shake and objects move.

The magic theatre
The first theatre in the world devoted wholly to magical entertainment was in Britain at the old Egyptian Hall, 170 Piccadilly, London, in the nineteenth century. This became the home of probably the greatest partnership in magic's long history — Maskelyne and Cooke.

John Nevil Maskelyne (1839–1917), the founder of the greatest family of magicians in history, was born at Cheltenham, Gloucestershire. As a boy he was apprenticed to a watchmaker and learned the tricks of working with springs and minute gears. Forming a friendship with George Cooke, a cabinet maker, he put together an act and performed locally. The two were soon hiring halls throughout the country, and in 1875 they gave a Royal Command performance before the Prince of Wales, later to become Edward VII. The prince was so pleased with their performance that he allowed them to use in their billing 'Maskelyne and Cooke: The Royal Illusionists and Anti-Spiritualists'. Their show at the Egyptian Hall ran for 34 years and the hall became widely known as 'England's Home of Mystery'.

This theatre was, as the programme stated, honoured by the presence of the 'Nobility, Gentry, Clergy and the Public'. In the late nineteenth century, the Egyptian Hall was pulled down and the magicians transferred to the St George's Hall in Upper Regent Street. Here, the earlier success was repeated and the hall was a home of magic until its closure during the Second World War.

Perhaps more than any other enterprise connected with magic, the two permanent homes brought fame and distinction to magic as a performing art. Jugglers, handshow artists, conjurors and illusionists performed there, drawn from all over the world. A wag of the Victorian age dubbed them 'medicine men in evening dress'. The conjuror Charles Bertram (1853–1907), a favourite magician of the Prince of Wales, was one of these performers, as was Martin Chapender, a youthful magician from Liverpool.

In 1905 the first society devoted to magicians was founded in Birmingham, England — the British Magical Society. This preceded the more famous British society, the Magic Circle, by barely six months. The Circle had its inaugural meeting at Pinoli's Restaurant, London, in the summer of 1905. The great David Devant (1868–1941) — a partner of John Nevil Maskelyne — was the Circle's first president. The following year, Nevil Maskelyne, the son of John Nevil Maskelyne, launched the Circle's first magazine, *The Magic Circular*.

Four years later the headquarters of the Magic Circle was transferred to the now demolished Anderton's Hotel in Fleet Street.

Magicians came to Anderton's from all over the world to perform their tricks before their fellows and, for the less well known, there was the chance to be noticed by one of the Maskelyne family, who never offered jobs at their homes of mystery without first seeing the magician in action.

The Magic Circle continues to thrive today and to promote the art of magic. In the USA its equivalent is the Magic Guild. This organization also furthers magic as a performing art — for example it sponsored the very last New York appearance of the famous American magician, The Great Raymond (1878–1948), in 1945.

The giants: Houdin and Houdini

Two giant figures stand out in the realm of magic. The first, Jean Eugene Robert Houdin (1805–1871), a French clockmaker, is regarded as the father of modern magic. He gained fame when he blindfolded his fourteen-year-old son, Emile, sat him in a chair on the stage, then collected objects from the audience which the boy described with amazing accuracy. A skilled machine-builder, he constructed an automated man — an early 'robot' — for a French exhibition in 1844. The mechanical figure wrote down answers to questions.

The second, Erich Weiss, took on a stage name based on Houdin's and became world famous as the Great Houdini (1874–1926), perhaps the greatest of all magicians, a master illusionist and escapist.

Many of Houdini's performances were under the Big Top and, as a circus performer, he was rated along with some of the leading circus artistes of the world. He would often alternate music hall and circus performances. One of his most famous illusions

Right Panzero is thought to have one of the best levitation acts in the world. He has appeared on television many times and he continues to astound his audiences. It is known that he sometimes uses as many as three different methods in one act, but the secrets of his illusions still remain a mystery to people outside the Magic Circle. In this act he appears to levitate a woman horizontally into the air. To show that she is not balanced on any anything, he then passes hoops around her body.

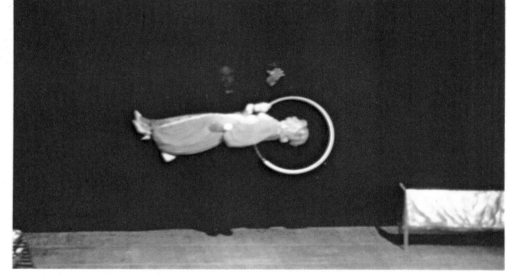

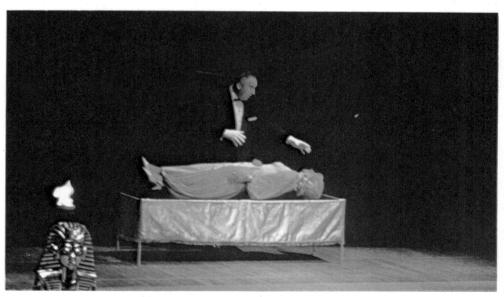

Above When magicians introduce live animals into their acts, they very often use a rabbit. This is because the rabbit is a docile animal with a quiet temperament. Whether it is hidden under a cloth or in a box, a rabbit will not make a sound but will sleep for hours wherever it is. White rabbits are used most as they show up well against a dark background.

Right Le Septembre are a French act who use animals and birds that are difficult to control. They usually work with cockerels and foxes.

was on horseback in the circus ring. Houdini appeared with a troupe of riders wearing a costume contrasting in colour with them. The riders would dismount and walk their horses round the ring, leaving Houdini, the sole mounted rider, galloping around. Suddenly there would be a cry of 'Lights' and the ring would be plunged into darkness. Three seconds later the lights came back on — but Houdini had disappeared along with his horse. All this had happened in an open circus ring, with no scenery to hide behind, and no trapdoors.

There is a simple explanation to this trick. Houdini's contrasting costume was made of paper and was torn off quickly when the lights went out, the sound drowned by the band playing. Houdini simply dismounted and merged with the other dismounted riders, walking their horses round the ring. No-one apparently ever counted how many riders — or horses — there had been in the first place.

The desire to be baffled

Audiences, it seems, really want to be tricked, whether they are gathered round a trickster in a bar or in a great audience in a music hall or theatre. If there is any resistance, it is soon dispelled by showmanship.

However, several tricks of the magician's art have now become so familiar that it is time to reveal how they are done.

Sawing a woman in half

One of the most famous stage tricks is sawing a woman in half. A girl is placed in a coffin-like box with her head, hands and feet

Above The Great Covari is a professional Hungarian illusionist. However, like many others, he is now restricted mainly to conjuring shows. Rising costs for travelling around with a large amount of equipment have forced him to abandon most of his illusions. Here, he has produced a multi-coloured scarf out of a bottle.
Above right Ali Bongo is a British comic magician.

Right Maldino is a German illusionist who specializes in sword cabinets. For obvious reasons, magicians try to keep their techniques secret. However, it is known that Maldino uses various mirrors to create illusions.

protruding. The magician then saws the box in half. The two halves are pulled apart so that the audience can see that it has really been cut in two. When the two halves are pushed together again and the lid opened, the girl walks out unharmed.

This was usually how this trick was presented some years ago by all the famous illusionists. But magicians are great improvers, never content until they reach the ultimate. Robert Harbin was among the first in the field with the illusion where a girl was not only cut into three pieces but her midriff was moved from the rest of her body. In America, Doug Henning actually moves parts of the girl's body from one side of the stage to the other. A British inventor, Jack Hughes, sawed a lady in two without a box, the girl's midriff encased in a slim frame — he even used an electric buzz saw.

This is how the trick was originally done. The box is shorter than the girl and rests on a hollow platform. The box lid is closed and the girl allows her body to sink down into the platform which supports the box. Because of the size of the box, no change is noticed as the girl extends her feet, head and hands. A central panel is dropped to hide the middle of the platform, hiding the girl's body. When the box is sawn down to the platform, two partitions are inserted in grooves so that each section of the box can be taken a short distance apart without the body being seen.

Finding the card

The find-the-card trick is much practised by both amateur and professional magicians. A brand new pack of cards is produced and shuffled. A member of the audience is invited to take any card, note what it is and then return it to the pack. The cards are shuffled again and then spread across the table. Inevitably the magician picks out the card at the first attempt.

Though there is nothing unduly complicated about this trick, it always fascinates the uninitiated. A member of the audience selects his or her card and looks at it, the magician diverts attention by repeating how important the card is, meanwhile the magician is carefully bending the rest of the pack in his hands. When the card is put back into the pack, it is not difficult to pick out the only straight one.

Coins, needles and cord

The big tricks got the illusionists their publicity, but some, like Houdini, put their best efforts into producing smaller wonders, often those that could be done impromptu. Can a coin be balanced on the edge of a piece of paper, for instance? The way a magician does this is to take a bank note and fold it in half, lengthways. Then he bends both ends round to form a V. The coin is then balanced on the pointed end of the V. Next, he takes hold of each end of the V and carefully pulls the note straight. The coin shifts and bal-

Above This nineteenth century pencil drawing depicts a conjuror performing in a Paris street. It was customary for entertainers to wander around with their props until they found a site suitable for their show. The audience here are watching the traditional cup and ball trick.

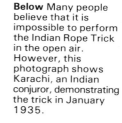

Below Many people believe that it is impossible to perform the Indian Rope Trick in the open air. However, this photograph shows Karachi, an Indian conjuror, demonstrating the trick in January 1935.

ances on the straightened edge of the folded note. The coin is on a tightrope. With a little practice this trick can be done without folding the note.

Then there is the trick of floating a needle in a glass of water. If you simply put the needle into a glass of water, it will sink to the bottom immediately. But try it this way: fill a glass to the brim with water, take a cigarette paper, tear it in half and place one half on top of the water. It will float. Take a needle and place it very carefully on the paper. Do not drop it on the paper or it may sink. Then slowly push the paper down until it sinks. The needle will be left floating. If the needle is placed very gently on the water the trick can be done without using the paper.

Another Houdini-like trick involves a piece of cord, about two feet long and a large curtain ring. The magician's wrists are securely tied leaving about 12 inches of space

between them. Two people hold up a small cloth in front of the shackled wrists and then the ring is passed over the cloth to the magician. Within seconds the ring is strung on the cord between the wrists.

Two identical rings are needed which are large enough so that one can be slipped over a wrist and up the arm under a jacket, out of sight. The other is passed around the audience for examination. When this is handed over the cloth, it is slipped into the inside pocket of the jacket. The other is slipped down the arm and becomes strung on the cord. This is all very simple, but effective when done quickly and efficiently.

Is it possible to hold both ends of a short piece of rope and tie a knot in the centre without letting go of one end of the rope? Anyone asked to try will quickly give up, but it can be done. Put the rope on a table; place the left arm diagonally across the chest; fold

Above In this painting by Bosch, a magician has amazed a crowd with the well-known cup and ball trick that dates back to 3,000 BC. He has deceived his audience with fast manipulation and skilful sleight of hand.

the right arm over the left and tuck it under the left armpit. The left hand rests on the right arm just below the shoulder. Lean over the table and pick up one end of the rope with the left hand and then the other end with the right. By unfolding the arms without letting go of the rope a knot will appear in the middle of it.

Magic continues to fascinate audiences of all ages as it has throughout the centuries. The audience will the magician to fool them and acquiesce happily in the illusions, sleights of hand and other tricks. The magician needs skill, dexterity and supreme confidence.

CIRCUS

FROM ROMAN GLADIATORS TO THE MODERN TOURING CIRCUS

One day in 1768, in a field called Halfpenny Hatch in Lambeth, London, a young horse-breaker and riding master made a fascinating discovery. He found that it was easier to stand on the back of a moving horse if he rode it in a circle and that the firmest, easiest balance was achieved when that circle was a fixed 42 feet (13 metres) in diameter.

Philip Astley, who was formerly a non-commissioned officer in a regiment of Light Dragoons, had invented the standard circus ring. It is the same basic size for bareback riding today. The young trick-rider went on to become the acknowledged father of the modern circus.

Horses have remained the centrepiece of all true circus (the word itself is Latin for 'ring') since the time of the first and largest circus of them all — the Circus Maximus in ancient Rome. The origins of this stadium are obscure, but it is known that it was rebuilt in the time of Julius Caesar (101–44 BC), to hold an audience of 150,000 on three sides of the course. Later emperors enlarged it still further until, by the time of Constantine (AD 280–337) the space occupied by arena, seating and accommodation for horses, beasts, charioteers and gladiators measured some 2,000 by 600 square feet.

Bread and circuses

There were numerous other spectacles besides chariot racing in Roman circus. During the reign of Augustus (27 BC–AD 14), around 4,000 beasts, wild animals mainly imported from Africa, are said to have been killed in staged 'hunts' in the arena. Human blood, too, was shed in abundance. No chronicler of the times kept account of the number of human beings who were slain in the rings and amphitheatres of ancient Rome. The Romans considered human blood — whether that of slaves or, in later times, political or Christian prisoners — to be cheaper than expensively-imported animal blood. Gladiators, entering the ring to kill their fellows or be killed by them, were the popular heroes of Rome, from the foundation of such contests, in 264 BC until their outlawry in AD 404. One circus billing of these bloodsoaked times promised a 'celebration' — probably in honour of one of the gods — during which 230 wild animals would die, together with, almost incidentally, 2,000 men.

Juvenal, the Roman poet and satirist (AD 60–130), in denouncing the political and social conditions of Imperial Rome, became the first circus critic when he sneered that all the Roman masses thought about were *panem et circenses* (bread and circuses). Indeed, some emperors, among them Caligula who reigned from AD 37–41, used the Roman games as a political distraction to conceal worsening economic circumstances from the populace. The number of spectacles and killings staged went up as the standard of living went down. However, despite the carnage and spectacle, which included the flooding of some Roman arenas to stage scaled-down naval battles, the circus was really centred on horses. Two, three, four, or even more, galloped round the dust-and-dirt arena. The vehicles they drew were unsprung two-wheeled chariots, which were little more than oversized buckets with cutaways for the charioteers.

These horsemen, mainly slaves, carried the colours of their owners. They wore leather and metal helmets and were draped from neck to knees in lengths of rein, knotted around their waists for greater security. Each man carried a short, sharp knife. This was — hopefully — to enable him to slash himself free from the sliding mass of reins and ropes caused when the inevitable collisions with opponents overturned the frail chariots.

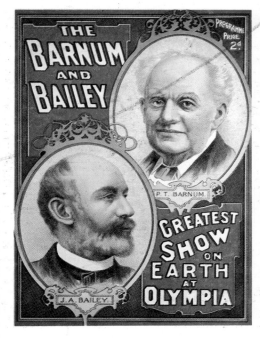

Modern circus has been dominated by families — both as circus proprietors and as performers. The Ringling Brothers **(above right)** owned and dominated American circus in the middle of this century. By 1929 the Ringlings owned 11 major American circuses. They had earlier taken over the influential circus owned by Barnum and Bailey. In 1871 P.T. Barnum founded 'The Greatest Show on Earth' **(above)**, one of the first international circuses. Barnum brought his show to London in 1889.

This selection of flamboyant circus posters illustrates the range of acts presented by circuses earlier this century. The Ringling Brothers feature the act of their horse-riding acrobats, the Lorch Family **(above right)**. Circuses also included static displays like the elephant exhibited in 1917 **(far right)**.
The Barnes' poster of the tiger **(right)** emphasizes the animal's ferocity while the horse poster **(right centre)** draws attention to the horseman's skills.

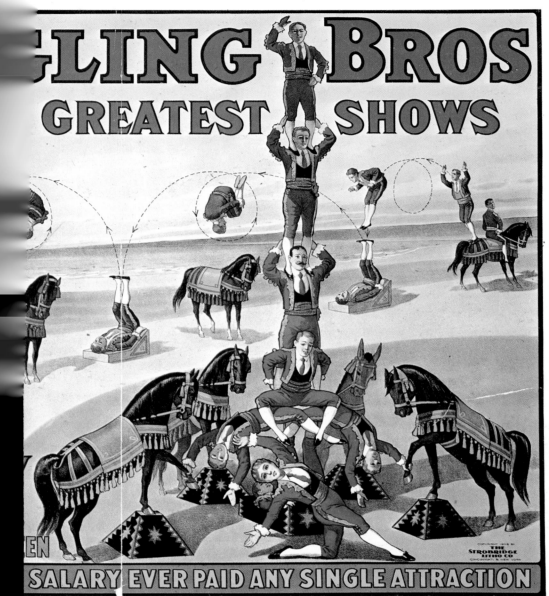

GLING BROS GREATEST SHOWS

SALARY EVER PAID ANY SINGLE ATTRACTION

JUNGLE TIGER

AL. BARNES G. BARNES WILD ANIMAL CIRCUS

WORLD'S FINEST HORSES

BIG BINGO

BIGGEST BRUTE THAT BREATHES

GIANT TWO-STORY ELEPHANT

NOW EXHIBITED BY

RINGLING BROS

Circus on the move

Ancient circus came to an end with the break-up of the Roman Empire. No definite date can be ascribed to this, but Edward Gibbon, the eighteenth-century British historian in his *Decline and Fall of the Roman Empire*, put its fall towards the end of the third century AD. For the next 1,500 years, there was no organized circus, but the Roman links with modern ringcraft never died. Trick riding, often performed by 'barbarians' (non-Romans), between chariot races, continued. In addition, those showmen and performers who had beguiled coins from the purses of Roman citizens on their way to the circuses and hippodromes — street jugglers, slack-rope dancers, acrobats and contortionists — resumed their wanderings, singly and in groups, throughout Europe, Asia and northern Africa.

The appeal of circuses to men of power and position also survived. Two British examples serve to illustrate this theme. King Alfred the Great of England (849 – 899) was, according to the chronicles of the time, entertained by a 'wild beast display', which almost certainly included bears, those dangerous, but endearing, knockabout clowns of the animal world. William the Conqueror who reigned from 1066 to 1087 brought troupes of ropedancers, tumblers, jugglers and 'strongmen' from France to Britain to amuse his new English court.

From the fall of the Roman Empire to the late fifteenth century, wandering bands of players, mimes, slack-rope dancers, jugglers and puppet-masters, together with trainers of horses, dogs, monkeys and bears, became an integral part of street fairs and fair grounds in Europe. Yet, even though all the essential elements of circus were alive, these were not due to be brought together into their romantic and irresistible whole — the circus ring — for many centuries. Even medieval pageantry, with its side-shows around the tournament arena and its displays of consummate horsemanship, cannot be counted among the true ancestors of circus. It lacked that factor which links audience and performers in a strange, binding intimacy — the ring itself.

There were clowns in plenty. Included among their number were gleemen, merrymen, jesters and fools — the second most important ingredient of circus after horses. The wisdom of clowns, who embarrass to amuse, is celebrated in many of the plays of Shakespeare.

The return of the ring

Circus had to wait until the eighteenth century for the return of the ring. As has been seen, this was the work of Philip Astley and its starting point came in 1768, when this 26-year-old son of a Midlands cabinetmaker, who had just bought himself out of the army, set up his makeshift arena in a Lambeth field. Following this, he was quick

Philip Astley was the father of modern circus. He founded 'Astley's Riding School' near Blackfriars in London in 1769. The original building **(right)** was a simple wooden amphitheatre. The arena **(far right)** consisted of a ring for the horses and room for the audience around the circumference.

Left Gladiators were only one element of Roman circus. This nineteenth century painting shows the vanquished fighter being given the 'thumbs down' — the death sentence. Roman circus was brutal and violent.

Below left Modern circuses have tried to imitate the Roman chariot race. This 1898 drawing of the Barnum and Bailey circus shows the final between the winners of the evening's two previous races — the male winner of the four-horse race and the female winner of the two-horse race.

to capitalize on his discovery. He advertised a trick riding show in which he, his wife and three others would execute 'extraordinary feats on one, two, three and four horses.'

Astley prospered on the pennies collected from the standing audience and the following year bought some land near Westminster Bridge. There, he built a ring with a large shed attached and charged for admission on a regular basis. Outside, he would sit astride his fiery charger, an imposing figure in full-dress Dragoon uniform and, with his sword, wave people towards the entrance of 'this here Riding School'.

Other turns — jugglers, wire-walkers, acrobats, slack-rope dancers, strong men — soon joined the equestrians in Astley's ring. So did the first true clowns of the circus — or merrymen, as they were known then — getting in the way of the horsemen, annoying the ring-master and amusing the audience between acts.

By 1778, Astley's was fully roofed, and had become famous in both Britain and Europe. In 1794, this building was burned down and Philip Astley scored another 'first' in circus history — the first proprietor to know the terrible hazard of a circus fire.

Expanding boundaries

The show had already paid its first visit to Paris, where it was a huge success. Thus Astley, in a sense, became the father of French as well as British circus. For several years he ran shows in 'double harness', travelling between Paris and London. He also had an amphitheatre in Dublin.

When, with the outbreak of the French

The circus of Philip Astley **(above right)** expanded considerably after its beginnings in Blackfriars. Circuses began to include wild animal acts. One of the most successful early trainers was the American Van Amburgh, shown here **(left)** battling with a 'panther'.

clown with Astley, had opened a Royal Circus at Blackfriars, just downriver from the Westminster 'Riding School' of his former boss.

When the Royal Circus closed and Hughes took his troupe to Europe, one of his equestrian stars, John Bill Ricketts, crossed the Atlantic. He built an amphitheatre in Philadelphia, and gave his first public performance there in 1792.

Ricketts moved to New York City and Boston, accumulating acts to supplement his feats of horsemanship. President George Washington was one of his patrons, and it was possible for him to announce proudly that 'The PRESIDENT and his LADY will honour the CIRCUS with their Company this Evening'. Ricketts is today acknowledged as the father of American circus – the forerunner of such internationally famous names as Barnum and Bailey and the Ringling Bros.

Tenting circuses

In Britain, for many years after its founder's death, the magic name 'Astley's' remained synonymous with permanent circus. From 1824 until he died in 1842, the show was run by Andrew Ducrow, said to be an even greater horseman than Astley, and possibly the finest trick rider ever known. One of his acts, 'The Courier of St. Petersburg' is still seen in circuses today. With one foot on each of two horses cantering side by side, he rode around the ring while other horses, decked in the flags of those nations through which the 'courier' passed, galloped between his legs.

Among his audience one day in the early 1830s was a small boy named George Sanger. Many years later, as the self-styled 'Lord' George Sanger, Britain's greatest Victorian circus showman, he was to recall the occasion and the vow he then made: 'One day,

Revolution, his visits became impossible, the great showman leased his interests to Antoine Franconi, an exiled Venetian and fellow trick rider. What had been commonly known as 'L'Amphithéâtre Astley' became 'L'Amphithéâtre Franconi' – and the Franconi circus dynasty began. A Franconi was still in charge when the Cirque Olympique, the most celebrated French circus of the mid-nineteenth century, finally came to an end in 1862.

When Philip Astley died in 1814, aged 73, his New Royal Amphitheatre had been running successfully in Covent Garden for eleven years. This was the 'Astley's' fondly remembered by Charles Dickens in his *Sketches by Boz* (1835).

The first American circus

Even before the turn of the century, circus had spread from Britain and Europe to America. In 1782, Charles Hughes, a former

149

Astley's will be mine'. The pledge was fulfilled in 1871 when he bought the premises as a permanent winter quarters.

By the middle of the century, tenting or 'rolling' circuses were popular in Britain, America and Europe. Russia had also been invaded by travelling circuses under the direction of the French showman Jacques Tournaire. He found much native talent to join his shows — clowns, acrobats and tightrope walkers, who were the ancestors of the great Soviet circus performers of today.

The great Barnum

The greatest showman in all circus history, however, was the American Phineas T. Barnum (1810–1891). He was already known in Europe at this date, but not in connection with circus. He was then the proprietor of The Great American Museum in New York City, a collection of curiosities, freaks and 'marvels'. These included the so-called General Tom Thumb, a perfectly formed midget less than three feet in height whom Barnum brought to London and introduced to Queen Victoria in 1844.

America in general greatly influenced circus development during this period. In 1854, the Sanger travelling circus, still small and struggling, got the boost it needed. One of America's biggest tenting shows, Seth B. Howes and Cushing's American Circus came to England. George Sanger borrowed their techniques, out-advertising these masters of ballyhoo advertising; within six years the Sanger name and ever-growing circus was known throughout Britain.

Every spring in the 1860s, the Sanger Circus would take to the road for a nine-month touring season, visiting around 200 towns in the course of a 2,000 mile journey. The routine was to perform two shows every day except Sunday. The appearance of the circus on the road was a show in itself — a two-mile caravan of some 70 horse-drawn wagons, including 20 which carried wild beasts. By now, a menagerie had been added to the circus. Behind this procession came the ring horses, and then a herd of up to 100 Shetland ponies. Elephants and camels were allowed to follow on at their own slower pace — a separate little show.

Throughout these years, George had been in partnership with his less flamboyant brother, John. After buying Astley's in 1871, so realizing his childhood dream, George broke amicably with John. From 1874 to 1885, George Sanger toured Europe during the summer, returning to Astley's in winter. He left the roads and towns of Britain to John.

International circus

By now, circus was truly international. The first full circus to cross the Atlantic is believed to have been that of Thomas Taplin Cooke, who took his company of 150 — including 40 members of the Cooke family — from Britain to America as far back as 1836. Cooke is still one of the great circus names on both sides of the Atlantic.

Towards the end of the century, exchange visits were commonplace. In 1889, Phineas T. Barnum, who had been drawn into the world of true circus in his sixties, brought his 'Greatest Show on Earth' to London's huge Olympia Stadium. It included the 'Original Stupendous Historical Spectacular Classic Drama of Nero or the Destruction of Rome'. This had a cast of 1,200 people and 380 horses. Though Barnum died two years later,

Below The circus has held a fascination for many artists including the French artists Degas and Toulouse-Lautrec. This drawing by Lautrec shows classic circus trick riding as well as conveying the atmosphere of the circus.

Clowns' make-up
Since the nineteenth century, clowns have tended to have very stylized make-up. Indeed some clowns even 'patented' their faces by drawing them on eggs. **(right)**. The clown as a figure developed partly from the *zanni* of the Italian *commedia dell' arte* tradition. The first clown to use a white face was Grimaldi.

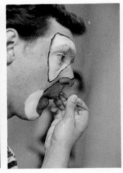

Applying a clown's make-up is a complicated process. A wide selection of greasepaint and make-up is needed **(left)**. It takes some time for a new clown to develop his face. Once it is established, he tends not to change the make-up substantially. Here the white greasepaint is applied first **(above)** and the face gradually painted in **(above right, right)** The finished face **(above far right)** is complemented by the traditional clown's wig and bowler hat.

aged 81, his partner, James A. Bailey, did not let the name die. The circus became 'The Barnum and Bailey Greatest Show on Earth.'

Circus continued to flourish in Edwardian times, but the First World War brought a golden age to an end. After the war, many smaller travelling circuses were unable to carry on, faced with the rising cost of motorized transport. Even the bigger tenting shows ran into financial trouble as the newly-born cinema whittled away their audiences.

Then, in 1920, a big revival began. It was the work of one man, then unknown in the circus world – Bertram Mills. The owners of Olympia had suggested to Mills, a wealthy 45-year-old horse-man, that a circus might fill their great hall.

Mills approached John Ringling – of the now-combined Ringling Bros and Barnum and Bailey Circus – but no shipping could be found to bring over the new 'Greatest Show on Earth.' Not to be beaten, in six months, Bertram Mills somehow organized the seating, found the British and European artists, arranged brilliant press publicity and opened his Great International Circus on December 17, 1920, for a five-week season. It was the beginning of 47 years of Bertram Mills' Circus. A tenting circus was started in 1930, supplementing the annual Olympia shows. It was the first tenting show in Britain to travel by rail.

Bertram Mills, 'the Guv'nor' as he was known to all his employees, died in 1936. His sons, Cyril and Bernard carried on, keeping the Mills circus dormant, but alive, during the Second World War, and resuming business in 1946.

Circus today

A world view of circus today shows that it is still thriving in America, where big tenting circuses can still be seen, although most run through circuits of permanent stadiums. Europe's smaller circuses, where the emphasis is more on the finesse of performers than spectacle, draw big crowds to both tents and permanent buildings. In Russia, where circus has been officially elevated to the status of an art, students from the Moscow Circus School perform in 100 or so circus rings across the country.

Britain has about a dozen large circuses and perhaps as many smaller ones. Permanent circuses include those at Blackpool Tower and Kelvin Hall, Glasgow. Names of long repute in show business and the circus appear in tented shows – the Chipperfields and the Fossetts. A newer name in British travelling circus is Gerry Cottle. He started in a small way in 1971; six years later, the whole Gerry Cottle Circus was flown to the Middle East for a four-week season. The Circus World, a new show started in 1979, claims to have more animals than any other tented

circus in Britain. The *Festival International du Cirque*, which started in Monaco in 1974, now draws more than 40 of the best acts in the world from up to 20 different countries. So international circus, perhaps the most universal of the popular arts, is still splendidly alive.

Horses – the circus mainstay

Horse acts, mainstay of all circus, are divided into three main types. These are *haute école* or high school; liberty horses; and voltige, or acrobatic riding.

In *haute école*, the rider takes the horse through the most elaborate dressage movements. These include walking to set rhythms, dancing on its hind legs, pirouetting, walking sideways, and making controlled, graceful leaps. These and other actions are known as airs and each has its own special name. The *capriole*, for instance, comes from the Italian *capro*, meaning goat. In it horse and rider make a goat-like leap.

The best-known centre of *haute école*, however, is not a true circus, but the Spanish Riding School in Vienna, where beautiful snow-white Lipizzaners are trained. Many of these enter the circus proper. The Lipizzaner, bred from Spanish and Moorish stock, has stronger hindquarters than the Arab – ideal to bear the horse and give freer play to its expressive forelegs.

Liberty horses, free from riders but obeying in symmetrical unison the gestures of their trainer, make a delightful circus act. Gestures are made with a long ring-whip – rise up, turn round, move on. In the trainer's other hand is the shorter, thicker guider, used to control the forequarters of each animal – slow down, stop, change direction, kneel. Very rarely is either whip seen to touch an animal, and then only extremely lightly.

Horses for voltige or bareback riding are quite different from the stately *haute école* and liberty horses. They must be solid, broadbacked and above all, placid enough to provide a steady moving platform for the rider-acrobat. Resin is liberally applied to the back of the horse and the shoes of the rider, to prevent slips – which is why voltige horses are often known as resinbacks.

Forward and backward somersaults – sometimes on one leg – were the stock-in-trade of many mid-nineteenth century voltige riders. In modern times, the Cristiani family perfected what they called a 'suicide' trick. Three of the family stand on the backs of three horses moving in line one behind the other. Simultaneously, they all turn a backward somersault. Two land on the backs of the horses behind. The third one lands on the ground.

The timeless clown

If horses can be described as the mainspring of circus, clowns can surely be called the oil in the works. Yet Joseph Grimaldi (1779–1837), the first true clown, in the modern sense of the word, never appeared in circus at all. He was a man of the theatre, a pantomime artist.

It was from his miming, grotesque dress and fantastic make-up that circus clowns have taken their inspiration from the middle of the nineteenth century – the end of the merrymen era – up to the present day. Grimaldi also gave clowns the name by which they are known within the circus world; there a clown is always a 'joey'.

Although the categories often mingle, and activities are mixed, there are four basic clown acts. Entrée clowns are the kings: these are the soloists such as the immortal Grock, Coco, and Oleg Popov of the Moscow State Circus. Then there are musical clowns, who may play an amazing variety of instruments; reprise clowns, who amusingly interrupt serious acts; and carpet-clowns, who rush and tumble into the ring to amuse the audience – and often mix with them – while props are being changed between acts.

The aerialists

In 1859, Jules Léotard demonstrated his recent invention, the flying trapeze, in Paris. On June 30 of the same year another Frenchman, Jean-Francois Gravelet – the great Blondin – crossed the Niagara Falls on a tightrope. In the late 1920s, Alfredo Cordona became the first man consistently to perform the triple somersault on the flying trapeze. And Con Colleano executed the first forward somersault on the tightrope (or high wire, as it is mainly now termed).

One of the most spectacular aerialists of the century, and one of the best-loved by audiences, was Lillian Leitzel, less than five feet tall, but with the shoulders and upper arms of a boxer. Her speciality was the 'plange'. She fixed her right wrist in a canvas loop at the end of a rope high in the big top. Then, at full arm's length, she swung her body round in a complete, almost vertical circle, using her shoulder socket as a pivot. At the end of each complete gyration, her shoulder was actually dislocated, but by sheer muscle power she hauled it back into place for the next turn, spinning from the rope like a catherine wheel. With the audience below shouting the number, she occasionally made more than 100 turns.

Of the many spectacular high wire troupe performers in modern times, the Wallendas – who as a family have been passing on their skills from generation to generation since 1928 – are thought to be the greatest. As the highlight of their act, four Wallendas, in two pairs, cross the wire. Between each pair is a pole. On each pole stands another member of the troupe. Between these two is another pole. In the centre of this, a chair is balanced – with a girl standing on the chair. All seven of this incredible pyramid carry their long, steel balancing poles. It is a feat of combined, perilous balance that has never been equalled or surpassed.

Tragedy struck in 1962 when two of the Wallendas were killed during the pyramid act in Detroit. And the veteran Karl Wallenda died, aged 73, when high winds knocked him from a wire between two buildings in Puerto Rico during a stunt in 1978.

Animals in the ring

Fear and brute force were the basis of many of the first great animal acts. On a visit to Britain, an American beast tamer, Isaac Van Amburgh, told the Duke of Wellington: 'When my pupils are no longer afraid of me, I shall retire from the wild beast line.'

Fear, instilled with an iron bar, was the basis of Amburgh's lion-taming. But this menagerie-owner, known as the 'Lion King' in the 1830s and 1840s, also had a strange power over animals. He is said to have been the first man to put his head in the jaws of a lion – and live. Tigers and panthers were also in his various taming acts, but a lion mauled him to death in 1846.

Since the late years of the last century, however, the training of most wild animals for circus performances has been based on the 'gentling' techniques devised by a German, Carl Hagenbeck. In these, sympathy, patience and understanding of animal psychology play a major part. But predatory animals, especially the big cats, will always be unpredictable.

Asked about the dependability of big cats, Clyde Beatty, the famous American trainer who once appeared in a cage alone with 42 lions and tigers, said simply: 'Cat animals are not built that way.'

Some 'jossers' – circus slang for non-circus people – suggest that the big cats are fed just before a performance to make them more docile. A lion that had eaten up to 18 pounds of meat, which is its daily ration, would not just be docile but probably too sleepy to go through with its part of the act. The usual practice is to feed the cats after the matinée and well before the evening performance takes place.

There is no method of treating wild animals to make the acts less inherently dangerous. Toothless lions and drugged tigers are myths. There will always be risks, the spice of circus, in the arena cage.

Because of their intelligence, curiosity, energy and innate sense of fun, bears are natural circus performers; and once a bear act is perfected, trainers say the animals can almost be left to run it themselves, or put in the temporary charge of a strange trainer.

Because of their size and build, the ring tricks of individual elephants are rather limited. They can sit up and beg, kneel, stand on their hind legs, even pirouette after a fashion, do head stands, 'dance' with their forelegs and lie down. But round these basic movements, ingenious trainers have built apparently complicated acts.

Elephants, like bears, enjoy their work. So do those fine mimics, chimpanzees, while sea-lions delight in showing-off their natural catching and balancing abilities. Naturalists have seen sea-lions in the wild balancing driftwood on their noses for fun.

Circus trainers agree that there is probably only one familiar animal that cannot be satisfactorily taught to obey set commands in a circus act. This is the domestic cat.

Stunts in the arena

Apparatus for arena acrobatics and stunts is contantly being improved. That most skilful, adaptable and versatile of all performing animals – man himself – also keeps pace with such improvements.

The Circus World Championships were inaugurated at Monaco in 1974. Most of the photographs here show artistes performing in the 1977 championships which were held in London. **Left** The White Devils, French high wire artistes, perform one of their most dangerous feats in which they cross the wire on bicycles. **Left, below left** High wire artist, Manfred Doual comes from Germany and performs his daring balancing act solo. **Left, below middle** Samson and Delila are a British couple who entered the championships with a 'strong man' act. **Left, below right** The aim of this juggling act is to keep as many hoops as possible spinning at once. **Below** The Mohawks are a British trick riding act. Members of the team stand on horses' bare backs and then jump from one horse to another as the horses canter around. **Right below** Large cats are always popular with audiences who are attracted by the dangerousness and unpredictability of the animals. Here Mary Chipperfield is controlling a tiger. **Right above** These two clowns are performing a stand-up comic routine between two acts. Clowns have now become used to speaking into microphones which are used when the Big Top is large and when the show is televised. **Right middle** Norman Barrett is the ringmaster at the famous Blackpool Tower circus in England. Here, he is doing an act with tame budgerigars.

H.L. Oakley.

'Lady Alphonsine', the stage name of a performer who 'walked' a large wooden ball up – and down – a spiral ramp in the closing years of the nineteenth century, would probably have appreciated the spectacular act of the Diors Sisters, trundling their three enormous plastic spheres up a light, open-sided ramp with a right-angled bend in it at the Blackpool Tower Circus in Britain.

The unicycle, basis of many popular modern acts, including a 'football match' with dogs as goalkeepers, was invented in 1869. It is doubtful if the early machines were as strong, light and manoeuvrable as those used by today's master of the unicycle, Rudi Horn. His most famous act is to ride one-footed while flipping cups and saucers up to nest in a growing pile on his head.

Jugglers, inheritors of what is possibly the most ancient 'show' art, seem constantly to be devising more difficult positions from which to practice their already difficult tricks. Slack-wire walkers balance on one foot to juggle. The top man in a head-to-head or hand-to-head balancing act further enlivens the remarkable performance by juggling. In the centuries-old perch act, where an acrobat is balanced aloft on a swaying pole by his equilibrist partner, both men may juggle.

Foot-juggling is a popular act – especially when the 'objects' juggled are human beings. The performer lies in a trinka, an upholstered cradle, leaving his legs, with their powerful thigh muscles, raised up to deal with far heavier weights than can be managed by arm-strength. A lighter partner is spun, tossed, whirled and tumbled – often at fantastic speed – by the juggler's feet. In one Russian act, partners are thrown from the feet of one performer to those of another.

With the growth of gymnastics, including tumbling, as a spectator sport, circus tumbling has declined in popularity. But no amateur gymnasts could hope to compete with the great circus acrobats such as the Merkels, with their incredible feats on a framework of fixed trapezes; or the Putzai troupe, who send man after man spinning up from a see-saw spring-board to land, four or five high, on each other's shoulders.

Programming and touring

In smaller family circuses, the bill is fairly predictable. It usually consists of knock-about clowns, a cage act with two or three lions, wire-walking, unicyclists, jugglers, perhaps one elephant (beloved, but expensive), single trapeze work, fire-eating – more spectacular than dangerous – knife-throwing, rope-spinning, dog acts, a one-horse *haute école* act, and even a small liberty horse act. These give variety and thrills enough for a two-hour show. Most members of a small circus can do more than one act and double for each other in emergencies. With quick changes of costume, the woman wire-walker might well be the fire-eater or the knife-thrower's 'target'. Even in bigger circuses the performers, unless they are recognized as stars by the management, might be asked to sell programmes or do other duties. In some cases their contracts require them to help move the circus.

The large-scale tenting circuses rely almost as much on quantity and spectacle as on thrills and skills. But for all types, it is essential to have an authoritative ringmaster. He must be both a compère and a glorified stage manager. He is responsible for coordinating the whole programme, ensuring that the props are set and the show moves smoothly. Long before he strides before the public, however, a complex pattern of management and sheer hard work has taken place.

Once a show has been put together, its touring route is worked out. Sites are more

difficult to find today as open space is becoming scarcer and scarcer. A public relations team moves ahead of the show, billing towns and advertising in local newspapers. The advance team also has to ensure that such things as water supplies and stocks of animal food are available. An advance box office is usually set up in a prominent local store.

A host of administrative problems can arise as soon as a circus arrives. The site will be visited by local health authorities, police and health and fire inspectors. The work schedule has to include the laying out of the site, rehearsal time, and time for maintenance and feeding. The animals have to be settled down after the journey and minutely inspected. An eye has to be kept on the weather – a circus tent can double in weight if it is soaked by rain, and this makes it difficult to put up or dismantle.

Most circuses today favour a four-pole tent which gives better resistance to high winds than the older two-pole variety and provides a square ceiling area from which to hang lighting and aerial rigging. Tents are usually coloured blue, enabling imaginative lighting effects to be used at the afternoon shows. Inside, an area is curtained off to provide storage space for props and waiting room for the performers. A bandstand is positioned – usually on a trailer. Other trailers are wheeled into place with seats built upon them. The larger shows will have an extra tent as a foyer with room for sales kiosks such as candy floss and soft drinks stands, to provide an important source of additional revenue. A diesel generator is set up to give power to the tents and the circus caravans.

The central lighting system is then focussed upon the area which has not changed in basic traditional layout through the years. The ring, with its levelled surface of earth, shavings or sawdust, is still basically much the same as when it was invented just over two centuries ago.

PUPPETS

FROM JAVANESE SHADOW PUPPETS TO THE MUPPET SHOW

The origin of the puppet theatre is shrouded in the past. The critic and puppet expert, Max von Boehn, has said that the first child to play with a doll invented the puppet; and certainly some modern techniques of manipulation, when the live actor is seen handling his puppet, call this picture to mind.

The origins of puppetry

Without doubt the use of the puppet as a theatrical form sprang up independently in many countries, often in primitive religious ceremonies when the figures represented divine personages, or in fertility and harvest rites, of which there is a strong African tradition. From China there is an account of priests who made their idols move, activating eyes and mouths to create a 'miracle' to impress their flocks, and this may be regarded as early puppetry.

However, most scholars tend to place India as the likely home of the oldest puppet tradition surviving today. Dramatizations of the *Ramayana*, the ancient Indian epic, are found in the shadow and rod puppet performance of Java, the Wayang Kulit and the Wayand Golek, and elements of these stories can also be traced in some of the sagas of the Chinese shadow theatre.

In Eastern countries puppets appear to have preceded the human theatre. The curi-

Above This detail from a medieval romance shows a group of women watching a puppet show. The puppets are fighting each other in a similar fashion to Punch and Judy who were introduced to Britain in the seventeenth century.

Below These shadow puppets of four Brahman daughters in prayer were made by Lotte Reiniger.

Although they are modern puppets, they are manipulated in the same way as traditional shadow puppets.

Right This collection of Javanese Goleks or rod puppets shows that the style of these puppets has not changed through the ages. They are still made with elaborately carved heads and a flowing dress over the main rod.

ous sideways movements of the traditional dances of Java and Cambodia are accepted as being copies of puppet movements, and there is an Indian phrase for a stage producer, 'Sutra Dhari' which literally means the 'puller of strings'. So the puppets came first.

These ancient shows have preserved the legends and myths of early peoples. But there are other more recent puppet dynasties: the Turkish Karagoz show, offering satirical and social comment rather than moral teaching or religion, originated in the fourteenth century; the Japanese Bunraku, with its highly classical literature, had its brilliant beginnings in the seventeenth century; our own Punch and Judy, first recorded in England in 1667, is one of the many theatrical descendants of the Italian *commedia dell' arte*. Puppet versions of the *commedia* characters were toured throughout Europe by Italian showmen — hence we have Punch's 'cousins', Polichinelle in France and Petrushka in Russia.

There are even more recent folk traditions, dating from the early nineteenth century, when many cities in Europe presented puppet shows featuring local characters. Most famous perhaps is Guignol, the lace-maker's apprentice from Lyons, who spread through the whole of France, his name becoming almost synonymous with the glove puppet theatre in that country. Similar characters are Tchantche in Liège, Hannechen in Cologne, Lafleur in Amiens and many others. There are also the great serial dramas about Charlemagne and his knights which were introduced about the same time both in Sicily and Belgium.

Some of these figures are glove puppets, some rod puppets, some shadow puppets and some marionettes. (A marionette is a figure worked by strings from above — except in France where the term is used for all types of puppet.)

Shadow puppets

Probably the oldest form of puppet is the shadow puppet. These are flat, jointed figures held against a cotton or silk screen by rods, with a lamp behind them so that their shadows appear to the audience on the other side.

The figures are traditionally cut from skin — in Java from buffalo hide, in Turkey from camel, in China and India from donkey or goat — though plastic and cardboard are sometimes used today. They are generally very elaborately decorated with stencil-like perforations indicating facial expression and costume detail. Each puppet is a work of art in itself. The thinner skins are dyed with vegetable dyes and the colours shine through the screen like a stained glass window. The Chinese and Indian figures are particularly colourful.

The Javanese puppets are equally colourful, but not transparent. They are painted in

Above, left The marionettes pictured here are part of the famous Toone puppet theatre in Brussels, which was founded in 1815. The production is *The Three Musketeers* and the detailed costumes that are needed for such a play are all made at the theatre.
Not only the costumes, but also the puppets themselves and the scenery for every show is designed and made in the theatre workshop. The Toone puppet theatre differs in several ways from other such theatres. For example, the puppets often talk in dialect and the plays show a coarse sense of humour. Another individual feature is that at the end of the performance one puppet who has been made up to resemble the founder of the theatre, Mr Toone, takes a curtain call in his honour **(above)**.

reds, blues and golds for the benefit of the men who traditionally sit behind the screen on the same side as the puppets, only the women see them as shadows.

The Javanese figures are often quite large, sometimes over 2ft tall, and are stiffened with a stem made of horn, which becomes the handle by which they are held at the base. This handle can be stuck into a split bamboo running along the base of the screen so that the puppet may be left in position. Normally there are two other rods, one for each hand, which are held vertically below the puppets. The legs are not articulated. The showman sits cross-legged behind the screen, with a single light — traditionally an oil lamp, but now more often a bare electric bulb — behind and above his head.

The Indian figures are much bigger, up to 4 or 5ft tall, but they are very thin and transparent. The head and the moving parts are attached to very short handles which the operator grasps, standing quite close to the screen, allowing just sufficient space for a row of lights above the screen to hit the figure without casting a shadow of himself.

The smallest and most delicate shadow puppets are the Chinese, particularly those from Peking which are often only 8 or 9in tall, compared with those from Szechuan, which run to about 18in. Though thin and bendy, they are extraordinarily strong, and often a face is cut out leaving only a hair-breadth profile. They are not stiffened but pressed against the screen by thin bamboo rods ter-

minating in a wire loop stitched to the figure. Unlike the Javanese method, these rods are held at an angle of 45° and the manipulator works in a standing position.

The Turkish Karagoz show uses rods firmly fixed in a horizontal position, which allows added facility in manipulation by twisting the rods. Screen sizes vary according to the size of the puppets, but are often 12ft or more wide. In this case a row of lights is used near the screen as in the Indian shows, but placed beneath the showman's arms instead of over his head.

The possibilities offered by modern materials — such as perspex, polythene and other plastics — and by spot lamps, strip lamps (which kill rod shadows), coloured mediums and even polarization, have opened up new avenues for the art of shadow puppetry.

Today's best-known exponent is undoubtedly Australia's Richard Bradshaw (born 1938), but there are many groups experimenting in this field, though as yet no theatres exclusively devoted to shadows have sprung up. It is essentially an itinerant art, though in the 1880s there was a famous café in Paris, the *Chat Noir*, which specialized in this form of entertainment. In the film work of the animator Lotte Reiniger (born 1899), shadow puppetry can be seen at the highest artistic level.

Rod puppets

The rod puppet has an equally ancient history. Java again offers the oldest surviving

technique. The puppet's head, beautifully carved in wood, is fixed on a long rod which passes through the shoulders and body and is held by the manipulator inside the figure's skirt or sarong. There are also rods for each hand. The showman is hidden behind a screen and works the puppet above his head. As the main rod is turned the figure's head turns from side-to-side. The tilt of the rod gives body attitude, and the hand rods provide gestures.

This simple technique gives very dignified and effective movements. The great Russian puppetmaster S. V. Obrastzov (born 1901) has adapted it and developed it out of all recognition, with springs and levers inside the figures and ingenious methods of concealing the rods so that his figures (often manipulated by several people) appear able to do anything. When they are placed in front of well-designed and well-lit decor in his vast custom-built puppet theatre in Moscow, the effect is breathtaking. This technique is now being used with many variations all over the world.

There is, however, one serious limitation. It is not possible to present this type of show in a theatre with circles or tiers, for if the audience is too high they can look over the top of the various screens and see the puppeteers' heads. An auditorium with a gentle rake is necessary. In Eastern Europe many cities particularly in Hungary, Poland, Czechoslovakia and Rumania, have permanent theatres for this type of show.

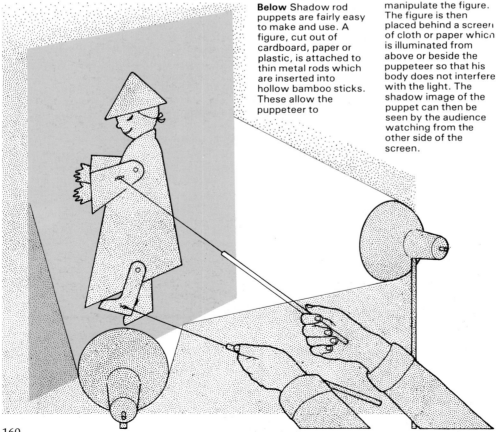

Below Shadow rod puppets are fairly easy to make and use. A figure, cut out of cardboard, paper or plastic, is attached to thin metal rods which are inserted into hollow bamboo sticks. These allow the puppeteer to manipulate the figure. The figure is then placed behind a screen of cloth or paper which is illuminated from above or beside the puppeteer so that his body does not interfere with the light. The shadow image of the puppet can then be seen by the audience watching from the other side of the screen.

Below The shadow hand puppet is used for one of the most simple puppet shows. The puppeteer only needs a white wall with light directed onto it. When the puppeteer places his hand some way in front of the light, a shadow image of his fingers and fist is projected onto the screen as a figure of an animal or person. The distance between the light, hand and screen determine the sharpness of the shadow. The closer the light and hand are to the screen the clearer the shadows will be.

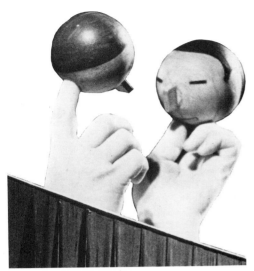

Right This photograph shows the famous Australian marionette troupe, The Tintokie, in performance at the Princess Theatre, Melbourne in 1975. Everything in these shows is done on a grand scale. The company has a large repertoire and they often stage productions that involve over 100 puppets. The puppets are sometimes three feet high and are worked from a bridge above, by at least 10 people.

Left This picture shows Sergei Obraztsov's finger puppets. Obraztsov is a highly regarded skilful puppet master, who has developed puppet theatre in Russia.

Below The string puppet, or marionette, is the most versatile and complicated of all puppets. All its strings are tied to a bar of wood called a control, perch or crutch, which takes the main weight of the puppet through the head string. The puppet's movements are achieved by tilting the horizontal bar carefully, rather than plucking individual strings. The length of the strings can be varied to suit the taste of the puppeteer and the layout of the stage scenery.

Below Unlike the shadow rod puppets which are flat, rod puppets have elaborate heads and a cloth body without legs. The puppeteer stands behind a screen beneath the puppet. He works the head with the main rod that passes down through the body and the arms are moved by two smaller rods. When the main rod is tillted, the body moves and the expression of the puppet is provided by its hand gestures. The puppeteer moves the figure's head by turning the main rod.

Below There are many techniques employed by glove puppeteers. The drawing below shows a combined technique with the puppet's head controlled by a rod. However, the most popular method is to put the index finger into the head and the thumb into the arms. Very few glove puppets have letgs and feet, but when they do the puppeteer controls them with his other hand and they are left hanging over the edge of the booth when they are not being used.

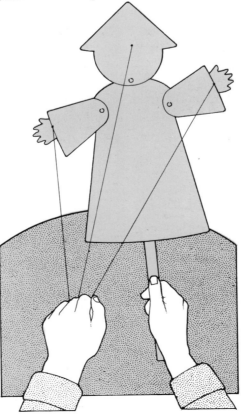

Right This watercolour shows Mr Punch with his traditional hooked nose and chin, hunchback, pot-belly and brightly coloured clothes. Mr Punch, who is the major character in Punch and Judy shows, is thought to be the English version of the Italian Pulcinella from the *commedia dell'arte*. He is a thoroughly unpleasant, cruel and boastful character. However, although he beats and sometimes even kills his wife, Judy, Mr Punch is the most popular British puppet.

Glove puppets

Mr Punch is a typical glove puppet. This technique is not of very ancient origin, and was probably invented by an Italian showman in the seventeenth century. The normal procedure is to put the first finger into the puppet's head and the second finger and thumb into its arms. But there are many variations. Some puppeteers put three fingers into an arm. The Catalan puppets, which are very heavy, require three fingers in the head. Some people put two fingers into the head, which makes it possible for them to turn their heads slightly.

Many puppeteers use a mixture of rod and glove techniques. They grip a short handle coming from the neck inside the puppet's chest instead of using the finger, or by using

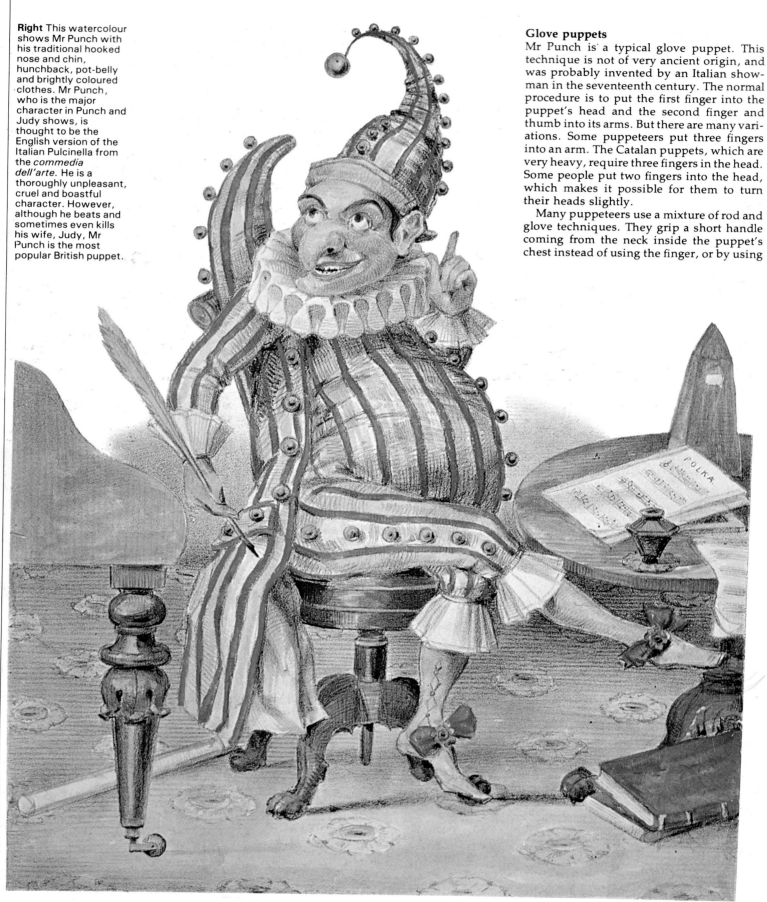

rods on the hands, which allows the arms to be made longer.

Although Punch himself is normally seen in a small booth, the glove theatre can be quite big and elaborate, employing many manipulators, with flies for the scenery, a front curtain and footlights. However, the same limitations apply as for rods concerning an audience in a high circle.

The Ferrari family of Parma are one of the few companies who present glove puppets in the grand style. Nevertheless gloves are used by many children's entertainers, and small permanent Guignol theatres can be found in many parks in France, while Mr Punch and his portable booth are often seen on beaches and in parks in Britain. The man-ipulative skill of the glove puppeteer is perhaps most remarkable in China. Here they stage a grand battle in which a figure is flung into the air to be accurately caught on the hand of another operator.

Marionettes

The origin of the marionette is uncertain. It was known very early in India, and jointed figures with holes, apparently for strings, have been found in ancient Egyptian tombs. Early references to puppets in literature give no indication of what type of figure was employed.

The marionette is undoubtedly the most difficult and most versatile of all puppets. There are people who consider that the remoteness of the puppeteer — separated by strings from the figure, rather than in the direct contact of the glove or precise control of the rod — makes him unable to give free or spontaneous expression in performance. This is quite untrue. Modern puppeteers such as Ann Hogarth (born 1910) with her Muffin animals or Albrecht Roser (born 1930) with his Gustaf and Grandma are shining examples of what can be accomplished given sufficient talent. The whole art of puppetry is the art of acting, and, with the marionette, a greater variety of roles, from comic to tragic, through mime or dialogue, is possible.

Basically, the figure is suspended from a wooden cross by seven strings, two for the head (taking its weight), one for each leg

Above Javanese rod puppets are very different. Since all the movements are made by manipulation from beneath, the show must always be staged from behind a screen.
Left Dan Leno is most famous for his performances in pantomime, but in this watercolour he is making puppets dance to bagpipe music. The puppets are strung together and attached to one of Leno's legs so that when he taps his foot the puppets seem to be dancing in time.

Above This photograph shows a collection of string puppets hanging backstage at the Harlequin Puppet Theatre. The detailed costumes here are wide in range — from a frogman to a Japanese lady.
Left These Italian glove puppet heads are much more primitive. The faces are carved from wood and then painted in bright colours to highlight the exaggerated features.

(often going to a separate bar), one for each hand and one for the back. Many extra strings may be required according to what the puppet is to do. Strings may go to elbows, heels or shoulders, for example. But it is a golden rule to use as few as possible. Sometimes the cross is held vertically, sometimes (always for animals) horizontally. Generally speaking both hands are required to work a marionette, whereas with gloves the puppeteer can work one on each hand.

The strings may be short, with the manipulator working behind the scenery on the same stage level as the puppet. They can be longer to allow the puppeteer to be raised a foot or two in order to obtain a greater reach; or they can be very long so that the operator can work on a bridge high above the puppet stage with the scenery underneath him. The puppets can be operated from either side of this bridge.

Some very elaborate marionette theatres have two high bridges, and a further bridge over the proscenium, which conceals the puppeteers. Long strings allow a high proscenium opening, which means that the puppets can play successfully in a normal human playhouse. Figures for this type of show average between 2 and 3ft in height. But

Above This picture shows the marionette theatre in Venice. As in most puppet theatres, everything in the production has been carefully scaled down to size so that the puppets and the props are as realistic as possible.

Below These Turkish shadow puppets are made of camel skin dyed pale orange and brown. The elaborate perforations outline the features of the puppet so that its shape is well defined on the screen.

considerably smaller figures can be very successful — 18in is a popular size.

There has been a tendency in the last 20 years to abolish the proscenium altogether and allow the manipulators to be seen above their puppets, though in shadow, and sometimes the puppeteers even address the puppets and take part in the performance. This style of 'open stage' presentation can be shown almost anywhere, from cabaret floor shows to large theatres.

A good hunting ground for permanent marionette theatres is Germany. Munich has two — as well as the biggest and finest collection of puppets of all kinds from all over the world in its City Museum. There are permanent marionette theatres in several other cities and towns — those at Stuttgart and Steinau are particularly interesting. Austria is the home of the famous Salzburg Marionette Theatre; and in London there is John Wright's Little Angel Theatre. Prague is noted for the Hurvinek and Spejbl Theatre founded by the great puppeteer Skupa .

Japan's Bunraku Puppets
The Japanese Bunraku have developed a style that is quite unique. The beautifully dressed figures are about 3ft high and are

operated by three manipulators who handle them in full view of the audience. The chief manipulator, clad in black but with his expressionless face uncovered, operates the head and the right hand. The head frequently has eye, eyebrow and sometimes mouth movements controlled by levers on a short handle continuing from the neck inside the costume. The second manipulator is hooded and is responsible for the right hand — which often has a moving thumb to allow the figure to hold objects, controlled by a short handle concealed in the sleeve. The third manipulator, also hooded, works the legs.

The plays are mostly poetical classics of love and violence by the famous seventeenth century author Monzaemon Chikamatsu, often referred to as the Japanese Shakespeare. The stories are told by a narrator in highly stylized old Japanese, accompanied by samisens. A samisen is a three-stringed instrument played with a plectrum. The

movements are so perfect that stage actors go to these puppet performances to study gesture. It takes 30 years to become a chief manipulator. As the performance progresses the presence of the manipulators becomes no more noticeable than an actor's shadow.

The Bunraku is perhaps the most perfected form of puppetry and is having an effect on puppet presentation all over the world. More and more often one sees the manipulators, who would a few years ago have been hidden, handling their figures, whether by rods or strings, or even just holding them like dolls and pushing them into attitudes in full view of the audience. Modern plastics, synthetic rubber and rubber foam — which makes possible moving facial expression — are so much lighter than the traditional wood for heads and bodies that puppets are becoming bigger and bigger and are no longer dwarfed by their human operators — sometimes the reverse is the case, and thus puppeteers can play to larger audiences.

One new technique now used by several groups in Britain is to hang the figures from the heads of the operators. They stoop forward slightly. As the operators turn or raise their heads, the puppets respond similarly. The hands are worked by means of short handles extending from the figures' wrists. The operators sometimes put their feet into the puppets' shoes.

Puppets on TV
Television and film offer the puppet theatre even larger audiences, but so far TV producers seem to have been unable to make the most of their possibilities — except in the case of the popular *Muppet Show*, directed by Jim Henson. Most puppet TV activity is given over to rather silly children's shows which does not exploit the medium.

Of course in film and television the proscenium can be done away with and the camera can wander over a wide setting, framing the picture at will in close up or long shot. There is also the possibility of using different-sized figures for different shots — for example, a large head with moving eyes and mouth for close-up work and a small, full-length version of the character for dance movement. Indeed it is quite practical to use different puppets with different manipulative techniques to present the same character in different shots, according to the movements required.

With cutting and editing the problems of stage continuity do not arise. It is even possible now to wipe out completely a manipulator handling his figure, leaving just the puppet against a background which is shot with another camera.

Puppet festivals
UNIMA — *Union International de la Marionette* — founded in 1929 and associated to UNESCO has centres and representatives in 40 countries all over the world. A big international congress and festival of puppet theatres and puppeteers is held every four years, alternating between major cities in West and East Europe.

The WEEPING AUDIENCE.

Above This humorous nineteenth century engraving satirizes the extent to which an audience may be moved by a puppet show.

Left This engraving shows one unusual way that the Cantonese in China developed the glove puppet theatre. The man standing on the stool operated the puppets above his head.

PANTOMIME

FROM HARLEQUINADES TO PANTOMIME IN THE EIGHTIES

Americans have the musical for their national theatrical form, Italians have the opera and the British have that strange and endearing, though insular ragbag called pantomime. The musical stems from the nineteenth century operetta and opera itself from the seventeenth century masque, but the roots of pantomime go as far back as the bacchanale of ancient Rome, with its broad comedy and its passion for dressing men as women, or vice versa. The plays of Plautus have comedy scenes in them that could easily be recognized in modern pantomime.

The history of pantomime

In medieval times the miracle plays emphasized the characters in the cast who were good, and who bad, by having the good characters, such as Archangel Gabriel, enter from the right of the stage and bad characters, such as Mephistopheles, from the left. Pantomime still uses this convention and so the Good Fairy enters from the right and the Demon King from the left.

When the art of ancient Rome was rediscovered during the Renaissance, so was the bacchanale. This developed into the *commedia dell'arte*. An early form of pantomime, called the harlequinade, which was popular in Britain during the eighteenth and early nineteenth centuries, had developed from the Italian *commedia dell'arte* − most of the characters were the same. The 'father' of British pantomime was the theatre manager John Rich (1682−1761) who founded the Covent Garden theatre in 1732. He regularly played Harlequin in the harlequinades which proved extremely popular with theatre audiences.

By 1800 a pantomime audience were offered a fairly straight presentation of some traditional fairy story such as *Cinderella* or *Mother Goose*. At the climax of the plot, when all seemed lost for the hero and his friends, the Good Fairy would enter and transform all the principals into the characters of the harlequinade − and then the fun would start. Cinderella would become Columbine, Prince Charming, Harlequin, but most important of all Baron Hardup, the 'heavy' character, would become Clown. It was the adventures of the Clown that the audience was waiting for. By comparison, the adventures of Harlequin, the traditional hero, were considered romantic but a bit dull, even if his sword or 'slap stick' was the signal for the acrobatic comedy of the harlequinade to begin.

The harlequinade reached its peak about 1815. The first real pantomime star was the brilliant clown Joseph 'Joey' Grimaldi (1778−1837). All clowns are named 'Joey' in his memory. One of the highlights of Grimaldi's career was his *Mother Goose*, and scenes from it were successfully presented all over Britain. The show itself was even presented at the Bowery Theatre, New York after its season in London's Covent Garden.

Above and **below**
These nineteenth century engravings by Alfred Crowquill show scenes from pantomimes performed at the famous Olympic, Adelphi, Haymarket, Surrey, Princess's and Lyceum theatres. The productions staged were usually fairy stories but during the climax of the play the whole cast would be transformed into the characters of the harlequinade. This ingredient was derived from the Italian *commedia dell'arte* and was a feature of all pantomimes. For this reason, some shows were given two titles such as *Romeo and Juliet or Harlequin Queen Mab*, or *Nell Gwynne or Harlequin Merrie Monarch* (**above left** and **centre**).

Right This watercolour shows the genie from *Aladdin* in a nineteenth century production.

Right This portrait of Joseph 'Joey' Grimaldi making his final stage appearance at Drury Lane shows him wearing the clown's wig and painted white face which he pioneered. Grimaldi was the first great stage clown and he created many routines for pantomime which are still used by clowns today. These included dancing and acrobatics that were often dangerous. Not only did Grimaldi influence the role of the clown in pantomime, he also made an impact on other performing arts such as variety and the circus.

Grimaldi played Squire Bugle, who later became Clown, and it was his comedy work more than anything that made for the show's popularity. It was said that the Lord Chancellor of the day saw this pantomime nine times so that he could study the various ways that Joey stole the fish from the fishmonger in the comedy shopping scene. Grimaldi invented many pantomime routines which were handed down to later generations, and some of his routines survive today. They can be seen virtually unchanged, for example, in the film routines of Laurel and Hardy.

When the kind-hearted but exceedingly accident-prone Grimaldi died, no-one could be found to succeed him. Grimaldi had been acrobat, singer, dancer, mime and satirist, no-one else could replace this multiplicity of talent, and the comic element in pantomime became less important.

Spectacle became increasingly important in pantomime. Theatres vied with one another to achieve spectacular results. In particular the 'transformation scene' became an excuse for extravagant and varied stage effects. This is the moment when, for example, Cinderella sees the pumpkin turn into a coach, or when Aladdin discovers that the

sinister cave is really a cavern of jewels. By 1890 it was nothing for a Drury Lane pantomime to have 20 scenes and a procession of 300 artists in the grand transformation scene at the interval curtain.

However, even these glittering displays began to pall and comedy returned. Dan Leno (1860–1904), a music hall clog dancer and comic, realized, with help from his writer – named in true pantomime style J. Hickory Wood – that Mother Goose, Widow Twankey, Mrs Sinbad and company were not just 'panto dames' but were individual characters with personalities of their own. Dan Leno had a serious and dedicated approach to pantomime comedy. His detailed study of the comical and pathetic old country woman Mother Goose was, like Grimaldi's version of the same character, one of his triumphs.

Dan Leno was an important figure in the history of pantomime. His comedy techniques are still used to this day by veteran 'dames' such as Arthur Askey (born 1906), George Lacey (born 1904) and Nat Jackley (born 1909). Leno was also one of the first pantomime stars who was primarily an actor, rather than a clown or comedian, and

Right This watercolour shows the results of the hard backstage work being enjoyed by an audience, predominantly of children, at Drury Lane Theatre. Most pantomimes included lavishly costumed dances, like the one being performed here by the traditional looking fairies. The picture also shows the sumptuous scenery. The Drury Lane pantomime was famous for its extravagant productions.
Left This 1870 picture shows two artists adding the final touches to the props for the Christmas pantomime. All theatres aimed at producing spectacular stage effects, which were best achieved by extravagant masks, costumes and colourful scenery. The grotesque masks, such as the one on the easel, would probably have been used for a procession of giants.
Below Stage devices were also used to impress audiences. This amusing engraving shows a group of fairies being raised from beneath the stage to make a magical entry.

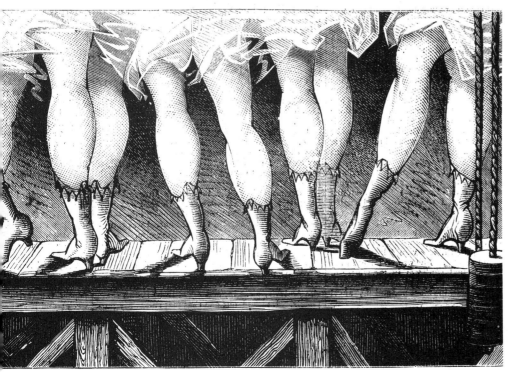

who had a scriptwriter and a director to help him to success.

By this time, around 1900, pantomime had more or less settled down and the general format has remained much the same. The emphasis has changed, however. The series of music hall acts, such as trapeze artists or comics, which were interpolated at regular intervals throughout the action, have disappeared. The audience earlier this century expected and enjoyed these acts and paid little attention to the actual plot, while the modern audience seems to take the adventures of Goldilocks or Crusoe more seriously.

After Dan Leno, pantomime retained its hold on the British theatre beyond its traditional Christmas season. During the First World War, London's biggest theatrical success was *Chu Chin Chow*, which is a reworking of the story of *Ali Baba and the Forty Thieves*. It opened in London in 1916.

In the 1920s and 1930s musical comedy had also caught the pantomime disease. There were only faintly disguised versions of pantomimes with titles such as *Mr Cinders, Princess Charming, Mr Whittington, The House that Jack Built*, and in the straight theatre *Alf's Button*, the story of a button made from Aladdin's lamp.

Pantomime is a highly stylized form of theatre in its presentation and content. Fairy tales and folklore provide the material. Today the standard parts still include the role of the hero, a 'britches part' — for a principal boy, played by a girl; the Dame — an old woman played by a male comic actor; the heroine — derived ultimately from Columbine; the 'baddie' — often a Demon King or similar figure; plus a series of comics. Staging still demands spectacular effects. The happy ending is likewise an essential feature of pantomime.

Modern performers

Almost all the famous artistes from the light entertainment world have appeared in pantomime. Before the Second World War, Will Fyffe (1884–1947) and Sir Harry Lauder (1870–1950) appeared regularly in pantomimes. Today, many British television stars, such as the comedians Frankie Howerd (born 1921) and Stanley Baxter (born 1928) regularly play pantomime.

More unlikely people are also attracted to pantomime. The dancers Alicia Markova and Anton Dolin once went straight from a season of *Les Sylphides* to appear in a Drury Lane pantomime. More recently, Twiggy (born 1946), the well-known model of the 1960s, portrayed a cockney Cinderella. Fay Compton (born 1894), the distinguished Shakespearean actress, once played Prince Charming. Many actors specialize in pantomime. One particularly long-lasting career was that of Dorothy Ward (born 1895). She first appeared as a pantomime principal boy in 1910 and was still playing that role in 1960. Her routine of Jack saying the sad goodbye to

British Christmas pantomime is dominated by tradition. For example, the hero, called the principal boy, is always played by a woman, and the comic old lady, called the Dame, by a man. The Citizens' Theatre in Glasgow produces a traditional pantomime every year. These pictures of *Puss in Boots* show aspects of the production on stage and backstage. Both costumes and scenery are lavish, even the extras need help with dressing **(left)**. The Dame is seen dressing **(below far left)** and in costume **(below left)**, and the heroine making up **(below)**. In a show designed to appeal particularly to children, spectacular lighting is another essential — the good fairy **(bottom left)** appears in red light with extra effects from a revolving glitter ball. Scenery is also colourful and traditional, as can be seen where Puss and the heroine wait to enter **(bottom right, right centre)**. In the picnic scene by the river **(right bottom)** the scenery is also elaborate and a lavish production number is staged. Pantomimes have happy endings with all the characters in harmony — both literally and figuratively as the Dame and King show **(far right)**. The final scene is normally a lavishly costumed procession **(right)** followed by a tableau.

his dear old cow in *Jack and the Beanstalk* was so highly rated that she was invited to perform it at a Royal Command Performance. She retired because she felt it had become absurd for her at the age of 60 to be seen as a fairy tale hero, but audiences disagreed and cheered her until the very end.

Staging
The traditional techniques remain, but only if they continue to entertain. If a theatre has a trapdoor, even though it is unused for the rest of the year, it is given a brush-down at Christmas so that the pantomime demon can rise mysteriously through the floor.

In the early days of pantomime many such devices and effects were positively harmful to the artists. For example, the notorious star trap, which shot the comic up on to the stage to a height of about four feet, is now considered too dangerous. Indeed, Grimaldi was forced into an early retirement in his mid-forties, crippled as a result of his pantomime acrobatics.

Safe trapdoors let into the scenery are still used and an audience is not getting its money's worth unless the walls of Widow Twankey's laundry are covered in traps that fly open when the Chinese police chase her and her son Aladdin in and out.

Songs and stories
By 1900, popular songs had ousted the spe-

cially written music and this tradition of using up-to-date songs has stayed. It is not considered anachronistic or illogical for Dick Whittington to wake up from his dream at the milestone on Highgate Hill and then to sing 'The Impossible Dream' from the American musical *Man of la Mancha*. A pantomime audience, although it has gone to the show principally for a good laugh, is nevertheless dimly aware of the historical background. Although throughout the nineteenth century pantomime was popular in the United States, as can be seen from contemporary prints, in the twentieth century its appeal has faded.

One reason for this is perhaps that many of the pantomime stories are British folklore. Incredibly, many of them are also true. Dick Whittington was indeed Lord Mayor of London, Robinson Crusoe was based on a Scottish sailor called Alexander Selkirk; Humpty Dumpty was Richard III. Moving further afield, Sinbad did live in twelfth century Persia and the Old Man of the Sea was one of the hairy apes of Formosa Mother Goose was named *La Mère d'Oie* and was the grandmother of Charlemagne.

Cinderella is an international character — in the Turkish version of her story, she makes an omelette which is turned into a flying carpet to take her to the ball. Only in the British and American versions does she wear a glass slipper, due to a charming accident in the translation from the French. The word *vair* (fur) was mistranslated as glass (*verre*).

Pantomime today

Although nineteenth century pantomime was popular in the USA, pantomime is now a peculiarly British form of entertainment. The Christmas plays popular, for example, in Germany, do not have the bawdy humour which is a prerequisite of British pantomime. The plots, characters and staging all remain the same — except for the occasional interpolation of a pop singer.

Pantomime — in spite of sophisticated sniggers — remains an extremely popular form of entertainment in Britain. Its yearly run of about two months over the Christmas period, guarantees packed houses, and many who attend will admit to never entering a theatre for the rest of the year. Pantomime remains a family entertainment, a spectacular three-hour show with singing, dancing and broad comedy.

Left This amusing 1870 cartoon by Cruikshank gives his view of a contemporary pantomime. The audience are watching the harlequinade that appeared in most pantomimes performed in the nineteenth century.

Above This painting shows Dan Leno in the title role of the much loved pantomime *Mother Goose.* Leno pioneered a more subtle characterization of pantomime 'Dames' at the end of the nineteenth century.

JAZZ AND POP

FROM NEW ORLEANS JAZZ TO CONTEMPORARY ROCK MUSIC

JAZZ

Events need not be distant to be mysterious. Jazz took on a separate identity as music no longer ago than the start of this century, but its beginnings and its origins are tantalizingly hard to pin down. At the end of the nineteenth century musicologists were not much concerned with what was happening in the lowest strata of American society. Very little information was recorded about the worksongs of the black field labourers of the South, or about the way in which gospel music, sung on the plantations, differed from the spirituals tidied up for Victorian audiences. We do not know exactly how and when blues acquired the pattern and characteristics that we recognize. All these forms of music were Afro-American, created by mixing the scales and musical procedures brought to America by the slaves with the Anglo-Saxon hymns and songs of the white settlers. This combination, thrown together with brass band music and ragtime — which has Afro-American syncopation, too — created jazz.

The ingredients for this musical fusion existed throughout the South. Jazz, in fact, may well have surfaced first in areas other than New Orleans, that cosmopolitan seaport which is normally credited as the birthplace of jazz. New Orleans simply had all the right conditions to encourage jazz and to allow it to flourish. It had the necessary basics of a mixed population of settlers and slave descendants, but it also had the benefits of earlier occupation by French and Spanish colonists with their own musical culture. One result of this was the tradition

of clarinet playing which the coloured Creoles brought to jazz.

The early days

Initially there was little to distinguish jazz from ragtime, the popular instrumental music of the 1890s from which it sprang. Buddy Bolden (1868 – 1931), the first king of the New Orleans trumpeters and the first name in jazz history, almost certainly played a music nearer to ragtime than the jazz that was recognizable as a separate entity later.

The earliest group to get on record, the Original Dixieland Jazz Band, made up entirely of white musicians and immortalized by the gramophone in 1917, had a style that reflected ragtime's clean-cut phrases and rhythms. The band, like most authentic New Orleans groups, used a front-line of cornet, clarinet and trombone. What they lacked was the blues feeling which gives emotional intensity to the finest black New Orleans bands, even when they are not playing formal blues.

The Twenties and Thirties

It is all there in the work of Joe Oliver (1885 – 1938), another king of New Orleans trumpeters. The band Oliver took to Chicago at the start of the 1920s brought collective improvisation, the real craft of New Orleans music, to new heights of turbulence and excitement. Playing second cornet in that band was a youngster who was called Louis Armstrong.

Armstrong (1900 – 1971) was to become the first virtuoso soloist of jazz. He switched from the cornet to the more brilliant-sounding trumpet and created improvisa-

tions that had immense imaginative breadth and emotional tenseness. An outstanding example of Armstrong's talent is his 1928 recording of 'West End Blues'.

Another New Orleans musician, Jelly Roll Morton (1885 – 1941), became the first composer of jazz. It was not a simple matter of writing tunes, but of devising pieces which made orchestral use of the dynamics and disciplines of the New Orleans front-line. Morton was recording in Chicago with his Red Hot Peppers at the same time that Armstrong was with his Hot Five and Seven.

Jazz remained a regional music right through the 1920s. It was heard on records and, to a lesser extent on radio, but most of the changes arose through musicians working alongside each other.

Chicago saw the most dramatic developments, but there were others, equally significant, that occurred in New York. A school of pianists sprang up in the city, playing a style that was described as Harlem 'stride' piano. They simplified the classic piano rags, at the same time turning them into vehicles for improvisation. The leaders of this piano style were James P. Johnson (1891 – 1955), Fats Waller (1904 – 1943), and a young man who had moved to the big city from Washington, Duke Ellington, (1899 – 1974).

Ellington's most lasting achievement in jazz was to be his work as a composer. Morton had harnessed the techniques of the New Orleans ensemble. Ellington built pieces around the sounds and style of his principal soloists, composing as much with people as with notes and harmony. By the early 1930s, Ellington was using an orchestra of three trumpets, three trombones, four sax-

Raymond Derry

ophones, and a rhythm section (piano, guitar, bass, drums). Ensembles of this sort had first appeared in the 1920s, using arrangements instead of collective improvisation. The first was brought together by Fletcher Henderson (1897–1952), performing many arrangements written by Don Redman (1900–1964), who later became a distinguished band leader himself.

Apart from the Original Dixieland Jazz Band, all these developments were the work of black musicians. But there were plenty of talented white jazz men around. They included the trombonist Jack Teagarden (1905–1964) and cornet player Bix Beiderbecke (1903–1931), who was greatly influenced in both solos and piano compositions by European harmonic practices. In Chicago a group of musicians, including tenor saxophonist Bud Freeman (born 1906), drummer Dave Tough (1908–1948) and clarinetist Frank Teschemacher (1906–1932) devised a way of playing 'Chicago style'. This was based on the music they heard on the city's South Side and included the singing of Bessie Smith, the improvising of Joe Oliver and the solos of Louis Armstrong.

Another white musician, Benny Goodman, brought jazz clarinet playing to a new level of virtuosity. But Goodman's greatest impact on jazz history was as the leader of the most popular band of the 1930s, a focus for what was to become known as the swing era. A new dance craze coincided with the easing of the great economic depression and provided a ready-made audience for Goodman's blending of jazz solos and orchestrations with the pop songs of the day. Most black bands and the early jazz musicians had

not previously found a way to get across to the vast white public. Goodman made it – but his band's orchestral style, a constant alternation between brass and saxophones, was fixed by arrangements mostly written by the black musician, Fletcher Henderson.

Jazz had reached Europe by the 1920s. In 1919, the Original Dixieland Jazz Band arrived in London and was followed by a band that included the New Orleans reed player, Sidney Bechet (1897–1959). He later wandered all over the continent and even visited Russia. Louis Armstrong toured Europe in 1932, and the following year Duke Ellington did the same with his band. In 1934, Coleman Hawkins (1904–1969), the first great tenor saxophonist made his headquarters in Europe and stayed until the outbreak of the Second World War. That period also saw the emergence of the first great jazz soloist to be born outside America, the guitarist of gypsy descent, Django Reinhardt (1910–1953).

The 1930s was a decade in which a remarkable number of virtuoso soloists emerged. They included Johnny Hodges (1906–1970), Duke Ellington's alto-saxophonist; Art Tatum (1910–1956), the pianist still most admired by other jazz pianists; vibraharpist Lionel Hampton (born 1909); the trumpeters Roy Eldridge (born 1911) and Bunny Berigan (1908–1942); and Billie Holiday (1915–1959). She was a singer who could, by the slant of her voice and the tilt of her phrasing, raise nondescript songs to the level of poetry.

In Kansas City Count Basie (born 1904) was leading an orchestra which transformed big band jazz when it arrived in New York in the winter of 1936-7. The 14-piece band

moved with the springiness of a small group, playing plenty of blues, often at a fast pace, and simple riff themes. Its rhythm section was more buoyant than any that had been heard before. One of its tenor saxophonists was Lester Young (1909–1959), whose laconic, sinuous style was to influence jazz playing for the next 20 years.

There were other smart swing bands besides Goodman's, notably those led by Artie Shaw, Tommy Dorsey, Jimmy Lunceford and Charlie Barnet. But there were also many others producing music that was becoming more and more predictable. This left many young musicians discontented and they reacted in two quite different ways.

One group, mostly white musicians on the West Coast, looked backwards, preaching and practising a fundamentalism based on the merits of early New Orleans music. They rallied around Bunk Johnson (1879–1949), a cornet-player who went to New York in 1945 with a band of elderly musicians, including clarinettist George Lewis (1900–1968) and the sounds created by these veterans exerted an enormous influence on young European musicians during the years immediately after the Second World War.

The second group was much more significant for the future of jazz. They were young black musicians from in and around New York who began meeting, first at Clark Monroe's Uptown House, later at Minton's Playhouse. They had no conscious policy of changing the course of music, but they were trying out new ways, new ideas. It was not so much a revolution, more a take-over. They did not abandon the practices of the previous

generation, they set about complicating them. The harmonies became tighter, full of passing chords, and intricate rhythms developed.

The music became known as bebop — an onomatopoeic way of describing its typical rhythmic phrasing. And it was Charlie Parker (1920–1955), an alto saxophonist from Kansas City, where he had spent nights as a teenager listening to Count Basie's Band at the Reno Club, who suddenly imposed his sound and style upon his contemporaries every bit as completely as Louis Armstrong had done 15 years before. There were others who played a vital part in the development of this music — the trumpeter Dizzy Gillespie (born 1917), the pianists Bud Powell (1924–1966) and Thelonious Monk (born 1920), and the drummers Kenny Clarke (born 1914) and Max Roach (born 1925).

All jazz innovations have been the work of the soloists. Composers move in later, rationalizing and providing an orchestral counterpart. It happened with bebop. By the start of the 1950s a change of mood, more thoughtful and less extrovert, was being expanded by a band, led briefly during 1949, by the trumpeter Miles Davis (born 1926). The band used scores contributed by three

men who were to become much better known in the next decade: Gerry Mulligan (born 1927), John Lewis (born 1920) and Gil Evans (born 1912). Evans's subsequent collaborations with Miles Davis rank among the classics of jazz, yet he worked more spasmodically than the others. Mulligan, playing baritone saxophone, led one of the most popular quartets of the 1950s. John Lewis devised pieces for the Modern Jazz Quartet of which he was pianist. This group, paradoxically, improvised more than most but frequently within frameworks that were highly formal. During this period Lewis and a number of other writers produced works which the musicologist and composer Günther Schuller described as 'Third Stream' — neither jazz nor symphonic pieces, but a combination of both.

The Sixties and after

New and earthier elements of music were drawn into jazz before the end of the Cool Decade, as the 1950s were known, drew to a close. The results were described as 'funk' or 'soul music'. The move was spearheaded by Charles Mingus (1922–1979) and the groups led by Art Blakey (born 1919) and Horace Silver (born 1928). Mingus was a superb bass player, but even more important as a band leader and composer. He would sometimes alter the direction of one of his pieces while on the bandstand, calling out instructions to his sidemen as they played. He made a sub-

tler and more compelling use of gospel rhythm and blues than most of his contemporaries. His groups included such dazzling solo performers as the alto saxophonist Eric Dolphy (1928–1964) and the multi-instrumentalist Roland Kirk (1936–1977).

There were even more radical departures at this time. The saxophonist John Coltrane (1926–1967) and Miles Davis, both dissatisfied with the complex ground plan of bebop, began cutting down harmonies to just a few chords, using them as a basis for scales upon which soloists improvised in a manner not unlike that of Indian classical musicians manoeuvring around a raga. Side by side with this exploration of 'modal jazz' came the even more drastic methods of Cecil Taylor (born 1933), a classically trained pianist, who developed his own style of atonal playing, and Ornette Coleman (born 1930), principally an alto-saxophonist, and leader of a quartet which dropped harmony altogether and either built their solos on a thematic fragment or related to an implicit tonal centre.

As the 1950s closed, the best of the newer European jazz musicians were proving themselves capable of rivalling the finest Americans. These included the German trombonist Albert Mangelsdorff, the British saxophonist John Surman, the Danish bass player Niels-Henning Orsted Pedersen, the Canadian trumpeter Kenny Wheeler, who settled in Britain.

Eddie Edwards, Larry Shields, Tony Sbarbaro, J. Russell Robinson, Nick LaRocca

Left The Original Dixieland Jazz Band were the first to record 'jazz' in 1917. This white quintet was based in New Orleans.
Below Buddy Bolden with his band was playing jazz in New Orleans as early as 1895.
Right The Hot Club of France featured Stephane Grappelli and Django Rheinhardt **(centre)**.

Chicago, too, produced a fresh school of performers, black musicians this time who shared with such British musicians as Evan Parker on saxophone and Derek Bailey, guitar, a fastidious and economical approach to the most experimental aspects of jazz. This school's most distinguished performer and composer is Anthony Braxton, most at home, like Ornette Coleman, on the alto saxophone.

Jazz has been a popular music at several times in its history, and it has always kept a close rapport with the pop world, consistently borrowing the better pop tunes as vehicles for improvisation. Coleman Hawkins's most famous solo recording is of Johnny Green's 'Body and Soul'. Jazz composers such as Duke Ellington have even written successful pop songs, like his 'Sophisticated Lady' and 'I Let A Song Out Of My Heart'.

Some time in the early 1960s pop music ceased to be a mere matter of songs and became, like jazz, much more concerned with the performing techniques. Jazz, inevitably, began borrowing some of its methods and accessories. The amplified guitar had already been assimilated, and, indeed, jazz had already produced its own virtuoso in Charlie Christian (1919–1942). But groups like Weather Report, which included several of Miles Davis's sidemen, and some larger ensembles, such as the bands led by the Rhodesian-born composer and arranger Mike Gibbs, not only deployed rock rhythms and bass guitar lines, but also used electronic instruments like the synthesizer.

There was a period after the Second World War when audiences in America demanded only jazz that was new or archaic. It was a tough time for the musicians whose style fell in between these two extremes. Happily, the situation has changed — and, in any case, it was never a problem that existed in Europe. So, in the 1960s, splendidly passionate playing was being heard from such relative veterans as the tenor-saxophonist Ben Webster (1909–1973), and trumpeter Roy Eldridge. The two musicians probably best-known to present-day jazz fans are Oscar Peterson (born 1925), the Canadian-born pianist whose roots lie close to Art Tatum, and the French violinist Stephane Grappelli (born 1908), who was Django Reinhardt's partner in the pre-war Quintet of the Hot Club of France. Grappelli has never played better than he did in the 1970s. For despite all its changes of style, jazz remains a music in which the genre is never so important as the gifted individual who is interpreting it.

Jazz in Performance

Jazz differs from other kinds of music in a number of important respects. It is basically a melodic improvisation on an harmonic theme, and it depends very much on the art of the individual performer, the idiosyncracies of the musician — his timing and phrasing as well as his timbre. It is decidedly an art of performance, never to be completely captured by notation. It is one of the luckier accidents of history that the gramophone was invented in time to preserve at least some of the music. Jazz is unique, too, in its use of vocalized tone, the way the brass or reed players allow their instruments to recreate the flexible characteristics of the human voice, even, occasionally, its raucousness. But its definitions are more than just musical. It sprang from a whole way of life . . .

A wagon trundles through the streets of turn-of-the-century New Orleans. It moves slowly, giving the crowd on the sidewalk plenty of time to read the placards and posters that deck it. Four men stand on the back. One plays a banjo, one a string bass, the leader is a cornettist and sticks most closely to the tune, while the clarinettist weaves a high-up counterpoint.

Sitting with his legs dangling over the tailboard of the wagon is the band's fifth member, the trombonist, using the full

Right Charlie Parker was the founder of modern jazz. **Below** The blues singer, Billie Holiday as a young girl is shown here with Ben Webster on the left.

This diagram shows the development of jazz, from its early roots in Africa to modern bands.

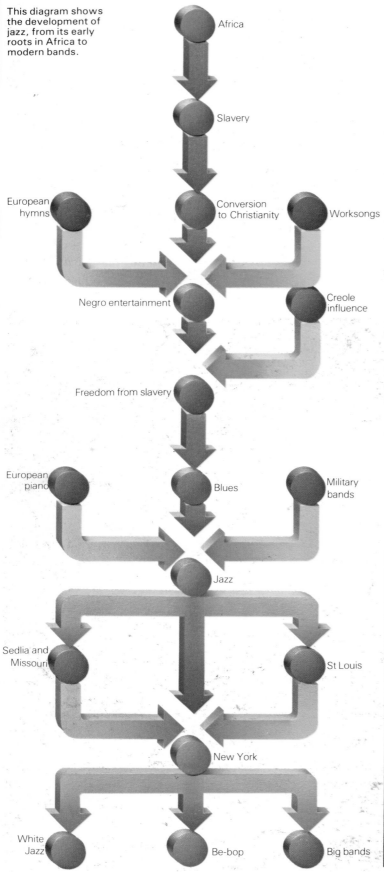

Africa

Slavery

European hymns — Conversion to Christianity — Worksongs

Negro entertainment — Creole influence

Freedom from slavery

European piano — Blues — Military bands

Jazz

Sedlia and Missouri — St Louis

New York

White Jazz — Be-bop — Big bands

Above This map shows those areas in the USA where jazz either originated or developed.

Among the most prominent figures in American jazz were Duke Ellington (**above left**), saxophonist Ornette Coleman (**left**), and Louis Armstrong (**right**). Ella Fitzgerald (**above**) was unrivalled among female jazz singers. **Below** Street musicians perform in New Orleans.

stretch of his slide to produce slurs and *glissandi*, helping to push the music forward as well as providing harmonic buttressing. History is in the making . . . that way of playing the trombone came to be called 'tailgate style', simply because this was a scene that was enacted time and time again. It was not just some odd, out-of-doors performance, but a real part of day-to-day living in New Orleans.

Almost everything was done to music in those early days down South. Guitarist Danny Barker recalls: 'There were countless places of enjoyment in New Orleans that employed musicians. There were balls, soirées, banquets, marriages, deaths, christenings, Catholic communions, confirmations, picnics at the lake front, country hay rides, and advertisements for business concerns.'

Jazz went wherever it was needed or wanted, and the musicians were not just musicians. Zutty Singleton, the drummer, remembered: 'They were bricklayers, and carpenters and cigarmakers and plasterers. Some had businesses of their own – coal and wood or vegetable stores. Some worked at the cotton exchange and some were porters.' King Oliver, one of the finest trumpeters to come from the city, once worked as a butler.

From a distance it looks idyllic, with music serving a functional purpose, in tune with its society. But it had an uglier side. Violence, even killings, occurred at cabarets and dance halls on the rougher side of town; and there were big changes during and after the First World War. At the same time that industry began to boom in the northern states, agriculture slumped in the South, with the boll weevil savaging the cotton crop. Thousands and thousands of Southern blacks went northwards, especially to Chicago, to work in the factories, steel mills and stockyards. They took their music with them. Jazz not only moved out of its birthplace, but it went indoors, too.

The musicians who had marched or ridden through the streets of New Orleans could find work in New York and Chicago only in the night clubs, theatres or dance halls. The music changed. 'High Society', customarily played as a march in New Orleans, was recorded by King Oliver's band in Chicago in 1923 as a rag, with four beats to the bar instead of two. Musicians reared in the New Orleans tradition of polyphony had to fit into brass and saxophone sections as the bands got bigger.

Even so, jazz contrived to operate as a social music, especially in the black ghettos. Skiffle parties were held in Chicago's South Side, while in Harlem, rent parties raised money to pay the landlords. Willie 'The Lion' Smith, remembers playing at many of them: 'A hundred people would crowd into one room until the walls bulged'. James P. Johnson played at rent parties in his early days – so did Fats Waller and even Duke Ellington.

The solo

Louis Armstrong's success heralded a new phase for jazz, with the soloist assuming greater importance, winning praise for originality rather than for the authenticity looked for in the folk musician – and early jazz had much in common with folk music.

Performers began to experience the responsibility of the artist, sharing a commitment to an aesthetic set of values, while continuing to operate in show business. It was not easy for a performer like Armstrong, accustomed to playing for black dancers in New Orleans and Chicago, to find himself the star of a revue on Broadway or appearing at the London Palladium, where white audiences, unfamiliar with the subtleties of black music, reacted to the novelty of his act rather than to its lyricism and emotional power. Armstrong, not surprisingly, sought refuge in technique, unleashing a succession of high notes. Later on he used the avuncular charm of his singing.

Circumstances often forced musicians to develop techniques that later became a part of their styles. Pianist Earl Hines, almost as remarkable a figure in the Chicago jazz of the 1920s as Armstrong, found himself in an era before the microphone, struggling to be heard amid the noise of a big band. His solution was to play melody notes as octaves at the upper end of the keyboard, the intervals ringing in a way that later became integral to his more complicated way of playing. Blues singer Joe Turner, trying to get his voice through the rowdy din of a Kansas City bar, came up with a recitative style, often inaccurately described as blues shouting.

Even the great Ellington can be said to have had his composing style shaped by the basest of commercial pressures. His early ambition was to become a songwriter. He

took a band into the Cotton Club at the end of 1927, but he found himself faced with the need to produce music for floor shows. These were elaborate, sensual affairs, designed to convince the white patrons that Harlem was only a handspring away from primeval Africa. New Orleans was not the only city to have brass players who used mutes to produce freak effects – the 'preaching trumpet' was probably the most popular. Ellington had two virtuosi of that sort in trumpeter Bubber Miley and trombonist 'Tricky Sam' Nanton. Their growls and snarlings became part of an armoury of bizarre timbres that Ellington went on using until his death half a century later. Many pieces now accepted as Ellington classics, 'Rockin' In Rhythm' and 'The Mooche', for example, were originally written to go behind exotic dance acts. Earl 'Snakehips' Tucker wriggled through one of his most startling routines to Ellington's 'East Street Louis Toodle-Oo'.

Social dancing, too, provided an impetus for a good deal of jazz playing. The repertoire of Buddy Bolden took in mazurkas and quadrilles – one got turned into 'Tiger Rag' – as well as stomps and blues. At Harlem's Savoy Ballroom, 'The home of happy feet', Chick Webb's Orchestra provided the music that was paralleled by the virtuosity developed on the dance floor itself. Webb's musicians never produced in a recording studio the swing and excitement that playing for the jitterbug dancers conjured out of them. Benny Goodman's band experienced something similar at the height of the swing craze. They played a short season at New York's Paramount Cinema, appearing between films. Queues formed first thing in the morning and the audiences stayed all day to jitterbug in the aisles.

In the early days, the people who just wanted to sit and listen to jazz were rare. But in the 1930s, the serious jazz fan emerged not only in America but – and with even more fervour – in Europe. Britain was dotted with rhythm clubs. France had its Hot Clubs. All of them presented record recitals and often jam sessions, too.

Travelling players

The jam session was originally an informal gathering of musicians, relaxing after a regular job by simply playing how they wanted to. But they took on the character of a medieval joust, and became a testing time for champions. Especially in Kansas City.

Jo Jones, Count Basie's drummer, recalls 'Some places never closed. You could be sleeping at 6 a.m. when a travelling band arrived in town. They would wake you up to make a session with them until 8 a.m.' If the Fletcher Henderson band was passing through, Coleman Hawkins or Chu Berry would be busy defending their reputations while local tenor-saxophonists Ben Webster, Dick Wilson and Lester Young tried to cut them down to size.

These touring bands were originally playing one-night stands, travelling often 400, 600 or even 800 miles from one job to the next. The most luxurious way to travel was by rail. In her wealthiest days, Bessie Smith had a special coach for her entourage which could be hooked on to the rear of a convenient train. Benny Goodman travelled the same way later on.

However, most musicians went in band coaches. In 1937, Billie Holiday toured with Count Basie's orchestra for 14 dollars a day. She hated it. Years later she would quote Lester Young's classic summing up of the band coach travel: 'At night we would pull into the town, pay two or four bucks for a room, shave, and take a long look at the bed, go play a gig, come back and look at the bed again, and then get in the bus.'

If a band earned too little to keep its bus in order the results could be tragic. King Oliver, in the 1930s, after pyorrhea had wrought havoc with his trumpet playing, had a rather different kind of bad luck. In a small Texas town in 1931, Oliver experienced another recurring hazard. He said: 'Everyone rushed to see the boys get off the bus. They were struck dumb because we were coloured. We unpacked and started to play, but no one came in. They did not dance to coloured music.'

There was normally no colour bar among the musicians themselves. The earliest mixed recordings had taken place before the end of the 1920s. Yet Benny Goodman still experienced problems with bookings in Southern states in 1935 when he recruited the black musicians Lionel Hampton on vibraharp and pianist Teddy Wilson, to play in his quartet.

The festivals

In 1938 there was a mixed jam session in Carnegie Hall as part of what amounted to the first jazz performance in an American concert hall. Musicians from the Goodman, Basie and Ellington orchestras performed. That same summer, the first jazz festival was held on Randall's Island, near the meeting point of the Harlem and East Rivers. This Carnival of Swing was organized to raise funds for the local branch of the American Federation of Musicians. It was a huge success, and 24,000 people turned up to hear 24 bands. The hit of the afternoon was Ellington's orchestra performing 'Diminuendo and Crescendo in Blue'. Eighteen years later, Ellington scored a second triumph with it at the Newport Jazz Festival.

The 1938 festival lasted for six hours. Jazz had to wait until 1948 for a full-scale event spread over several days. The first International Jazz Festival was held at Nice on the French Mediterranean coast, with Armstrong performing for a new and awe-struck generation of European jazz fans.

Not until six years later was the first proper American jazz festival held at Newport,

Left Sidney Bechet, the New Orleans clarinettist, achieved immense fame in Europe and the US. **Below** Dave Brubeck's 'classical' jazz was very popular in the 1950s. **Opposite** Jelly Roll Morton blended Latin-American music with ragtime and jazz.

Rhode Island. It later became an annual event, shifting to New York in 1972.

Large festivals, usually held outdoors, have become an even bigger part of the European jazz scene than they have in the United States. Berlin, Paris, Montreux, London, even cities behind the Iron Curtain such as Prague and Warsaw have staged elaborate presentations, featuring American as well as local musicians. The Arts Council of Great Britain is just one of a number of subsidizing bodies in these countries, which have enabled works to be commissioned from jazz composers especially for these events. Stan Tracey's 'Bracknell Suite' and 'Salisbury Suite' are successful examples.

Jazz as art

European critics were the first to apply the word art to jazz. Constant Lambert, for example, spoke of it when writing about Duke Ellington, and as long ago as 1921, Ernst Ansermet used the word in hailing the then unknown Sidney Bechet as a genius. But in the 1920s and 1930s, the jazz performers regarded themselves as entertainers. Although acutely aware of what they could get away with, they never questioned the rights of the paying customer.

The first real change in the psychology of the jazz musician came in the 1940s, when the beboppers persisted in playing a style of jazz that, at first, many people disliked. The fans complained: 'You can't dance to it'. The players ignored the public reaction and stuck to their aesthetic convictions — and by doing so, they had begun to think for the first time of themselves as artists and what they played as art. The difference lay not in the music — Armstrong, Ellington, Hawkins and Tatum had all created performances of equal value — but in their attitude to it.

The withdrawal from function, the retreat from the dance floor, meant a change in audience. Jazz ventured more and more into the concert hall in the 1950s, not as a novelty like Goodman's 1938 concert, but as a normal way of working. A kind of jazz came to be played that often could be heard at its best only in concert hall surroundings. It would be hard, for example, to imagine the performance which the Gil Evans orchestra gave in London in spring 1978, using electronics as well as traditional horns, taking place in a more suitable setting than the Royal Festival Hall. At the same period, Dave Brubeck, one of the big names of the 1950s, discovered a new audience for jazz on the campuses of American colleges.

The urge to become respectable and to record, for example, with strings, has often been strong among jazz musicians, especially those who emerged when the music was dominated by show business. It is an ambition that can be seen in some of the attempts — but not all — at Third Stream composition, especially among those more concerned with dignifying rather than experimenting.

Duke Ellington even fared disastrously when he tried to work with a symphony orchestra. He came off much better when he took his own band and a team of singers into American and British cathedrals for a succession of sacred concerts.

The concert hall was used in a very different way by entrepreneur Norman Granz, when he mixed musicians of both the swing and bebop era in a series of what were virtually public jam sessions. These began with a concert at the Los Angeles Philharmonic Hall in 1944. Later, Dizzy Gillespie, Roy Eldridge, Lester Young and Charlie Parker were just some of the musicians who took part in these informal concerts, which Granz titled *Jazz At The Philharmonic*. Critics denounced the performances as circuses pandering to audiences that wanted honking saxophones and flashy drum solos. Others recognized that, in addition to providing some instant and harmless excitement, Granz was reviving the cut-and-thrust of that old Kansas City jousting as well as presenting some solid and sober playing.

Concert halls, cathedrals and campuses have taken jazz a long way from its New Orleans origins. Yet in Harlem in 1965, an event took place that echoed those far-off days. The Jazzmobile, invented to advertise a festival of the arts, caught on as a good idea.

Since then New York and its environs have frequently seen a large bandstand, mounted on a truck, being towed through the streets en route for a one-hour concert. Performers as diverse as Dizzy Gillespie, Herbie Mann and the entire Count Basie orchestra have cheerfully re-enacted a scene of 60 or 70 years back — even if no one was prepared to dangle his legs over the back and play the role of the tailgate trombonist.

POP

The origins of pop

What is now termed 'pop' music is of more recent origin than jazz, but its roots reach back into the past. In Roman times, for instance, there were what today could be termed 'hit' tunes. These were usually songs which had been performed in the theatre and struck a chord with the Roman public. It was not unknown for the crowd in the Coliseum to interrupt the gory proceedings with a spontaneous chorus of some current hit.

Such songs can be classified as pop music, which has tended to be urban and lies somewhere between folk music with its essential country background and classical, or salon, singing.

There were singers at the medieval trade fairs and market places of Europe, but even if their songs became popular within the limits of medieval communications, they were almost certainly songs that sprang from folk music. Pop music in its modern manifestation is part of the world of growing towns, of people crowding together, of the Industrial Revolution, and of speeding communications. It was influenced, like so much of modern entertainment, by the *commedia dell'arte* of the Italian Renaissance, but its growth has been entirely conditioned by its vigorous environment.

The Industrial Revolution spawned congested communities and a swift growth in population. In the eighteenth and nineteenth centuries there was an increasing demand for noisy, sociable entertainment in the towns that was answered by the music hall, a place of drink, jokes — and song. Boisterous satire poking fun at bosses, wives and bailiffs was loved by the audiences, and performers found that if they kept the music down to a simple octave everyone would join in the chorus. Charles Dibdin (1745–1814), one of the great music hall innovators, wrote no less than 1,000 pop songs. As the railways spread in the nineteenth century, London day-trippers, passing for an evening through the great, 2,000-seater music hall palaces of the city, went back to the towns taking the popular songs of the day with them. This was a music culture that was rude and cheerful. It retained narrative elements from folk music tradition and, musically, assimilated the more sophisticated tonal phrasing and lyricism of salon singing.

Music in the air

New sounds heralded the dawn of the twentieth century. In New Orleans, street musicians were creating, with a curious blend of

Below Bill Haley started the rock 'n roll era with his recording of 'Rock around the Clock' in 1954.

Right The Beatles, who split up in 1970, were the world's most successful pop group. They excelled both at performance and on record.

African beat and Victorian gospel harmonies, the music that was to become jazz and affect the whole course of pop. On Broadway, impresarios had invented the musical, and were turning to a succession of talented composers to create the scores. They added a technical breadth to popular music that lifted the songs away from the simple, stylized tunes of the music halls to the level of a sort of pop opera.

Jerome Kern, George and Ira Gershwin, Irving Berlin, Richard Rogers and Oscar Hammerstein and Lorenz Hart were to create musical shows that became legendary and hit songs that were to become the first classics of pop – 'Make Believe', 'There's No Business Like Show Business', 'Can't Help Lovin' That Man', 'They Say Falling In Love Is Wonderful'.

The new century brought not only new sounds which altered the course of popular music, but also three developments that transformed it into a major performing art and created the age of pop. The three revolutionary steps were: cinema, the gramophone, and radio.

All three were to spread pop music to a world-wide audience. The film-makers of Hollywood immortalized on celluloid the great musical shows of the 1920s and 1930s, and produced the world's first pop superstars, Al Jolson (1886–1950), whose 'Swanee' became a pop classic, and Bing Crosby, whose laconic style crossed generations. Crosby (1903–1977) reached a wider audience through the record industry, which boomed in the 1930s. His unforgettable rendering of 'White Christmas' by Irving Berlin, passed sales of 100 million in the 1940s, and has outsold any other record by millions. Crosby's main rival as the world's major pop singer of the 1940s was Frank Sinatra (born 1915), whose 'Chicago' and 'The Lady Is A Tramp', remain popular music classics. Sinatra's brilliant, almost poetic intonation enabled him to hold his place as a world pop superstar right into the 1970s, despite the enormous changes of the post-war period, which took pop on a new and exciting course away from the romantic ballads of the musical shows.

One other important development took place in the 1930s. The ragtime music of New Orleans had become pure jazz by the 1920s, and spread its way northwards across the States and eventually to Europe, helped by the growing gramophone business.

Pop, like jazz, had leaned heavily on rhythm and blues, but it was written music, clear and identifiable, not a spontaneous improvisation like some jazz. It was inevitable that, as both these branches of popular

Right Chuck Berry, one of the most influential figures of rock 'n roll, has delighted audiences since the 1950s. His music is influenced by blues, and country and western. Many of his songs have been recorded by others, including the Beatles.

Left Elvis Presley was justifiably called the 'King' of rock. His performances and records remained popular throughout his life, while his record sales benefitted from the wild adulation and grief after his death in 1977.
Above The Rolling Stones in concert always provide an exciting visual spectacle which enhances the impact of their music.

Pop music terms
It is impossible to categorize the many types of popular music. As one style becomes established, musicians adapt it so that a new sound gradually emerges. So, these definitions necessarily only give a general outline of some of the main terms in popular music. *Blues* originated among American negroes. The tempo of the music is usually slow and rhythmic. *Rock 'n' Roll* was a new style of music with a heavily accentuated rhythm, which emerged in the late 1950s. It was related to the blues form. The first exponent of rock 'n' roll was Bill Haley.

Country and Western has always been connected with the cowboy image of Southern USA. Jim Reeves and Tammy Wynette are famous exponents of Country and Western. *Folk music* is based on traditional music. There was a major folk revival in the early 1970s. *Punk* marked a revolution in pop music in the late 1970s. Punk musicians like the Sex Pistols tried to shock with their performances and songs. *Reggae* originated in Jamaica. It can be identified by its steady beat and heavily amplified bass tempo. Bob Marley and The Wailers are the most famous reggae group.

music developed, the distinctions between them would become blurred. The first steps were taken by the big bands of the 1930s. Clarinettist Benny Goodman was essentially a jazz man, but as his big band played to wider audiences in concert halls and the dance halls of Chicago and New York, he began to popularize jazz and to play jazzed-up pop tunes. The move was crystallized by trombonist Glen Miller (1904–1944) and his band in their immortal 'In The Mood'. Miller's blend of jazz and pop had enormous breadth of appeal. His 'Chattanooga Choo Choo' clocked up sales of a million, and in February 1942, Miller became the first person to receive a golden disc — a record specially sprayed with gold by RCA Victor for presentation to acknowledge his million sales. Miller died in a wartime air crash, but his style lives on, and he has had numerous imitators.

Boom time
The affluent 1950s brought a new phenomenon — millions of teenagers with money to burn. The record makers were all ready to help them spend it. They offered them a new sound that was to take pop even closer to jazz, rock and roll.

The first hero of this new wave was a most unlikely idol for teenage swingers. He was chubby, 30 years old, and he had a kiss curl and a squint. His name was Bill Haley. Haley's 'Rock Around the Clock' swept the

Western world and became the first anthem of the Rock Age. Haley (born 1927) had started playing hill-billy music with only moderate success. As soon as he turned to the stronger rhythm and blues beat of rock, he hit the very chord the youngsters wanted. Rock created an age and became a way of life, a way of dressing and talking.

Haley pointed the way. Buddy Holly, killed in a plane crash in 1959, Chuck Berry and Fats Domino — who both still draw huge audiences — followed. It was an age of exuberance, and it gave birth to an all-time great, whose musical appeal was to leap the national barriers of language and style.

In 1956 in Mississipi, a youngster walked into a local recording studio and made a recording of 'My Happiness' as a birthday present for his mother. His name was Elvis Presley. He was 21, and he was to die 21 years later, the biggest name of all in pop music, and the unrivalled King of Rock.

Presley (1935–1977) drew heavily on black music for his style. There was the deep rhythm and blues of the old South which Haley had so brilliantly turned to pop. Presley added another vital ingredient to his style — his individual performance was as important as the music. Presley became the first great sex symbol of pop with the wild gyrations that earned him the tag 'Elvis the Pelvis'.

An astute former fairground showman,

Colonel Tom Parker, skilfully guided Presley to the top and kept him there until the teenagers of the 1970s were idolizing him as their parents had 20 years before. America dominated the pop world of the 1950s. The motivation came from Presley. It was exploited during the 1960s by Berry Gordy Junior who came from the motor town of Detroit. He founded Motown, the first really successful black record company to produce an original sound, and such artists as Stevie Wonder, The Supremes, Temptations, Marvin Gaye and Smokey Robinson and his Miracles.

Britain had few rockers of her own. Marty Wilde and Billy Fury had their followers, but they could claim nothing like the popularity of the great American stars. All that changed in the 1960s. A brilliant pop manager, Brian Epstein, picked up four young men from the Cavern Club in Liverpool and launched the Mersey Sound on the world.

The Beatles and after

The Beatles — Paul McCartney (born 1942), bass guitar; John Lennon (born 1940), rhythm guitar; George Harrison (born 1943), lead guitar; and Ringo Starr (born 1940), drums — drew most of their inspiration from the rhythm and blues origins that had created the Detroit sound of Berry Gordy's Motown team. They also owe a musical debt to Little Richard and Chuck Berry.

The Beatles first — albeit small — success was 'Love Me Do' in 1962. The hits poured out. 'Please Please Me', 'From Me To You' and 'She Loves You' made them international idols by the end of 1963. In March 1964, their newest song, 'Can't Buy Me Love' soared into the charts. The Beatles smashed the British record with 1,000,000 advance sales for their next record 'I Want To Hold Your Hand'.

The 1960s pop boom began, as record companies flocked to buy up groups. The biggest rivals to the Beatles were British, too, but so, so different from the smiling, boysnext-door image of the Liverpool four. Mick Jagger (born 1943) led his Rolling Stones on to the pop stage, pulling faces, shouting outrageous things. They looked the bad boys of pop — but they were good musicians. They built up a following of fans with almost a religious fervour and packed concerts and huge, open-air, one-night stands all over the world. The first few bars of Jagger singing 'Satisfaction' became enough to set the fans screaming.

As the 1960s wore on, the great beat boom softened. There were voices of disenchantment from The Who with 'Can't Explain', and, in a different vein, from Bob Dylan, whose style opened a path back to the folk music scene. Born in Minnesota in 1941, Dylan emerged from New York's Greenwich Village with his protest songs like 'Blowin' In The Wind' and 'A Hard Rain's Gonna Fall'. He was joined by Joan Baez, and Peter, Paul and Mary in echoing the growing awareness

Above American singer and guitarist, Bruce Springsteen attracted a select following in the mid 1970s.
Far right Led Zeppelin were one of the major rock bands of the 1970s. They place great emphasis on live performance and, indeed, rarely appear on television.

Right The world's main pop and rock music centres are shown on this map: Liverpool (1), Hamburg (2), London (3), Isle of Wight (4), New Orleans (5), New York (6), Woodstock (7), Detroit (8), Chicago (9), Los Angeles (10), Monterey (11), San Francisco (12) and Altamont (13).

of a literate generation of youngsters. It was the first time such serious subjects had crept into pop.

A new technology was sweeping pop along new avenues. Bands became more proficient with their instruments, electronics and studio techniques became more and more sophisticated. By 1967 and 1968 the politics had softened into a Peace and Love message from the flower power people of San Francisco. The Byrds, Jefferson Airplane and Grateful Dead preached happiness.

The huge, open air festivals of music

sprang from this movement. There had been jazz festivals for years, but pop, perhaps typically, did it all on an enormous scale. At Woodstock for three days in August, 1969, 450,000 people sat around peacefully to listen to pop music. Six months later at Altamont, 400,000 turned up to hear The Rolling Stones top the bill in what was not such a peaceful celebration. Four years later at the Tampa Stadium, Florida, another British group, Led Zeppelin passed all records for the highest takings for a single group when 560,000 people paid to hear them. It was the largest pop audience ever.

Even more than the 1960s, the 1970s was a decade of constantly changing and shifting fashions and enthusiasms, of brief ascendancies and equally swift eclipses of fame. Technology gave pop and rock ever more sophisticated lights, lasers and aural impact. Many individual artists and groups made important contributions to pop as a performing art. David Bowie (born 1947), for example, was highly influenced in his early days by theatrical techniques, particularly mime. His career began in the late 1960s and by the mid 1970s he was a major force in rock music with a varied series of albums and visually exciting live performances. Bowie's style changed and by the end of the decade he was regarded rather as a spent force.

The 1970s have also seen a splintering of pop and rock music into different genres. Reggae, for example, is based on West Indian music; while folk and its offshoots have remained popular. Punk rock blossomed briefly during the late 1970s and there were numerous 'New Wave' bands in Britain and, to a lesser extent, in the USA. Groups such as the Sex Pistols, Clash and the American group the Ramones came to the fore in a similar — but less lasting — upsurge of youthful enthusiasm to the pop group boom of a decade earlier.

As the 1970s closed, pop was firmly settled in the world of discos and flashing lights, using all the electronic brilliance of the space age to excite its adherents and shock their parents.

Records and the road

The future of pop as the 1980s begin lies in records and touring performances. In 1978, in Britain alone, the total for record sales was a staggering £304,113,000. World-wide it was £5,000,000,000.

Touring encompasses the extremes of the pop and rock world. On the one hand, successful groups such as Genesis travel in some style. On the other, thousands of struggling and unknown musicians, paying their own travelling expenses and carting scant equipment from hall to hall and begging a chance at the recording studios, fight to get into this cut-throat business. For every one who will make it, probably 100 others will end up back home with some out-of-date equipment and a pile of bills. Big business

claims most of the rewards, and a performer needed not only to be original, but also able to write his or her own songs to be sure of ending up with a fortune from royalties. Former Beatle Paul McCartney is estimated to receive as much as £10,000 a day from publishing companies.

Concerts pull in great crowds and what seems like vast receipts, but they are enormously expensive to stage, and without record sales to follow, they can exhaust a group — and leave them penniless as well.

Musicians today have to produce as good a live sound as possible, and with the technical excellence of records and sound production improving all the time, a concert group hoping for the vital disc sales, has to carry about with it a vast amount of equipment, even computers.

Most top bands have toured, sleeping in their props van, the only economical way to make it. They can even tell you the finest details about the best and cheapest freeway restaurants. Promoters know that there are endless struggling groups desperate for a chance, so the fees are small — often expenses only. With a flood of hopefuls always ready to stand in there is no incentive for the small-time promoter to raise his rates.

Pop group on tour The complexities of touring with a pop group are illustrated in the picture **(below)**. This shows the members of Genesis who toured Europe in 1978 **(right)**. Genesis are a British group, who use a large amount of props and lighting effects in their performances. No fewer than 71 people took the road for the tour. The road crew of 52 was made up of 3 light riggers, 5 band, 10 sound crew, 15 electricians, 2 computer operators, 2 production engineers, 1 laser beam operator, 2 bus drivers, 12 truck drivers. The rest of the entourage consisted of the families of the band, managers and an accountant. The equipment travelled in 11 articulated lorries and the road crew in 2 buses. They had to build a 40ft square stage with a lighting

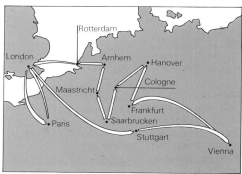

gantry and 500 lamps. The rest of the party travelled in 8 cars. The cost of keeping the show on the road was approximately £90,000 ($200,000) per week, so even playing to crowds of 100,000 did not leave much room for profit. Touring also involves much moving of heavy equipment **(below left)**. Here Wings prepare to set off on tour. Logistics become very important on such a tour. For example,

each of the 11 Genesis articulated trucks had to be checked at every international border. In the interests of maintaining international harmony and of not antagonizing customs officials, it was advisable for all the trucks not to arrive at the border together.

Above left Paul McCartney formed Wings in 1971. After some changes in personnel, Wings developed into one of the major touring and performing bands of the 1970s. During 1975 and 1976 they made a successful world tour.

HAPPENINGS AND EVENTS

FROM ONE-MAN SHOWS TO BUSKING AND FEATS OF DARING

HAPPENINGS AND EVENTS

No art is purer than live art — a performance that springs, unaided by intellect, from the soul or from the unconscious. This belief, or perhaps it should be called a feeling, grew strongly among artists in all fields in the early part of the twentieth century. It gave rise to an amazing succession of happenings, the aim of which was to break down the barriers between the various arts and to add a new dimension to the visual arts.

It started from a simultaneous revolution against the classical artistic tradition — against ballet in the form of modern art dance inspired by Isadora Duncan (1878–1927), against painting in the abstract and surrealistic world of Pablo Picasso and Salvador Dali; against the theatre in the free or unwritten productions or happenings prompted by Oskar Schlemmer (1888–1943) at the Bauhaus School in Germany in the 1920s.

In its pure state, performance art is, perhaps, the truest performing art — a simple, straightforward performance of what the artist feels like performing at the time.

As a revolutionary demonstration, a deliberate artistic protest, it has faded somewhat since Andy Warhol (born 1930) built his long, wind-blown plastic fence, the great Exploding Plastic Inevitable, in the late 1960s. But the underlying principle, the simple belief that the performance is as important as the words, the sounds or the design of a work of art, has been a prime motivation of many artists in the twentieth century.

It exists most independently in jazz, in which the improvisation, the musical feeling of the player, is the real work of art. It exists in modern dance, in which performers such as Merce Cunningham (born 1922) have chased chance and indeterminacy to the sound of experimental music. It exists in art such as that of the American Jackson Pollock (1912–1956) who allowed his paint to drip at random on the canvas. It existed in the pop of Elvis Presley (1935–1977), whose performance was more important than the song.

The beginnings

Happenings started in Zürich, Switzerland in 1917, with a group of disillusioned Germans. Hugo Ball (1886–1927) and Emmy Hemmings (1885–1948), unhappy with life in wartime Germany, left Munich for Zürich, and set up there the *Cabaret Voltaire*. Their aim was to develop their own brand of satire, but these artists found themselves in a city teeming with an assortment of artists and exiles. The prevailing aims were to shock and be anti-establishment. They used whatever came to hand to shock and to attack — poems, dance, plays, paintings, music of every kind, even puppets.

The artists even fell out among themselves, and their performances became shambolic, almost public theatrical disagreements — the first 'happenings.' Tristan

Spontaneous performances have long delighted audiences. These pictures, taken outside the Pompidou Centre in Paris, show a variety of street performances. The fire eater **(top)** clearly owes much to the circus for his act, as do the acrobats **(middle)**; while the person lying on the bed of glass **(bottom)** perhaps bases his act on similar Eastern performances.

Tzara (1896–1963) gave the movement, Dada, its name from his native Rumanian 'da, da', meaning 'Yes, yes,' and symbolizing a sort of childish open-mindedness.

The idea of spontaneous action as a work of art spread across Europe. Happenings reached such extreme moments as the lone walk along Berlin's Kurfürstendamm in 1919 by the poet and caricaturist George Grosz (1893–1959) attired as Death, or the massive, and most spectacular happening of all time, when 10,500 people re-enacted the storming of the Winter Palace in Leningrad on its third anniversary in 1920.

The people surged, in an amazing art performance, around the city's streets and squares under the direction of Nikolai Yevreinov. This astonishing demonstration of participation theatre was still being recreated on a small scale in the 1950s, by a New York company, Living Theatre. This was founded by Julian Beck and Judith Malina. Both actors and audience took part in their staged productions of the Winter Palace storming.

The link between art and technology, which is often at the heart of performance art in the 1970s, was most strongly forged half a century earlier at the Bauhaus School in Germany, founded by the German educator and architect Walter Gropius (1883–1969). It was conceived as an artistic community with a wide variety of disciplines, including painting, architecture, sculpture and an assortment of crafts. Theatre was always part of its manifesto, and there were ideological disputes involving both Lothar Schreyer and Oskar Schlemmer, who were basically artists rather than theatre people.

Schlemmer believed that space was the unifying factor in both painting and theatre and his productions, if they could be called that, concentrated on this aspect. His happenings experimented with puppets, masks and mechanically operated figures. But the events became so complex that they needed such close direction, that eventually their essential spontaneity was lost.

The Nazis eventually closed down the Bauhaus, and the teachers Josef Albers and Xanti Svhawinsky moved to the Black Mountain College in North Carolina to lay the foundations of American performance art. It was there that Merce Cunningham (born 1922) and musician John Cage (born 1912) collaborated with music and movement in the 1930s.

Cage's music was often played on what he called a 'prepared piano'. It was an ordinary instrument that had the strings jammed with miscellaneous material like rubber bands, paper, and pieces of metal. It gave out an **avant-garde** sound. In 1952, Cage 'wrote' his famous silent piece of music 4' 33", in which no sounds were produced, the interpreter merely moving his arms to indicate the start of each of three movements. This, according to Cage, enabled those present to hear the

Carnival is a form of street entertainment which has extremely old roots. The word 'carnival' is taken from the Latin meaning 'farewell to meat' — carnival celebrations are traditionally a associated with the period before Lent. Some of the most famous carnivals are held annually in New Orleans and Rio de Janeiro. In Germany the carnival season runs from January to Lent. It is called *Fasching* and is celebrated with fancy dress parties, and large parades of floats through the streets of Cologne and other cities. In recent times carnival has come to refer to any type of general communal celebration. These pictures were taken at the carnival in Notting Hill, London, which is held every Autumn.

music which is in their own heads all the time.

That same year, another happening took place at Black Mountain. Cage, Cunningham, Robert Rauschenberg and David Tudor – who had 'conducted' the first 4' 33" – staged a completely unstructured event in which the spectators were seated in four triangular areas, while the various performers filled moments of time as indicated by Cage.

The move was swiftly followed up by the New School for Social Research in New York, where Allan Kaprow, Claes Oldenburg and Jim Dine were all pioneers of live art. They took over the Rueben Gallery in 1959 and 'performed' paintings, readings, music and projected slides in three different rooms at the same time.

In some of these events there had to be a certain amount of background planning, but essentially, the performances reflected the personal views of the artists concerned. They were each spontaneous outbursts of creativity, even though there was constant contact between the people involved and certain similarities in their techniques. There were many experiments with films and slides and the flashing lights that have now become standard disco backings.

Cage brilliantly experimented in this field with photo cells. Dancers, leaping at random across a stage, broke the beams, causing lights to flash on and off in spectacular happenings.

The 1970s have seen more concentration on individual performance and an upsurge of dance activity, prompted mainly by Cunningham, Ann Halprin and Yvonne Rainer. These dancers place considerable emphasis on dance as a way of life, improvisation and the use of body language – which has an historical precedent in Isadora Duncan. Dance performances capture spontaneity and the flavour of a happening, but they are restricted by space.

Happenings are more prone, by their nature, to fall between the two stools of true spontaneity – which must be their essence – and the prepared scenario. Dada believed that art could rise out of chaos, the complete overturning of accepted forms. The Bauhaus, on the other hand, eventually moved around to working within a carefully laid out set of geometrical rules. Both were essentially concerned with performance, as are what we think of today as happenings.

The common feature of happenings lies in their ability to stimulate and to shock people into seeing outside the accepted terms of an art form. Extraordinary things happen in ordinary places, often very ordinary indeed. In London, Ken Ellis has created plays on the Underground trains. Jeff Nuttall, another British writer, has caused consternation in Yorkshire pubs by setting up situations in front of unsuspecting customers. And an English touring group, Welfare State, adver-

tised themselves as 'celebratory engineers'. They build upon existing outdoor environments to create big productions based on myths and legends that often last for days. In 1974 at Wath-upon-Dearne, Yorkshire, they put up a 50ft long Giant Ice Man, who was calculated to melt away to nothing during their performances throughout the whole of the Christmas holiday period.

The great happenings of the 1960s have not been sustained in the decade that followed, and Andy Warhol's forays into film-making seem to have been designed for posterity rather than as a one-off protest. But Dada still has influence, particularly in the world of pop, where the performance may become as important as the music. It is a prime motivation of Dadaism – a conscious destruction of conceived boundaries. Much of the thinking behind the happenings of the twentieth century have been, however genuinely spon-

taneous, an unconscious revolt against or expression of fear about science.

The visual and acoustic shock in happenings has been a recurring statement that art is something that should be seen only once, that belongs as much to time as to space and invention, and that, outside its momentary creation, it cannot be properly understood.

The protest of the happening may be fleeting, but it brings its lasting impact to art. The happenings of the 1960s were so essentially of the avant garde, that they remained apparently elitist. However, they have not been without value or influence, although they have become diffused.

Above Yoko Ono sits in her work of art 'Half a Bedroom' which was exhibited in New York during the 1960s in a show entitled 'Half a Memory'. Other exhibits included 'Half a Dream' and 'Half a Sky'. In the 1960s happenings were very varied. Some, like this piece by Ono, simply tried to undermine the onlooker's ideas and assumptions about art. Others involved much more active participation from both the 'artist' and the audience.

Right The Danish artist Jens Jorgen Thorsen puts himself on exhibition in a Copenhagen gallery in 1966. The artists showing at the gallery wanted to exhibit the results of 50,000 years of progress — in short, themselves! Interests in happenings and other similar performances has rather waned since the heady days of the 1960s.

FEATS OF DARING

Roll up, roll up . . . The world loves a hero, and crowds have been flocking for centuries to watch daredevils defy death, disaster or serious injury to perform 'the impossible'. Millions have gazed in awe at the fire-eaters, the sword-swallowers, glass-chewers and high-wire walkers. Breathless crowds still gasp at the gravity-defying acrobats of the circus and the man with his head in the lion's mouth.

It all goes back a long way. St. Simeon Stylites (AD 390–459) spent at least 30 years – some sources say 45 years – on top of a 75ft high stone pillar near Antioch in what is now Turkey. The astonishing La Quebrada divers who leap 120ft off the jagged cliffs near Acapulco, Mexico, into 12ft of rocky water are risking their lives in a feat that has remained unchallenged for generations. It is only in the last century that feats of daring and endurance have been commercially turned into a money-making branch of the performing arts. Today, thousands will turn up to watch high-speed motor cycle leaps

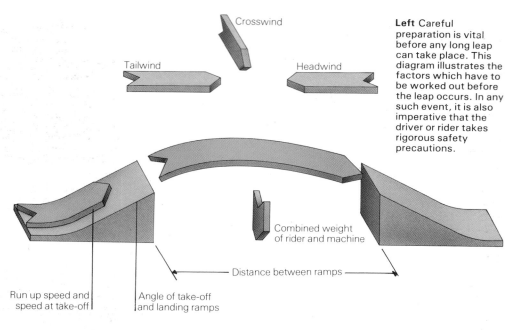

Crosswind

Tailwind

Headwind

Combined weight of rider and machine

Run up speed and speed at take-off

Angle of take-off and landing ramps

Distance between ramps

Left Careful preparation is vital before any long leap can take place. This diagram illustrates the factors which have to be worked out before the leap occurs. In any such event, it is also imperative that the driver or rider takes rigorous safety precautions.

Left High-wire walking is a popular form of daring. This contemporary illustration shows Blondin's varied exploits on the high wire – carrying a heavy load, standing on a chair, having a nap, carrying another person, walking blindfold, sitting, standing on his head, and riding a bicycle. Blondin was the first great exponent of such feats; he walked across Niagara Falls in 1860. He then made a career of performing daring feats in different places. His last appearance was in Belfast in 1896.

that do not always defy death.

The spread of feats of endurance owes much to the world of films and television. Both demand realistic stunts for dramatic scenes. The stunt man is usually standing in for a big name star in a dangerous scene. This anonymity created a need in the daredevils for self-expression that is satisfied by staging dangerous feats.

Many feats of daring can be performed only once – then they become routine or are turned into a commercial act like wall of death riding at amusement parks. It is the first man or woman to perform the feat who goes into the record books and the hall of fame. Successors are mere emulators. After the first time, the crowd knows it can be done, and so much of the element of daring has gone.

The circus is a confined world of daring, of endurance and injury-defying acts and it is from the circus that many of the people who have performed the great, outdoor spectaculars have come. One of the first was the amazing tightrope walker, Charles Blondin (1824–1897). Blondin, whose real name was Jean-Georges Gravelet, was a professional who found his horizons limited by merely crossing from one side of the arena to the other.

Blondin went outside to perform a staggering feat that drew world-wide publicity in 1855. He walked for 1,100ft on a 3in rope 160ft above the surging water of Niagara Falls. The feat won him international acclaim and crowds flocked to see him whenever he performed. Once was not enough for this remarkable man. He went back and walked across Niagara several times later. Perhaps the most astonishing walk of this born showman was his second defiance of the great Falls in 1860. Blondin made the crossing while carrying pick-a-back — his agent, Harry Colcord.

Since then other performers have surpassed Blondin both for bravery and endurance. Another Frenchman, Henri Rochetain (born 1926), has made the longest walk on a tightrope. In July 1969 he covered 3,790 yards on a wire stretched across a gorge at Clermont Ferrand, France, taking 3 hours and 20 minutes. Rochetain was back on a wire four years later and astonishing the world. He spent 16 days on a rope stretched 82ft above a supermarket in St. Etienne. He took regular exercise, covered about 300 miles and even managed to sleep on the rope.

Others have defied greater heights. American Steve McPeak walked a wire suspended 1,800ft above the Yosemite Valley Falls in California, and also holds another strange record — for an ascent on a wire. He made a one-in-four climb over 2,400ft on Sugar Loaf Mountain in Rio de Janeiro. It took him just over an hour.

Another Frenchman, Charles Elleano, was the first to cross the Thames in London on a wire in 1951. But London has seen nothing to

Right Houdini was renowned for escaping from chains and impossible situations. This young follower in Paris has an appreciative audience as he is tied up and left to escape from his bonds.

Left American unicyclist Steve McPeak travelled over 2,000 miles on a unicycle on a circus promotion trip. He is seen here in Chicago. Long distance and endurance events are one type of daring feat which, because of their record-breaking potential, never cease to appeal to the public.

compare with Blondin's feat in 1861, when he crossed a rope stretched across the central transept of the Crystal Palace while wearing stilts. He even performed several somersaults on the way. Blondin bowed out — in more modest style it must be admitted — with a high wire performance in Belfast in 1896 at the age of 74.

Another daring activity that has become a permanent part of the performing arts is escapology, and no-one has made a bigger name for himself at this than Harry Houdini (1874–1926). Houdini, born Erich Weiss, son of a Budapest rabbi, was a brilliant magician and illusionist and took his stage name from that of the great French magician, Houdin. Houdini began as a trapeze artist. By the time he was in his early twenties he was appearing as a magician, assisted by his wife, on the stage and in circuses in America. His amazing feats of escapology grew from his work as an illusionist and as the publicity swelled, the tricks he performed became more and more elaborate. Houdini extricated himself from ropes, chains, handcuffs and strait-jackets while hanging upside down. His great innovation was to pioneer underwater escapes. Houdini, with brilliant facility, slipped from seeming certain death after being shackled with irons, locked and tied inside a weighted box and dropped into water. The British escapologist Alan Alan has escaped from a strait-jacket while hanging upside down from a blazing rope. In America, Bill Shirk got out of a strait-jacket in a mere 5 seconds, then took only 22 seconds to escape from one while hanging from a helicopter over Indianapolis. He was later locked in a jail cell at Hamilton, Indiana, shackled with three pairs of handcuffs, a set

of footcuffs and 44lb of chain. He was free in four hours.

Age of the stuntmen

The new pioneers of the performing art of daring are the motorbike stuntmen, who drew huge crowds in the 1970s. Their skill stems from the world of films. It was stunningly exploited by Robert Craig, whose gift for publicity as the reckless rider Evel Knievel, won him world fame. Knievel's leap across the Snake River Canyon in Ohio was brilliant, and his success encouraged many emulators. In 1978, the Londoner Robin Winter-Smith set up a world record ramp jump when clearing 31 parked cars. Thousands of expectant fans have filled old airfields or large parks to watch these spectacular events. Motorbike jumping requires more than just physical expertise. Ramp angles, projections, speed, wind resistance and timing are critical. Mistakes are fatal. Winter-Smith died in 1979 trying to clear a line of parked Rolls-Royces at Elstree Aero Club in England.

Stuntmen are also experts at daredevil diving. The Briton, Don Lindbergh plunges head first into shallow tanks covered in burning oil. In America, Ron Nix dived into a pile of blazing cardboard boxes in 1975.

And the art of St. Simeon has been revived too. In 1966, John Stokes, a Birmingham man, spent 32 days in a barrel on top of a 45ft pole. Frank Perkins did even better. He went up a telegraph pole at San Jose, California in June, 1975, settled down in an 8ft by 8ft wooden box, and stayed there until July 1976. In this particular feat, modern man is definitely not getting better than his ancestors. St. Simeon's record looks pretty safe.

Right Evel Knievel has stunned the world with his daring feats on a motorcycle. Here he is jumping over buses.

Far right American Steve McPeak varied the convention of carrying the bride over the threshold — he carried his bride across a tightrope.

Below The original feat of daring — Blondin crosses the Niagara Falls on tightrope. After Blondin's achievement, others followed, each trying to outdo the other.

STREET PERFORMERS

It may seem a long way from the wandering minstrel of the medieval fairs to the street busker of the twentieth century, strumming his amplified guitar in a subway beneath the traffic-packed street of a modern city. For all the apparent change, they stem from an unchanging tradition and both players, divided as they are by almost 1,000 years, would recognize each other unhesitatingly. Buskers play what they want, sing what they want, often of their own composition, and the audience pays if it wishes. If people do not like what they hear they can just walk on.

It is out there in the open air where the buskers are today that live performance began. If most of them strum their way to unknown graves, unsung and probably not missed, they keep an independence that eludes their famous colleagues of the boards.

Light entertainment owes a lot to the early traditions of the open air musicians, tumblers and magicians, cajoling a living from those historic fairgoers of Norman times and before. They often performed from the back of an open cart, like the mystery and miracle players who carried their message of Christianity through the streets of such English cities as Coventry, Chester and Wakefield.

London has long been considered a stronghold of street entertainment, though it often suffers more from quantity than quality. Even this quantity has been pared down in recent years, due in no small way to harassment by the police. Fines, usually on charges of causing an obstruction, have turned many buskers' pitches into unprofitable beats. The term 'busker' in its true definition really means an out-of-work artist who entertains a queue of people waiting for seats at a West End theatre. Its meaning has become much broader, and many of the performers who masquerade as buskers outside theatres, train stations and in the subways are now often not performers at all, but mere beggars, whose minimal ability with an instrument is just enough to protect them from a charge of vagrancy.

Some of the great street acts of recent years have abandoned the flagstones to these shades of artists. The thronging crowds who stroll through London's Leicester Square in a summer season can no longer enjoy the brilliant improvisation of the Road Stars, a group of two dancers and an accordionist, led by Ronnie Ross, who built up their quick-fire song, dance and joke act on the lines of Wilson, Keppel and Betty, a classic music hall trio.

The Road Stars could gather a crowd in seconds. With luck they might do a couple of routines and make a quick collection before their look-out roared up with a warning: 'The Law!' As quickly as they had set up their act, the Road Stars melted into the crowd and took refuge in a nearby restaurant until the coast was clear. Then out they came again.

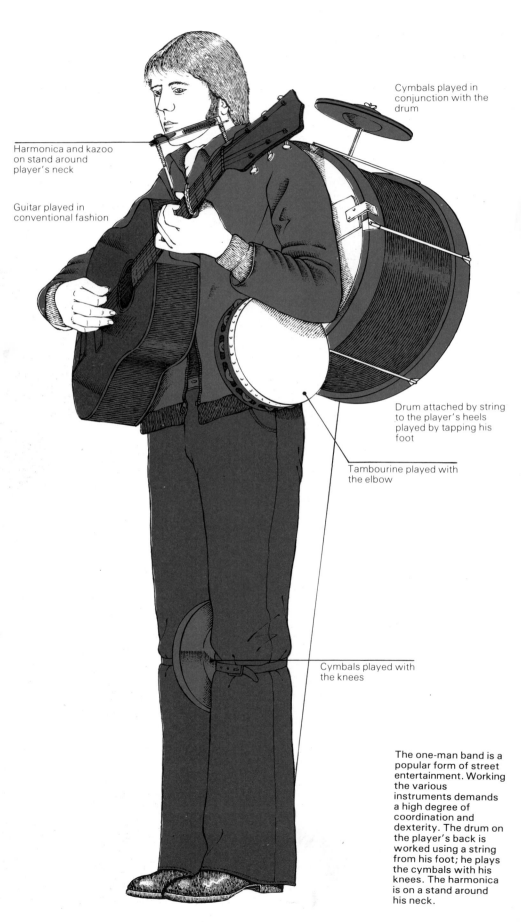

Cymbals played in conjunction with the drum

Harmonica and kazoo on stand around player's neck

Guitar played in conventional fashion

Drum attached by string to the player's heels played by tapping his foot

Tambourine played with the elbow

Cymbals played with the knees

The one-man band is a popular form of street entertainment. Working the various instruments demands a high degree of coordination and dexterity. The drum on the player's back is worked using a string from his foot; he plays the cymbals with his knees. The harmonica is on a stand around his neck.

Right The solo instrumentalist is a frequent sight in the streets of many cities. This picture of a saxophonist was taken in New Orleans. Many street musicians are highly skilled in their craft — others are simply trying to beg money.

The Road Stars say that continual police pursuit has driven them into retirement. Another professional busker, the eccentric Earl of Mustard, a notable tap-dancer and one of the best-known London street performers, reckoned he spent more time dodging police than entertaining the crowds.

A new type of street performer is found among the buskers today. These are young men and women who are studying for a serious musical career and play the streets to help pay for their keep and studies. Their favoured pitches are in the subways, which often have excellent acoustics. The music of some of these street players is of a very high standard and remarkably diverse, ranging from baroque classics on the flute or violin to folk and pop. The guitar is especially popular because it is easy to carry, the case can make an excellent collecting box .

The best pitches are greatly in demand, and there is often a queue of artists waiting in the vicinity to perform. Some subways might even be able to boast of a bill of varieties!

One or two familiar figures of the pop world and the folk singing scene have supported themselves in the past by busking — even if they are reluctant to admit it.

Few performers, in fact, regard busking as a stepping stone to discovery and the big time. The only artist in recent years to make it directly from the kerb to the recording studio is Don Partridge. He wrote and played a number one hit in the 1960s called 'Rosie. Partridge was a one-man band with guitar, harmonica, kazoo and a drum strapped on his back. He enjoyed a brief spell in the limelight which took him into radio, television, cabaret and even fringe theatre.

Then, dramatically and almost as quickly as he shot to the top, Partridge slipped back into obscurity. Whether or not he preferred the anonymity of the pavement, he never said. Perhaps he is still happily amusing the crowd along some street somewhere.

Europe and America

Many other major cities seem less favourably disposed to the street entertainers than London and even Paris which has many busking musicians, has lost its tradition of the itinerant balladeer – sad for a city that produced from its pavements one of the great post-war entertainers, Edith Piaf (1915–1963).

New York, too, has produced a great star from the shadows of its skyscrapers. The extraordinary blind musician, calling himself Moondog, conjured an amazing range of

exotic sounds from a collection of percussion instruments. He never left the sidewalks where he created his own brand of entertainment for the big lights around the corner in Broadway, but he stamped his unmistakeable style on a number of records that are enthusiastically collected.

One outstanding form of American street entertainment has passed in a body from the roadways into the culture of the nation. It is the blues. During the first 30 years of this century the travelling blues singer, often blind, was a familiar sight in the southern states. Thanks largely to Alan Lomax and his programme for the Library of Congress, and to other collectors and enthusiasts such as Sam Charters, the work of these men has been carefully annotated. Some were even launched on new careers in clubs and concert halls, among the best-known being the vocal

and harmonica pairing of Sonny Terry and Brownie McGhee.

New Orleans was also the home of that other great street music tradition in the United States, the famous marching bands. They were hired mainly for funerals, marching to the ceremony with a slow, mournful dirge, and returning with joyful tunes.

Street entertainment today

Apart from the subway serenaders, there is little left in the way of street performers. Attempts have been made to revive strolling outdoor theatre companies, but modern traffic conditions may well have tolled the knell of passing plays − and players.

Street theatre companies have been re-established in Britain and the United States as well as in Europe. This marks a revival in a tradition which stretches back to the Middle

Ages. Many of these groups have a strongly defined political or social purpose. Many aim mainly at a sympathetic audience in the under-privileged areas of large cities, an audience well away from the buskers of the showbiz world. For example, London's most active unit is the Covent Garden Community Theatre. Many other major cities have at least one group which devotes some of its time to street or outdoor performances, even if most of their productions are done inside a theatre. Many municipal authorities, to their credit, have recognized the importance of such groups and opened parks and open spaces to the players.

However, even if the medieval minstrel and the subway busker are really one and the same type, much else has changed or gone for ever. For example, the pierrots and minstrels who once toured the British beaches in summer time, often doing six shows a day, have vanished as the tourists fly to more exotic excitements in the Mediterranean. A few resorts still hire a Punch and Judy man to amuse the kids. With the disappearance of the pierrots and minstrels, another seaside tradition has vanished too. These itinerant entertainers always passed a bottle around the audience for a collection − it was easy to put the money in, and not so simple to get it out! Street performers today still talk of 'bottling' but − alas − not many know what it means.

Left Don Partridge, a busker who entered the charts , is seen in London's Regent Street warming up the audience for a musical show − in which he himself will play. Buskers have traditionally played to theatre queues in London.
Below New York also has buskers — like this saxophonist.

ONE-MAN SHOWS

In recent years, one-man shows have been extremely popular throughout the world. From the impresario's point of view, the reasons for this are simple; it is obviously easier and cheaper to mount a one-man show than a lavish musical or a twelve character one-set play. From the audience's viewpoint, the reasons are far more complex.

The Victorian man of letters, Thomas Carlyle (1795–1881) came close to the truth when he wrote about Charles Dickens' (1812–1870) solo readings from his work, which began in 1853. 'I had no conception, before hearing Dickens read, of what capacities lie in the human face and voice', he wrote, 'No theatre stage alone could have had more players than seemed to flit about his face, and all tones were present.'

Origins and history

The history of the one-man show dates back to the eighteenth century when a German actor, Johann Christian Brandes invented what is known as the monodrama, a short solo piece for an actor or actress supported by silent figures or by choruses. Between 1775 and 1780 Brandes popularized the form particularly in his version of *Ariadne auf Naxos*. In the nineteenth century, Dickens earned a small fortune from public readings of his works until his doctors forbade him to continue for health reasons.

Dickens was only the forerunner of a long line of one-man performers. For many years,

Bransby Williams (1870–1961) toured the music halls giving solo presentations of characters from Dickens and Shakespeare. In October 1951, at the Lyric Theatre in Hammersmith, London, Emlyn Williams (born 1905) gave the first of his many readings from Dickens which amounted both to a full-scale impersonation of the author, even down to white gloves and immaculate evening dress, and a dramatization of the stories. Where Williams led, other serious actors quickly followed. These included the Irish actor Micheál macLiammoir (born 1899) who, complete with green carnation, re-created the spirit of Oscar Wilde. Max Adrian (1902–1973), spritely and red-bearded, performed an intoxicating blend of Bernard Shaw's memoirs, letters, diaries and journalism. Roy Dotrice (born 1923) became the seventeenth century diarist, John Aubrey, in an astonishingly cluttered set, and took his audiences through Aubrey's day.

These were what could be termed literary one-man shows, since they were all drawn from the works of single authors. But within

that format, there is great variety as Roy Dotrice has demonstrated and explained 'During the interval of *Brief Lives* when I sit on the stage pretending to be asleep, I work out what kind of audience I've got and the stories that I tell in the second half depend on what kind of material they are responding to: the bawdy jokes or the historical references.'

There is, however, a completely different solo entertainment that relies on songs and sketches rather than on a re-creation of the life and work of a dead author. Interestingly, it is a field in which women, or men impersonating women, have triumphed. The most famous of the former was the American actress Ruth Draper (1884–1956) who relied on a bare stage, a minimum of props and the idea of herself responding to invisible companions. 'Long ago', she once said, 'a man who knew a great deal about the theatre told me that the old advice to actors — that you must put it over — was wrong. What is really important is not to put anything over but to bring the audience up on the stage and into the scene with you.'

One-man shows are very demanding on the actor. Two twentieth century figures who have excelled at this form of presentation are the Americans Ruth Draper (**right**) and Bransby Williams (**below**). Williams is here impersonating a Chinaman.

The Russian director, actor and teacher, Konstantin Stanislavsky (1863–1938) said that the key to all great acting was the art of public solitude. Ruth Draper, an American by birth, certainly possessed this quality. So, too, did the Canadian-born Beatrice Lillie (born 1898), who filled theatres for months on end with her strange songs and sketches. 'Her gift,' said the English critic Kenneth Tynan, 'is to reproduce on the stage the idiocy with which people behave when they are on their own: humming and mumbling, grimacing at the looking glass, perhaps even singing to it . . . looking, definitely batty.'

The latest star arrival on the solo scene is, however, a quietly-spoken man from Melbourne who sports dark suits and a club tie. He is Barry Humphries, who created a monstrous Australian expatriate in bats-wing spectacles and outrageous garb wearing the form of Dame Edna Everage. Starting off as a garrulous suburban housewife, Edna has now achieved the status of a privileged superstar who turns her venom on her adopted country, Britain, like some vaude-

Right Another successful solo performer was Canadian born actress Beatrice Lillie, who delighted audiences with her show *An Evening with Beatrice Lillie* which she first performed in 1952.

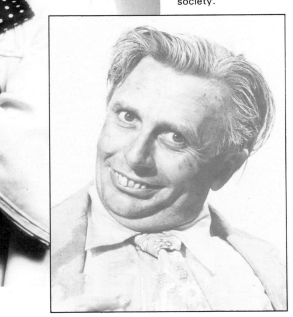

Through the figures of housewife-superstar, Dame Edna Everage **(left)** and the Australian cultural emissary, Les Patterson **(below)**, Barry Humphries turns a satirical eye on society.

ville equivalent of the classic eighteenth century satirist, Jonathan Swift.

Members of the audience, always female, are ruthlessly interrogated about their clothes, address and personal habits, as some lady editors of magazines published in London found out when they invited the lady, or gentleman, in question, to one of their monthly luncheons in 1979. Edna is a monster whom the British, and perhaps to a lesser extent the Australian public, have clasped to their bosoms — possibly the most suicidal mammary gesture since Cleopatra embraced an asp.

In America, one-man shows have similarly flourished. The US has produced not only Ruth Draper but also another famous *diseuse* in Cornelia Otis Skinner (born 1901). Charles Laughton (1899–1962) toured America with solo readings from the Bible, while the distinguished actor Hal Halbrook (born 1925) has presented an evening with Mark Twain that is an affectionate blend of impersonation biography and criticism.

All these and many more one-man shows have succeeded for one inescapable reason. In them the audience surrenders to the primal lure of the magnetic, outsize star performer. And for the artist there is always the advantage, as Barry Humphries once pointed out, that 'they can't start without you'.

POETRY READING

Although there has been a great revival of spoken poetry this century, and particularly in the last 20 years, the tradition is as old as poetry itself.

Poetry has its roots in ancient tribal culture, where the poet had an agreed place in society – part entertainer, part historian, part moral philosopher and part visionary and prophet. The poetry of old – such as the work of Homer and Virgil and the much later English epic, *Beowulf* – was recited. It was devised for immediate enjoyment and edification. Much of it was chanted or sung, often accompanied by music and sometimes combined with mime, dance or drama.

We have grown accustomed to thinking of a poem such as Virgil's *Aeneid* as being a sophisticated piece of literature, yet we know that it was being read aloud by the author at the court of Augustus and was not published until after Virgil's death.

Decline of the oral tradition

The reason for the decline of spoken poetry was the spread of the printed word and with it, the new habit of silent reading. However, even at the height of this revolution there were some who urged caution. When the Scottish poet Walter Scott (1771–1832) was collecting ballads for his *Minstrelsy of the Scottish Border* early last century he talked to the poet James Hogg's mother after she sang him one of the old ballads. She disliked the

idea of putting them in print, telling Scott that they were made for singing, and not for reading.

The old woman was right. Ballads were being printed in anthologies and read in schools simply as poems and it was being forgotten that they had tunes and were meant to be sung. It is only recently, along with the renewed interest in spoken poetry, that the ballads have again been recognized as songs.

The growing realization of what has been lost or overlaid by the print culture of the last 500 years does not mean outright opposition to written poetry, but rather a sense that it should once more be complemented by an oral culture.

Performing poets

When Virgil was writing 2,000 years ago a public or semi-public reading was the usual method of first 'publication'. Today this is again quite often the case. Many poets will try out a new work at a poetry reading, with publication proper in a magazine or book coming later.

This trend has been particularly strong in Russia. As Andrei Voznesensky said in an interview in 1972: 'New poets come from the platform in Russia, from readings. Before poems are published they become known by being read aloud. Akhmadulina, Yevtushenko. Okudzhava and myself became known through our readings.'

Even in the absence of formal readings,

poets have long been in the habit of reciting new work to friends before publication. The British poet and critic Samuel Taylor Coleridge (1772–1834) records how he had been an awed listener to the 'deep voice' of William Wordsworth (1770–1850) reciting evening after evening the whole of his new long poem *The Prelude*.

Later in the nineteenth century Alfred, Lord Tennyson (1809–1892) read his poems on many occasions, both to small groups and to large country house gatherings, and he was evidently a dramatic and gripping performer. He was equally convincing in standard English or Lincolnshire dialect and during his reading of *St Simeon Stylites* he would interject weird laughs to underline the work's black comedy.

In reciting his long poem *Maud* he would burst into tears or, as on one occasion recorded by his grandson, Charles, Tennyson performed 'with such intensity that he seized and kept quite unconsciously twisting in his powerful hands a large brocaded cushion which was lying at his side'.

Tennyson's committed, emotional style contrasts with the sheer professionalism of the Welsh poet Dylan Thomas's (1914–1953) famous performances, particularly in America. Thomas's biographer John Malcolm Brinnin says that Thomas's first reading in New York in 1950 brought 'a whole new conception of poetry reading. The enormous range and organ-deep resonance of his voice as he read from Yeats, Hardy, Auden, Law-

Far left In 1965 the Albert Hall was crammed with 7,000 people avidly listening not to the hall's usual orchestral or musical fare but to poetry reading. The 'International Poetry Incarnation' was a sign of the rise in popularity of poetry reading during the 1960s. The poets who read at the Albert Hall event included the British poets Adrian Mitchell and Michael Horovitz, the Austrian poet, Ernst Jandl and the Russian Alexander Trocchi **(below)**. The event was so popular that several hundred people had to be turned away from the hall.

Left Aristide Bruant recites one of his verses in Montmartre. Bruant was one of the leading figures in Parisian cabaret at the turn of the century. The casual setting of the cabaret club suited Bruant's socially committed verse.

the American Allen Ginsberg (born 1926) or the Russian Yevgeny Yevtushenko (born 1933) try to restate the importance of the platform.

The culmination of this renewed belief in the power of the spoken word and the importance of the presence of the living poet was the famous 'International Poetry Incarnation' on 11th June 1965 when 7,000 people packed the Albert Hall in London to hear four hours of poetry read by, among others, Ginsberg, Lawrence Ferlinghetti, Gregory Corso: and Adrian Mitchell.

Sound poetry
In the 1970s perhaps the most challenging development has been sound poetry, in which the voice is combined with recorded tapes, movement or some visual element, the performance often edging out towards becoming music. International festivals of sound poetry have been held in London, Stockholm, Amsterdam and Glasgow, and sound poets have been particularly active in Sweden, France, Canada and Britain.

The sound poetry movement has its roots in the experimental writings and performances earlier this century of Velemir Khlebnikov and Alexey Kruchonykh in Russia, Filippo Marinetti in Italy, Hugo Ball in Germany and Pierre Albert-Birot in France. Today performers such as Bob Cobbing, bp

rence, MacNeice, Alun Lewis and Edith Sitwell gave new music to familiar cadences and, at times, revealed values in the poems never disclosed on the page.'

What Tennyson would have disliked in Thomas's performance was the elocutionary polish, the ease with which he might make Alun Lewis and Edith Sitwell sound as good as Yeats and Hardy, and even more disturbing, the ease with which he could switch from professionally reading others' poetry to professionally reading his own.

Tennyson would have condemned this style as artificial and insincere. It is indeed a frequent reaction among those who listen to Thomas's recordings today to waver between enormous admiration and an underlying but persistent suspicion or distaste. The novelist and poet Kingsley Amis put his finger on it when he said of a Thomas reading in Swansea in 1951: 'Although obviously without all charlatanry, he did here and there sound or behave like a charlatan.'

The undeniable triumph of Thomas's readings was very much a part of the postwar period – the period, also, of the popularity of the verse plays of Christopher Fry and T. S. Eliot. Thomas died in 1953 and ten years later he would not have made the same impact.

The new impetus
The new conception of poetry reading which emerged during the late 1950s and reached its peak in the 1960s demanded something

much less dependent on beauty of delivery, something more exposed and vulnerable, a sense of the poet being wholly there in the reading of his own work, with much less of a disjunction between the everyday man and the platform personality.

This new sincerity had obvious links with Beat poetry in America, the Liverpool poets in England and with the poets of the 'thaw' in Russia and Eastern Europe, but it was part of a general change which cannot be identified too closely with any one movement.

As Vladimir Mayakovsky (1894–1930) had stirred, provoked, inspired and interacted with his audiences in the 1920s so now, at a time of rapid social and political change, did

Nichol, Ernst Jandl, Henri Chopin, Bernard Heidsieck, Tom Leonard and Jerome Rothenberg can produce effects sufficiently spellbinding to win over even sceptical audiences.

Arranging readings
Poetry readings today are often professionally organized. In Britain, for example, the National Poetry Secretariat guarantees fees and expenses to poets on their list and there are various Arts Council schemes for funding visits of poets to schools. The administrative side of readings is similarly well-organized in other parts of Europe, in America and Australia.

CHRONOLOGY

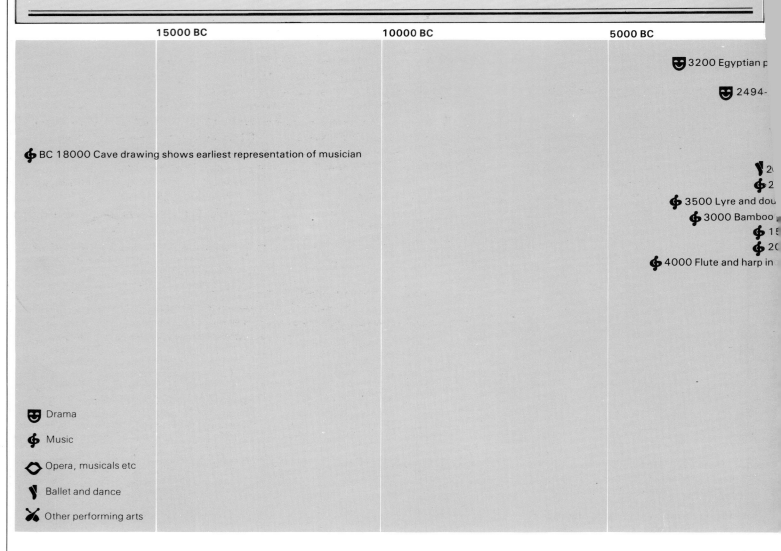

15000 BC	10000 BC	5000 BC

😀 3200 Egyptian p

😀 2494-

♪ BC 18000 Cave drawing shows earliest representation of musician

🎻 2(
𝄞 2
𝄞 3500 Lyre and dou
𝄞 3000 Bamboo
𝄞 1ξ
𝄞 2(
𝄞 4000 Flute and harp in

😀 Drama

𝄞 Music

◇ Opera, musicals etc

🎻 Ballet and dance

✗ Other performing arts

Aeschylus
(c.525-c.456 B.C.)
Greek tragic
dramatist. Only seven
of his plays survive,
the most famous of
which are
*Agamemnon, Seven
against Thebes,
Persians* and
Prometheus Bound.
He not only appeared
in his own plays but
also directed the
chorus.

Aristophanes
(c.445-c.385 B.C.)
Greek comic
playwright. His 11
surviving plays are
shrewd social satires,
boldly written and
with much coarse
humour. His most
famous works are *The
Clouds, The Wasps,* a
satire on Athenian
litigation, *The Birds*
and *Lysistrata.*

Armstrong, Louis
(1900-1971) American
jazz trumpeter and
composer. His career
began in New Orleans

where he started
playing at the age of
12. In 1922 he moved
to Chicago, and then
to New York where
he achieved
considerable success
as a solo trumpeter
and made numerous
recordings. By 1946
he had gained
international fame
both as a trumpeter
and gravel-toned
singer of folk jazz.
Affectionately known
as 'Satchmo', he is
considered one of the

greatest jazz
musicians of his age.

Ashton, Frederick
(born 1904) British
dancer and
choreographer.
Ashton was born in
Ecuador, and after
seeing Pavlova dance
in Lima, Peru, in 1917
decided to become a
dancer. In the 1920s
he studied with
Massine and Marie
Rambert and in 1935
joined the Vic-Wells
Ballet as dancer and
choreographer. His

Balanchine, George
(born 1904) Russian
dancer, ballet master
and choreographer.
Balanchine studied
music at the
Petrograd
Conservatory of
Music before turning
to ballet: his
choreography is noted
particularly for its
musicality. He left
Russia in 1924 and
went to Paris where

association with
Margot Fonteyn, for
whom he created
some of her greatest
roles, began at this
time. He was
knighted in 1962 and
was director of the
Royal Ballet from
1963 to 1970. His
notable works include
Wedding Bouquet
(1937), *Symphonic
Variations* (1946),
*Marguerite and
Armand* (1963) and
Enigma Variations
(1968).

he became Diaghilev's
principal
choreographer
producing important
works such as
Prodigal Son (1929)
and *Apollo* (1928).

Since 1934 he has
been mainly
associated with the
New York City Ballet
as its artistic director.
He is one of the most
prolific and influential
of twentieth century
choreographers.

Barnum, Phineas T.
(1810-1891) American
theatre manager and
showman. He was
America's first great
show business
personality. He
founded the American
Museum in New York
in 1842 but is best
known for 'The
Greatest Show on
Earth', a combination
of circus, menagerie
and museum which
he created in 1871
and with which he
toured the world.

Barrymore, John
(1882-1942) American
actor. A member of
the talented
Barrymore family, he
was the younger
brother of the actor
and actress, Lionel
and Ethel. He began
his career playing in
light comedies and
popular farces but
later found his real
metier in such
classical roles as
Richard III, Hamlet

BC	800 BC	600 BC	400 BC	200 BC	0

creation of the world

🎭 c. 600 Tragedies performed as part of Festival of Dionysus Athens

🎭 441 Sophocles *Antigone* 🎭 205 Plautus *Miles Gloriosus*

drama of death of God Osiris performed in Egypt

🎭 Pindar (c. 518-438) Greek musician and poet

🎭 472 Aeschylus *The Persians* 🎭 191 Plautus *Pseudolus*

🎭 534 First drama contest in Athens won by poet Thespis 🎭 166 Terence *Andria*

🎭 720 The Pear Garden drama school established in Nanking China 🎭 300 Records of earliest religious plays

◆ 580 Dramatization of stories in China with singing and dancing

Religious dances in Crete

🎭 Aeschylus (525-456) Greek dramatist founder of European drama

ussion instruments in Egyptian orchestral music

✗ 5th century BC Puppets mentioned in Xenophon

net in Egypt ◆ 800 Development of Greek choral dramatic music 🎭 458 Aeschylus *Oresteia* 🎶 50 Oboe in Rome

nina 🎭 431 Euripides *Medea* 🎭 Plautus (251-184) Roman dramatist

o in Egypt 🎶 700 Seven string lyre introduced 🎭 330 Theatre of Dionysus built at Athens

mpet in Denmark

🎶 309 Earliest known industrial dispute in music —
Ariostos, Greek musician in Rome, brings his
players out on strike

pt. Accompanied liturgical chant in Mesopotamia

◆ 500 Zenith of Greek choral music

🎶 400 Greek trumpet-playing competitions

🎶 c. 550 Pythagorus introduces octave in music

🎶 340 Aristotle founds musical theory in Greece

---

and Romeo, which he played in both New York and London in the 1920s.

The Beatles British pop group. The group consisted of George Harrison (born 1943), John Lennon (born 1940), Paul McCartney (born 1942) and Ringo Starr (born 1940). In 1961 Brian Epstein became their manager after seeing them perform at The Cavern, Liverpool. With their 1963 record 'Please Please Me', they had a hit and from then on had one spectacular success after another. They achieved an acclaim unprecedented in the history of popular music and greatly influenced not only the music of their time but also the attitudes of young people throughout the world.

Beckett, Samuel (born 1906) Irish dramatist and a novelist. Born in Dublin, he went to Paris in 1928 to teach and study. He has lived there permanently since 1938 and many of his plays were first written in French, notably *Waiting for Godot* (1952) and *End Game* (1957). Other works include *All That Fall* (1957), *Krapp's Last Tape* (1959) and *Embers* (1960). His

plays which, at times, are both enigmatic and funny, focus on the absurdity of human nature. He was awarded the Nobel Prize for Literature in 1969.

Beecham, Thomas (1879-1961) British conductor. The son of a wealthy manufacturing chemist, he began his conducting career in 1906. From 1910 he directed operatic seasons at Covent Garden and was responsible for the first English performances of Richard Strauss's *Elektra, Salome* and *Der Rosenkavalier.* He was one of the few British conductors of his time to achieve international fame.

Berlin, Irving (born 1888) Russian-born American composer. He achieved his first success with

'Alexander's Ragtime Band' in 1911 and went on to write a number of immensely popular stage musicals including *The Cocoanuts* (1925, with the Marx Brothers) and *Face the Music* (1932). He won international fame with *Annie Get Your Gun* (1946) and *Call Me Madam* (1950). Berlin is one of the most famous composers of American popular music.

Bernhardt, Sarah (1844-1923) French actress. She first appeared with the Comédie Française in 1862 and for the next 20 years acted off and on with the company, establishing herself as the leading actress of her time. She excelled in tragic roles such as Marguérite Gautier in *La Dame aux*

Camélias, as Hamlet and in Sardou's melodramas, *Fedora* and *La Tosca*. Her personality, physical

grace and exceptionally beautiful voice helped to make her one of the greatest tragediennes of all time.

Bournonville, August (1805-1879) Danish dancer, choreographer and ballet master. He received his early training in Paris and

after 1828 returned to Denmark where he worked as a dancer, choreographer and teacher. Not only was he a soloist of remarkable talent, but he also created more than 50 ballets for the Royal Danish Ballet including *Napoli, Ventana* and *Far from Denmark.* He was Denmark's leading choreographer and several of his romantic ballets are still regularly performed.

Brecht, Bertolt (1898-1956) German playwright, director, poet and theoretrician. Brecht's early plays, of which *Baal* (1918) is the first, are expressionist in technique. He achieved his first popular success with *The Threepenny Opera* (1928), but with the advent of Hitler he left Germany

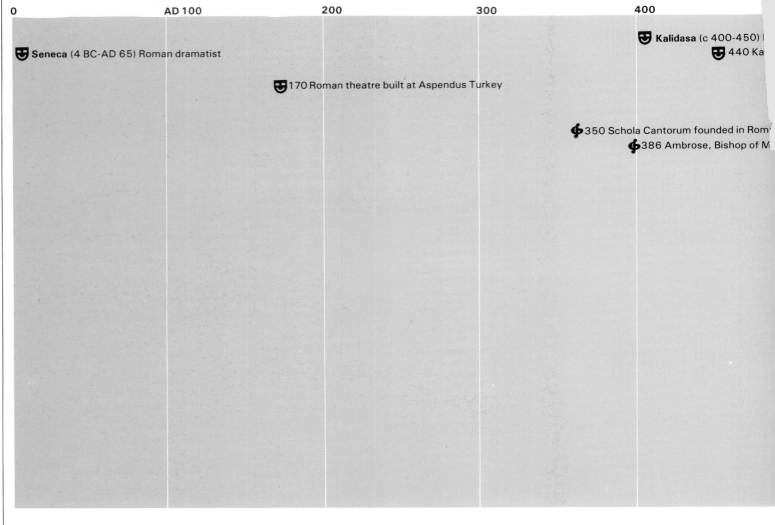

0   AD 100   200   300   400

☻ **Seneca** (4 BC–AD 65) Roman dramatist

☻ **Kalidasa** (c 400-450)

☻ 440 Ka

☻ 170 Roman theatre built at Aspendus Turkey

♫ 350 Schola Cantorum founded in Rom

♫ 386 Ambrose, Bishop of M

---

in 1933 to settle in Denmark, and then, in 1941, California. During his period of exile he wrote a series of important plays including *The Life of Galileo* (1937-1939). *Mother Courage* (1938-39), *The Good Woman of Setzuan* (1938-42) and *The Caucasian Chalk Circle* (1943-45). In 1949 Brecht returned to Germany and set up his own company,

the Berliner Ensemble, in East Berlin. Here he directed his own plays and sought to practise his theories about drama. He believed that neither the actors nor the audience should wholly identify with any character but should remain sufficiently detached to judge the action on stage critically and coolly. His plays do, however, work remarkably well in the theatre. Brecht soon became recognized as one of the most influential and important figures in twentieth century drama.
Britten, Benjamin (1913-1976) British composer and conductor. He wrote many operas, of which the most popular are *Billy Budd* (1951), *Peter Grimes* (1945), *Let's Make an*

Opera (1949) (for children), *A Midsummer Night's Dream* (1960) and *Death in Venice* (1973).

Calderon de la Barca, Pedro (1600-1681) Spanish dramatist. As Court poet and head of Philip IV's Court Theatre he wrote about 300 plays, many of them religious dramas as well as a number of secular plays. His

best-known works are *El alcalde de Zalamea (The Mayor of Zalamea)*, one of the first social dramas, and *La vida es sueno (Life is a Dream)*. He was a master of dramatic situation, a fine poet and one of the greatest of Spanish playwrights.
Callas, Maria (1923-1977) American-born Greek soprano. She made her professional debut at the age of 16 in Athens, although her later career was mainly in Italy. During the 1950s and early 1960s she gained an outstanding international reputation, especially in works by Rossini, Verdi and Puccini. She retired from the stage in the late 1960s to take up teaching. Her vocal technique was flawed, but she was an artist of

exceptional quality and one of the greatest operatic performers of her time.
Caruso, Enrico (1873-1921) Italian tenor. He made his debut in Naples in 1894 in Gounod's opera *Faust*, sang regularly at Covent Garden between 1903 and 1907 and towards the end of his career was mainly associated with the Metropolitan Opera House, New York. He was one of the most celebrated tenors of his age.
Chaliapine, Feodor (1873-1938) Russian bass singer. He made his operatic debut in 1890 but achieved the height of his fame when he was brought to London and Paris in 1913 by Diaghilev. Soon after the Russian Revolution, he settled abroad, and

died in Paris. His vocal mastery was unrivalled in the roles he sang from Russian opera and he was one of the great bass singers of all time.
Chekhov, Anton (1860-1904) Russian dramatist. While studying medicine at Moscow University he began writing short stories and then later turned to drama. Chekhov's most successful plays are *The Seagull* (1896), *Uncle Vanya* (1897), *The Three Sisters* (1901) and *The Cherry Orchard* (1904) of which the last two were written for the Moscow Art Theatre. Chekhov's major contribution to drama lies in the exquisite balance between tragedy and comedy that his plays achieve.
Chevalier, Maurice (1888-1973) French singer, actor and

600   **700**   **800**   **900**   **1000**

and dramatist

ntala

900 Beginnings of church drama

First Chinese plays with music c.960

The *The Maries* and the *Angels* dialogues performed in churches at Easter 925

th-10th century AD Travelling troupes of puppeteers in Europe

Guido d'Arezzo (995-1050)
Italian music teacher

gical song

600 Pope Gregory compiles collection of church chant

900 Organum (plainsong in
     fourths, fifths and octaves)
     develops

duces hymn-singing

Aethewold, Bishop of Winchester, writes of how to perform the Easter story dramatically in church 970

521 Boethius establishes Greek letter names for scale in Europe

800 Poems accompanied by music at Charlemagne's court

500 Boethius writes *De Institutione Musicae*

Hrotsvitha writes Latin comedies 995

790 Schola Cantorum establishes schools in Cologne, Paris,
     Metz and Soissons

850 Eight church modes established

Winchester Abbey has 400-pipe organ built 980

855 Birth of polyphonic music

750 Wind organs replace water organs

Antiphonarium Codex Montpellier written 980

750 Gregorian chant in France, England and Germany

---

dancer. He sang in cafés as a child but went on to become Mistinguett's partner at the Folies Begère in Paris. He first appeared in London in a revue, *Hullo, America!* in 1919. He went on to gain an international reputation in cabaret and appeared in revue, theatre and many films.
Coward, Noël (1899-1973) British actor, dramatist, composer and director. He started his career as a child actor in 1911 and went on to become one of the most popular and one of the most versatile figures in twentieth century theatre. As a playwright, his real talent was with elegant, high comedies such as *Hay Fever* (1925), *Private Lives* (1930), *Blithe Spirit* (1941) and *Present*

Laughter (1942). As the composer and librettist of his own songs for musical comedies and revues he was highly

inventive and extremely professional. As a performer, he had great wit and elegance.
Crosby, Bing (1904-1978) American singer. He sang with dance bands from 1925 to 1930 and from 1931 began to work in

radio and films. He soon gained enormous popularity as a crooner. He made thousands of recordings and appeared in a number of films. Known as the 'old groaner', he was the best-known popular singer of his generation.
Cunningham, Merce (born 1919) American dancer and choreographer. After early formal training in dance and theatre, he joined Martha Graham's company in 1939. He began giving solo concerts in 1942 and in 1959 set up his own studio. He has choreographed more than 60 new ballets and has toured extensively.

Dada Artistic movement of the 1920s. Founded in Zürich in 1916 it included among its

manifestations, theatre and cabaret. Dada rejected traditional moral and aesthetic values and advocated freedom and spontaneity of artistic expression. Its dramatic sketches lacked logical plot and were completely abstract, often making use of expressionist dance, grotesque costume and mechanical sound. Its most notable works were *Le Coeur à Gas* (1921), a play by its founder Tristan Tzara, and the ballet, *Relâche* with designs by Picabia and music by Satie.
Dauberval, Jean (1742-1806) French dancer and choreographer. An outstanding dancer, he made his debut at the Paris Opéra in 1761 and remained there as dancer and teacher until 1783. His major

contribution was as director of ballet at the Grand Theatre, Bordeaux (1785-90) where he staged the first production of *Fille Mal Gardée* in 1789.
Deburau, Jean-Baptiste (1796-1846) French mime artist. Born in Bohemia, he arrived in Paris in 1812 and soon after joined the troupe of jugglers and acrobats at the Théatre des Funambules. Here he created the melancholy clown, Pierrot, in which role he became the theatre's chief attraction. Deburau and his Pierrot soon became legendary figures in French theatre.
Diaghilev, Sergei (1872-1929) Russian ballet impresario. A scholar of painting and opera, he turned to ballet in 1909. In 1911 he set up his famous

company, Ballet Russes, in Paris and the ingenuity and splendour of his productions captivated Europe. His genius lay in his comprehensive grasp of all aspects of ballet and in his unique gift for spotting talent. His company made use

of the greatest contemporary choreographers (Fokine, Massine, Balanchine), designers (Picasso, Bakst,

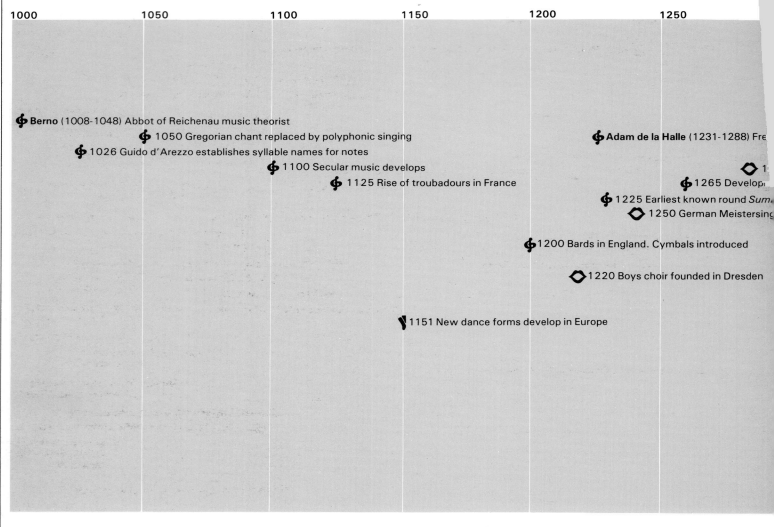

1000 1050 1100 1150 1200 1250

𝄞 **Berno** (1008-1048) Abbot of Reichenau music theorist

𝄞 1050 Gregorian chant replaced by polyphonic singing

𝄞 1026 Guido d'Arezzo establishes syllable names for notes

𝄞 1100 Secular music develops

𝄞 1125 Rise of troubadours in France

𝄞 **Adam de la Halle** (1231-1288) Fre

◇ 1

𝄞 1265 Develop

𝄞 1225 Earliest known round *Sum*

◇ 1250 German Meistersing

𝄞 1200 Bards in England. Cymbals introduced

◇ 1220 Boys choir founded in Dresden

❦ 1151 New dance forms develop in Europe

Braque), dancers (Nijinsky, Pavlova) and musicians (Stravinsky, Debussy, Prokofiev) and many of the works commissioned by him are among the finest of their kind. He is one of the most important figures in the history of ballet.

Dibdin, Charles (1745-1814) English dramatist, actor and song-writer. He is best remembered for his nautical songs of which 'Tom Bowling' is the most famous. He also produced several plays, including a popular ballad opera, *The Waterman* (1774). He was an important figure in the development of variety and music hall.

Donizetti, Gaetano (1797-1848) Italian composer. A composer of over 70 operas, his works, like those of his contemporaries, Bellini and Rossini, were enormously popular in opera houses throughout Europe. His work is characterized by beautiful melodies requiring virtuoso singing rather than dramatic action. His most popular operas are *Lucia di Lammermoor, The Daughter of the Regiment* and *Don Pasquale.*

Duncan, Isadora (1878-1927) American expressionist dancer. She rebelled against the formality of classical ballet and began giving concerts in New York society salons where she danced barefoot and in long flowing robes, taking her inspiration from nature and improvising her gestures from Greek vases. She made a successful tour of Europe, and in Russia in 1905 her natural, interpretative style influenced Fokine and Pavlova. She continued to tour Europe and the U.S. until, in 1921, she was invited to Russia to start an academy of dance. She left soon after, as her excessive drinking and self indulgence began to take its toll, and her popularity declined. Her influence on the development of modern dance has been enormous.

Durante, Jimmy (born 1893) American comedian. Known as 'Schnozzle', he had a long career in vaudeville and nightclubs. A rough and tumble comic, he was famed for his long nose, his stiff-kneed strut and his nasal voice. He also appeared in films and on TV and was one of the best-loved comics of his generation.

Dylan, Bob (born 1941) American folk singer. He started playing the guitar at the age of 12 and from 1961 in New York began singing in folk clubs where he attracted attention. His influence on popular contemporary music is rivalled only by The Beatles and his semi-visionary songs altered the attitudes of an entire generation.

Ellington, Duke (1899-1975) American dance-band leader and composer. He directed his own bands from about 1918 onwards and composed a number of memorable pieces, such as *Mood Indigo* and *Solitude*. His longer works, like *Creole Rhapsody* (1931) and *Green Apple* (1965) reveal a

distinctly individual jazz style. He was one of the most versatile of American jazz performers.

Euripides (c.480-c.406 B.C.) Greek poetic dramatist. He wrote about 92 plays, of which 17 tragedies survive, among them *Medea, Andromache, The Trojan Women* and *The Bacchae*. His plays are often critical and sceptical of society and humanity and his characters are drawn with great vividness and insight. He has thus been called the first of the realists.

Fonteyn, Margot (born 1919) British ballerina. After a childhood training in ballet she joined the Vic-Wells Ballet Company in 1934 and became the principal dancer at the Royal Ballet until 1959. During this period her association with Ashton was established and her dancing came to its peak. In such ballets as

	1350	1400	1450	1500	1550	1600

🎭 **Thomas Middleton** (1570-1627) English dramatist

🎭 **Zeam Motokiyo** (1363-1443) Most famous of Japanese *Noh* dramatists

🎭 **Juan del Encina** (1469-1529) 'Father of Spanish drama'

🎭 **Gil Vicente** (1465-1536) Portuguese poet and actor

🎭 **William Shakespeare** (1564-1616) English dramatist

poser

Guillaume de Machaut (1300-1377) French composer

o-opera *Le Jeu de Robin et Marion*

♭ **John Dunstable** (1385-1453) English composer

he motet

♭ 1437 Dunstable develops counterpoint

♭ **William Byrd** (1543-1623) English composer

cumen in in six parts

blished

♭ **Giovanni Pierluigi da Palestrina** (1525-1594) Italian composer

♭ **Guillaume Dufay** (1400-1474) French composer

♭ **John Taverner** (1495-1545) English composer

Nicholas Udall (1505-1556) English dramatist

♭ 1325 Pedals added to organ

♭ 1329 *Ars Nova* new musical style

♭ 1502 des Pres *First,Book of Masses*

◇ 1364 Machaut *Mass for Four Voices*

♭ 1473 First music printed (German book of plainsong)

♭ 1498 *Terminorum Musicae Diffinitorium* first musical dictionary

♭ 1385 First French court ball at wedding of Charles VI and isabella of Bavaria

♭ **Josquin des Pres** (1450-1521) French composer

♭ 1554 Palestrina *First Book!of Masses*

♭ 1535 Rise of the madrigalists

♭ c.1530 Andrea Amati makes first violin

✖ 14th century Karagoz Turkish puppet show

♭ 1537 First music conservatories founded in Venice and Naples

♭ 1499 Degrees in Music at Oxford University

♭ **Thomas Tallis** (1505-1585) English composer

♭ **Claudio Monteverdi** (1567-1643) Italian composer

ꕥ 1490 Beginnings of ballet at Italian Courts

Ondine and *Symphonic Variations* her dancing provided the best example of the British style of ballet. Although nearing retirement

age, in 1960 she embarked on a partnership with Nureyev, which was to prove her the greatest ballerina of her time.

Garrick, David (1717-1779) English actor, dramatist and theatre

manager. One of the greatest of English actors, his first major success was as Richard III in 1741. His foremost contribution was to introduce a simple, naturalistic approach to acting, hitherto dominated by the declamatory style. He also managed Drury Lane from 1747 to 1776 and introduced a number of important reforms such as banishing spectators from the

stage, using concealed lighting and realistic backdrops. He wrote a number of plays, and adaptations of Shakespeare and Wycherley.
Gielgud, John (born 1904) English actor and director. He made his stage debut in 1921 at the Old Vic but was soon recognized as an actor of formidable talent. His most outstanding qualities as an actor are his fine speaking

voice and his intelligent depiction of character. Some of his best performances have been in **Shakespearean** roles. His Hamlet (1934) is regarded as one of the greatest of this century. He has played Romeo, Richard II, Lear, and Othello, among many other roles.
Gilbert (1836-1911) and **Sullivan** (1842-1900) Respectively, English dramatist and composer. Together they created the Savoy Operas, a series of light operas with spoken dialogue, the first of which was *Trial by Jury* (1875). Most of them, including *H.M.S: Pinafore, The Pirates of Penzance, The Gondoliers* and *The Mikado* are still regularly performed today. Sullivan's melodic fluency together with Gilbert's

remarkable comic talent produced a unique contribution to the British musical stage.

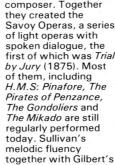

Goethe, Johann Wolfgang von (1740-1832) German poet, dramatist and novelist. Germany's greatest poet, he was also an important and influential playwright. His early plays include *Götz von Berlichingen* (1773), and *Egmont* (1796). His great

masterpiece, the poetic drama *Faust* (1808 and 1830) with its masterly combination of classical and romantic elements, has had a profound influence on world literature. As director of the Weimar Court Theatre from 1791 to 1817 he strove to increase the dignity and nobility of drama and here encouraged and collaborated with Schiller.
Goldoni, Carlo (1707-1793) Italian dramatist. The founder of realistic Italian comedy in succession to the *commedia dell' arte,* he wrote over 250 plays, of which *The Servant of Two Masters* (1746) is the best known today. His works, which are acutely observed, portray the life and manners of Italian society.

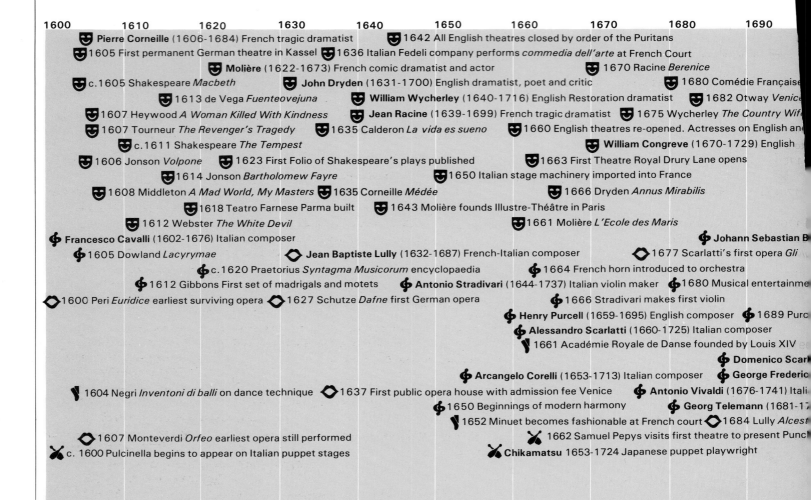

1600	1610	1620	1630	1640	1650	1660	1670	1680	1690

Pierre Corneille (1606-1684) French tragic dramatist

1642 All English theatres closed by order of the Puritans

1605 First permanent German theatre in Kassel

1636 Italian Fedeli company performs *commedia dell'arte* at French Court

Molière (1622-1673) French comic dramatist and actor

1670 Racine *Berenice*

c.1605 Shakespeare *Macbeth*

John Dryden (1631-1700) English dramatist, poet and critic

1680 Comédie Française

1613 de Vega *Fuenteovejuna*

William Wycherley (1640-1716) English Restoration dramatist

1682 Otway *Venice*

1607 Heywood *A Woman Killed With Kindness*

Jean Racine (1639-1699) French tragic dramatist

1675 Wycherley *The Country Wife*

1607 Tourneur *The Revenger's Tragedy*

1635 Calderon *La vida es sueno*

1660 English theatres re-opened. Actresses on English and

c.1611 Shakespeare *The Tempest*

William Congreve (1670-1729) English

1606 Jonson *Volpone*

1623 First Folio of Shakespeare's plays published

1663 First Theatre Royal Drury Lane opens

1614 Jonson *Bartholomew Fayre*

1650 Italian stage machinery imported into France

1608 Middleton *A Mad World, My Masters*

1635 Corneille *Médée*

1666 Dryden *Annus Mirabilis*

1618 Teatro Farnese Parma built

1643 Molière founds Illustre-Théâtre in Paris

1612 Webster *The White Devil*

1661 Molière *L'Ecole des Maris*

Francesco Cavalli (1602-1676) Italian composer

Johann Sebastian B

1605 Dowland *Lacyrymae*

Jean Baptiste Lully (1632-1687) French-Italian composer

1677 Scarlatti's first opera *Gli*

c.1620 Praetorius *Syntagma Musicorum* encyclopaedia

1664 French horn introduced to orchestra

1612 Gibbons First set of madrigals and motets

Antonio Stradivari (1644-1737) Italian violin maker

1680 Musical entertainme

1600 Peri *Euridice* earliest surviving opera

1627 Schutze *Dafne* first German opera

1666 Stradivari makes first violin

Henry Purcell (1659-1695) English composer

1689 Purc

Alessandro Scarlatti (1660-1725) Italian composer

1661 Académie Royale de Danse founded by Louis XIV

Domenico Scarl

Arcangelo Corelli (1653-1713) Italian composer

George Frederic

1604 Negri *Inventoni di balli* on dance technique

1637 First public opera house with admission fee Venice

Antonio Vivaldi (1676-1741) Itali

1650 Beginnings of modern harmony

Georg Telemann (1681-17

1652 Minuet becomes fashionable at French court

1684 Lully *Alcest*

1662 Samuel Pepys visits first theatre to present Punc

1607 Monteverdi *Orfeo* earliest opera still performed

Chikamatsu 1653-1724 Japanese puppet playwright

c.1600 Pulcinella begins to appear on Italian puppet stages

Graham, Martha (born 1894) American expressionist dancer. One of the founders of modern dance, she set up her own company in New York in the 1920s. Dancing barefoot and using her entire body she attempted to express modern psychological tensions. One of her most notable works was *Appalachian Spring* (1944). Success came only gradually; however, her influence on the development of modern dance in America is inestimable.

Grimaldi, Joseph (1778-1837) English clown. He was trained in pantomime from an early age by his Italian father and first appeared on stage as a dancer. From 1806 until his retirement in 1823 he performed at Covent Garden as a dancer, mime, actor and acrobat. He was one of the most famous of all clowns; indeed clowns are still traditionally called 'Joey', in memory of Grimaldi.

Guthrie, Tyrone (1900-1971) British director. He was associated with the Old Vic as director and administrator until 1952 when he left to found the Shakespeare Memorial Theatre at Stratford, Ontario, based on the ensemble pattern. His fame as a director rests on his Shakespeare productions, of which one of his most famous was *Hamlet* in modern dress with Alec Guinness in the lead (1938).

Houdini, Harry (1874-1926) American magician. Perhaps the greatest magician of all time, he was particularly famous for his escapes from handcuffs, sealed chests and so on. He was highly professional and well-versed in the literature of magic. He appeared in silent films and was also well-known for his exposure of fraudulent spiritualists.

Ibsen, Henrik (1828-1906) Norwegian dramatist. His early verse dramas, *Brand* (1866) and *Peer Gynt* (1867) brought him immediate success but it is the plays of his middle and later years which are the most significant. Of these, *The Pillars of Society* (1877), *Ghosts* (1881) and *An Enemy of the People* (1882) deal realistically with social problems, as does *Hedda Gabler* (1890),

are more obviously symbolic. In all his plays the naturalistic action symbolizes a deeper psychological situation in which his complex and often tragic characters are inevitably entangled. Ibsen has been called the father of modern drama and his influence on its course is inestimable.

his masterpiece. His later plays, like *The Master Builder* (1892)

Kemble, John Philip (1757-1832) English actor and theatre manager. The most eminent actor of his day, he played with great success such roles as Hamlet, Romeo, Brutus and Coriolanus. He had considerable dignity and a particularly fine voice and is best remembered as a distinguished tragic actor. He was also, for some time, manager of the Drury Lane and later Covent Garden Theatres.

Kern, Jerome (1885-1945) American composer. He acquired his musical training in New York and Europe. His early successes included *Sally* (1920) and *Sunny* (1925) but his most important work was *Show Boat* (1927). He was the father of the modern musical and is important for setting a

high standard of dramatic logic and musical unity in his works.

Lauder, Harry (1870-1950) Scottish singer and comic. He made his London debut in 1900 and soon achieved popular success. His famous songs include 'Roamin' in the Gloamin'' and 'Stop Yer Tickling, Jock'. During World War I he entertained the troops.

Leno, Dan (1860-

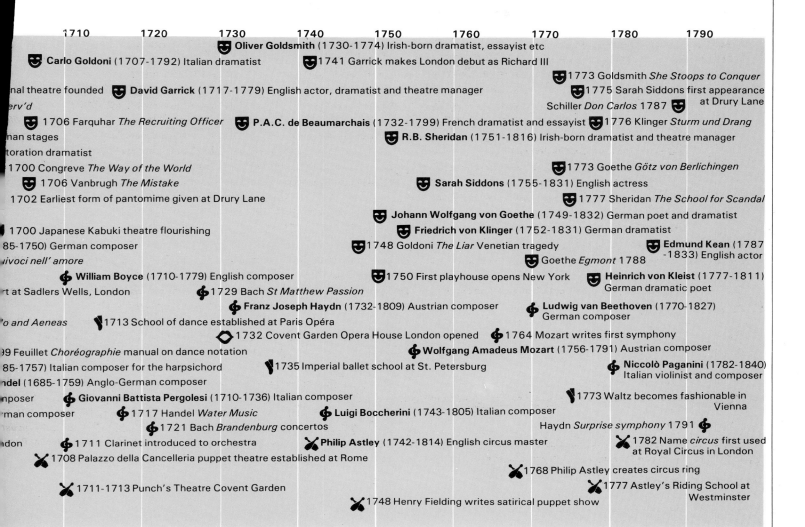

| 1710 | 1720 | 1730 | 1740 | 1750 | 1760 | 1770 | 1780 | 1790 |

Oliver Goldsmith (1730-1774) Irish-born dramatist, essayist etc

Carlo Goldoni (1707-1792) Italian dramatist

1741 Garrick makes London debut as Richard III

1773 Goldsmith *She Stoops to Conquer*

nal theatre founded   David Garrick (1717-1779) English actor, dramatist and theatre manager

1775 Sarah Siddons first appearance at Drury Lane

erv'd   Schiller *Don Carlos* 1787

1706 Farquhar *The Recruiting Officer*   P.A.C. de Beaumarchais (1732-1799) French dramatist and essayist   1776 Klinger *Sturm und Drang*

nan stages

R.B. Sheridan (1751-1816) Irish-born dramatist and theatre manager

toration dramatist

1700 Congreve *The Way of the World*

1773 Goethe *Götz von Berlichingen*

1706 Vanbrugh *The Mistake*   Sarah Siddons (1755-1831) English actress

1702 Earliest form of pantomime given at Drury Lane

1777 Sheridan *The School for Scandal*

Johann Wolfgang von Goethe (1749-1832) German poet and dramatist

1700 Japanese Kabuki theatre flourishing   Friedrich von Klinger (1752-1831) German dramatist

85-1750) German composer   1748 Goldoni *The Liar* Venetian tragedy   Edmund Kean (1787-1833) English actor

ivoci nell' amore   Goethe *Egmont* 1788

William Boyce (1710-1779) English composer   1750 First playhouse opens New York   Heinrich von Kleist (1777-1811) German dramatic poet

t at Sadlers Wells, London   1729 Bach *St Matthew Passion*

Franz Joseph Haydn (1732-1809) Austrian composer   Ludwig van Beethoven (1770-1827) German composer

o and Aeneas   1713 School of dance established at Paris Opéra

1732 Covent Garden Opera House London opened   1764 Mozart writes first symphony

99 Feuillet Choréographie *manual on dance notation*   Wolfgang Amadeus Mozart (1756-1791) Austrian composer

85-1757) Italian composer for the harpsichord   1735 Imperial ballet school at St. Petersburg   Niccolò Paganini (1782-1840) Italian violinist and composer

ndel (1685-1759) Anglo-German composer

nposer   Giovanni Battista Pergolesi (1710-1736) Italian composer   1773 Waltz becomes fashionable in Vienna

rman composer   1717 Handel *Water Music*   Luigi Boccherini (1743-1805) Italian composer

1721 Bach *Brandenburg* concertos   Haydn *Surprise symphony* 1791

ndon   1711 Clarinet introduced to orchestra   Philip Astley (1742-1814) English circus master   1782 Name *circus* first used at Royal Circus in London

1708 Palazzo della Cancelleria puppet theatre established at Rome

1768 Philip Astley creates circus ring

1711-1713 Punch's Theatre Covent Garden   1777 Astley's Riding School at Westminster

1748 Henry Fielding writes satirical puppet show

1904) British music-hall star. As an actor, singer, dancer and mime he appeared in music halls all over Britain. From 1886 he appeared in pantomime at Drury Lane and was particularly successful in comic women's parts such as Widow Twankey and Cinderella's stepmother. He was a versatile comedian and the leading figure of the Victorian music hall.

Lind, Jenny (1820-1887) Swedish soprano. One of the greatest singers of her age and one of the most popular, she was known as the 'Swedish nightingale'. She studied in Stockholm and then in Paris and sang in numerous opera houses. She was idolized by the public but retired from opera

in 1849, preferring to sing in concerts and oratorios.

Lloyd, Marie (1870-1922) British music-hall star. Her first major success came in 1885 with the song 'The Boy I Love Sits Up In The Gallery'. She then went on to conquer the music halls of England and Ireland with such songs as 'Oh! Mr Porter' and 'A Little Of What You Fancy Does You Good'. She remained in music hall right up to her death and was the best-known and loved of Edwardian music-hall performers.

Lope de Vega (1562-1635) Spanish dramatist. The first great writer of the Spanish theatre, over 470 of his works survive. He laid down the classic form for Spanish drama of three acts in both popular

and classical metres and drew his characters from all classes. He was an immensely popular writer and one of the world's great dramatists.

Marceau, Marcel (born 1923) French mime. After a brief period with the Compagnie Renaud-Barrault he left, in 1946, to concentrate on mime, creating his famous character, Bip, a white-faced, melancholy clown based on the nineteenth century Pierrot. He has also produced complete mime dramas, the most ambitious of which was based on Gogol's *The Overcoat*.

Marlow, Christopher (1564-1593) English Elizabethan dramatist. Educated at Cambridge, his earliest play, *Tamburlaine the*

Great (1587) was a great success on the London stage. This was followed by *The Tragical History of Doctor Faustus, The Jew of Malta* and *Edward II*. Had he not been killed in a brawl at the age of 29, he would have been Shakespeare's most serious rival. He greatly influenced the development of Elizabethan drama and the sheer beauty of his verse and imagery makes him one of the greatest of English playwrights.

Melba, Nellie (1861-1931) Australian soprano. After studying in Australia and then in Paris she achieved a major success as Lucia di Lammermoor at Covent Garden in 1888. She went on to have a long and brilliant international career as an opera

singer before returning to Australia as director of the Melbourne Conservatory. She is one of the most famous sopranos of all time.

Molière (1622-1673) French comic dramatist. After touring the French provinces with a small company of actors he won the favour of Louis XIV and settled in Paris where he began to write his

great series of comedies, the most notable of which are *Le Tartuffe* (1664), *Le Misanthrope* (1666) and *Le Bourgeois Gentilhomme* (1670). Molière's satires on human nature and society are both deft and subtle. He is one of the greatest comic dramatists of all time and established French comedy as a notable genre.

Monteverdi, Claudio (1567-1643) Italian composer. The founder of modern opera, his great works are *Orfeo* (1607); *Ritorno di Ulisse in Patria (Ulysses' Return to his Country)* (1641) and his masterpiece, *Incoronazione di Poppea (The Coronation of Poppea)* (1642). The first, and one of the great masters of opera, Monteverdi's works are still regularly

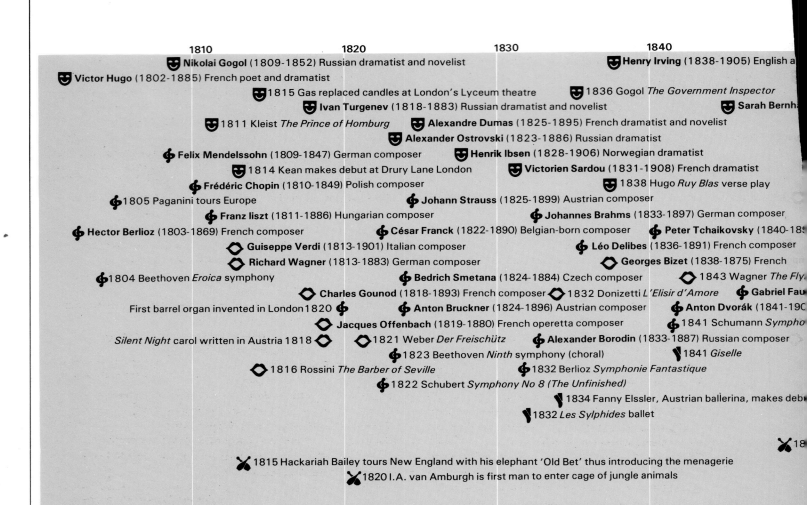

	1810	1820	1830	1840

Nikolai Gogol (1809-1852) Russian dramatist and novelist

Henry Irving (1838-1905) English a

Victor Hugo (1802-1885) French poet and dramatist

1815 Gas replaced candles at London's Lyceum theatre

1836 Gogol *The Government Inspector*

Ivan Turgenev (1818-1883) Russian dramatist and novelist

Sarah Bernh

1811 Kleist *The Prince of Homburg*

Alexandre Dumas (1825-1895) French dramatist and novelist

Alexander Ostrovski (1823-1886) Russian dramatist

Felix Mendelssohn (1809-1847) German composer

Henrik Ibsen (1828-1906) Norwegian dramatist

1814 Kean makes debut at Drury Lane London

Victorien Sardou (1831-1908) French dramatist

Frédéric Chopin (1810-1849) Polish composer

1838 Hugo *Ruy Blas* verse play

1805 Paganini tours Europe

Johann Strauss (1825-1899) Austrian composer

Franz liszt (1811-1886) Hungarian composer

Johannes Brahms (1833-1897) German composer

Hector Berlioz (1803-1869) French composer

César Franck (1822-1890) Belgian-born composer

Peter Tchaikovsky (1840-18

Guiseppe Verdi (1813-1901) Italian composer

Léo Delibes (1836-1891) French composer

Richard Wagner (1813-1883) German composer

Georges Bizet (1838-1875) French

1804 Beethoven *Eroica* symphony

Bedrich Smetana (1824-1884) Czech composer

1843 Wagner *The Fly*

Charles Gounod (1818-1893) French composer

1832 Donizetti *L'Elisir d'Amore*

Gabriel Fau

First barrel organ invented in London 1820

Anton Bruckner (1824-1896) Austrian composer

Anton Dvorák (1841-190

Jacques Offenbach (1819-1880) French operetta composer

1841 Schumann *Sympho*

Silent Night carol written in Austria 1818

1821 Weber *Der Freischütz*

Alexander Borodin (1833-1887) Russian composer

1823 Beethoven *Ninth* symphony (choral)

1841 *Giselle*

1816 Rossini *The Barber of Seville*

1832 Berlioz *Symphonie Fantastique*

1822 Schubert *Symphony No 8 (The Unfinished)*

1834 Fanny Elssler, Austrian ballerina, makes deb

1832 *Les Sylphides* ballet

18

1815 Hackariah Bailey tours New England with his elephant 'Old Bet' thus introducing the menagerie

1820 I.A. van Amburgh is first man to enter cage of jungle animals

performed today.
Mozart, Wolfgang Amadeus (1756-1791) Austrian composer. One of the greatest musical geniuses of all time, among his prolific output are seven superb operas, of which *The Marriage of Figaro* (1786), *Don Giovanni* (1787) and *The Magic Flute* (1791) are perhaps the most popular. In these, his

characteristic grace, elegance and purity of style is coupled with an emotional depth and intensity which places them among the greatest of all operatic works. His influence on the subsequent development of opera was profound.

Nijinsky, Vaslav (1890-1950) Russian dancer and choreographer. One of the greatest of all ballet personalities, he is principally associated with Diaghilev and the Ballet Russes. As a dancer, his brilliant technique and interpretive genius won him world wide acclaim. As a choreographer, he is a great pioneer of modern dance. His *L'Après-midi d'un Faune,* inspired by Greek art, is now

recognized as a masterpiece and his *Sacre du Printemps,* a work with dramatic but primitive gestures to Stravinsky's music, is a remarkable work of innovation. His insanity from 1919 terminated a brilliant career.

Noverre, Jean Georges (1727-1810) French dancer and choreographer. As ballet master in Stuttgart he had his first notable success with *Jason et Medée* (1763) and then at the Paris Opera with *Les Horaces* (1776). His great contribution to ballet was as a reformer. He introduced freer dancing and costumes and campaigned for safety devices on stage.

Nureyev, Rudolf (born 1938) Russian dancer. Principal dancer with the Kirov Ballet until

his defection to the West in 1961, he has danced to international acclaim all over the world. He formed a notable partnership with Margot Fonteyn in 1962 and some of his most memorable performances have been with her. His remarkably athletic technique, his dramatic stage presence and the versatility of his characterization have made him one of the

most outstanding of contemporary dancers.

Offenbach, Jacques (1819-1880) German-born French composer. He came to Paris as a boy and was conductor of the Théâtre Français before gaining immense success as a composer of operettas. He produced nearly 90 such works, of which the most popular are *La Belle Hélène, Orpheus in the Underworld* and *La Vie Parisienne.*

Olivier, Laurence (born 1907) English actor and director. One of the finest English actors of all time, he made his debut in 1922. He has played an enormous number of roles on both stage and screen, but is perhaps best known for his Shakespearean interpretations of

which his Hamlet, Richard III, Henry V and Othello are the most acclaimed. He was appointed director of Britain's first National Theatre in 1963 and was also the first director of the Chichester Festival Theatre.

O'Neill, Eugene (1888-1953) American dramatist. America's first major playwright, his success began with *Beyond the Horizon* in 1920. His most important works are *The Iceman Cometh* (1939) and his masterpiece, the autobiographical *Long Day's Journey Into Night* (1941), a powerful and moving work which is regularly performed.

Parker, Charlie 'Bird' (1920-1925) American jazz musician and

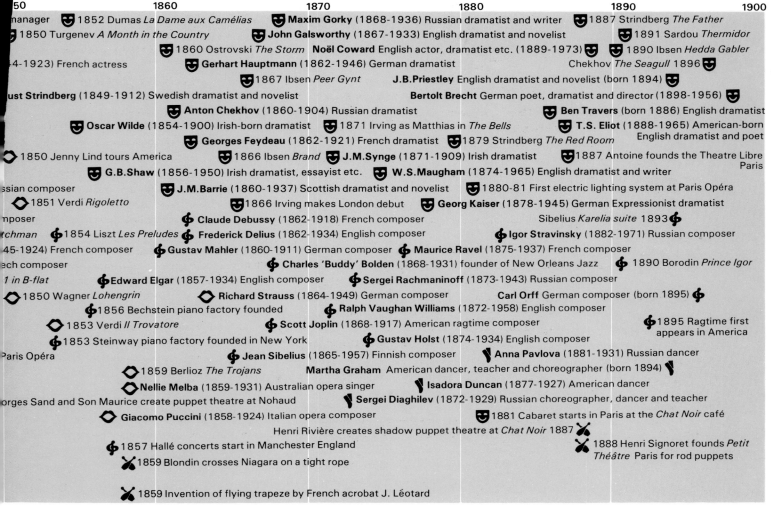

50	1860	1870	1880	1890	1900

🎭 1852 Dumas *La Dame aux Camélias*   🎭 **Maxim Gorky** (1868-1936) Russian dramatist and writer   🎭 1887 Strindberg *The Father*

🎭 1850 Turgenev *A Month in the Country*   🎭 **John Galsworthy** (1867-1933) English dramatist and novelist   🎭 1891 Sardou *Thermidor*

🎭 1860 Ostrovski *The Storm*   **Noël Coward** English actor, dramatist etc. (1889-1973) 🎭   🎭 1890 Ibsen *Hedda Gabler*

4-1923) French actress   🎭 **Gerhart Hauptmann** (1862-1946) German dramatist   Chekhov *The Seagull* 1896 🎭

🎭 1867 Ibsen *Peer Gynt*   **J.B.Priestley** English dramatist and novelist (born 1894) 🎭

ust Strindberg (1849-1912) Swedish dramatist and novelist   **Bertolt Brecht** German poet, dramatist and director (1898-1956) 🎭

🎭 **Anton Chekhov** (1860-1904) Russian dramatist   🎭 **Ben Travers** (born 1886) English dramatist

🎭 **Oscar Wilde** (1854-1900) Irish-born dramatist   🎭 1871 Irving as Matthias in *The Bells*   🎭 **T.S. Eliot** (1888-1965) American-born English dramatist and poet

🎭 **Georges Feydeau** (1862-1921) French dramatist   🎭 1879 Strindberg *The Red Room*

◇ 1850 Jenny Lind tours America   🎭 1866 Ibsen *Brand*   🎭 **J.M.Synge** (1871-1909) Irish dramatist   🎭 1887 Antoine founds the Theatre Libre Paris

🎭 **G.B.Shaw** (1856-1950) Irish dramatist, essayist etc.   🎭 **W.S.Maugham** (1874-1965) English dramatist and writer

ssian composer   🎭 **J.M.Barrie** (1860-1937) Scottish dramatist and novelist   🎭 1880-81 First electric lighting system at Paris Opéra

◇ 1851 Verdi *Rigoletto*   🎭 1866 Irving makes London debut   🎭 **Georg Kaiser** (1878-1945) German Expressionist dramatist

mposer   🎵 **Claude Debussy** (1862-1918) French composer   Sibelius *Karelia suite* 1893 🎵

chman   🎵 1854 Liszt *Les Preludes*   🎵 **Frederick Delius** (1862-1934) English composer   🎵 **Igor Stravinsky** (1882-1971) Russian composer

45-1924) French composer   🎵 **Gustav Mahler** (1860-1911) German composer   🎵 **Maurice Ravel** (1875-1937) French composer

ech composer   🎵 **Charles 'Buddy' Bolden** (1868-1931) founder of New Orleans Jazz   🎵 1890 Borodin *Prince Igor*

1 in B-flat   🎵 **Edward Elgar** (1857-1934) English composer   🎵 **Sergei Rachmaninoff** (1873-1943) Russian composer

◇ 1850 Wagner *Lohengrin*   ◇ **Richard Strauss** (1864-1949) German composer   **Carl Orff** German composer (born 1895) 🎵

🎵 1856 Bechstein piano factory founded   🎵 **Ralph Vaughan Williams** (1872-1958) English composer

◇ 1853 Verdi *Il Trovatore*   🎵 **Scott Joplin** (1868-1917) American ragtime composer   🎵 1895 Ragtime first appears in America

◇ 1853 Steinway piano factory founded in New York   🎵 **Gustav Holst** (1874-1934) English composer

Paris Opéra   🎵 **Jean Sibelius** (1865-1957) Finnish composer   ♪ **Anna Pavlova** (1881-1931) Russian dancer

◇ 1859 Berlioz *The Trojans*   **Martha Graham** American dancer, teacher and choreographer (born 1894) ♪

◇ **Nellie Melba** (1859-1931) Australian opera singer   ♪ **Isadora Duncan** (1877-1927) American dancer

orges Sand and Son Maurice create puppet theatre at Nohaud   ♪ **Sergei Diaghilev** (1872-1929) Russian choreographer, dancer and teacher

◇ **Giacomo Puccini** (1858-1924) Italian opera composer   🎭 1881 Cabaret starts in Paris at the *Chat Noir* café

Henri Rivière creates shadow puppet theatre at *Chat Noir* 1887 ✖   ✖ 1888 Henri Signoret founds *Petit Théâtre* Paris for rod puppets

🎵 1857 Hallé concerts start in Manchester England

✖ 1859 Blondin crosses Niagara on a tight rope

✖ 1859 Invention of flying trapeze by French acrobat J. Léotard

---

composer. One of the great jazz musicians of his generation, he became well known in the 1940s as a talented and imaginative saxophonist. With the trumpeter Dizzy Gillespie he helped create the jazz style known as Bebop.

Pavlova, Anna (1885-1931) Russian ballerina. The greatest solo dancer of her time she first danced her

acclaimed *Giselle* in 1903. Although she danced with Diaghilev she preferred working with her own company and from 1908 conducted world tours which brought her spectacular world fame. She was a supreme artist with a particular talent for mime and has become a legendary figure in the history of ballet.
Petipa, Marius (1818-1910) French-born dancer and choreographer. As chief ballet master at the Imperial Theatre, St Petersburg from 1869 he created the classic ballet as we know it today. He choreographed more than 60 ballets, including *Sleeping Beauty*, *Giselle* and *Swan Lake* and created the Imperial Russian Ballet.
Piaf, Edith (1915-1963) French cabaret

singer. She began singing as a young girl in cafés and in the streets of Paris. She was soon engaged in cabaret and her fame spread quickly. She made numerous recordings, several films and appeared in nightclubs all over Europe and America. Known as the 'little sparrow', her highly emotional and powerful voice made her one of the greatest artists of cabaret of her time.
Plautus (c. 254-184 B.C.) Roman comic playwright. He adapted Greek plays for the Roman stage and among his surviving works are *Miles Gloriosus*, *Menaechmi* and *Amphitrou*. The plots are simple and theatrical and contain boisterous, low-comedy portrayals of middle and lower class

life. His works have had a decisive influence on comedy since the Renaissance and have been imitated and adapted by many great dramatists, including Shakespeare.
Porter, Cole (1892-1964) American composer. He studied music at Harvard and in Paris but wrote little before 1928 when he wrote a revue, *Paris*, which was immediately successful. He wrote his own witty and sophisticated lyrics and his music is inventive and memorable. His most popular musicals were *Kiss Me Kate*, *Anything Goes*, *Can-Can* and *Silk Stockings*.
Presley, Elvis (1935-1977) American popular singer. He began playing the guitar as a teenager

and made his first recording in 1953. By 1956 he had achieved international fame as a rock 'n roll star and

was one of the dominant figures in pop music for just under a decade. He was the first performer to accompany his singing with pelvic gyrations on stage and his influence on the whole course of pop music is inestimable.
Puccini, Giacomo

(1858-1924) Italian composer. From 1884 when his first work was produced, he wrote a series of operas almost all of which were highly successful. His most popular works are *Manon Lescaut* (1893), *La Bohème* (1894), *Tosca* (1900) and *Madame Butterfly* (1904). He is one of the world's most successful opera composers and his work is characterized by strong melody, dramatic plot and powerful depiction of character.
Purcell, Henry (1659-1695) English composer. From 1677 to his death he was composer to the Chapel Royal. He wrote one true opera *Dido and Aeneas* (1689), which is still regularly performed today, and a number of semi-operas, including

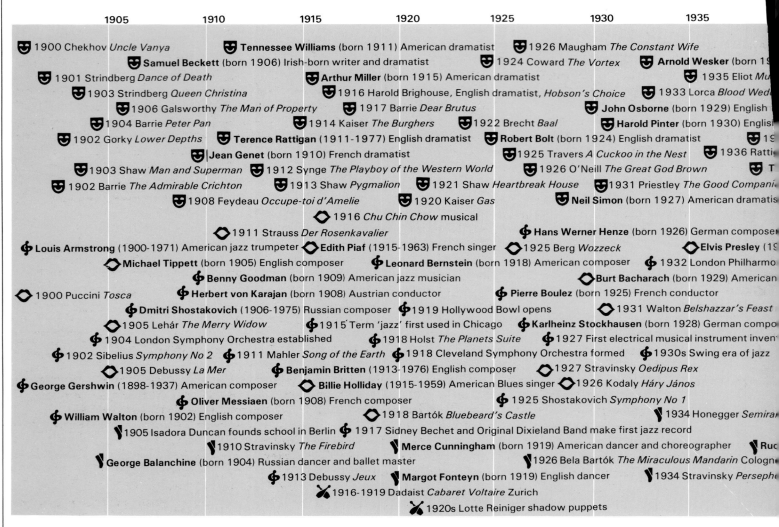

1905	1910	1915	1920	1925	1930	1935

1900 Chekhov *Uncle Vanya*
Tennessee Williams (born 1911) American dramatist
1926 Maugham *The Constant Wife*
Samuel Beckett (born 1906) Irish-born writer and dramatist
1924 Coward *The Vortex*
Arnold Wesker (born 1
1901 Strindberg *Dance of Death*
Arthur Miller (born 1915) American dramatist
1935 Eliot *Mu*
1903 Strindberg *Queen Christina*
1916 Harold Brighouse, English dramatist, *Hobson's Choice*
1933 Lorca *Blood Wed*
1906 Galsworthy *The Man of Property*
1917 Barrie *Dear Brutus*
John Osborne (born 1929) English
1904 Barrie *Peter Pan*
1914 Kaiser *The Burghers*
1922 Brecht *Baal*
Harold Pinter (born 1930) English
1902 Gorky *Lower Depths*
Terence Rattigan (1911-1977) English dramatist
Robert Bolt (born 1924) English dramatist
19
Jean Genet (born 1910) French dramatist
1925 Travers *A Cuckoo in the Nest*
1936 Ratti
1903 Shaw *Man and Superman*
1912 Synge *The Playboy of the Western World*
1926 O'Neill *The Great God Brown*
T
1902 Barrie *The Admirable Crichton*
1913 Shaw *Pygmalion*
1921 Shaw *Heartbreak House*
1931 Priestley *The Good Compani*
1908 Feydeau *Occupe-toi d'Amelie*
1920 Kaiser *Gas*
Neil Simon (born 1927) American dramatis
1916 *Chu Chin Chow* musical
1911 Strauss *Der Rosenkavalier*
Hans Werner Henze (born 1926) German composer
Louis Armstrong (1900-1971) American jazz trumpeter
Edith Piaf (1915-1963) French singer
1925 Berg *Wozzeck*
Elvis Presley (19
Michael Tippett (born 1905) English composer
Leonard Bernstein (born 1918) American composer
1932 London Philharmo
Benny Goodman (born 1909) American jazz musician
Burt Bacharach (born 1929) American
1900 Puccini *Tosca*
Herbert von Karajan (born 1908) Austrian conductor
Pierre Boulez (born 1925) French conductor
Dmitri Shostakovich (1906-1975) Russian composer
1919 Hollywood Bowl opens
1931 Walton *Belshazzar's Feast*
1905 Lehár *The Merry Widow*
1915 Term 'jazz' first used in Chicago
Karlheinz Stockhausen (born 1928) German compo
1904 London Symphony Orchestra established
1918 Holst *The Planets Suite*
1927 First electrical musical instrument inven
1902 Sibelius *Symphony No 2*
1911 Mahler *Song of the Earth*
1918 Cleveland Symphony Orchestra formed
1930s Swing era of jazz
1905 Debussy *La Mer*
Benjamin Britten (1913-1976) English composer
1927 Stravinsky *Oedipus Rex*
George Gershwin (1898-1937) American composer
Billie Holliday (1915-1959) American Blues singer
1926 Kodaly *Háry János*
Oliver Messiaen (born 1908) French composer
1925 Shostakovich *Symphony No 1*
William Walton (born 1902) English composer
1918 Bartók *Bluebeard's Castle*
1934 Honegger *Semira*
1905 Isadora Duncan founds school in Berlin
1917 Sidney Bechet and Original Dixieland Band make first jazz record
1910 Stravinsky *The Firebird*
Merce Cunningham (born 1919) American dancer and choreographer
Ruc
George Balanchine (born 1904) Russian dancer and ballet master
1926 Bela Bartók *The Miraculous Mandarin* Cologne
1913 Debussy *Jeux*
Margot Fonteyn (born 1919) English dancer
1934 Stravinsky *Persephe*
1916-1919 Dadaist *Cabaret Voltaire* Zurich
1920s Lotte Reiniger shadow puppets

The Fairy Queen (1692) and *King Arthur* (1690). He also composed much theatre and church music and a wide variety of songs and keyboard music.

Racine, Jean (1639-1699) French dramatist and poet. Regarded as the greatest of French tragic dramatists, his plays are based on classical themes and written in alexandrines. *Andromaque* (1667), *Berenice* (1670) and *Phèdre* (1677) are the most notable examples of his superbly organized tragedies which are written with economy, precision and great beauty of expression.
Rambert, Marie (born 1888) Polish-born dancer and teacher. After early training in Paris she joined

Diaghilev's company but came to London in 1914. Here she created *La Pomme d'Or* (1917), a ballet in which she also danced. Her work attracted attention and in 1920 she set up her own studio which later became the Ballet Rambert. She had a shrewd eye for talent and many of Britain's leading dancers and choreographers have been associated with her. As the grande dame of British ballet her influence has been considerable.
Rossini, Gioacchino (1792-1868) Italian composer. His early career was spent as director of the San Carlo Theatre in Naples. He had a successful opera career from 1810 although, ironically, his most famous work, *The Barber of Seville* (1816) was at first a

failure. Other notable works include *The Thieving Magpie* and *William Tell*. He was an immensely popular composer who combined a delight in comedy with a strong melodic line.

Salomon, J.P. (1745-1815) German-born musician and concert manager. A violinist of note, he settled in London in 1781. He brought Haydn to England in 1790 and 1794 and commissioned the 12 symphonies now known as the Salomon Symphonies for performance at concerts which he organized.
Schiller, Friedrich von (1759-1805) German poet and dramatist. This great master of Romantic historical drama wrote his first play, *Die Räuber (The Robbers)* at the age of

22. His later works, which include *Don Carlos* (1787) *Wallenstein* (1799), *Maria Stuart* (1800) and *Wilhelm Tell* (1804) revealed him as one of the most powerful writers in the history of drama.

Shakespeare, William (1564-1616) England's greatest dramatist and poet. Born in Stratford-upon-Avon, he lived in London from about

1592 to 1610 where he earned a successful living as an actor and playwright. He wrote 36 plays which can roughly be divided into comedies, tragedies, histories and romances. His greatest period was between 1600 and 1607 when he produced the comedies, *As You Like It* and *Twelfth Night* and his great tragedies, *Hamlet, Othello, King Lear* and *Macbeth*. He was first and foremost a writer for the popular stage and his plays have a unique and consistent dramatic impact, coupled with stunning beauty of language. His works have been translated into almost every language and are constantly performed throughout the world. His influence, not only on the history of drama, but also on

human thought and literature, is incalculable.
Shaw, George Bernard (1856-1950) Irish dramatist and critic. His plays cover a wide range of themes, most of them containing a moral, political or social message. His prolific output includes *Arms and the Man* (1894), *Man and Superman* (1903), *Heartbreak House* (1919) and *Pygmalion* (1913). In spite of his propagandist aims many of his plays are full of paradox, wit and acute observation and are regularly performed all over the world.
Siddons, Sarah (1755-1831) English actress. One of the greatest of all tragediennes, she did not achieve success in London until 1782. She played a number of tragic roles, the most

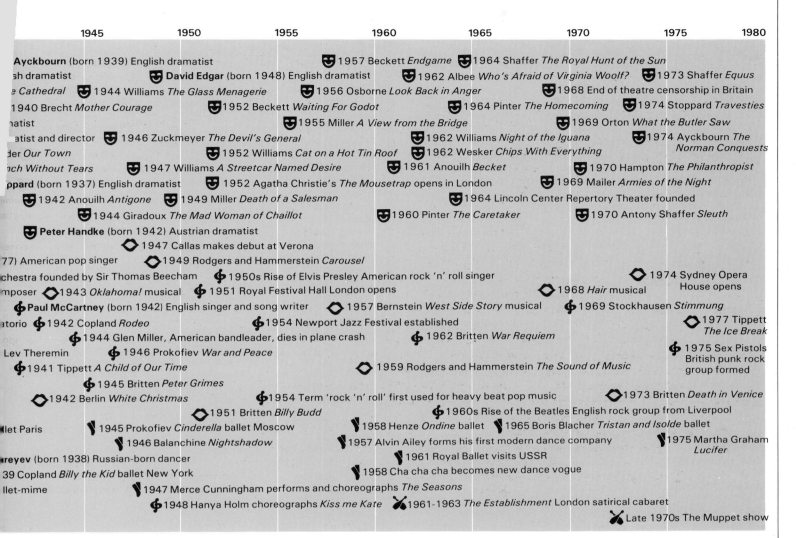

1945 1950 1955 1960 1965 1970 1975 1980

Ayckbourn (born 1939) English dramatist   🎭1957 Beckett *Endgame*   🎭1964 Shaffer *The Royal Hunt of the Sun*

sh dramatist   🎭 **David Edgar** (born 1948) English dramatist   🎭1962 Albee *Who's Afraid of Virginia Woolf?*   🎭1973 Shaffer *Equus*

e Cathedral   🎭1944 Williams *The Glass Menagerie*   🎭1956 Osborne *Look Back in Anger*   🎭1968 End of theatre censorship in Britain

1940 Brecht *Mother Courage*   🎭1952 Beckett *Waiting For Godot*   🎭1964 Pinter *The Homecoming*   🎭1974 Stoppard *Travesties*

atist   🎭1955 Miller *A View from the Bridge*   🎭1969 Orton *What the Butler Saw*

atist and director   🎭 1946 Zuckmeyer *The Devil's General*   🎭1962 Williams *Night of the Iguana*   🎭1974 Ayckbourn *The Norman Conquests*

der *Our Town*   🎭1952 Williams *Cat on a Hot Tin Roof*   🎭1962 Wesker *Chips With Everything*

ch *Without Tears*   🎭1947 Williams *A Streetcar Named Desire*   🎭1961 Anouilh *Becket*   🎭1970 Hampton *The Philanthropist*

ppard (born 1937) English dramatist   🎭1952 Agatha Christie's *The Mousetrap* opens in London   🎭1969 Mailer *Armies of the Night*

🎭1942 Anouilh *Antigone*   🎭1949 Miller *Death of a Salesman*   🎭1964 Lincoln Center Repertory Theater founded

🎭1944 Giradoux *The Mad Woman of Chaillot*   🎭1960 Pinter *The Caretaker*   🎭1970 Antony Shaffer *Sleuth*

🎭 **Peter Handke** (born 1942) Austrian dramatist

◇1947 Callas makes debut at Verona

77) American pop singer   ◇1949 Rodgers and Hammerstein *Carousel*

chestra founded by Sir Thomas Beecham   ♪1950s Rise of Elvis Presley American rock 'n' roll singer   ◇1974 Sydney Opera House opens

mposer   ◇1943 *Oklahoma!* musical   ♪1951 Royal Festival Hall London opens   ◇1968 *Hair* musical

♪ **Paul McCartney** (born 1942) English singer and song writer   ◇1957 Bernstein *West Side Story* musical   ♪1969 Stockhausen *Stimmung*

atorio ♪1942 Copland *Rodeo*   ♪1954 Newport Jazz Festival established   ◇1977 Tippett *The Ice Break*

♪1944 Glen Miller, American bandleader, dies in plane crash   ♪1962 Britten *War Requiem*

Lev Theremin   ♪1946 Prokofiev *War and Peace*   ♪1975 Sex Pistols British punk rock group formed

♪1941 Tippett *A Child of Our Time*   ◇1959 Rodgers and Hammerstein *The Sound of Music*

♪1945 Britten *Peter Grimes*

◇1942 Berlin *White Christmas*   ♪1954 Term 'rock 'n' roll' first used for heavy beat pop music   ◇1973 Britten *Death in Venice*

♪1951 Britten *Billy Budd*   ♪1960s Rise of the Beatles English rock group from Liverpool

llet Paris   ⚉1945 Prokofiev *Cinderella* ballet Moscow   ⚉1958 Henze *Ondine* ballet   ⚉1965 Boris Blacher *Tristan and Isolde* ballet

⚉1946 Balanchine *Nightshadow*   ⚉1957 Alvin Ailey forms his first modern dance company   ⚉1975 Martha Graham *Lucifer*

reyev (born 1938) Russian-born dancer   ⚉1961 Royal Ballet visits USSR

39 Copland *Billy the Kid* ballet New York   ⚉1958 Cha cha cha becomes new dance vogue

llet-mime   ⚉1947 Merce Cunningham performs and choreographs *The Seasons*

♪1948 Hanya Holm choreographs *Kiss me Kate*   ✄1961-1963 *The Establishment* London satirical cabaret

✄Late 1970s The Muppet show

---

celebrated of which was her Lady Macbeth.
Sophocles (c. 496-406 B.C.) Greek tragic dramatist. Author of more than 100 plays, the seven which survive are *Ajax, Antigone, Trachiniae, Oedipus Rex. Electra, Philoctetes* and *Oedipus at Colonus.* His plays represent the height of Greek tragedy and he is regarded as the epitomy of the classic dramatists.
Stanislavsky, Konstantin (1863-1938) Russian director, actor and teacher. After an early career as an actor and director, he founded the Moscow Art Theatre in 1898 where he developed a new approach to acting based on realism, ensemble playing and the actor's complete identification

with his character. His greatest triumphs as a director were with Chekhov's plays but he was also one of the greatest teachers of his day. He has had an enormous effect on modern theatre .
Strauss, Richard (1864-1949) German composer and conductor. His early career was devoted to the composition of orchestral works and symphonic poems In 1905, his opera, *Salome,* appeared and this was soon followed by *Elektra, Der Rosenkavalier* and *Ariadne auf Naxos.*

Thomas, Dylan (1914-1953) Welsh poet and dramatist. His finest dramatic work *Under Milk Wood,* a play for voices, had its first public hearing in 1953 in America when he

read it himself. His mellifluous voice was particularly suited to the reading of poetry in which he made a successful career. He died during a tour of America where he was lecturing and reading.
Toscanini, Arturo (1867-1957) Italian conductor. His important first performances includce Puccini's *La Bohème* and *Turandot* at La Scala, Milan. He settled in America in the 1930s. A great opera conductor, he demanded and got perfection from his singers and players.

Verdi, Guiseppe (1813-1901) Italian composer. Of humble origins Verdi studied music privately before turning to opera. His first major success was *Nabucco* (1842). Thereafter followed a series of operas with

bold, unforgettable melodies of which *Rigoletto, Il Trovatore, La Traviata* and *Aida* are the best known. The two operas of his later life, *Otello* and *Falstaff* are his acknowledged masterpieces. They contain few set arias and are almost symphonic in style. Verdi is a towering giant in the world of opera.

Wagner, Richard (1813-1883) German composer. One of the most revolutionary figures in the history of music, his fame rests on his operas, of which *Tannhäuser* (1843-44), *Lohengrin* (1846-48), *Tristan and Isolde* (1857-59) and his masterpiece, the great cycle of four music dramas, *The Ring Of The Nibelung* (1853-74) are the most famous. His operas are

written in a 'symphonic' form, using musical leitmotifs to represent different characters, ideas or emotions in the story. His singers, therefore, had no set-piece arias but were part of the orchestral whole. He also believed opera was a unified work of art and wrote his own libretti and supervised every detail of production. His influence on the course of music and

opera is probably greater than that of any other composer.
Webster, John (c. 1580-c.1625) English Jacobean dramatist. He is probably the greatest writer of tragedy in his age after Shakespeare. Very little is known about his life but he is justly famous for his tragedies, *The White Devil* and *The Duchess of Malfi,* which are still performed today.
Wood, Henry (1869-1944) British conductor. In 1895 he began the famous series of London Promenade concerts (the Proms), still one of the most important events in the London musical season. His conductorship was remarkable for introducing a large number of unfamiliar works and composers to the British public.

INDEX

V

ACKNOWLEDGEMENTS

12 top: Scala, below: BBC Hulton Picture Library; **13** Michael Holford Picture Library; **14** top: BBC Hulton, below left: Scala, below right: Scala; **15** Scala; **16** top, below and right: BBC Hulton; **17** top: Michael Holford, centre left: Alastair Campbell, centre right: Scala, below: Walter Rawlings; **18-19** Mansell Collection; **20** BBC Hulton; **21** whole page: Scala; **22** left: City Art Gallery Manchester, centre: Royal Shakespeare Co., photo Anthony Crickmay, right top: National Theatre, photo Nobby Clark, right below: RSC; **23** top: BBC Hulton, below left: RSC/Nobby Clark, below right: RSC; **24** Snark International; **25** BBC Hulton; **26-27** Ronald Sheridan Photo Library; **26** Michael Holford; **27** centre: Scala, below: Mansell; **28** BBC Hulton; **29** top left: BBC Hulton, top right and below: Mansell; **30** top and centre: Society for Cultural Relations with the USSR, below: Lincoln Center, NY, photo Ezra Stoller; **31** top left and right: Royal Exchange Theatre, Manchester; **30-31** National Theatre, photo Brecht-Einzig Ltd; **32** BBC Hulton; **33** top left and right: Robert Harding Associates Ltd, top centre. Royal Exchange Theatre, Manchester, centre: BBC Hulton, centre right: Robert Harding, centre left: Richmond Orange Tree Theatre, centre below: British Tourist Authority, below: Bildtjänsten Sverigehuset, below right: Metropolitan Opera House, NY; **34-35** top left: Novosti Agency, top centre: Mansell, top centre right: Austrian National Tourist Office, top right: Australian Information Service, centre left: Lincoln Center, centre right: Theatre Museum, at the Victoria and Albert Museum, London, below left: Mansell below centre: Scala, below right: E.N.I.T.; **36-37** Scala; **37** Mansell; **38** top: Mansell centre: G.L.C. Dept. of Architecture and Civic Design, below: GLC Photo Library; **39** top: Mansell, centre and below: Decca Record Company: **40** John Massey Stewart; **41** top: Finnish National Tourist Office, left: Brecht-Einzig Ltd, right: Austrian National Tourist Office; **42-43** Decca Record Company, photo Bob Lightfoot; **43** top and centre: Goethe Institute, below left: Carnegie Hall, below right: Lincoln Center; **44** whole page: Max Jones; **45** top: Max Jones, centre left and right: Valerie Wilmer, below: David Redfern; **46-7** both pages: Mansell; **48** top: Mansell, below: Marquis of Bath, Longleat House, photo Courtauld Institute; **48-49** top left, centre and right: Theatre Museum, centre left: Joe Cocks Studio, centre: RSC centre right: The Shakespeare Centre, below left: Thomas Holte, below centre left: Joe Cocks, below centre right: J.W. Debenham, below right: Theatre Museum; **50-51** Snark; **50** left and right: Mansell; **51** left and right: Mansell; **52-53** National Theatre photo Zoë Dominic; **52** below: BBC Hulton; **53** top and centre: BBC Hulton, below: National Theatre; **54** Zoë Dominic; **55** top: Bettman Archive Inc, below left and right: Jay Thompson; **56-57** BBC Hulton; **56** Mander and Mitchenson Theatre Collection; **58-59** (Costumes) Iona McLeish, (Production) Jon Wyand; **62** top left and below: Gordon McLeish, right: Michael Busselle (Wigs and make-up created by Kenneth Lintott); **63** top: Zoë Dominic, below: Kenneth Lintott Collection; **65** top left: Mansell, top centre and right: Theatre Museum, centre left: Linda Proud (Bernhardt Collection), Mander and Mitchenson, centre right: Shakespeare Memorial Theatre, Mander and Mitchenson, below left and right: BBC Hulton; **66** top, centre left and centre: Scala, centre right: BBC Hulton; **67** left: Mander and Mitchenson, centre and right: Scala, frieze: Stuart-Liff Collection; **68** top: Decca Record Company, below: BBC Hulton; **69** left: Stuart-Liff Collection, centre: BBC Hulton, right: Decca Record Company; **70** whole page: John Massey Stewart; **71** top: Theatre Museum, below: Mansell; **72** left: Theatre Museum, top and below left: BBC Hulton, centre: Stuart-Liff Collection, below right: BBC Hulton, below: Stuart-Liff Collection; **73** left to right: Stuart-Liff, Stuart-Liff, Theatre Museum, Stuart-Liff; **74-75** both pages: Guy Gravett, Picture Index; **76** top: BBC Hulton, below left and right: Metropolitan Opera, NY; **78** top: National Gallery London, centre: Scala, below: Decca; **78-79** Scala (Louvre); **80-81** BBC Hulton; **81** top: E.N.I.T. (photo E. Piccagliani), below: © BBC; **85** top: © BBC, centre and below: Decca Record Co; **86** top: BBC Hulton, below left and right: Mike Davis Studio, photo Jessie Davis; **87** top left and centre: BBC Hulton, top right: Michael Holford, below: Mike Davis/Jessie Davis; **88** BBC Hulton; **89** top: Festival Ballet, centre left: Popperfoto,

centre right: Australian Information Service, below left and right: Mike Davis Studio, below centre: BBC Hulton; **90** top left and centre: Mike Davis Studio, right: Cooper-Bridgeman Picture Library, below left: Michael Holford, below centre: Mike Davis Studio; **91** top left: Michael Holford, top right: Michael Busselle, centre left: Mike Davis Studio, below left: Cooper-Bridgeman, below centre: Michael Busselle, below right: Mike Davis Studio; **92** centre: Mike Davis Studio, Benesh: © Rudolf Benesh 1955, Choreology: © Glen Tetley 1979; **93** top: Australian Information Service, centre and below: Anthony Crickmay; **94** left: BBC Hulton, centre, top right and centre right: Mansell, below: BBC Hulton; **95** top left and right: Mansell, centre left: Popperfoto, centre: Mike Davis Studio; **94-95** Mike Davis, photo Jessie Davis; **96** BBC Hulton; **97** left: Anthony Crickmay, right: Peter Moore; **98** top left: Mike Davis, photo Jessie Davis, top right: Ballet Rambert photo Anthony Crickmay, centre, below left, centre top right: Mike Davis/Jessie Davis, centre right and below: Ballet Rambert, photo Gert Weigelt; **99** top left: Michael Holford, top right: Homer Sykes, centre top: KAW-Warsaw, centre left: Homer Sykes, all others: Mike Davis/Jessie Davis; **101** left and below: Popperfoto; **102** Ronald Grant Collection; **103** top and left: Mike Davis/Jessie Davis, right: Arthur Shafman International Ltd; **104-5** Ronald Grant **106-7** Michael Busselle; **108-9** KAW-Warsaw; **110** Theatre Museum; **111** left: Mansell, right: Theatre Museum; **112** top and below: BBC Hulton; **114-5** Zoë Dominic; **114** top: Zoë Dominic; **115** BBC Hulton; **116-7** BBC Hulton; **118-9** BBC Hulton; **120** whole page: BBC Hulton; **121** top: Mansell, below and right: BBC Hulton; **122** BBC Hulton, below: Theatre Museum; **123** top: Popperfoto, below left: Mansell; below right: Mansell; **124** top right: Roger-Viollet, all others BBC Hulton; **125** Roger Viollet; **126** top: BBC Hulton, bottom left and right: Cooper-Bridgeman; **127** left: Mansell, right: Roger-Viollet; **128** top: Dezo Hoffman, centre left and right: BBC Hulton, below left: Trends Management, below right: by courtesy of London Palladium; **129** left: by courtesy of The London Palladium, right: Australian Film Company; **130** Cooper Bridgeman; **131** Cooper Bridgeman; **134-5** both pages: Dezo Hoffman; **136** Atlantic Records/WEA; **137** Allied Artists/Pictures TV Corp. (British Film Institute); **138** Mary Evans Picture Library; **139** Magic Circle, photo: Mac Wilson; **140** Mary Evans/University of London, Harry Price Collection; **141** whole page: Mary Evans; **142** whole page: Magic Circle, photo: Mac Wilson; **143** centre left: The Great Kovari, all others: Magic Circle/Mac Wilson; **144** top and below: Mary Evans/Harry Price; **145** Mansell; **146** Scala; **146-7** top: Mansell, all others: Peter Cotes; **148** whole page: BBC Hulton; **149** top left: BBC Hulton, centre: Mansell; **150** Peter Cotes; **151** whole page: Nick Birch; **152** Mansell; **154-5** both pages: Nick Birch; **156** Peter Cotes; **157** top: BBC Hulton, below: Peter Cotes; **158** top: BBC Hulton, centre and below: Hogarth Puppets; **159** top and below: John Moss; **161** left: Novosti, right: Australian Information Service; **162** Theatre Museum; **163** top left and below right: Hogarth Puppets, top right: British Tourist Authority, below left: Theatre Museum; **164** top: Scala, below: Hogarth Puppets; **165** top: Theatre Museum, below: BBC Hulton; **166** top and below: Theatre Museum, centre: Mansell; **167** Michael Holford; **168-9** both pages: Mansell; **170-1** both pages: J. Barr; **172-3** Mansell; **173** BBC Hulton; **174-5** Q.E.D.; **176-7** both pages: Max Jones; **178** top: David Redfern, below: Valerie Wilmer; **179** top and below right: David Redfern, below left: Valerie Wilmer; **180** Max Jones; **181** top: Max Jones, below: David Redfern; **182** whole page: Popperfoto; **183** David Redfern; **184** Popperfoto; **185-7** both pages: David Redfern; **188-9** EMI Ltd; **188** Homer Sykes; **190-1** Alastair Campbell; **192-3** Popperfoto; **194** Mansell; **195** left: Associated Press, right: Alastair Campbell; **196-7** BBC Hulton; **197** top left and right: Associated Press; **199** Walter Rawlings; **200** Popperfoto; **201** Q.E.D., photo: Roger Pring; **202** left and right: BBC Hulton; **203** left and centre: Peter Thompson Associates, right: Mansell; **204** Contemporary Films; **205** top: Q.E.D., below: Contemporary Films.

Special photography throughout the book by Walter Rawlings, Jon Wyand, Michael Busselle and Michael Fear.